DAYTIME SHOOTING STAR

Story & Art by
Mika Yamamori

★4★

CONTENTS

STORY THUS FAR

Suzume Yosano is a first-year in high school. Born in the country, she grew up living a free and easy life. Due to family circumstances, she was forced to transfer to a school in Tokyo. Lost on her first day in the city, she is found by a man who later turns out to be her homeroom teacher, Mr. Shishio. Suzume gradually develops feelings for him.

The appearance of Mr. Shishio's ex-girlfriend Tsubomi and his everyday words and actions soon have Suzume declaring her love to Mr. Shishio, who turns her down. Later, when Mamura declares his love for her, Suzume realizes that it isn't easy being the one to turn down another's love declaration either.

During summer vacation on an outing to watch the fireworks with her classmates, Suzume runs into Mr. Shishio, who is there with Tsubomi. Thinking they have gotten back together, Suzume suddenly runs off. Mr. Shishio goes after her, but when he catches up, she tells him, "If you feel nothing for me, please don't be casually nice to me." But Mr. Shishio and Tsubomi's relationship has ended...

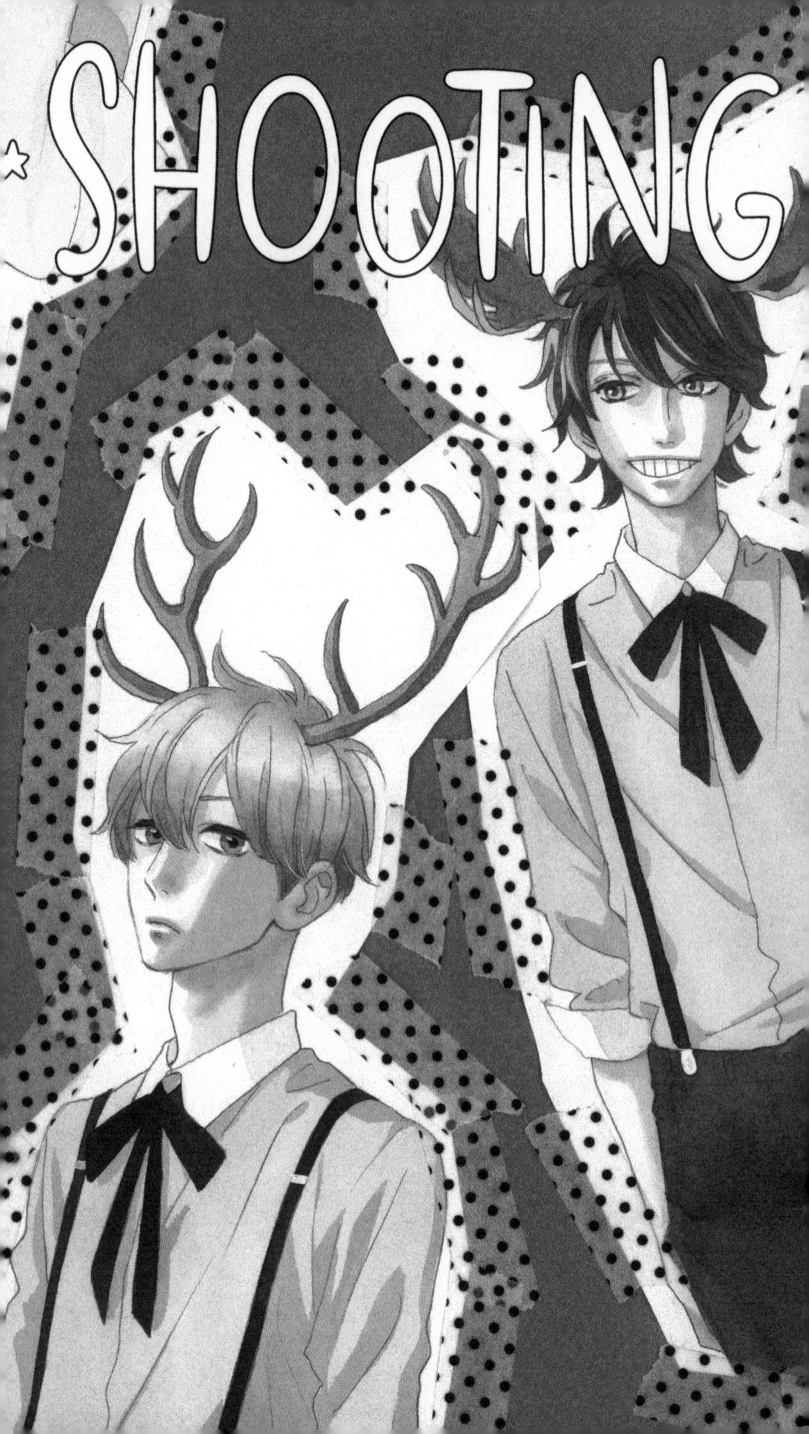
SHOOTING

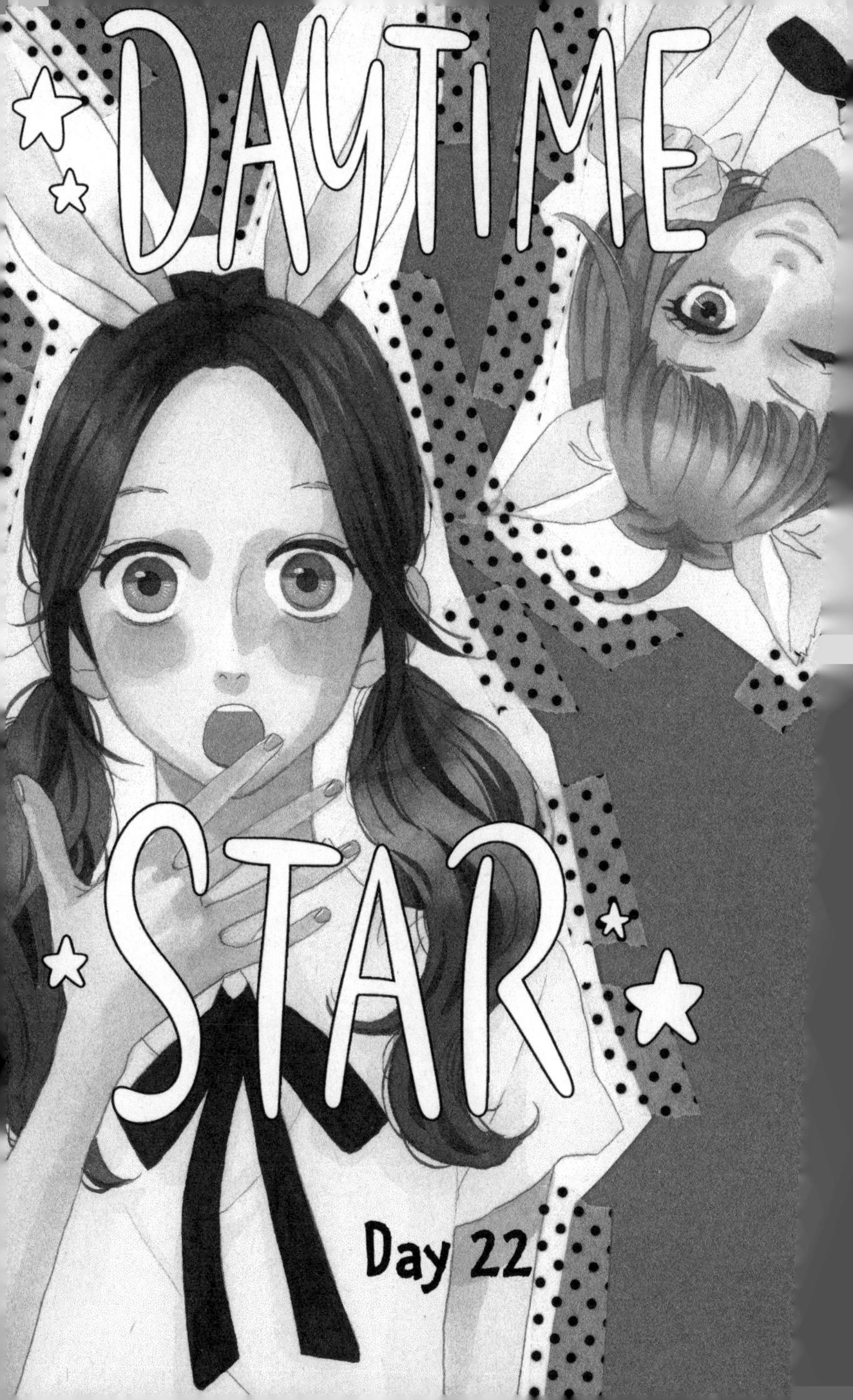
DAYTIME
STAR
Day 22

Want some juice?

Here is volume 4. Thank you all very much.
I am grateful to have received more illustrations of
Daytime characters. It's wonderful seeing others draw
the characters I've created. It feels like I'm sharing
my world will many different people.
Your fan letters are very heartening. I read each one,
grinning at times, feeling embarrassed at times or
even moved at times. It makes me very happy that I
became a manga creator. What? You say I'm being
uncharacteristically serious? Why, even I have my
serious moments. I just don't have the strength to be
that way right before my deadlines...

I hope you will enjoy volume 4 of *Daytime* Shooting Star! ☆✉

Mika♡

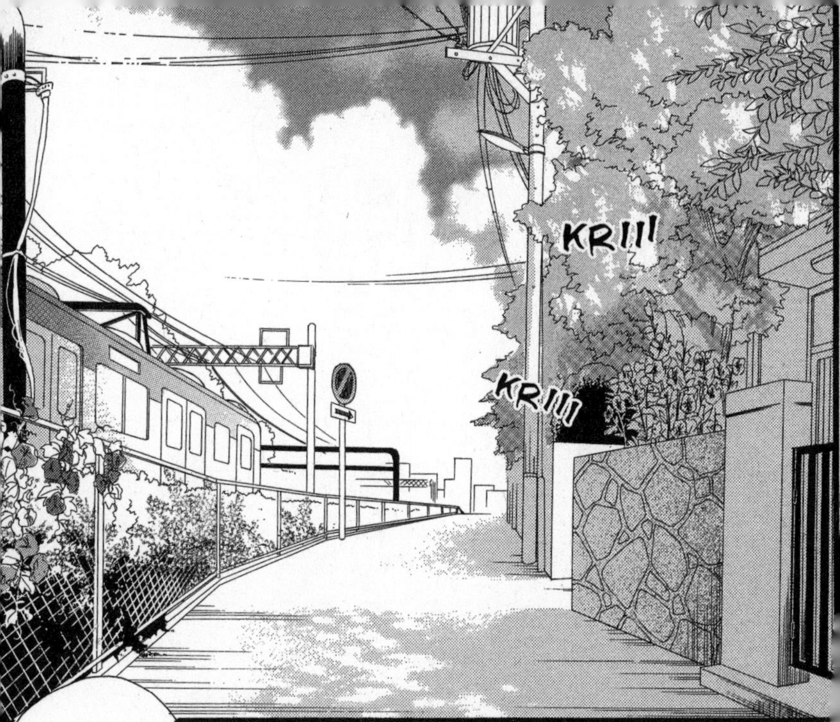
KRIII
KRIII

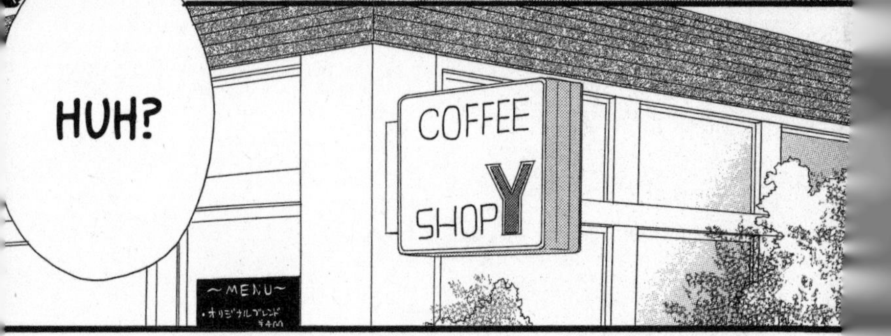
COFFEE SHOP Y
HUH?
~MENU~
・オリジナルブレンド

Mamura, Talking to Himself

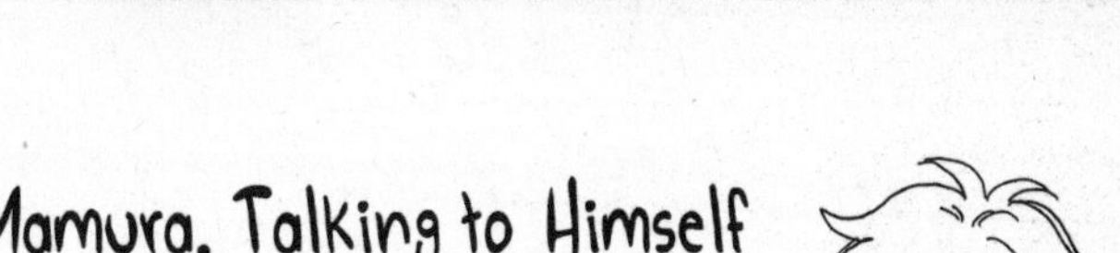
.....

It's great that his first name is finally revealed...

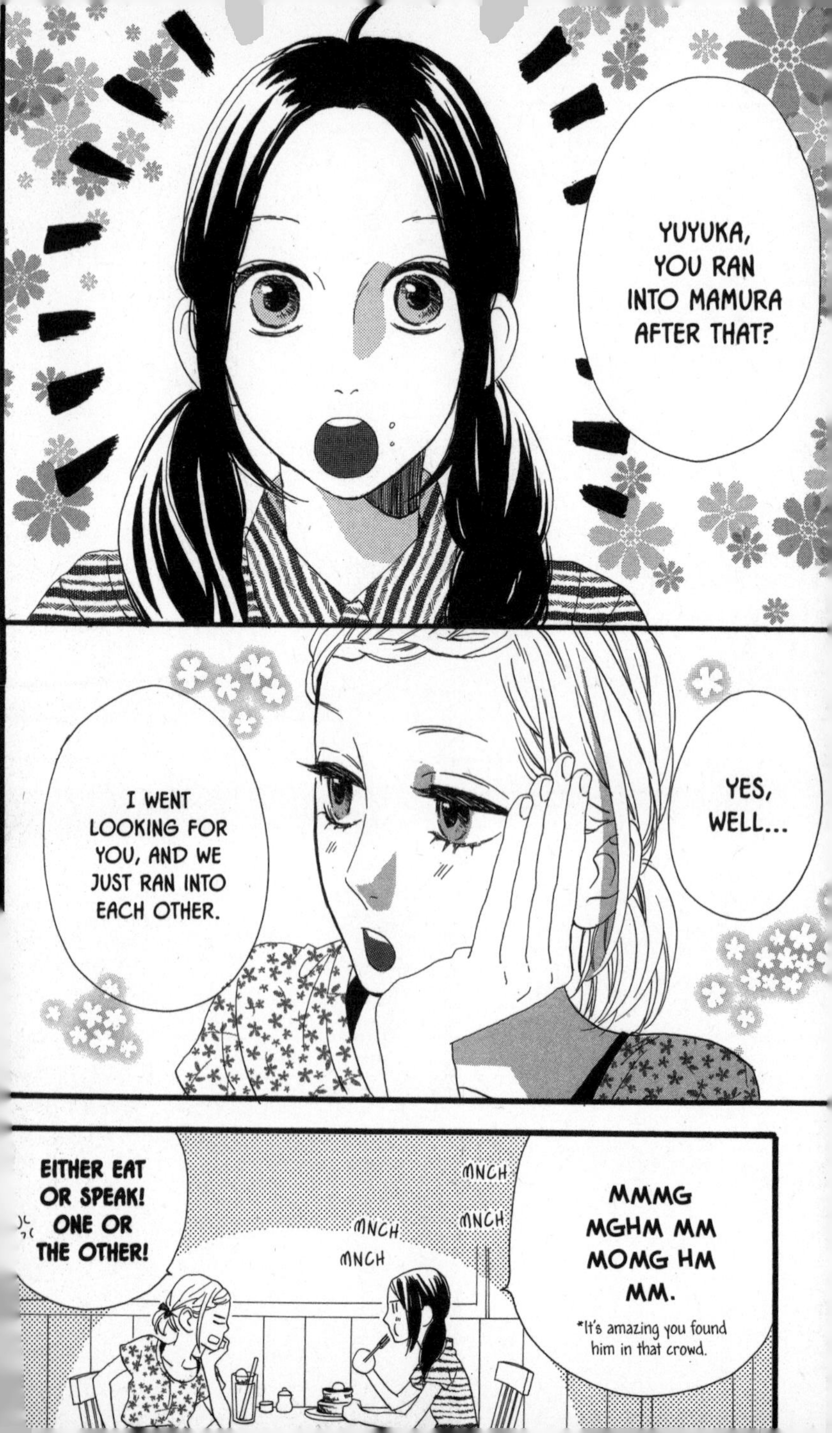

YUYUKA, YOU RAN INTO MAMURA AFTER THAT?
YES, WELL...
I WENT LOOKING FOR YOU, AND WE JUST RAN INTO EACH OTHER.
MMMG MGHM MM MOMG HM MM.
*It's amazing you found him in that crowd.
MNCH
MNCH
MNCH
MNCH
EITHER EAT OR SPEAK! ONE OR THE OTHER!

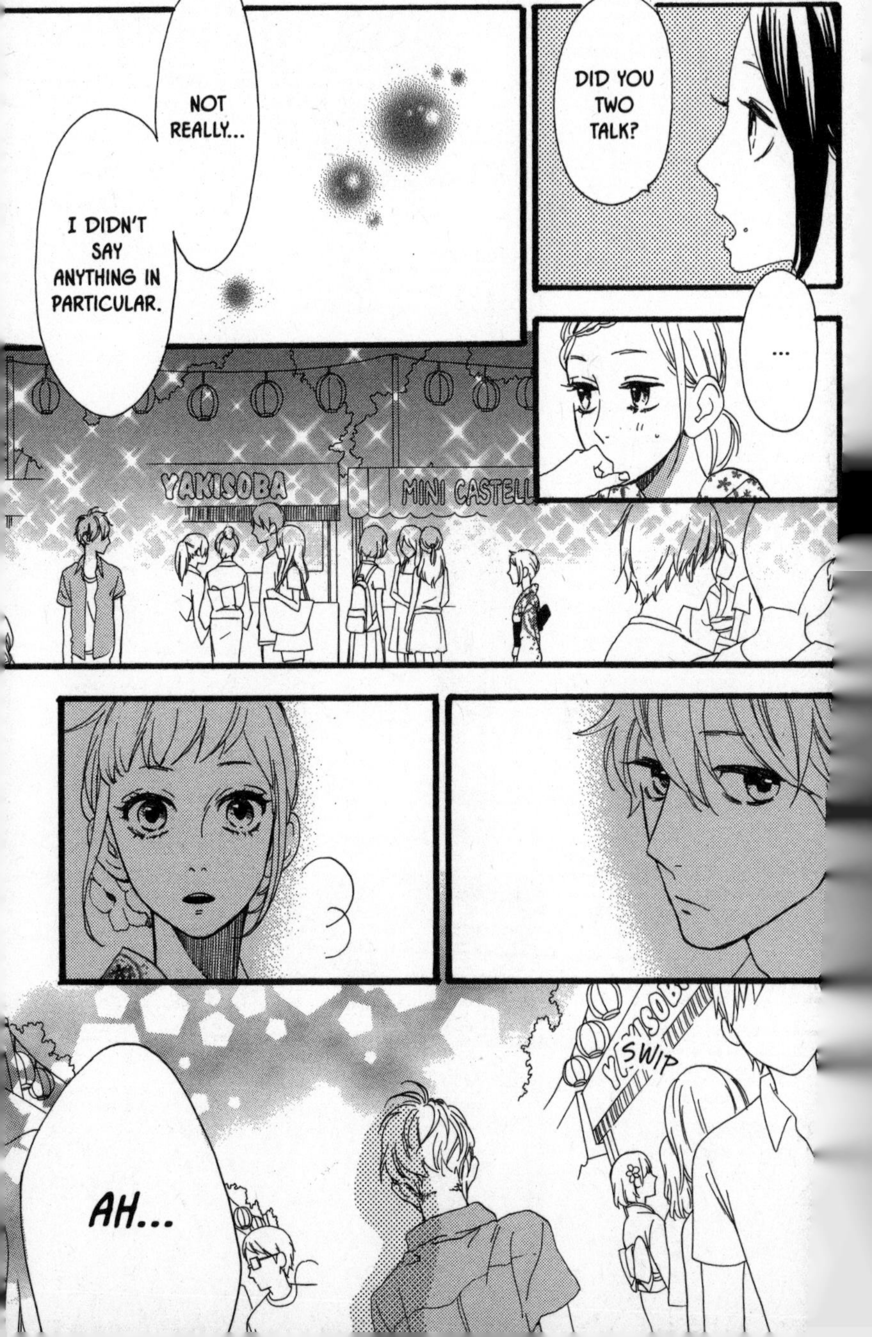
DID YOU TWO TALK?
...
NOT REALLY...
I DIDN'T SAY ANYTHING IN PARTICULAR.
YAKISOBA
MINI CASTELL
SWIP
AH...

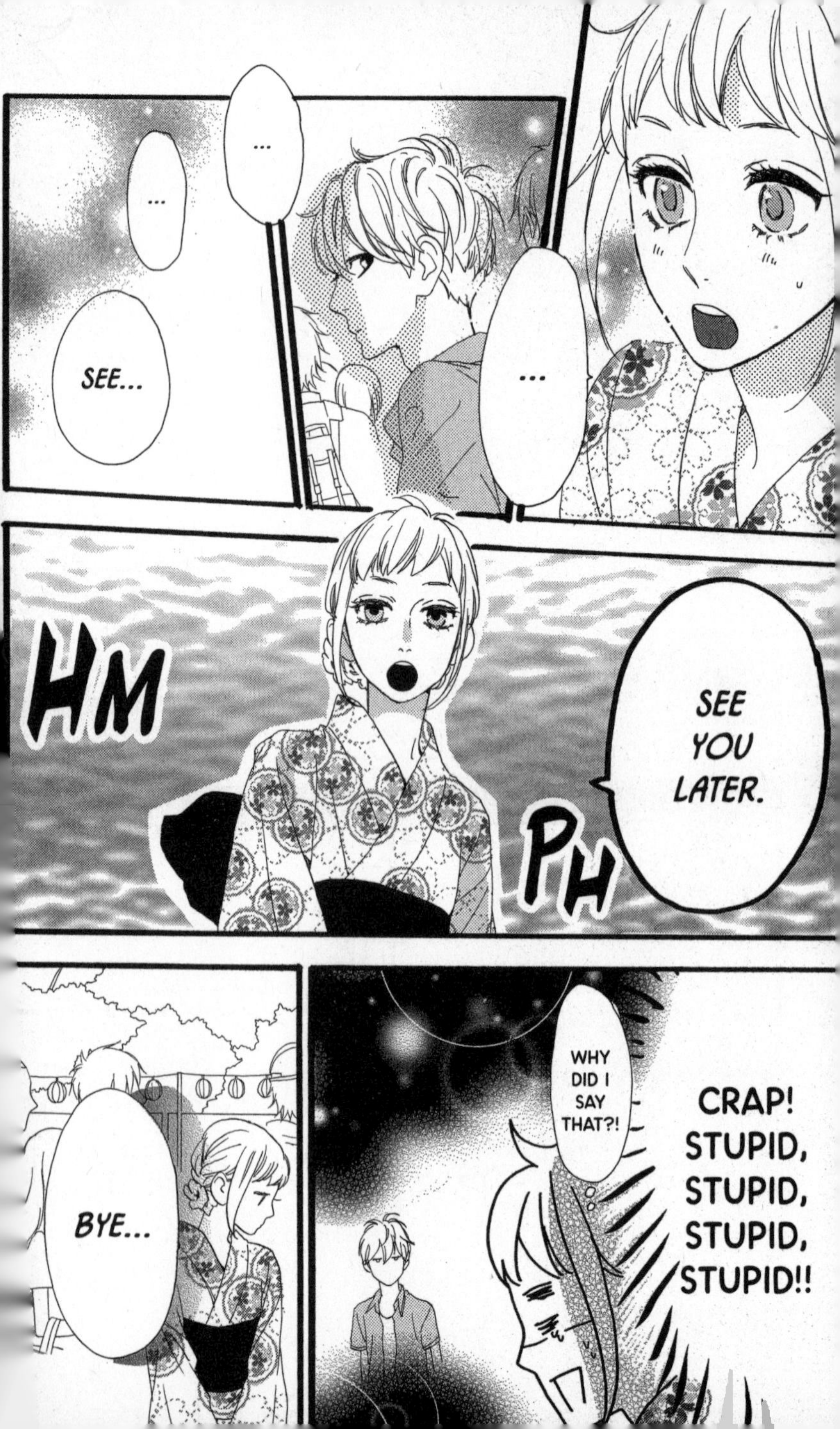
...
...
...
SEE...
SEE YOU LATER.
HM
PH
WHY DID I SAY THAT?!
CRAP! STUPID, STUPID, STUPID, STUPID!!
BYE...

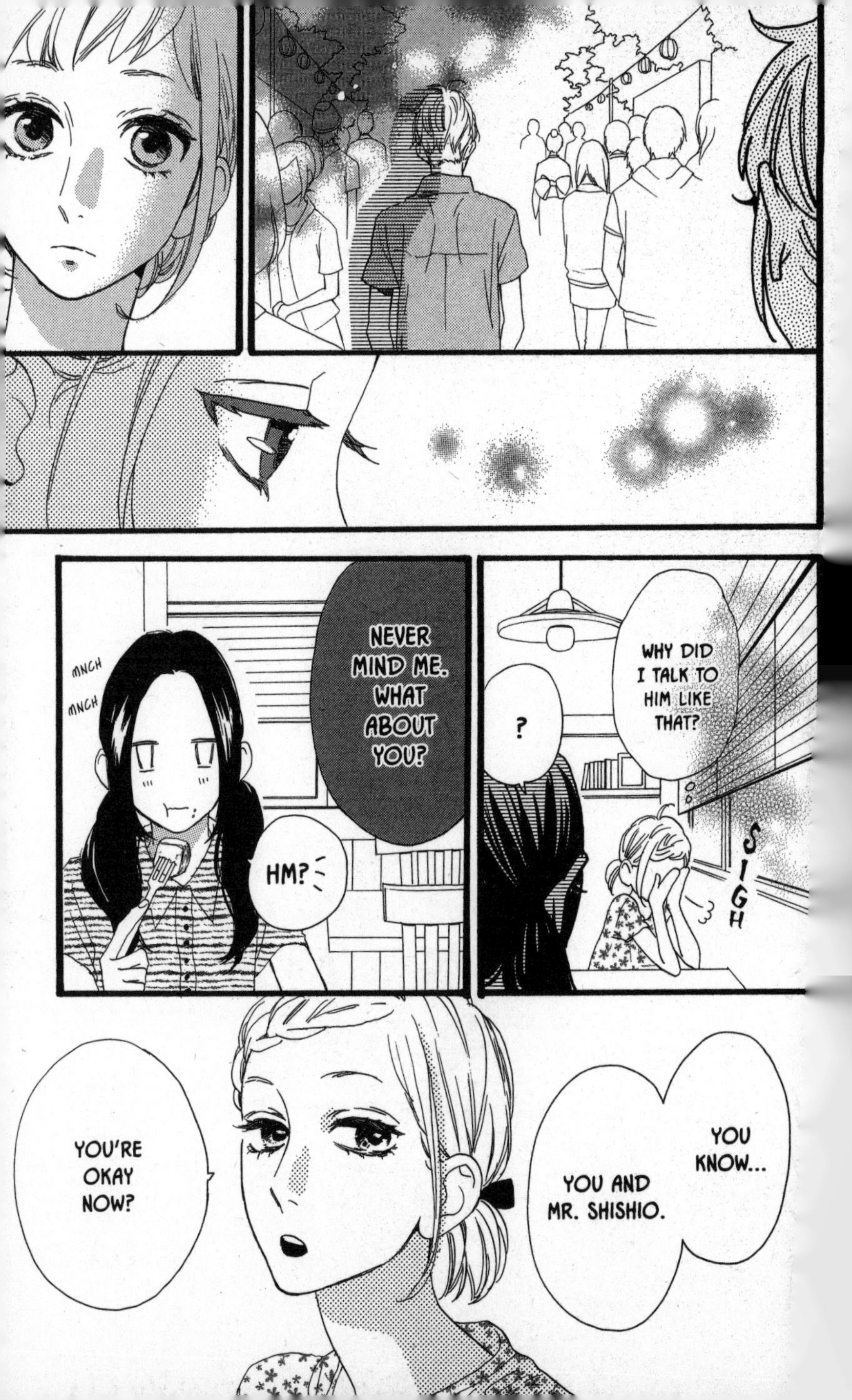
WHY DID I TALK TO HIM LIKE THAT?
?
SIGH
NEVER MIND ME. WHAT ABOUT YOU?
MNCH MNCH
HM?
YOU KNOW...
YOU AND MR. SHISHIO.
YOU'RE OKAY NOW?

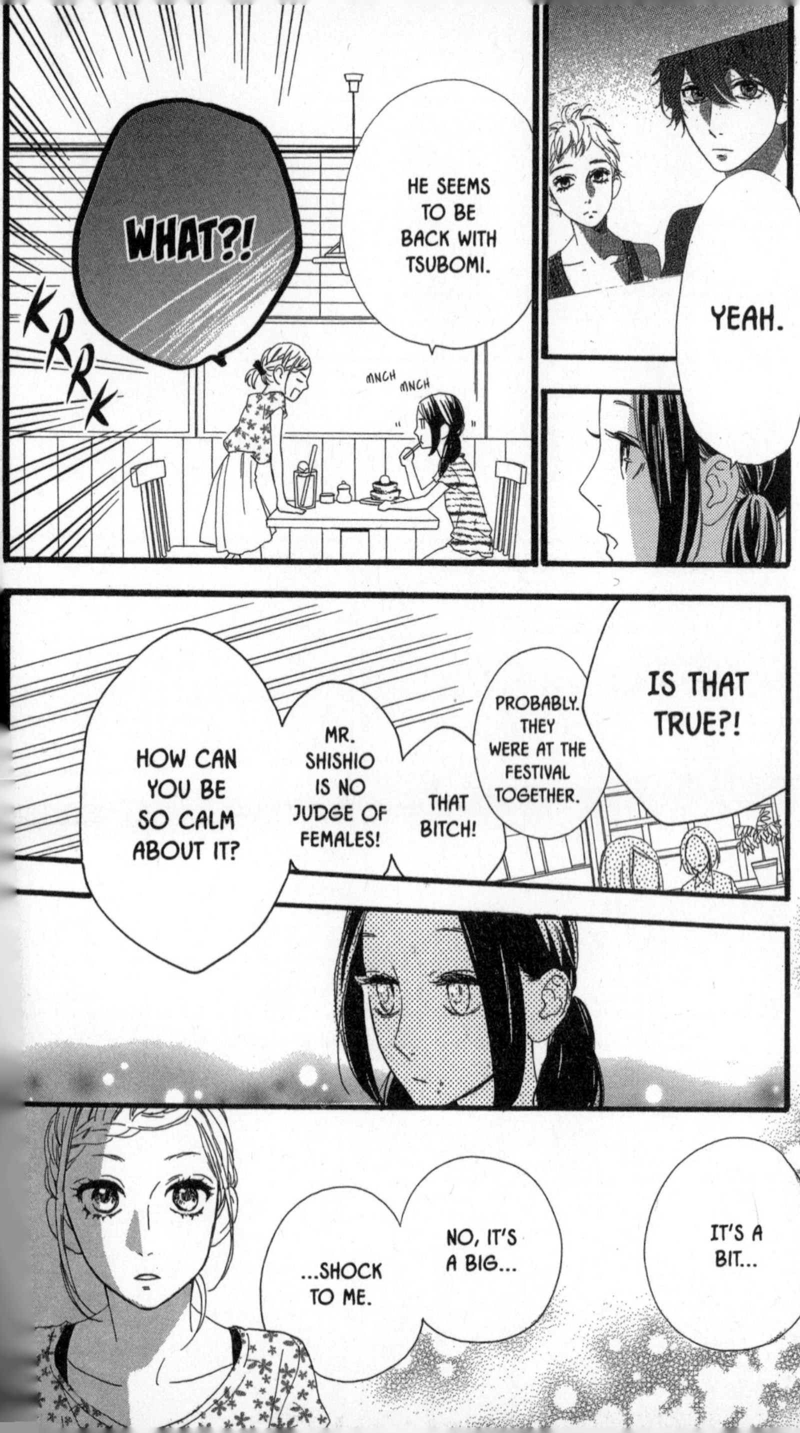
YEAH.
HE SEEMS TO BE BACK WITH TSUBOMI.
WHAT?!
KRRK
MNCH MNCH
IS THAT TRUE?!
PROBABLY. THEY WERE AT THE FESTIVAL TOGETHER.
THAT BITCH!
MR. SHISHIO IS NO JUDGE OF FEMALES!
HOW CAN YOU BE SO CALM ABOUT IT?
IT'S A BIT...
NO, IT'S A BIG...
...SHOCK TO ME.

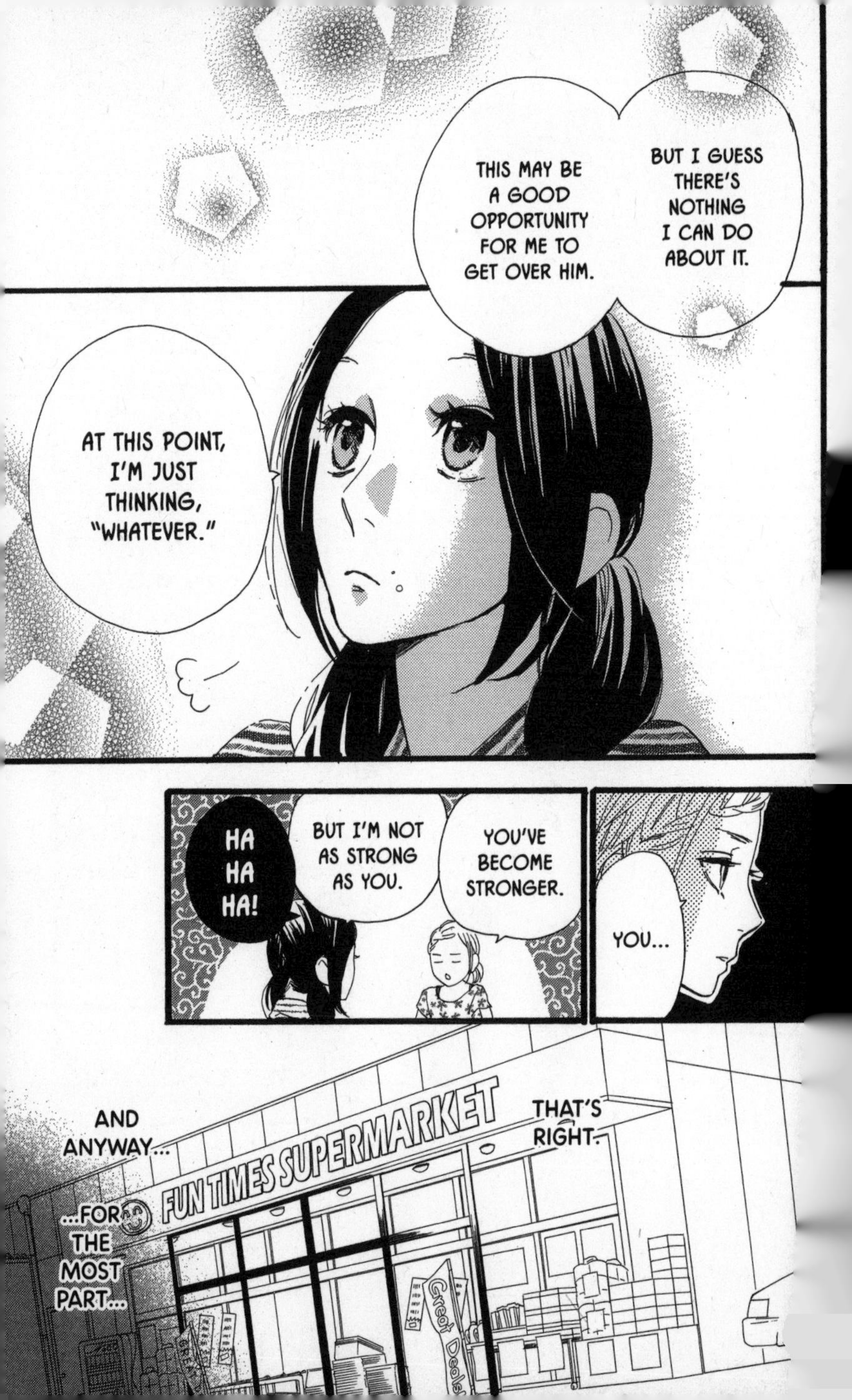
BUT I GUESS THERE'S NOTHING I CAN DO ABOUT IT.
THIS MAY BE A GOOD OPPORTUNITY FOR ME TO GET OVER HIM.
AT THIS POINT, I'M JUST THINKING, "WHATEVER."
YOU...
YOU'VE BECOME STRONGER.
BUT I'M NOT AS STRONG AS YOU.
HA HA HA!
THAT'S RIGHT.
AND ANYWAY...
...FOR THE MOST PART...
FUN TIMES SUPERMARKET
Great Deals

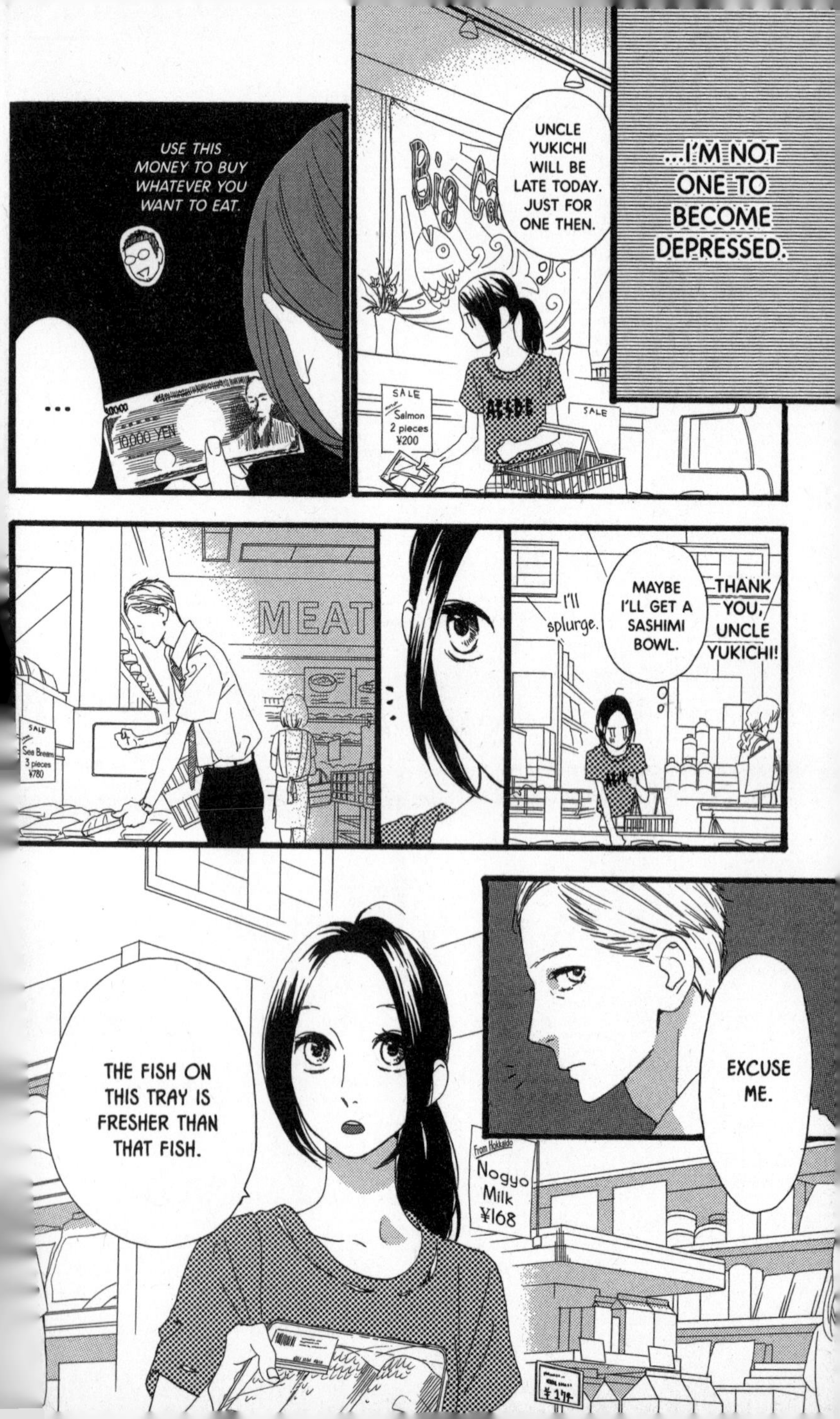
...I'M NOT ONE TO BECOME DEPRESSED.
UNCLE YUKICHI WILL BE LATE TODAY. JUST FOR ONE THEN.
SALE Salmon 2 pieces ¥200
SALE
USE THIS MONEY TO BUY WHATEVER YOU WANT TO EAT.
...
10,000 YEN
THANK YOU, UNCLE YUKICHI!
MAYBE I'LL GET A SASHIMI BOWL.
I'll splurge.
MEAT
SALE See Bream 3 pieces ¥780
EXCUSE ME.
THE FISH ON THIS TRAY IS FRESHER THAN THAT FISH.
From Hokkaido Nogyo Milk ¥168

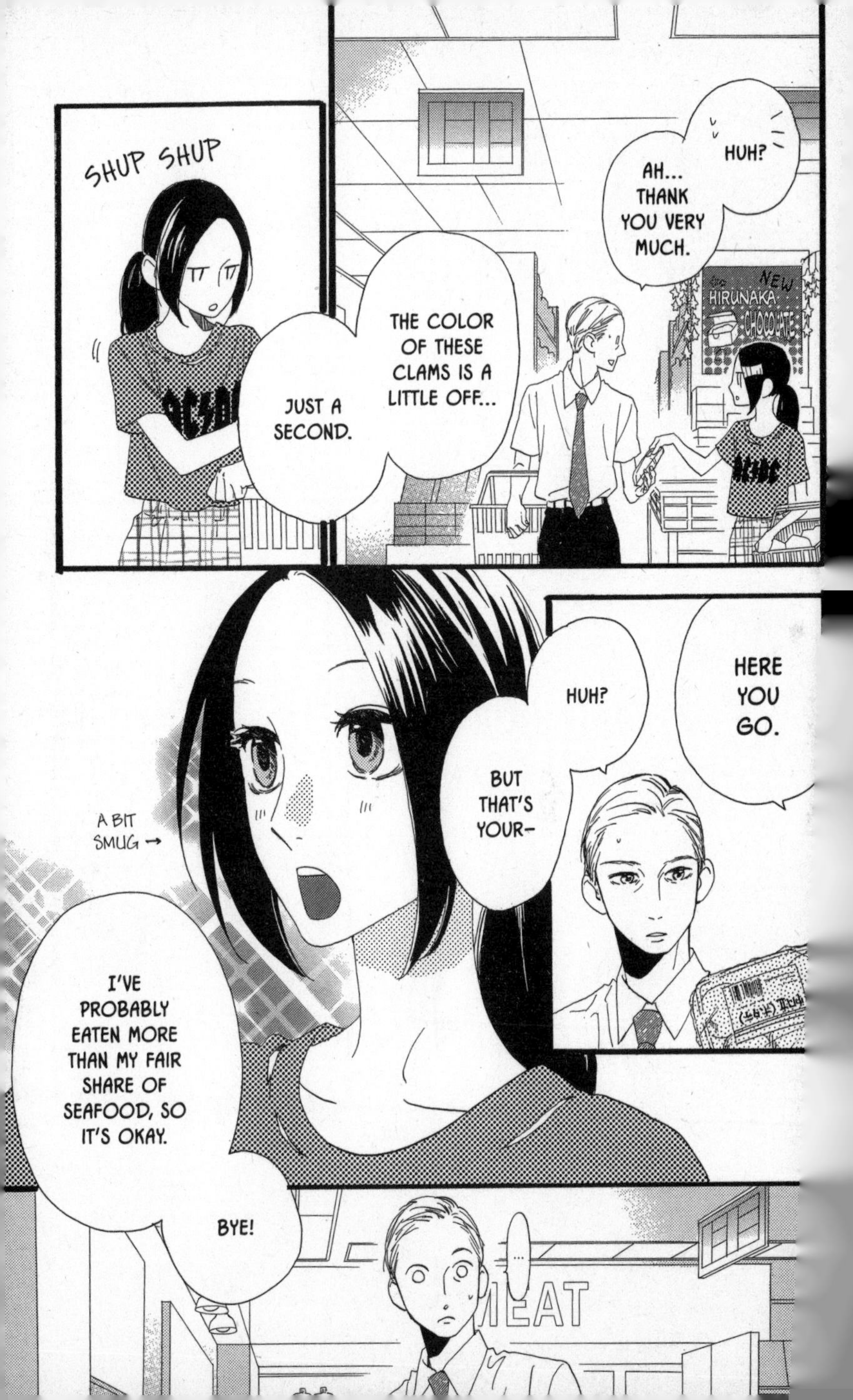
HUH?
AH... THANK YOU VERY MUCH.
NEW HIRUNAKA CHOCOLATE
THE COLOR OF THESE CLAMS IS A LITTLE OFF...
JUST A SECOND.
SHUP SHUP
HERE YOU GO.
HUH?
BUT THAT'S YOUR-
A BIT SMUG →
I'VE PROBABLY EATEN MORE THAN MY FAIR SHARE OF SEAFOOD, SO IT'S OKAY.
BYE!
...
MEAT

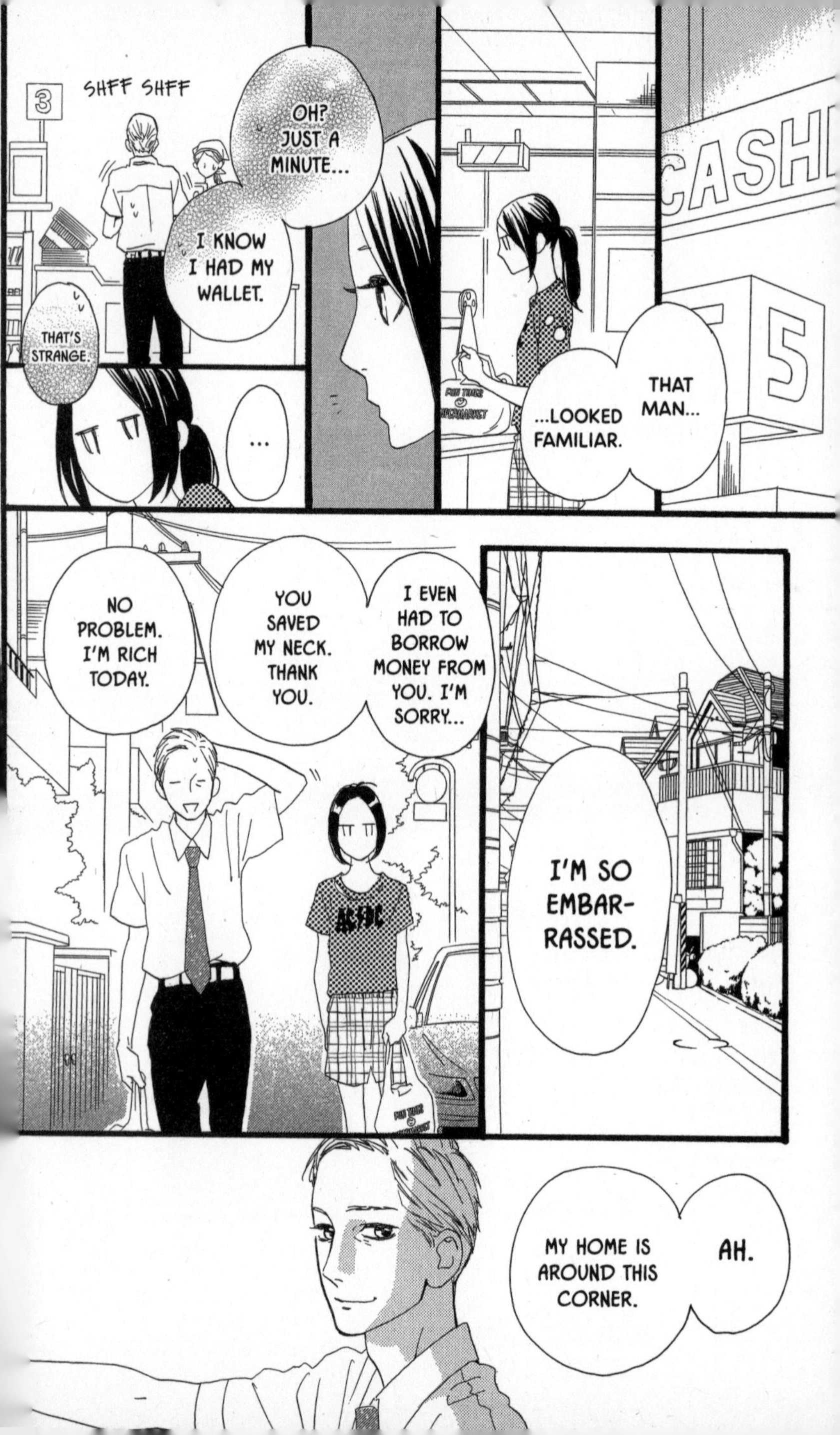
THAT MAN...
...LOOKED FAMILIAR.
3
SHFF SHFF
OH? JUST A MINUTE...
I KNOW I HAD MY WALLET.
THAT'S STRANGE.
...
I'M SO EMBARRASSED.
I EVEN HAD TO BORROW MONEY FROM YOU. I'M SORRY...
YOU SAVED MY NECK. THANK YOU.
NO PROBLEM. I'M RICH TODAY.
AH.
MY HOME IS AROUND THIS CORNER.

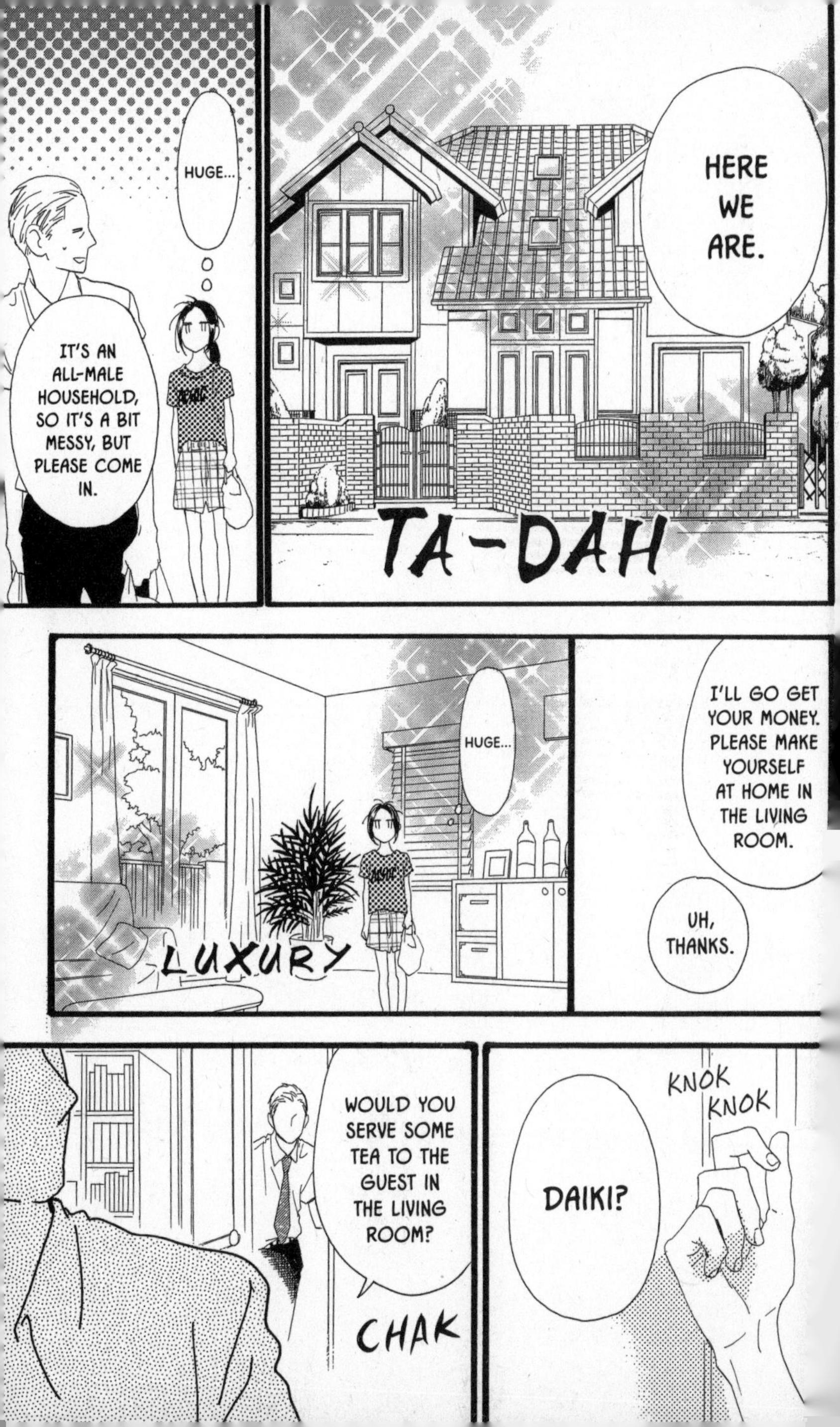
HERE WE ARE.
TA-DAH
HUGE...
IT'S AN ALL-MALE HOUSEHOLD, SO IT'S A BIT MESSY, BUT PLEASE COME IN.
I'LL GO GET YOUR MONEY. PLEASE MAKE YOURSELF AT HOME IN THE LIVING ROOM.
UH, THANKS.
HUGE...
LUXURY
KNOK KNOK
DAIKI?
WOULD YOU SERVE SOME TEA TO THE GUEST IN THE LIVING ROOM?
CHAK

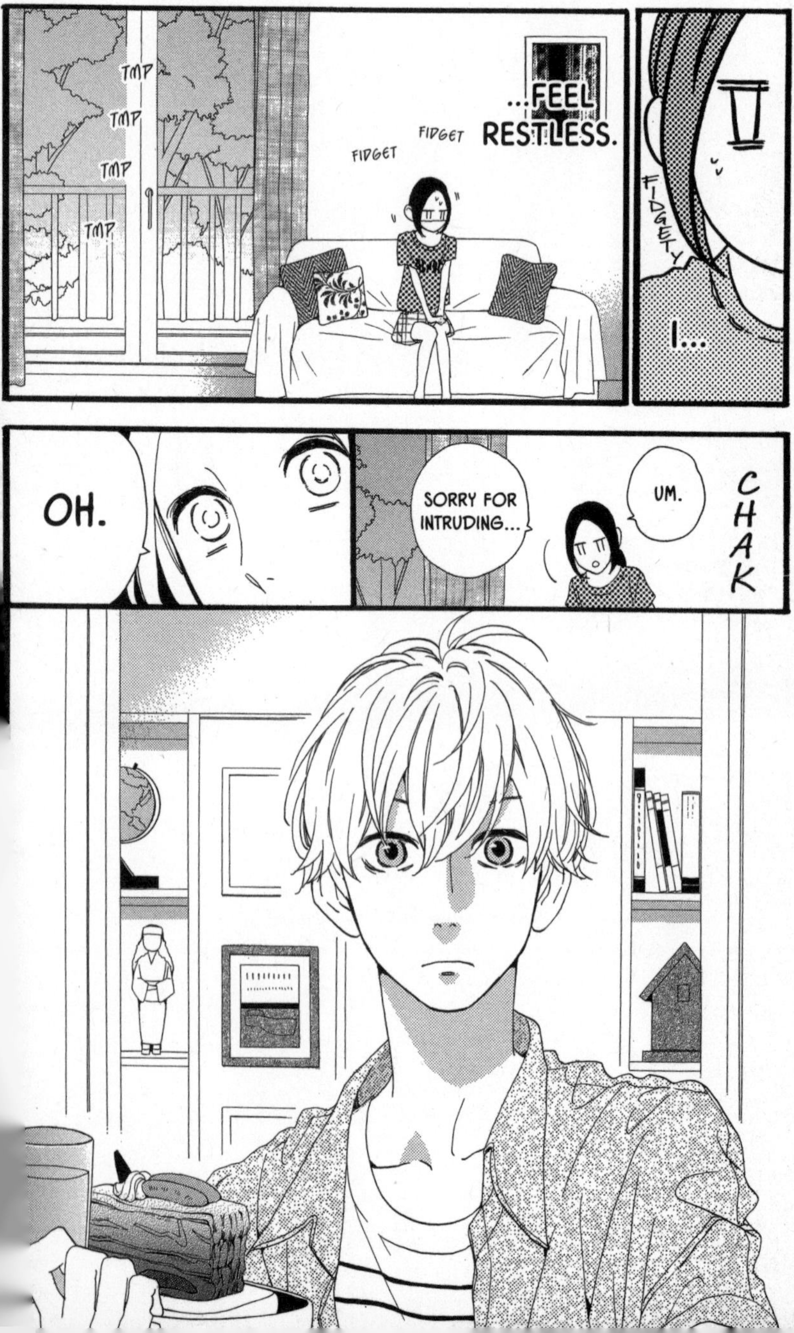
FIDGETY
I...
...FEEL RESTLESS.
FIDGET
FIDGET
TMP
TMP
TMP
TMP
CHAK
UM.
SORRY FOR INTRUDING...
OH.

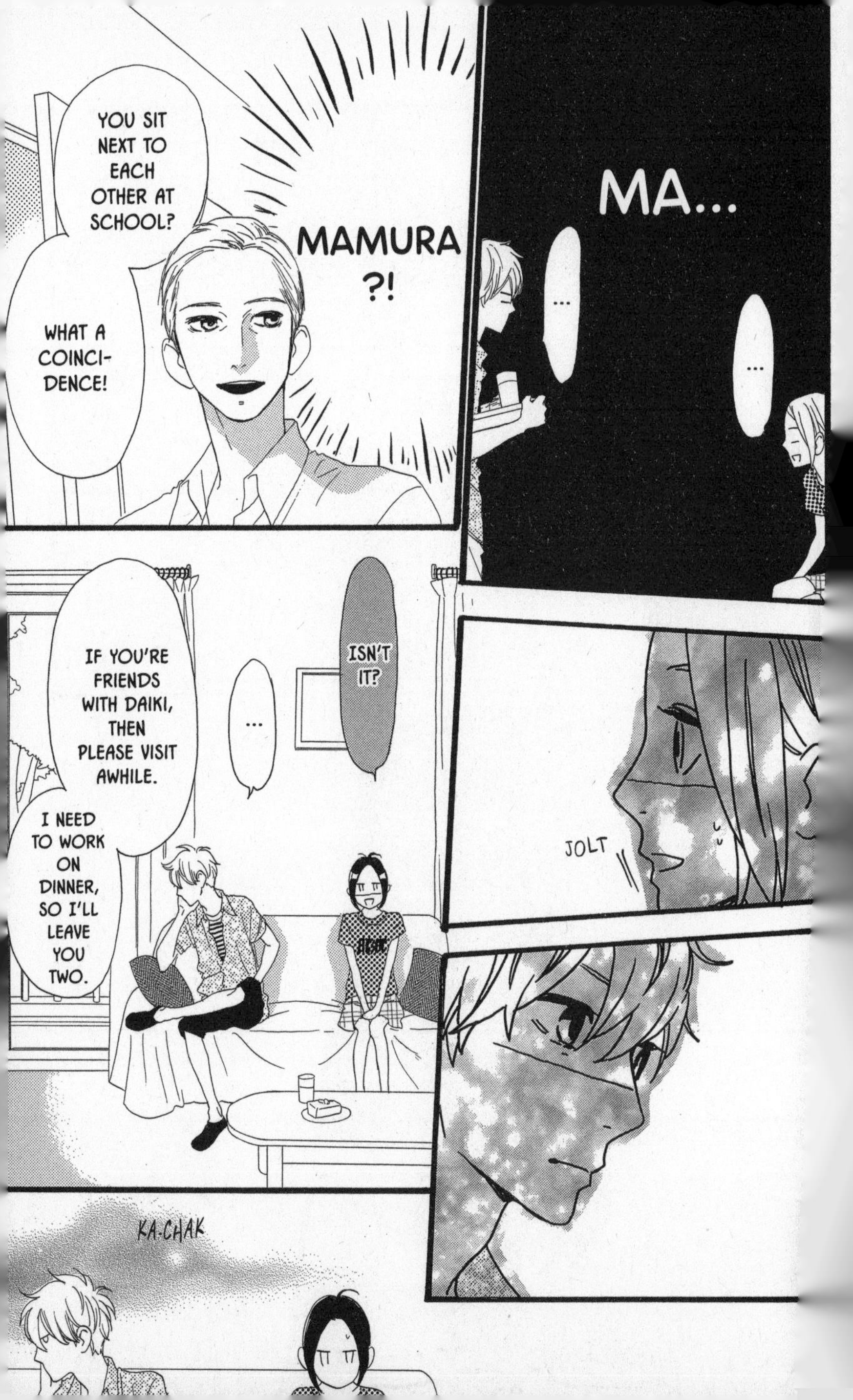
MA...
...
...
YOU SIT NEXT TO EACH OTHER AT SCHOOL?
WHAT A COINCI-DENCE!
MAMURA ?!
JOLT
ISN'T IT?
...
IF YOU'RE FRIENDS WITH DAIKI, THEN PLEASE VISIT AWHILE.
I NEED TO WORK ON DINNER, SO I'LL LEAVE YOU TWO.
KA-CHAK

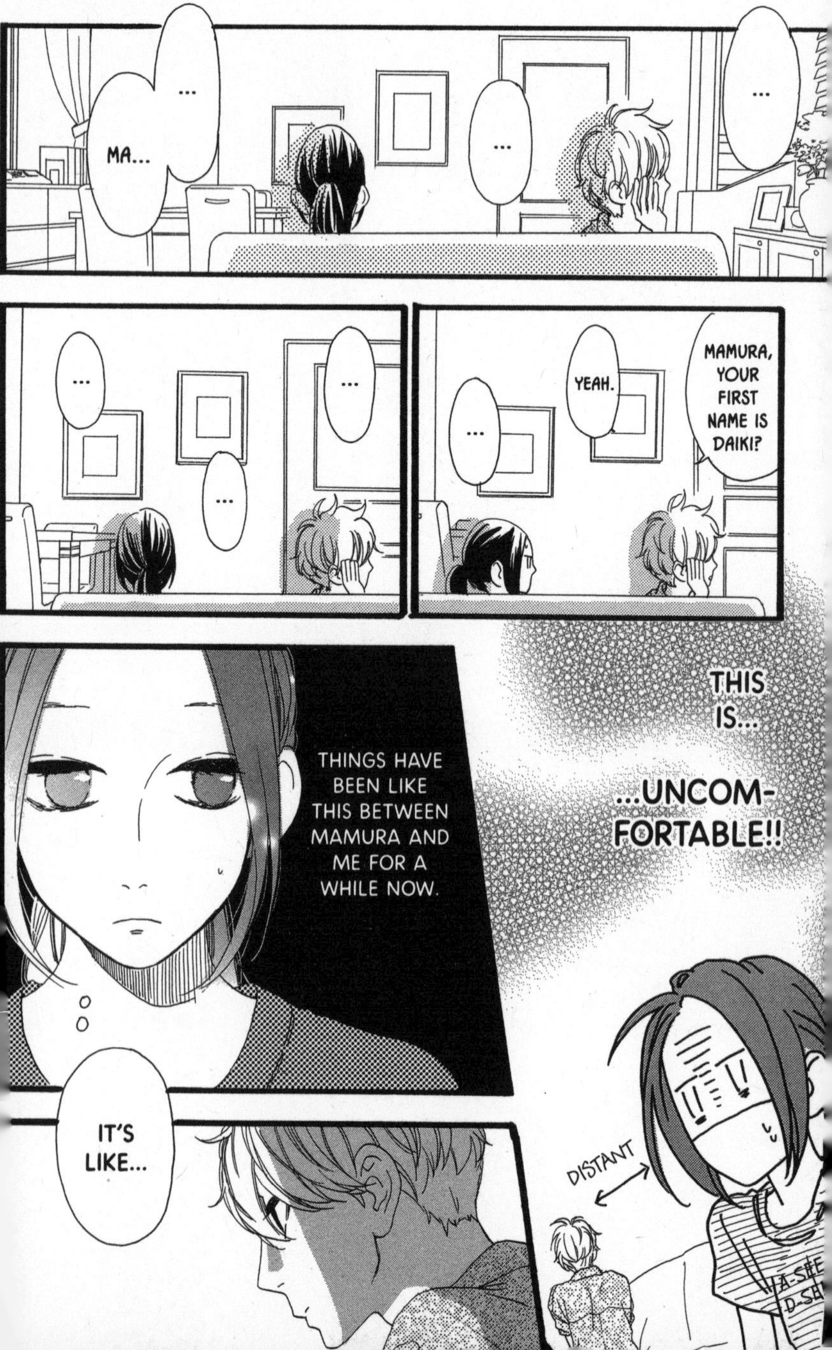
...
...
...
MA...
MAMURA, YOUR FIRST NAME IS DAIKI?
YEAH.
...
...
...
...
THIS IS...
...UNCOM-FORTABLE!!
THINGS HAVE BEEN LIKE THIS BETWEEN MAMURA AND ME FOR A WHILE NOW.
DISTANT
IT'S LIKE...

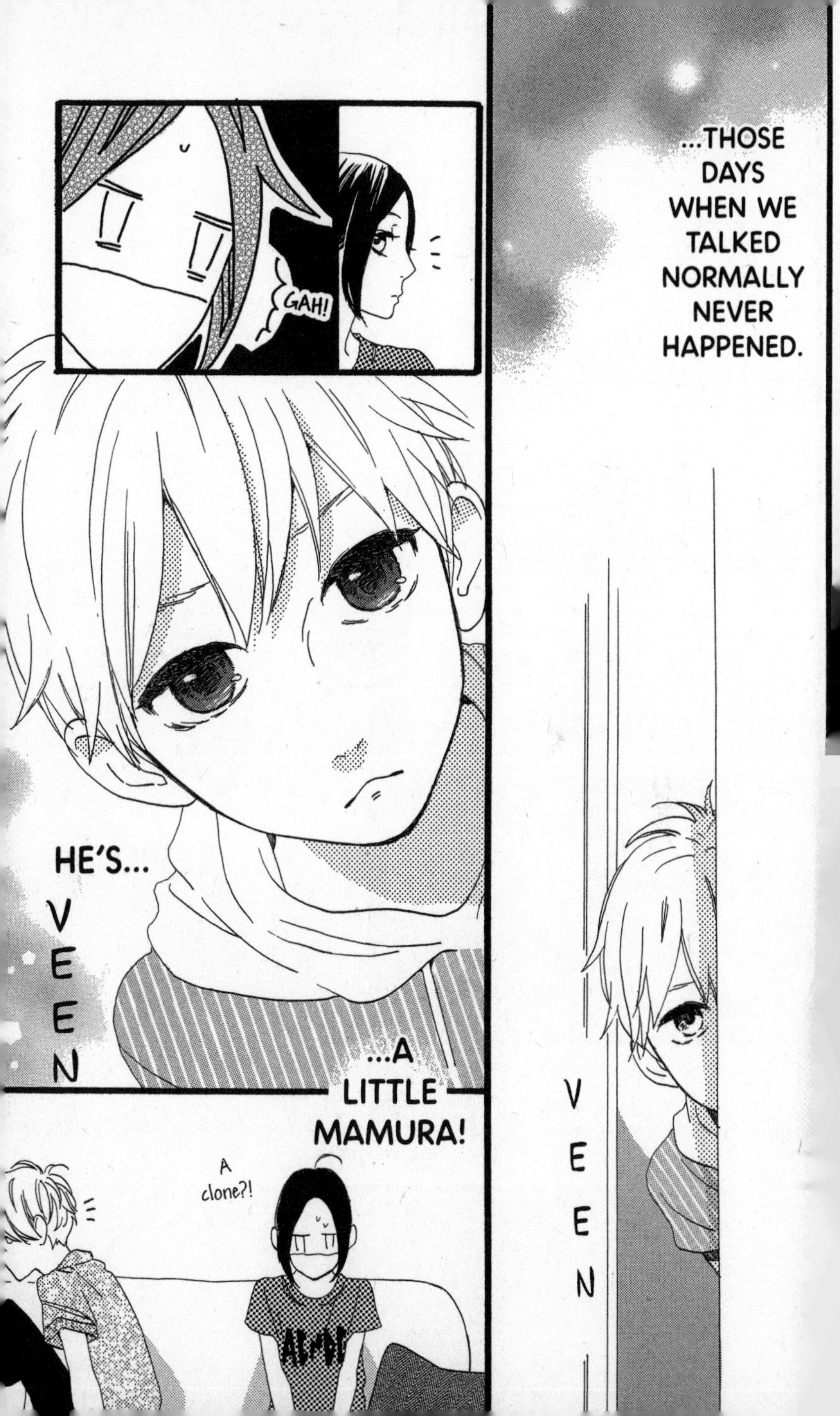
...THOSE DAYS WHEN WE TALKED NORMALLY NEVER HAPPENED.
VEEN
GAH!
HE'S...
VEEN
...A LITTLE MAMURA!
A clone?!

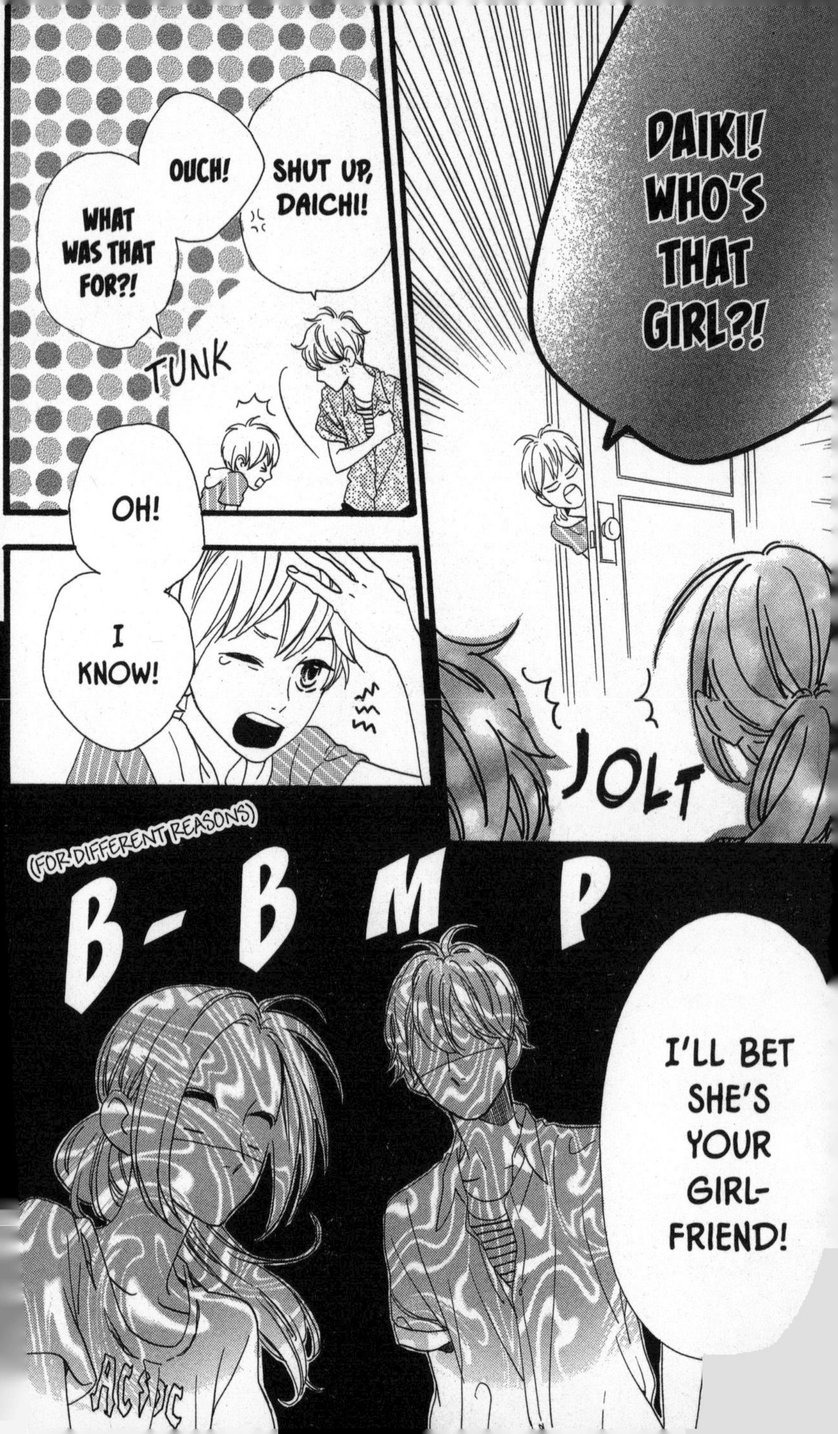
DAIKI! WHO'S THAT GIRL?!
JOLT
SHUT UP, DAICHI!
OUCH! WHAT WAS THAT FOR?!
TUNK
OH! I KNOW!
I'LL BET SHE'S YOUR GIRL-FRIEND!
B-BMP
(FOR DIFFERENT REASONS)

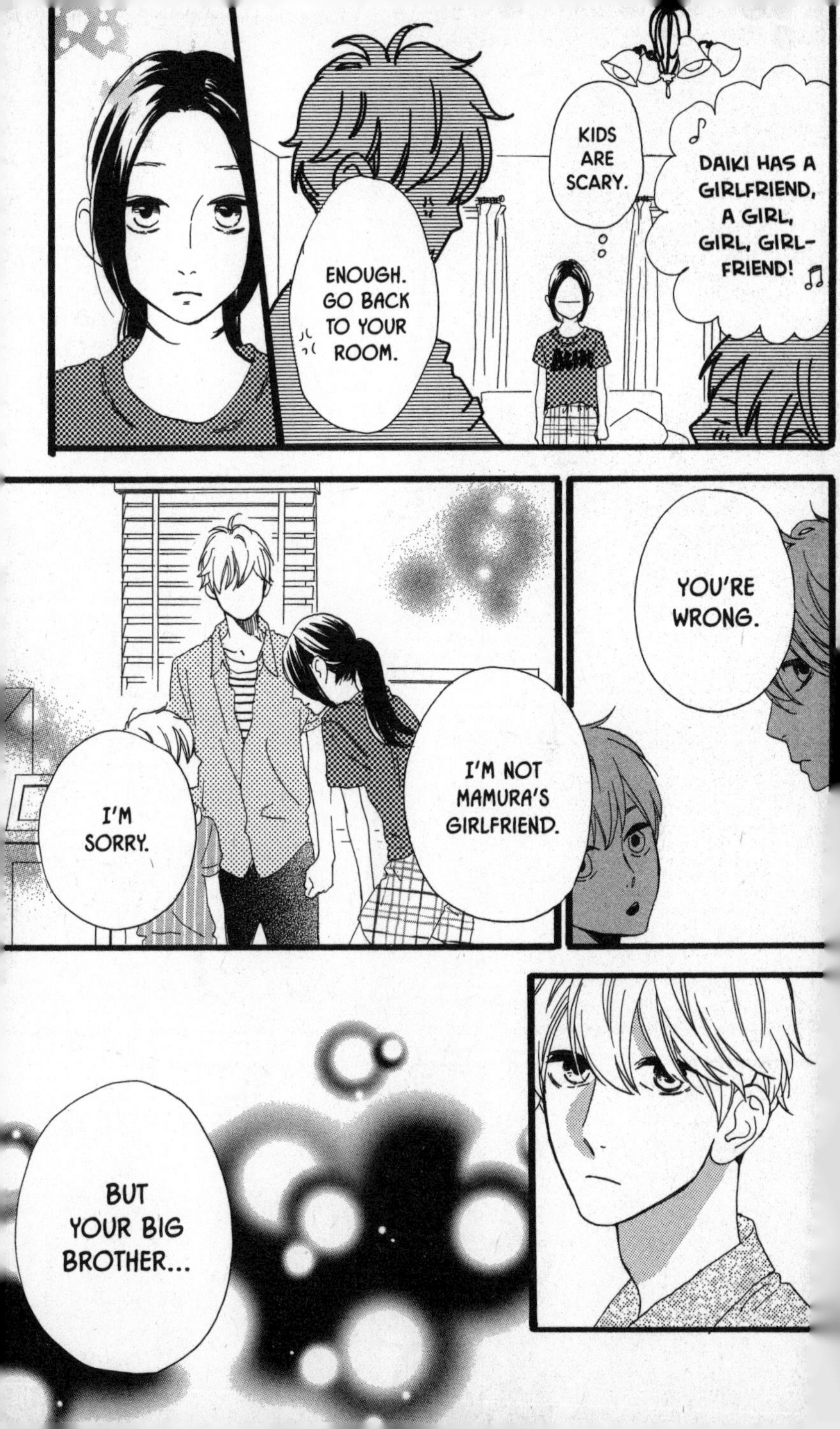
DAIKI HAS A GIRLFRIEND, A GIRL, GIRL, GIRLFRIEND! ♫
KIDS ARE SCARY.
ENOUGH. GO BACK TO YOUR ROOM.
YOU'RE WRONG.
I'M NOT MAMURA'S GIRLFRIEND.
I'M SORRY.
BUT YOUR BIG BROTHER...

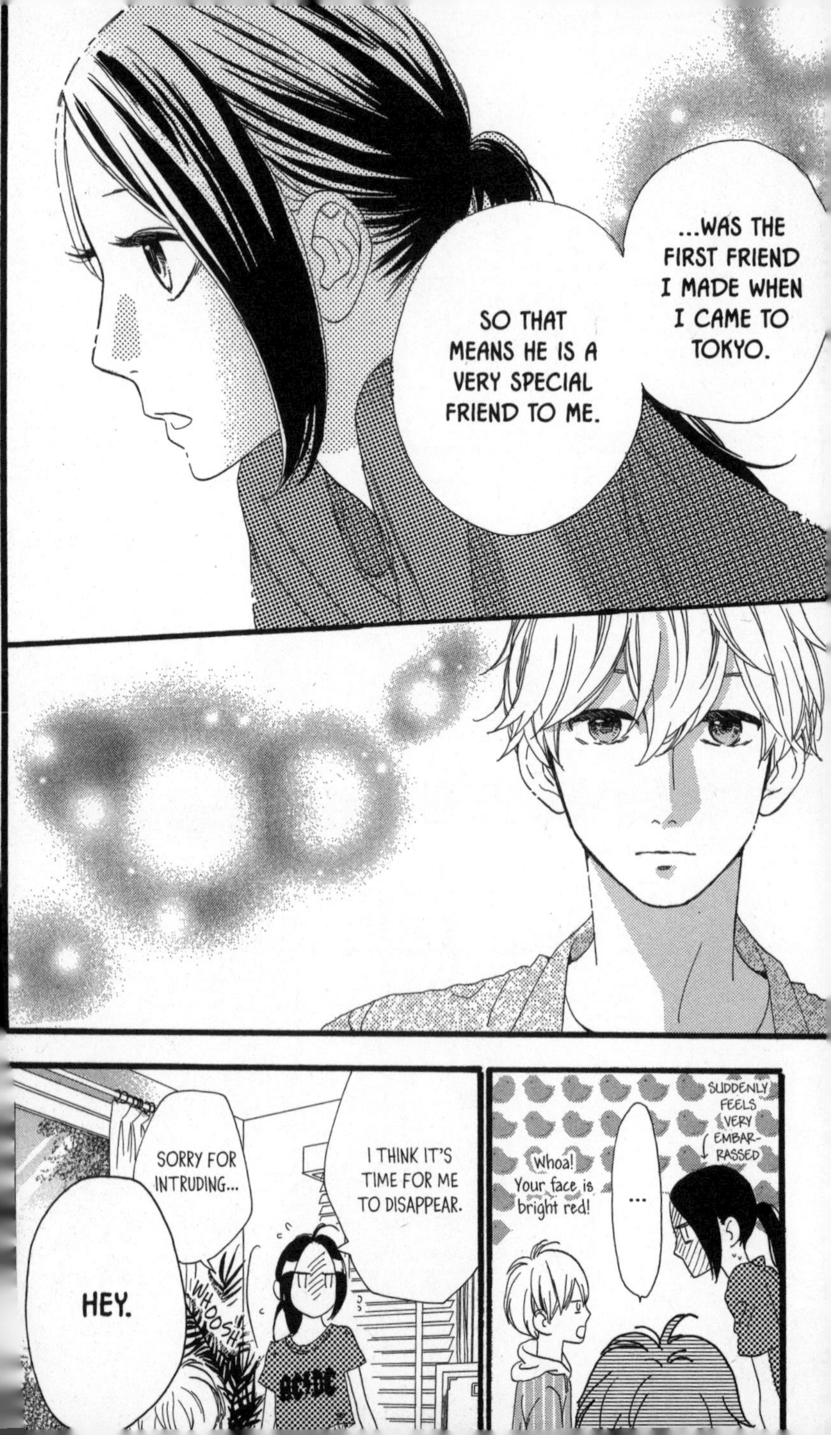
...WAS THE FIRST FRIEND I MADE WHEN I CAME TO TOKYO.
SO THAT MEANS HE IS A VERY SPECIAL FRIEND TO ME.
SUDDENLY FEELS VERY EMBARRASSED
...
Whoa! Your face is bright red!
I THINK IT'S TIME FOR ME TO DISAPPEAR.
SORRY FOR INTRUDING...
WHOOSH
HEY.

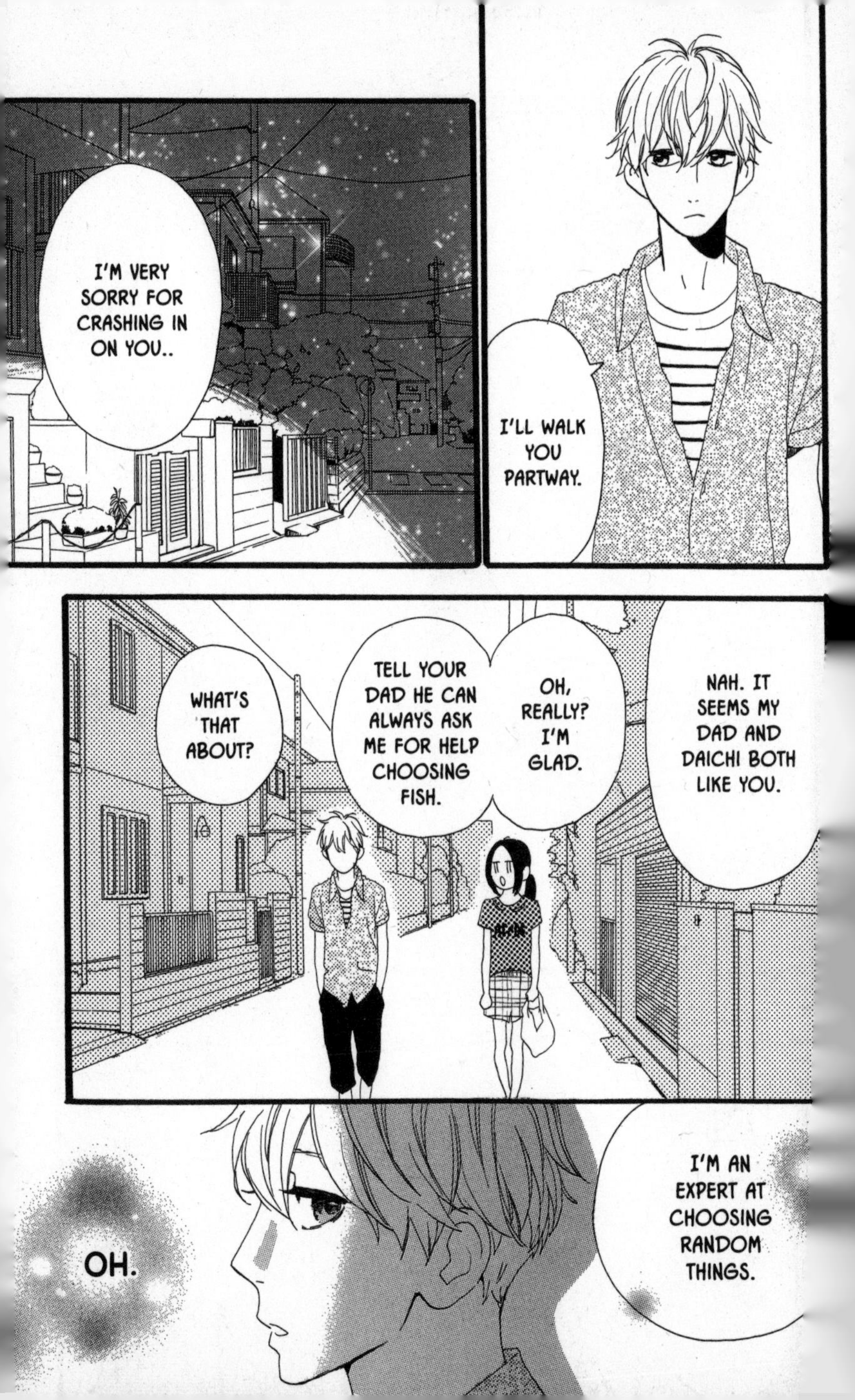
I'LL WALK YOU PARTWAY.
I'M VERY SORRY FOR CRASHING IN ON YOU..
NAH. IT SEEMS MY DAD AND DAICHI BOTH LIKE YOU.
OH, REALLY? I'M GLAD.
TELL YOUR DAD HE CAN ALWAYS ASK ME FOR HELP CHOOSING FISH.
WHAT'S THAT ABOUT?
I'M AN EXPERT AT CHOOSING RANDOM THINGS.
OH.

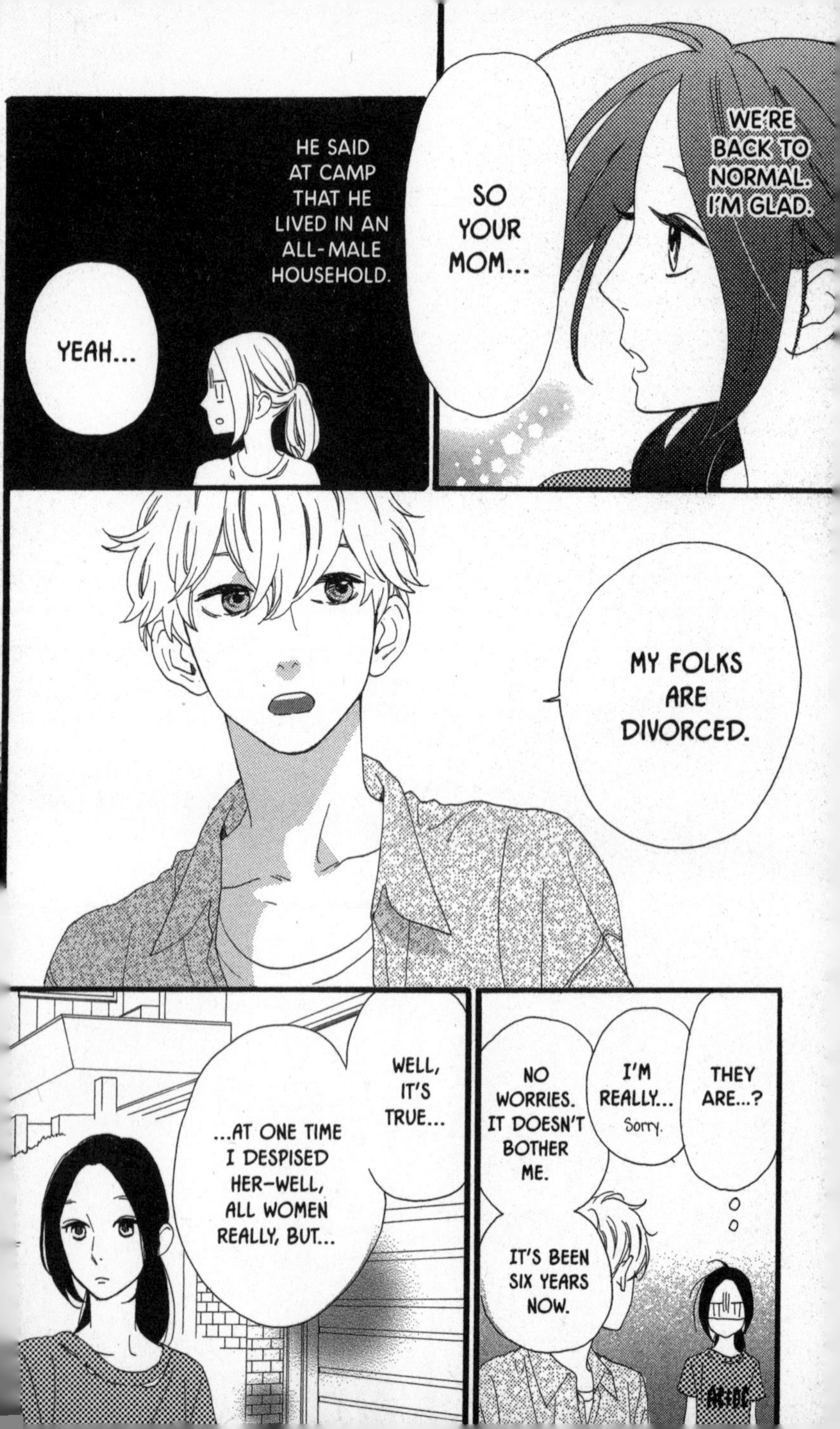
WE'RE BACK TO NORMAL. I'M GLAD.
SO YOUR MOM...
HE SAID AT CAMP THAT HE LIVED IN AN ALL-MALE HOUSEHOLD.
YEAH...
MY FOLKS ARE DIVORCED.
THEY ARE...?
I'M REALLY...
Sorry.
NO WORRIES. IT DOESN'T BOTHER ME.
IT'S BEEN SIX YEARS NOW.
WELL, IT'S TRUE...
...AT ONE TIME I DESPISED HER—WELL, ALL WOMEN REALLY, BUT...

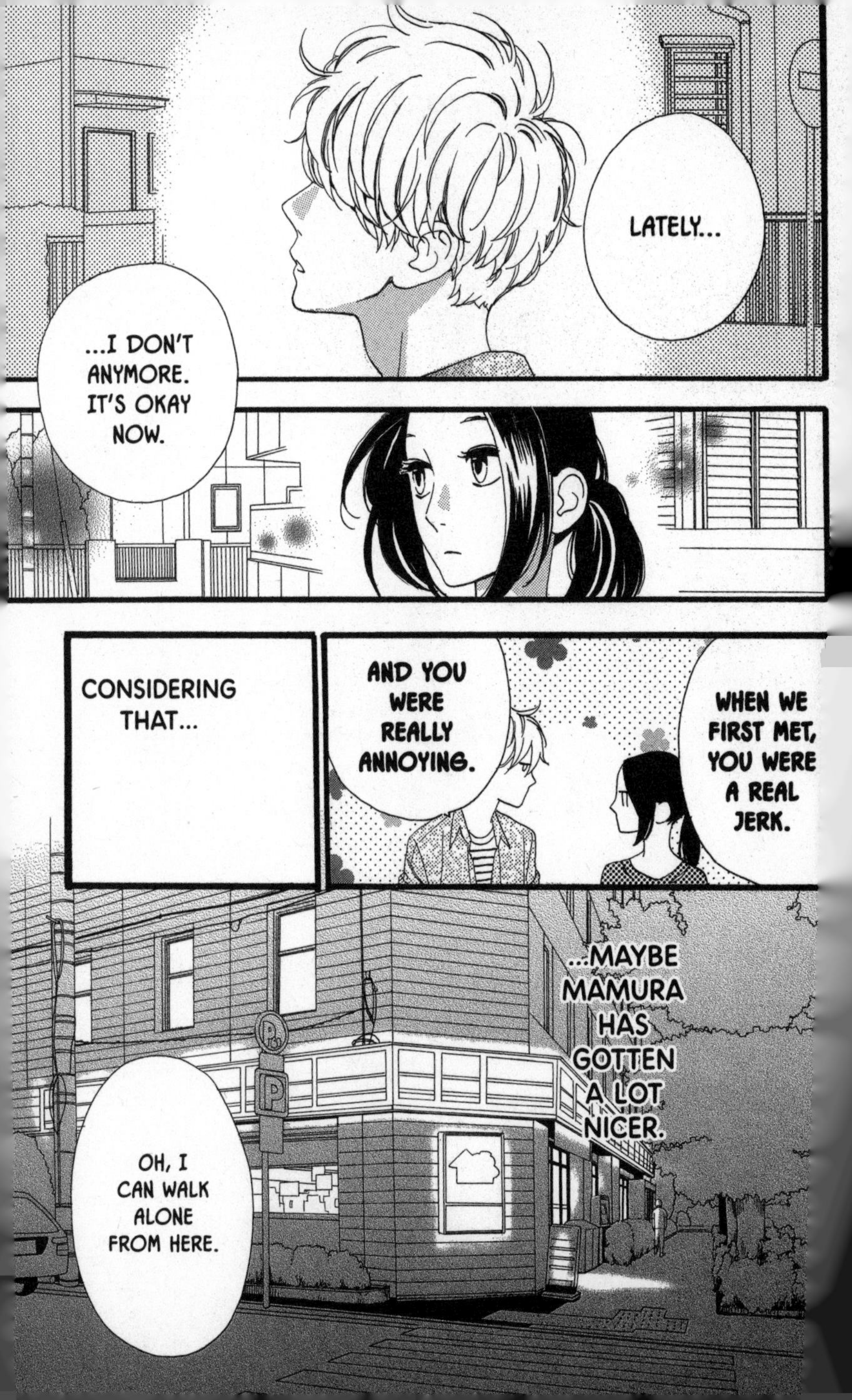
LATELY...
...I DON'T ANYMORE. IT'S OKAY NOW.
WHEN WE FIRST MET, YOU WERE A REAL JERK.
AND YOU WERE REALLY ANNOYING.
CONSIDERING THAT...
...MAYBE MAMURA HAS GOTTEN A LOT NICER.
OH, I CAN WALK ALONE FROM HERE.

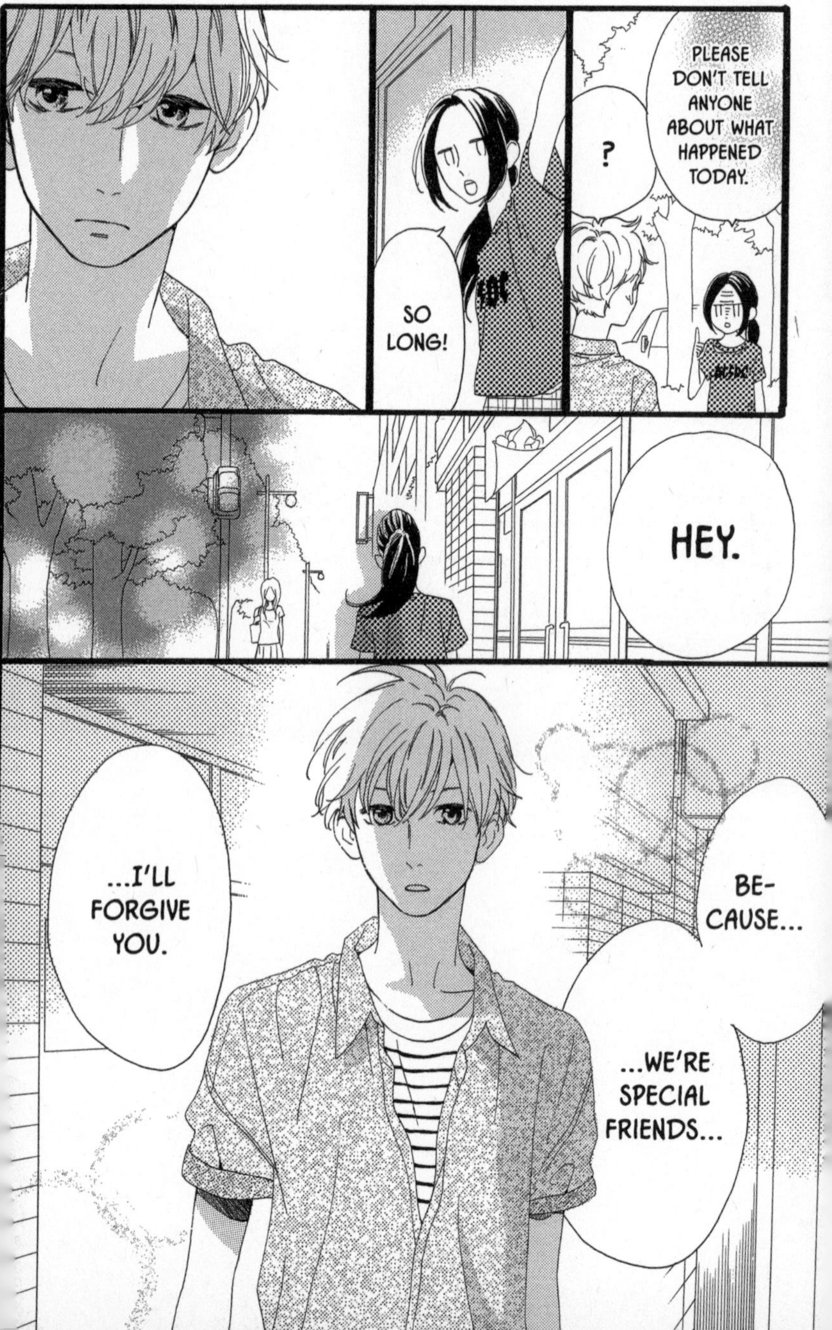
PLEASE DON'T TELL ANYONE ABOUT WHAT HAPPENED TODAY.
?
SO LONG!
HEY.
...I'LL FORGIVE YOU.
BE-CAUSE...
...WE'RE SPECIAL FRIENDS...

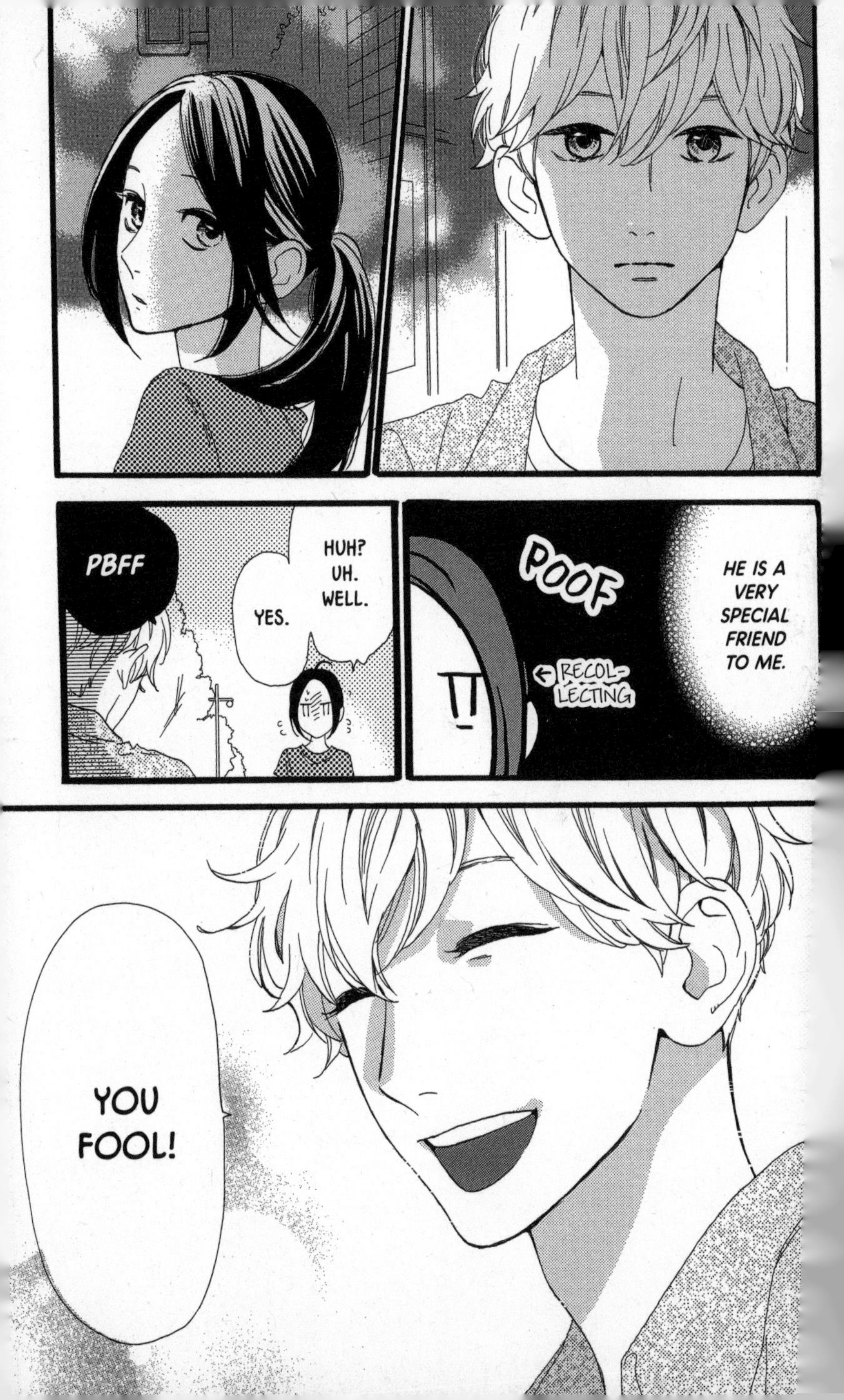
HE IS A VERY SPECIAL FRIEND TO ME.
POOF
← RECOL-LECTING
HUH? UH. WELL.
YES.
PBFF
YOU FOOL!

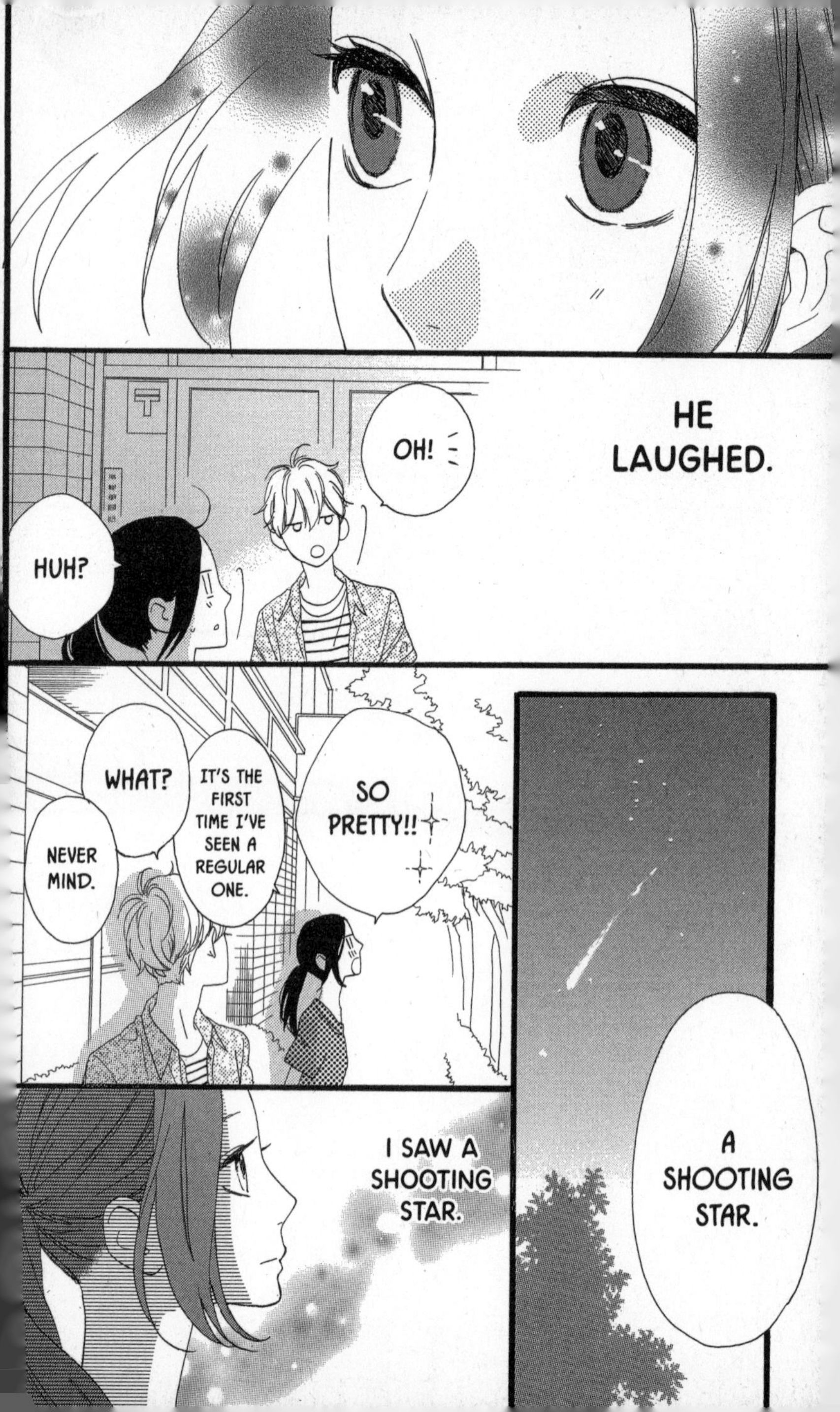
HE LAUGHED.
OH!
HUH?
A SHOOTING STAR.
SO PRETTY!!
IT'S THE FIRST TIME I'VE SEEN A REGULAR ONE.
WHAT?
NEVER MIND.
I SAW A SHOOTING STAR.

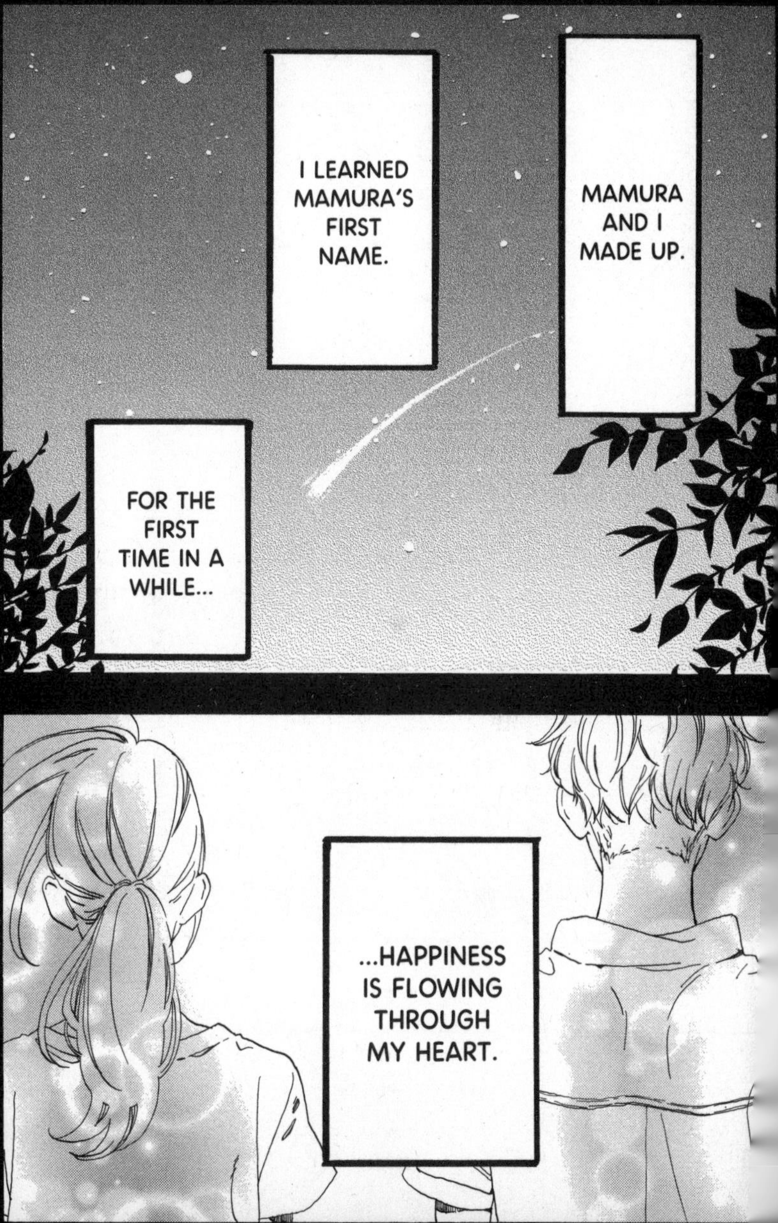
MAMURA AND I MADE UP.
I LEARNED MAMURA'S FIRST NAME.
FOR THE FIRST TIME IN A WHILE...
...HAPPINESS IS FLOWING THROUGH MY HEART.

Mamura's Everyday Life

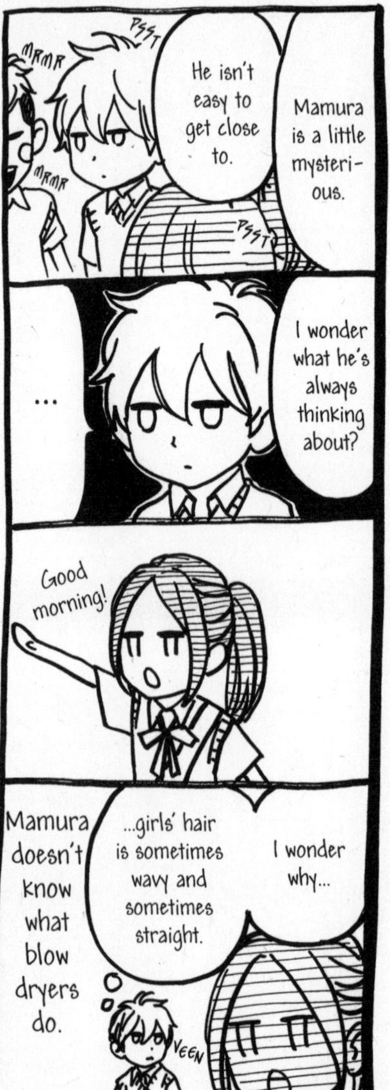
Mamura is a little mysteri-ous.
PSST
He isn't easy to get close to.
PSST
MRMR
MRMR
I wonder what he's always thinking about?
...
Good morning!
I wonder why...
...girls' hair is sometimes wavy and sometimes straight.
Mamura doesn't know what blow dryers do.
VEEN

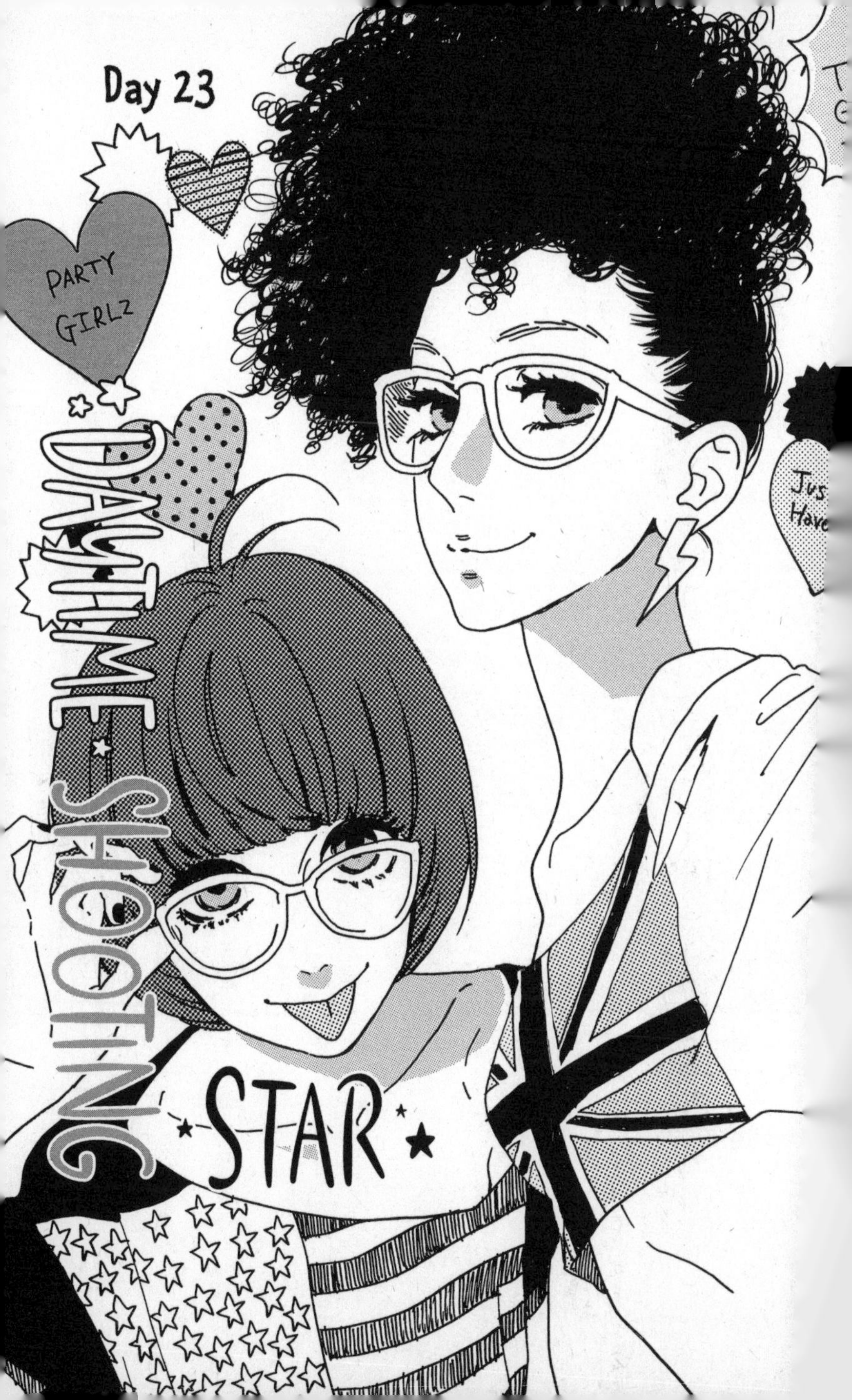
Day 23
PARTY GIRLZ
DAYTIME SHOOTING STAR

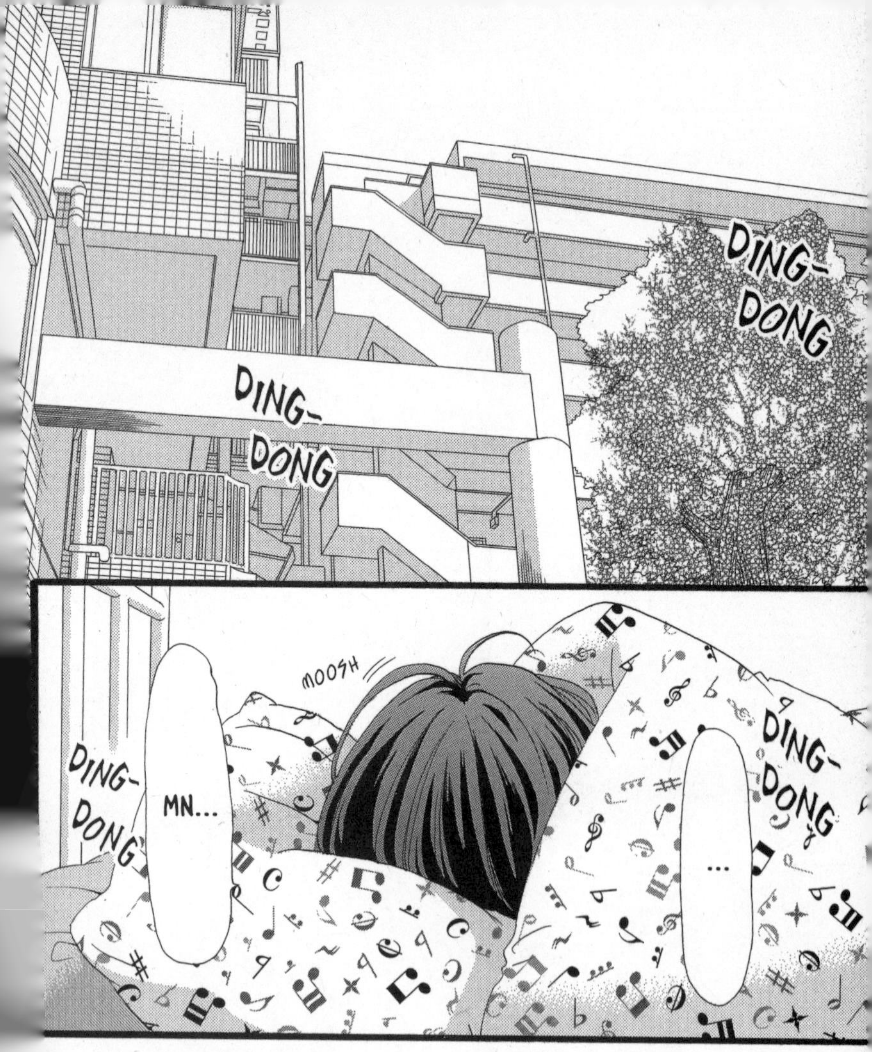
DING-DONG
DING-DONG
DING-DONG
...
MOOSH
MN...
DING-DONG

Tsubomi Kajima

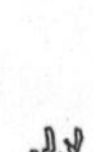

Let's watch digital TV!

Birthday: Sept. 7

Height: 5'3"

Weight: 104 lbs

he *ka* in Kajima means "deer." There is mascot for digital terrestrial television in Japan that is a deer.

Blood Type: AB

① Macadamia nuts. Dried cod with cheese snack.

② Camera. Othello.

③ She seems to have problems and yet not have them. But if you say she doesn't have any, it would be a lie. (She doesn't seem to use her camera much, does she?)

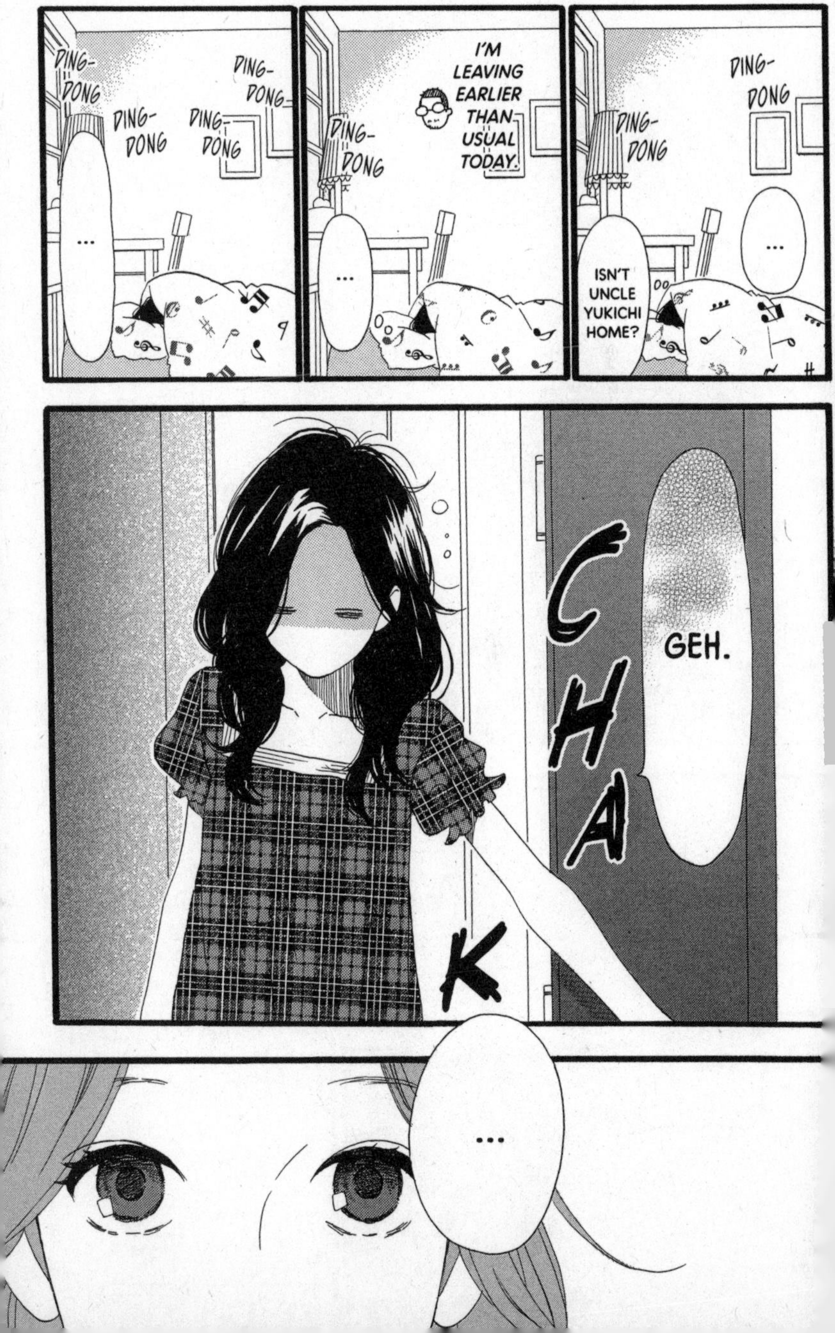
DING-DONG
DING-DONG
...
ISN'T UNCLE YUKICHI HOME?
I'M LEAVING EARLIER THAN USUAL TODAY.
DING-DONG
...
DING-DONG
DING-DONG
DING-DONG
DING-DONG
...
GEH.
CHAK
...

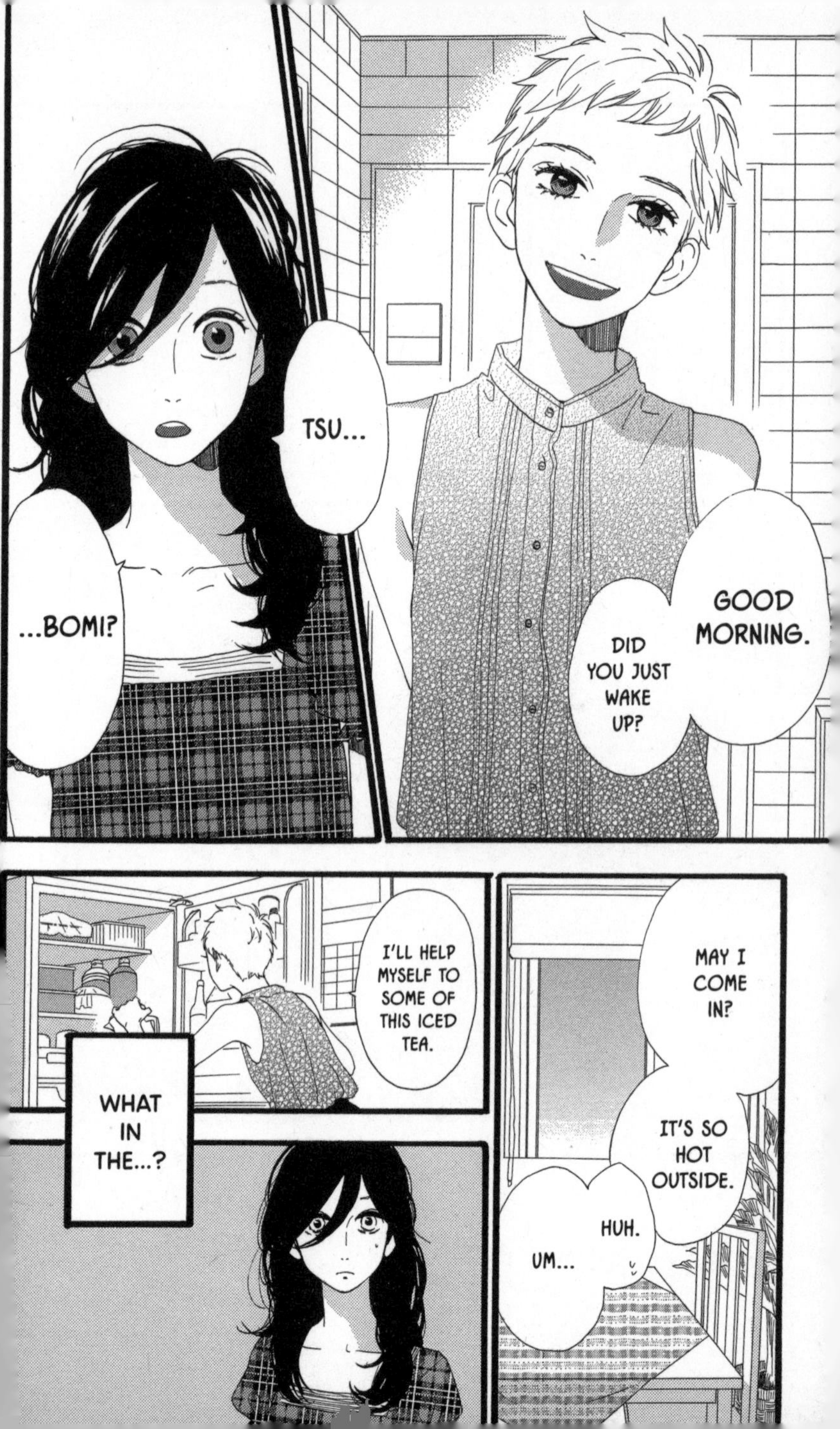
GOOD MORNING.
DID YOU JUST WAKE UP?
TSU...
...BOMI?
MAY I COME IN?
IT'S SO HOT OUTSIDE.
HUH.
UM...
I'LL HELP MYSELF TO SOME OF THIS ICED TEA.
WHAT IN THE...?

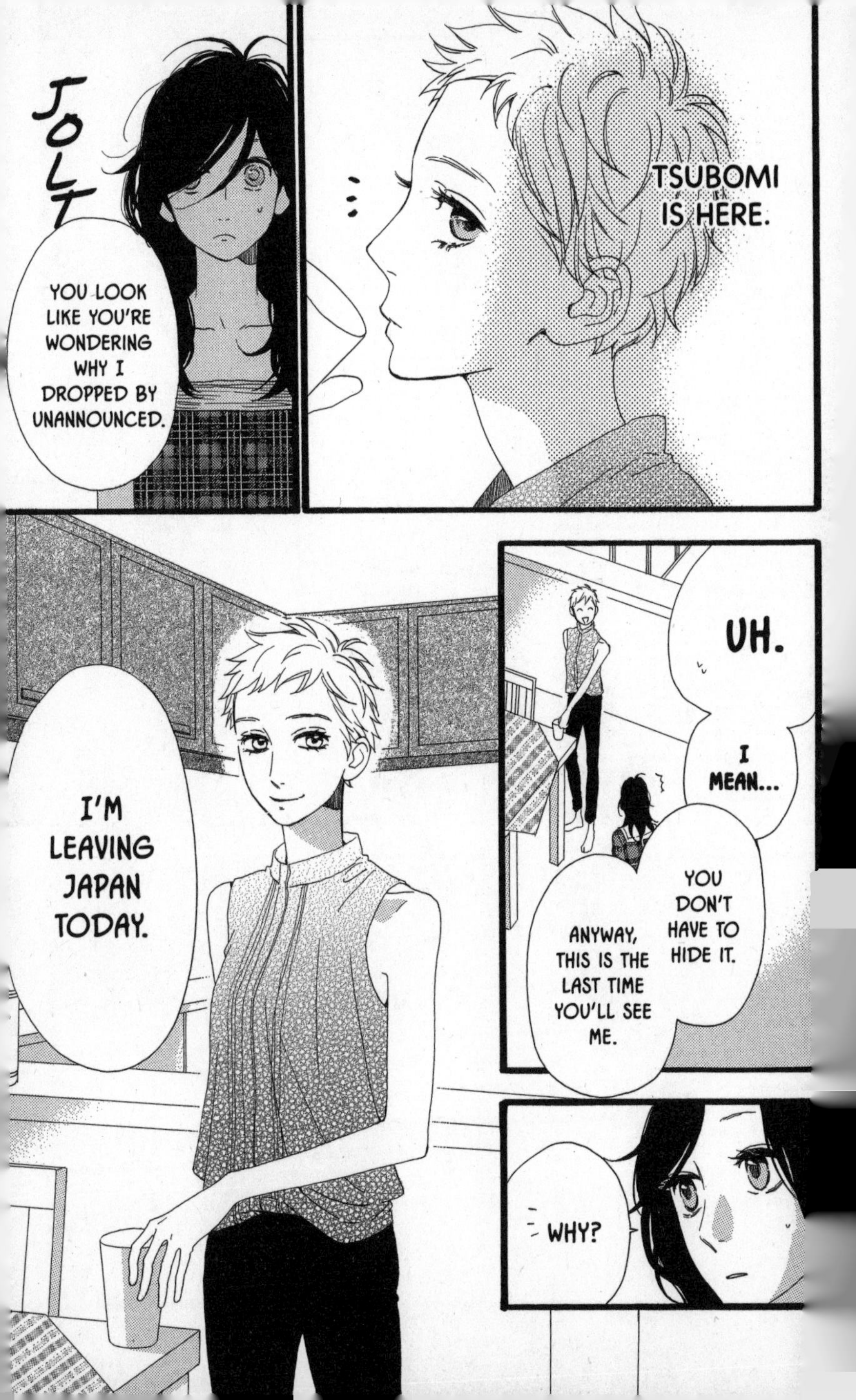
...
TSUBOMI IS HERE.
JOLT
YOU LOOK LIKE YOU'RE WONDERING WHY I DROPPED BY UNANNOUNCED.
UH.
I MEAN...
YOU DON'T HAVE TO HIDE IT.
ANYWAY, THIS IS THE LAST TIME YOU'LL SEE ME.
WHY?
I'M LEAVING JAPAN TODAY.

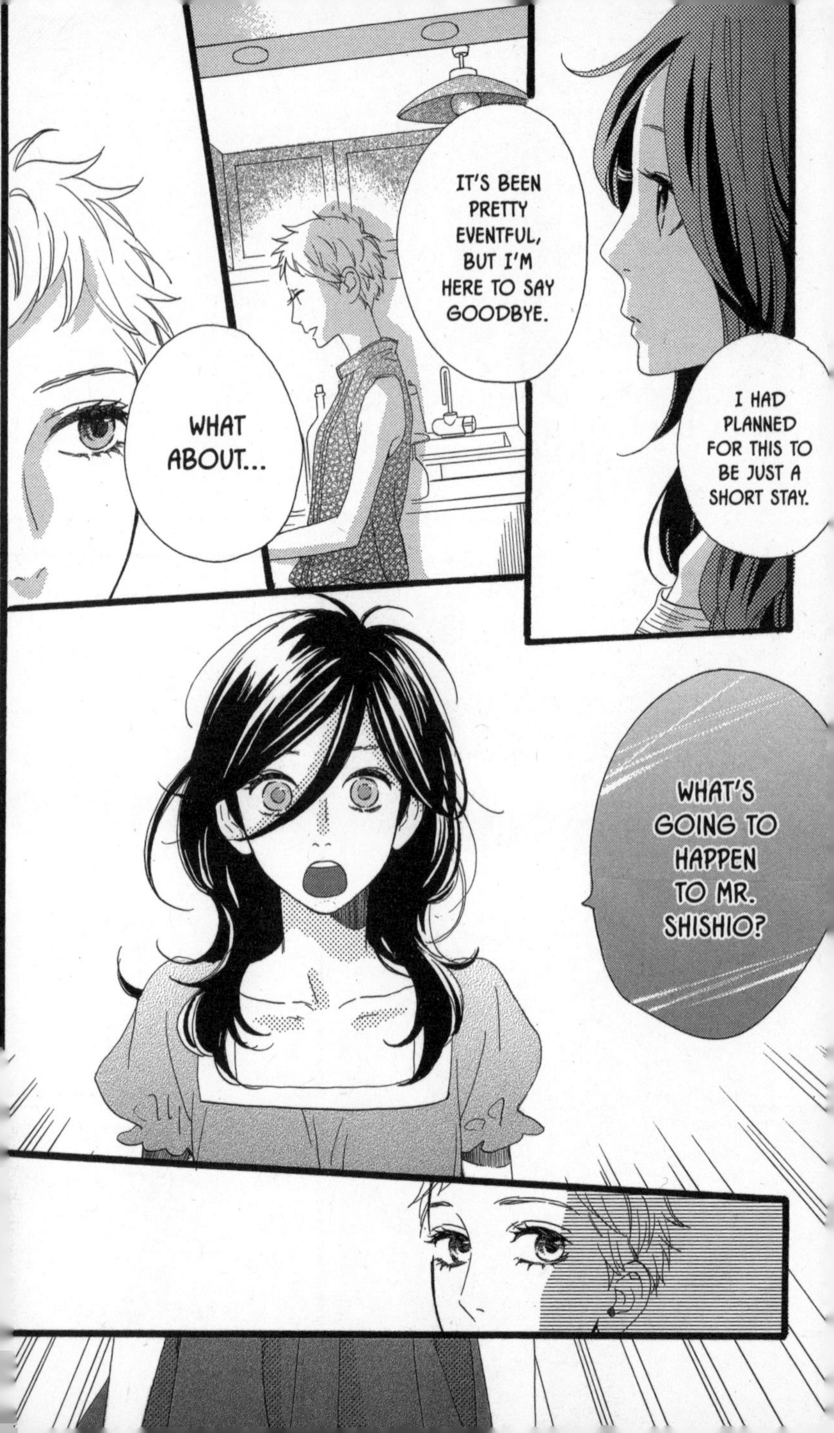
I HAD PLANNED FOR THIS TO BE JUST A SHORT STAY.
IT'S BEEN PRETTY EVENTFUL, BUT I'M HERE TO SAY GOODBYE.
WHAT ABOUT...
WHAT'S GOING TO HAPPEN TO MR. SHISHIO?

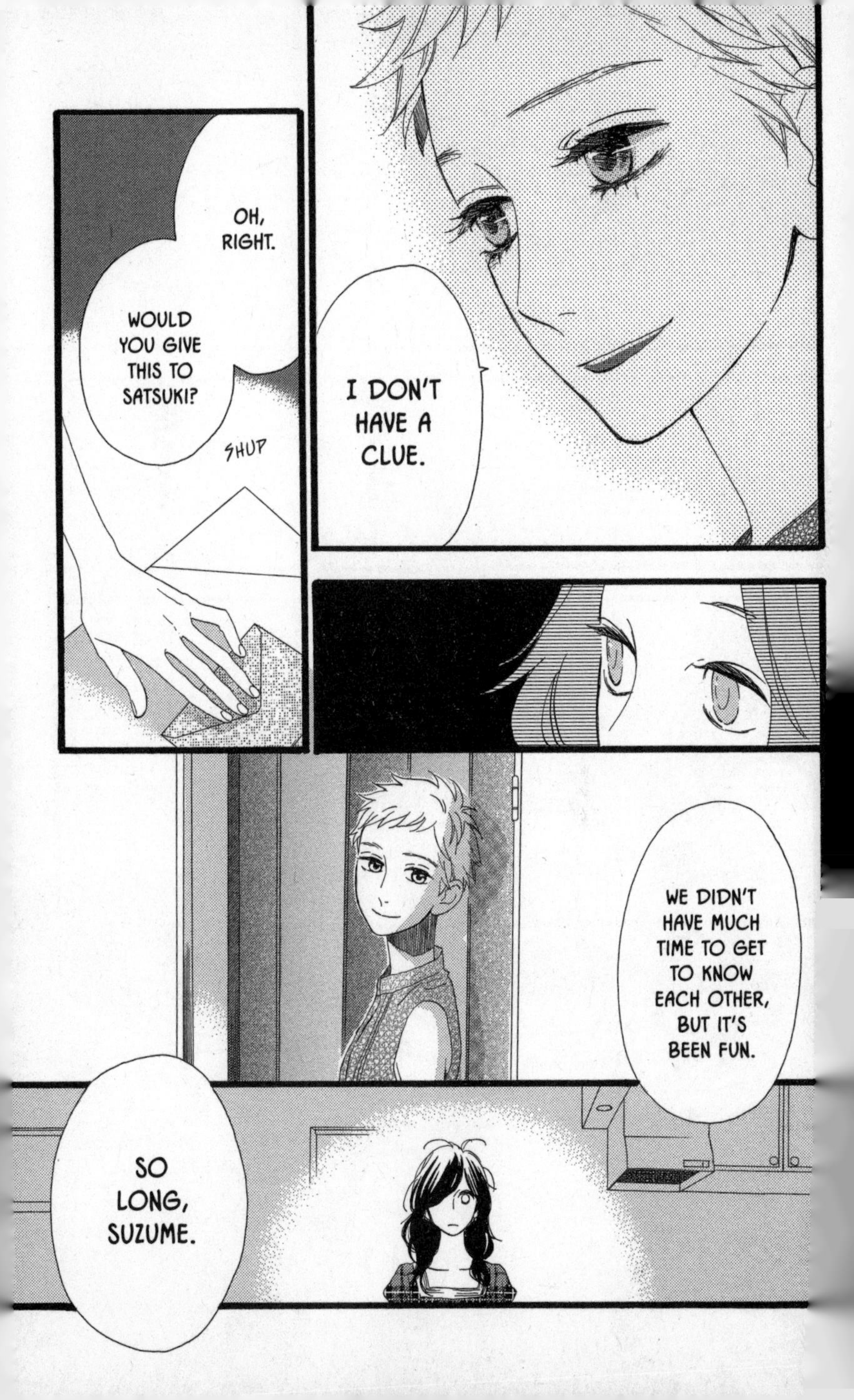
I DON'T HAVE A CLUE.
OH, RIGHT.
WOULD YOU GIVE THIS TO SATSUKI?
SHUP
WE DIDN'T HAVE MUCH TIME TO GET TO KNOW EACH OTHER, BUT IT'S BEEN FUN.
SO LONG, SUZUME.

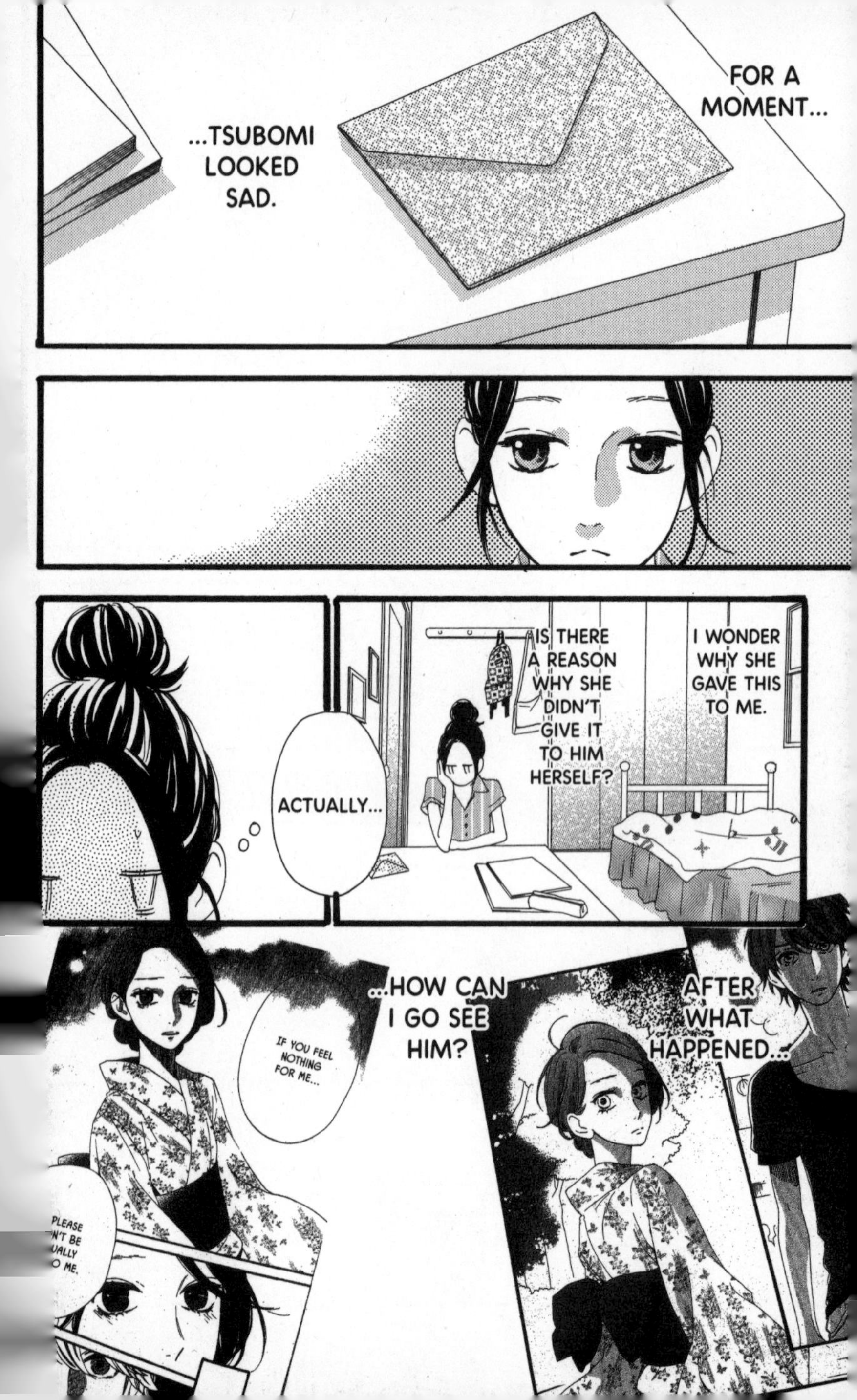
FOR A MOMENT...
...TSUBOMI LOOKED SAD.
I WONDER WHY SHE GAVE THIS TO ME.
IS THERE A REASON WHY SHE DIDN'T GIVE IT TO HIM HERSELF?
ACTUALLY...
AFTER WHAT HAPPENED...
...HOW CAN I GO SEE HIM?
IF YOU FEEL NOTHING FOR ME...
PLEASE

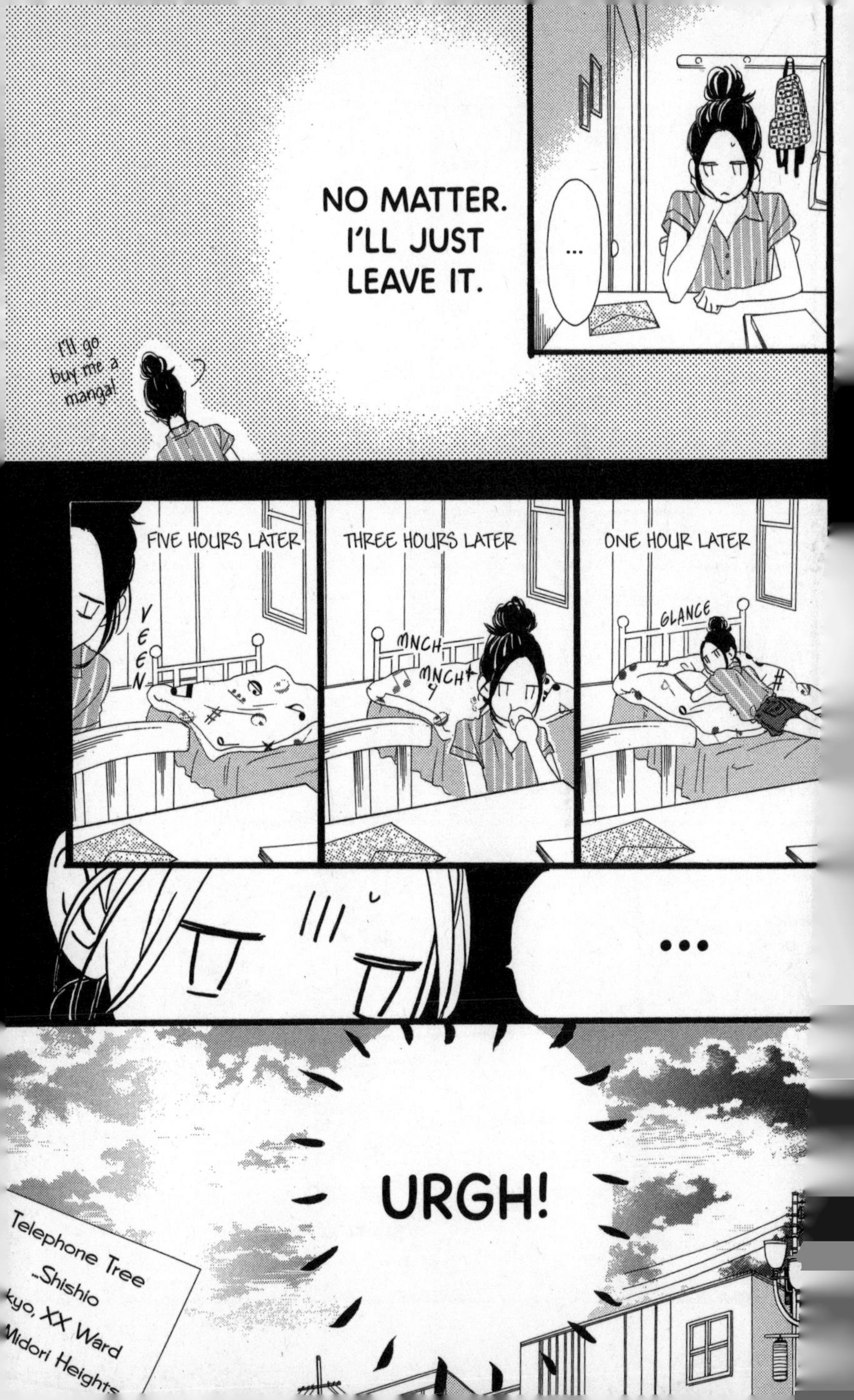
...
NO MATTER. I'LL JUST LEAVE IT.
I'll go buy me a manga!
ONE HOUR LATER
GLANCE
THREE HOURS LATER
MNCH MNCH
FIVE HOURS LATER
VEEN
...
URGH!
Telephone Tree
-Shishio
kyo, XX Ward
Midori Heights

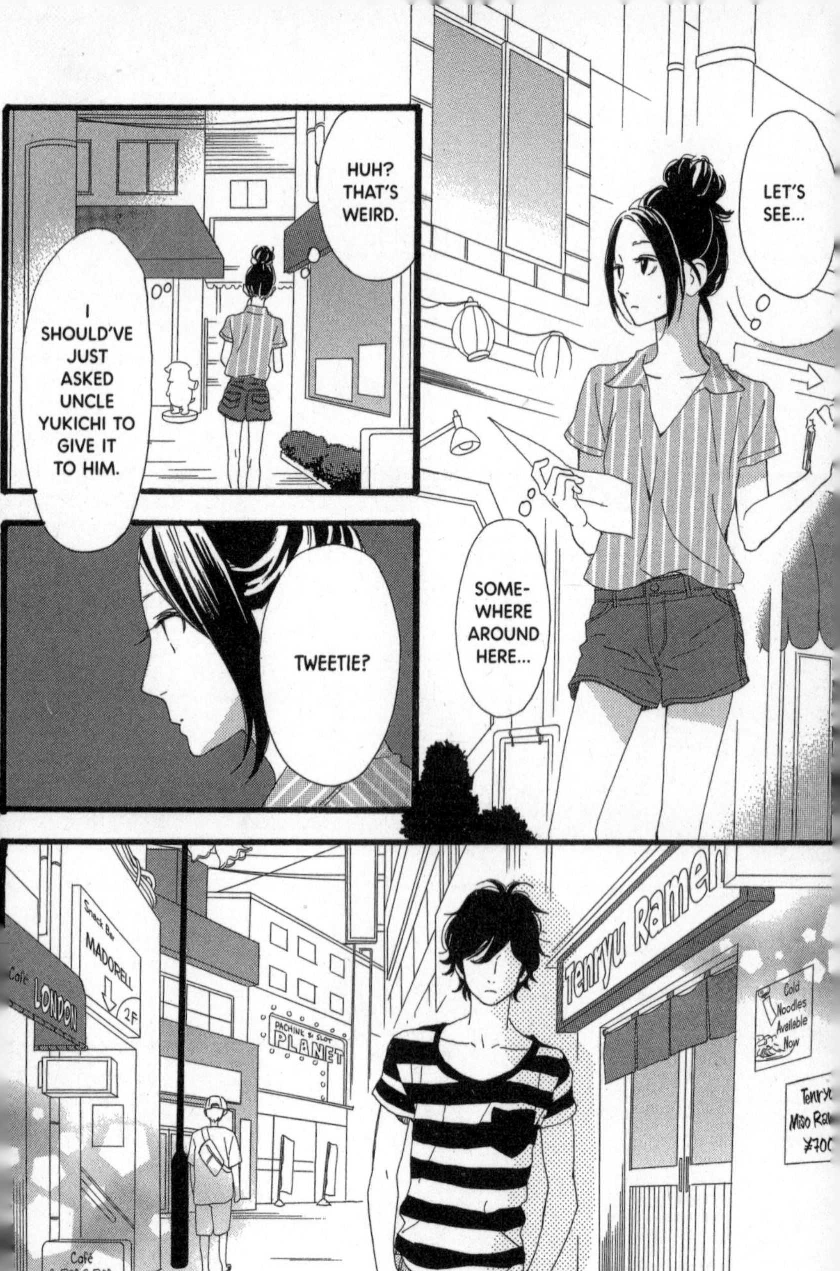
LET'S SEE...
SOME-WHERE AROUND HERE...
HUH? THAT'S WEIRD.
I SHOULD'VE JUST ASKED UNCLE YUKICHI TO GIVE IT TO HIM.
TWEETIE?
Tenryu Ramen
Cold Noodles Available Now
Snack Bar MADORELL 2F
Café LONDON
PACHINKO & SLOT PLANET
Café LONDON

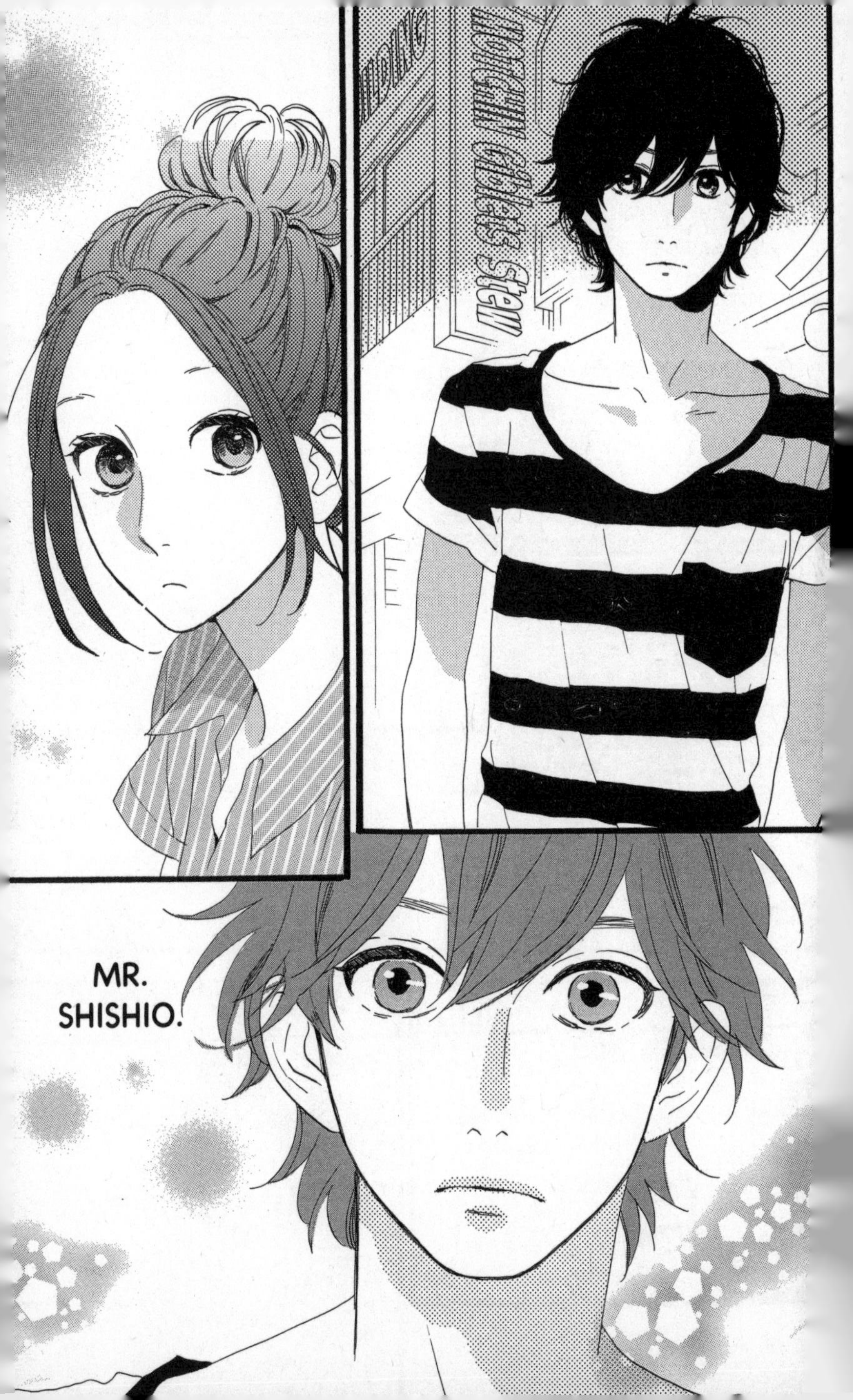
MR.
SHISHIO.

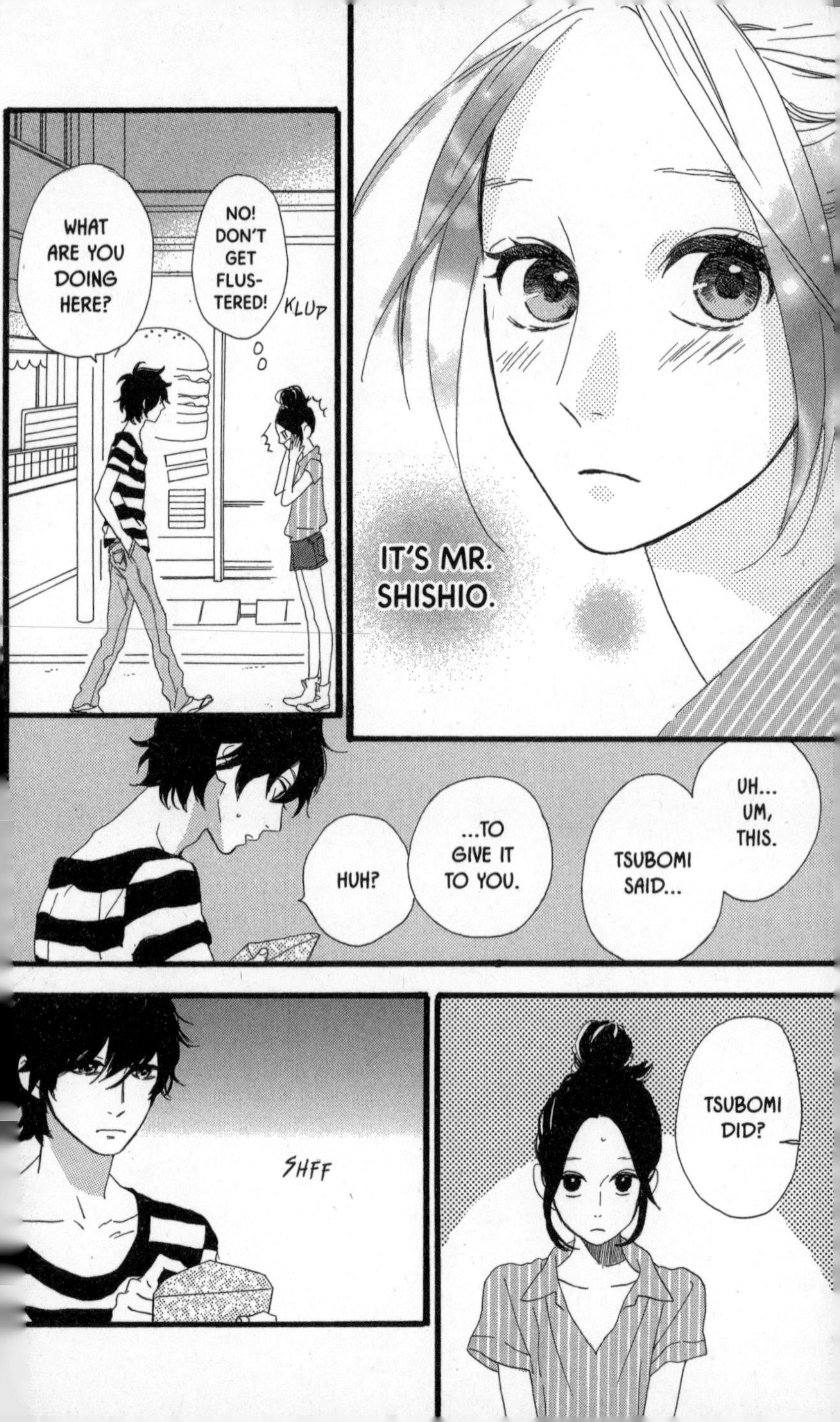
IT'S MR. SHISHIO.
NO! DON'T GET FLUS-TERED!
KLUP
WHAT ARE YOU DOING HERE?
UH... UM, THIS.
TSUBOMI SAID...
...TO GIVE IT TO YOU.
HUH?
TSUBOMI DID?
SHFF

I hope a girl will appear one day who will allow you to be your natural self.
XXX Tsubomi
W-WELL, I'D BETTER GO...
BYE
TWEETIE.

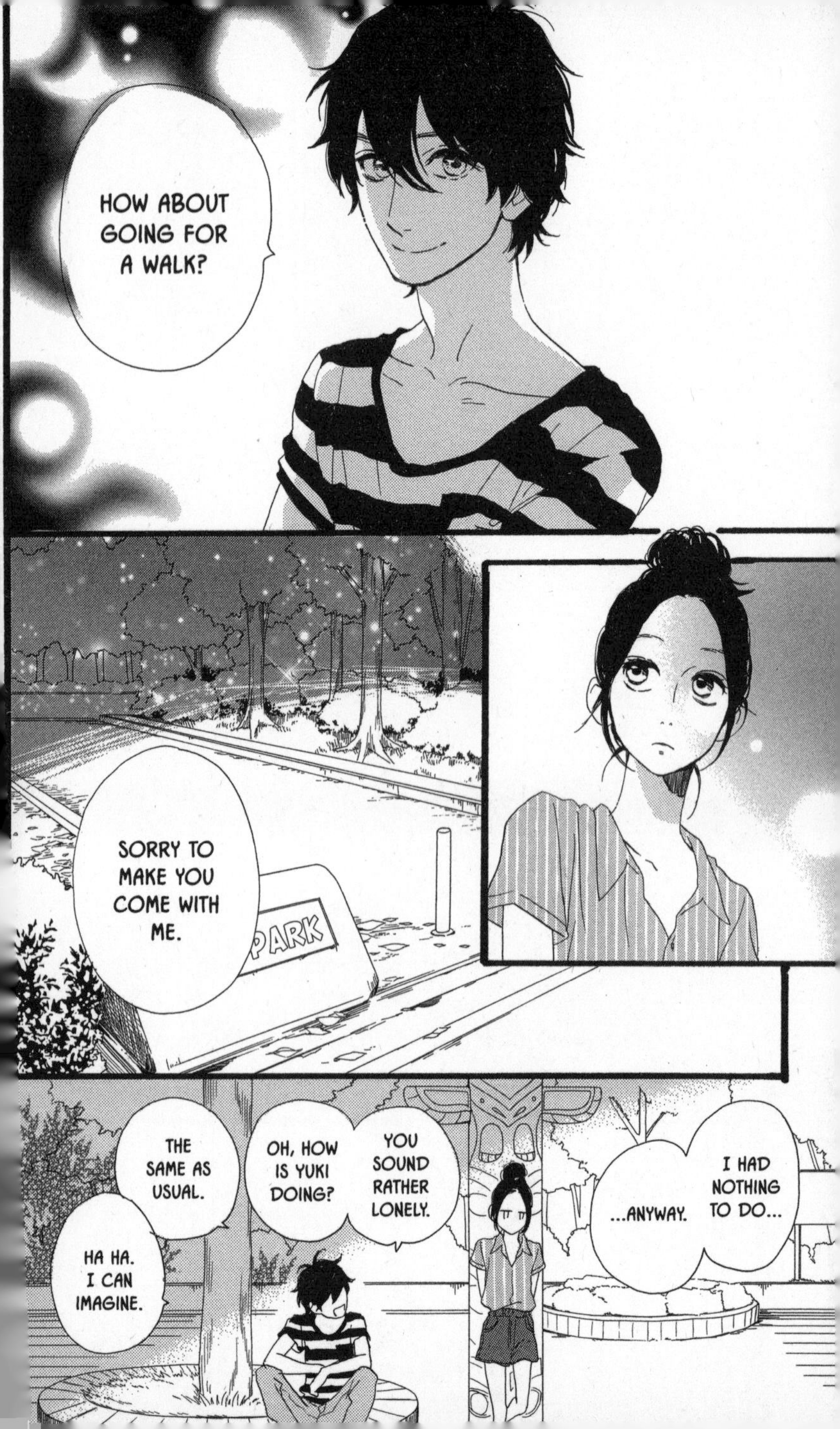
HOW ABOUT GOING FOR A WALK?
SORRY TO MAKE YOU COME WITH ME.
PARK
I HAD NOTHING TO DO...
...ANYWAY.
YOU SOUND RATHER LONELY.
OH, HOW IS YUKI DOING?
THE SAME AS USUAL.
HA HA. I CAN IMAGINE.

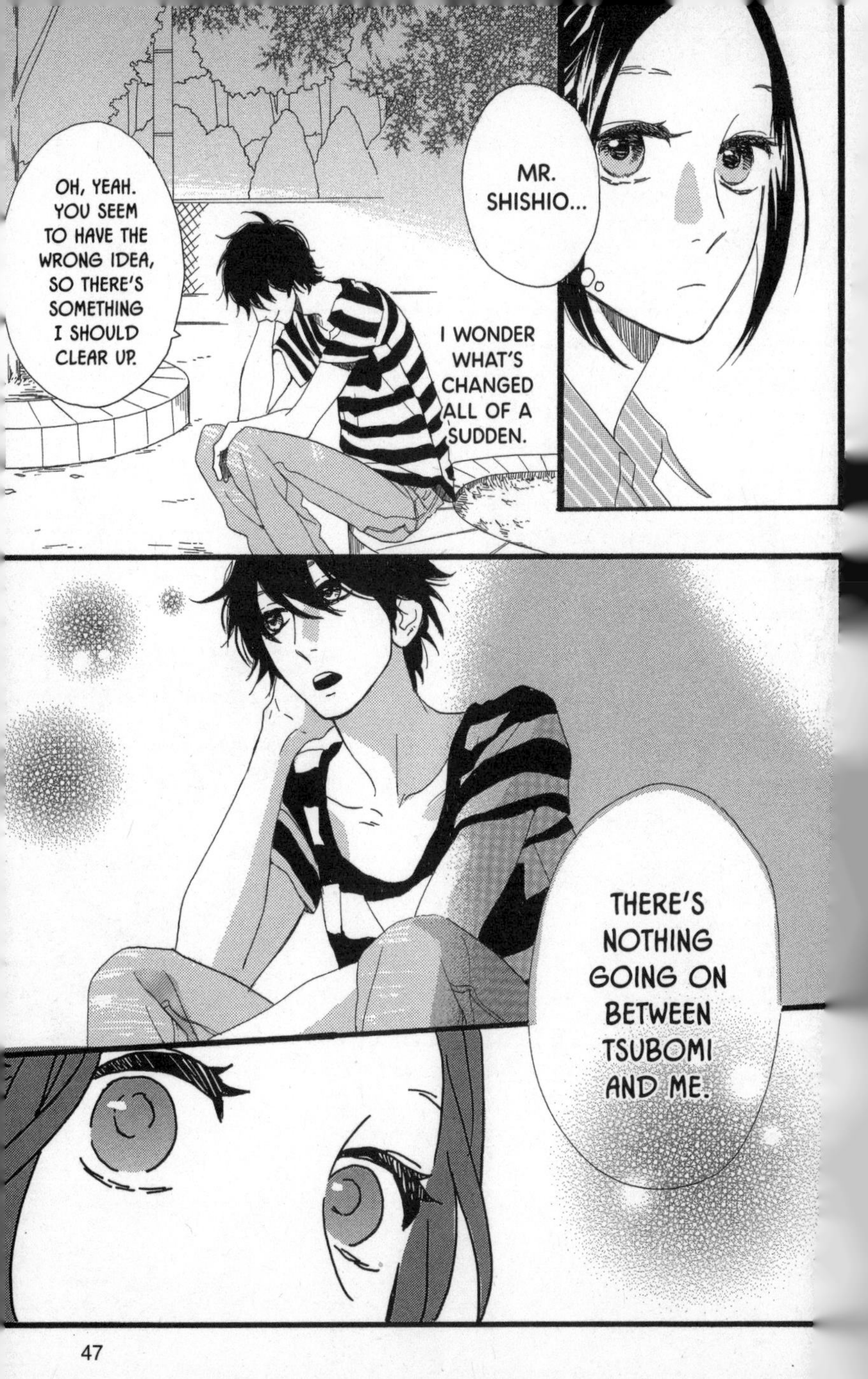
MR. SHISHIO...
I WONDER WHAT'S CHANGED ALL OF A SUDDEN.
OH, YEAH. YOU SEEM TO HAVE THE WRONG IDEA, SO THERE'S SOMETHING I SHOULD CLEAR UP.
THERE'S NOTHING GOING ON BETWEEN TSUBOMI AND ME.

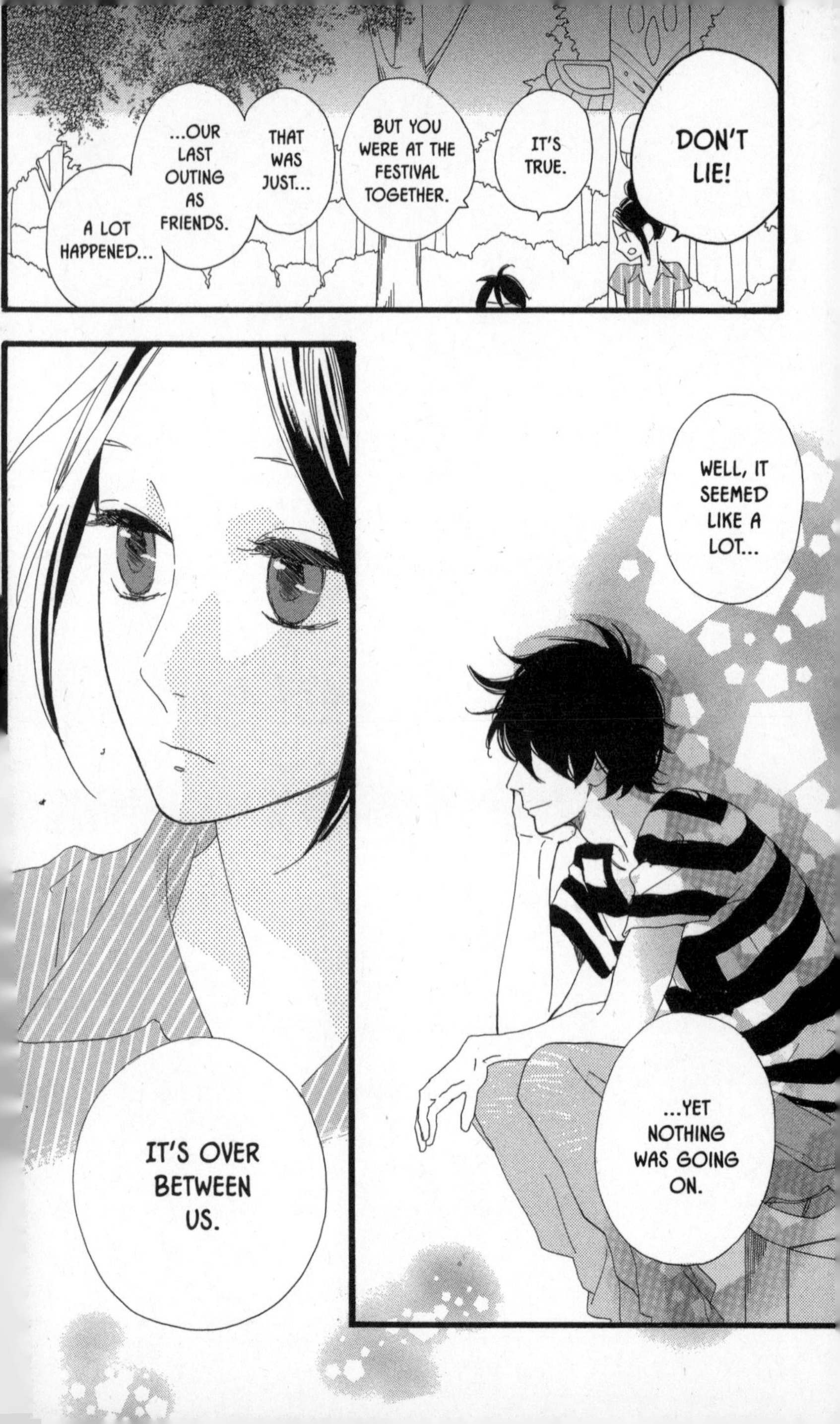
DON'T LIE!
IT'S TRUE.
BUT YOU WERE AT THE FESTIVAL TOGETHER.
THAT WAS JUST...
...OUR LAST OUTING AS FRIENDS.
A LOT HAPPENED...
WELL, IT SEEMED LIKE A LOT...
...YET NOTHING WAS GOING ON.
IT'S OVER BETWEEN US.

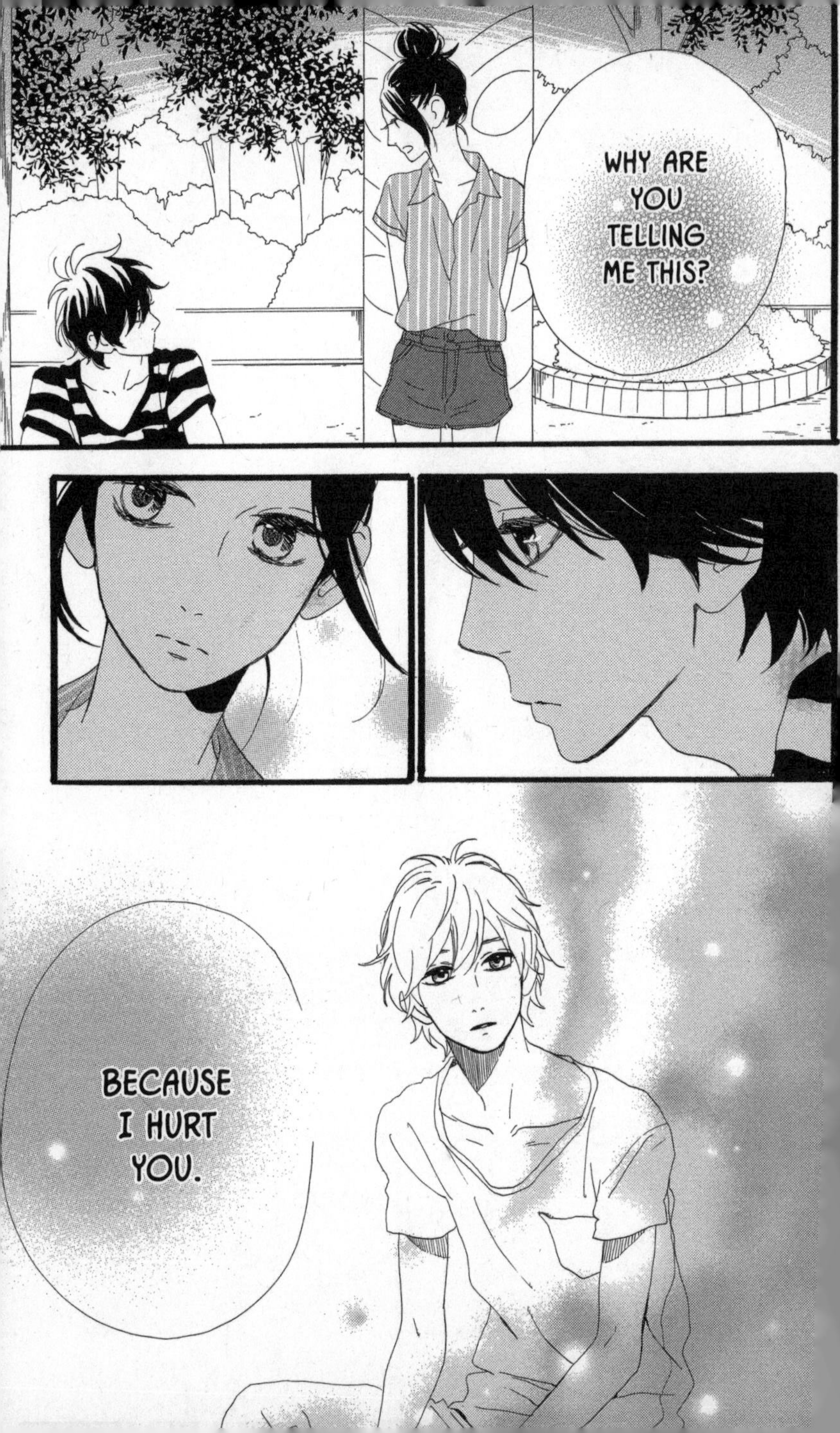
WHY ARE YOU TELLING ME THIS?
BECAUSE I HURT YOU.

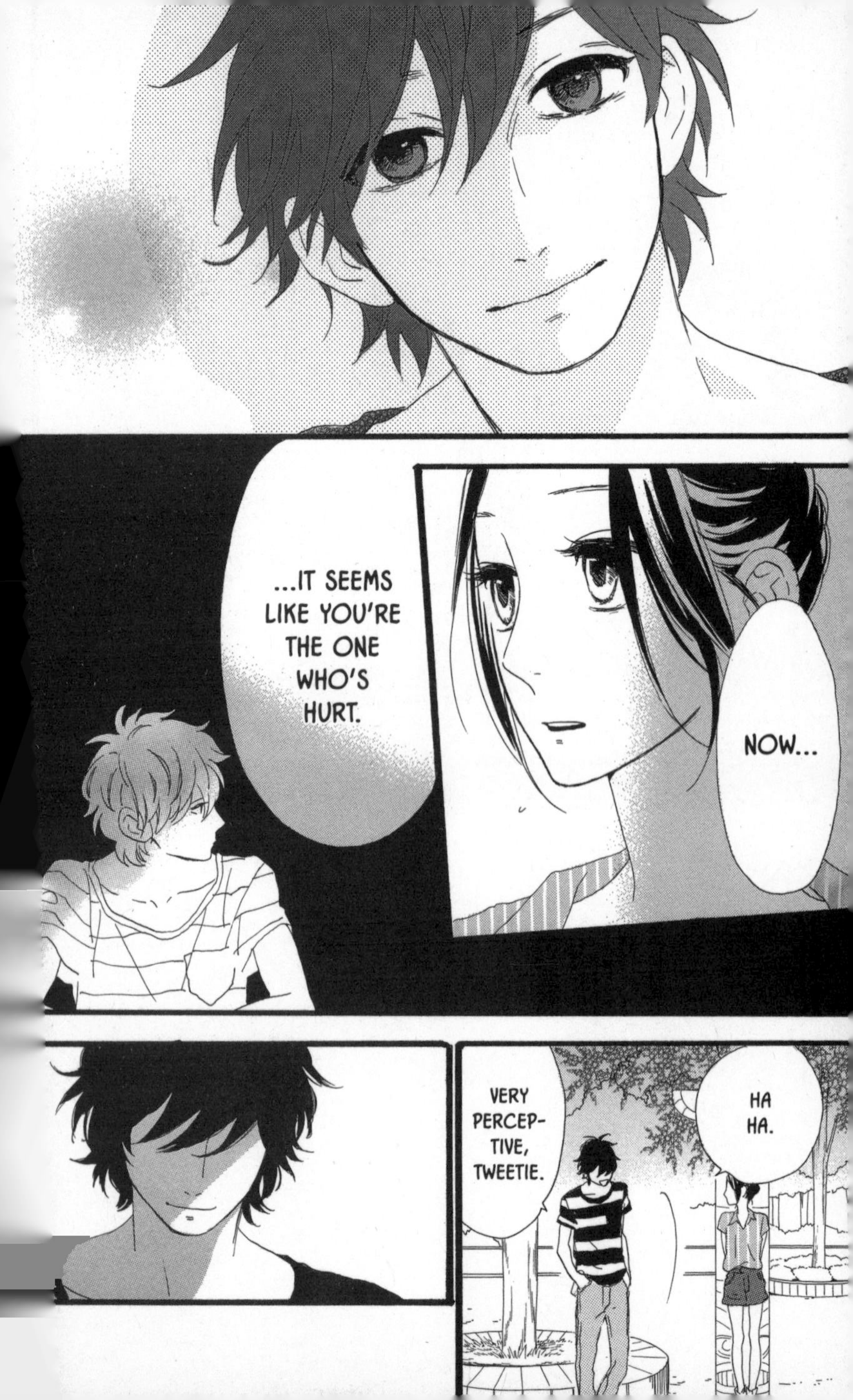
NOW...
...IT SEEMS LIKE YOU'RE THE ONE WHO'S HURT.
HA HA.
VERY PERCEP-TIVE, TWEETIE.

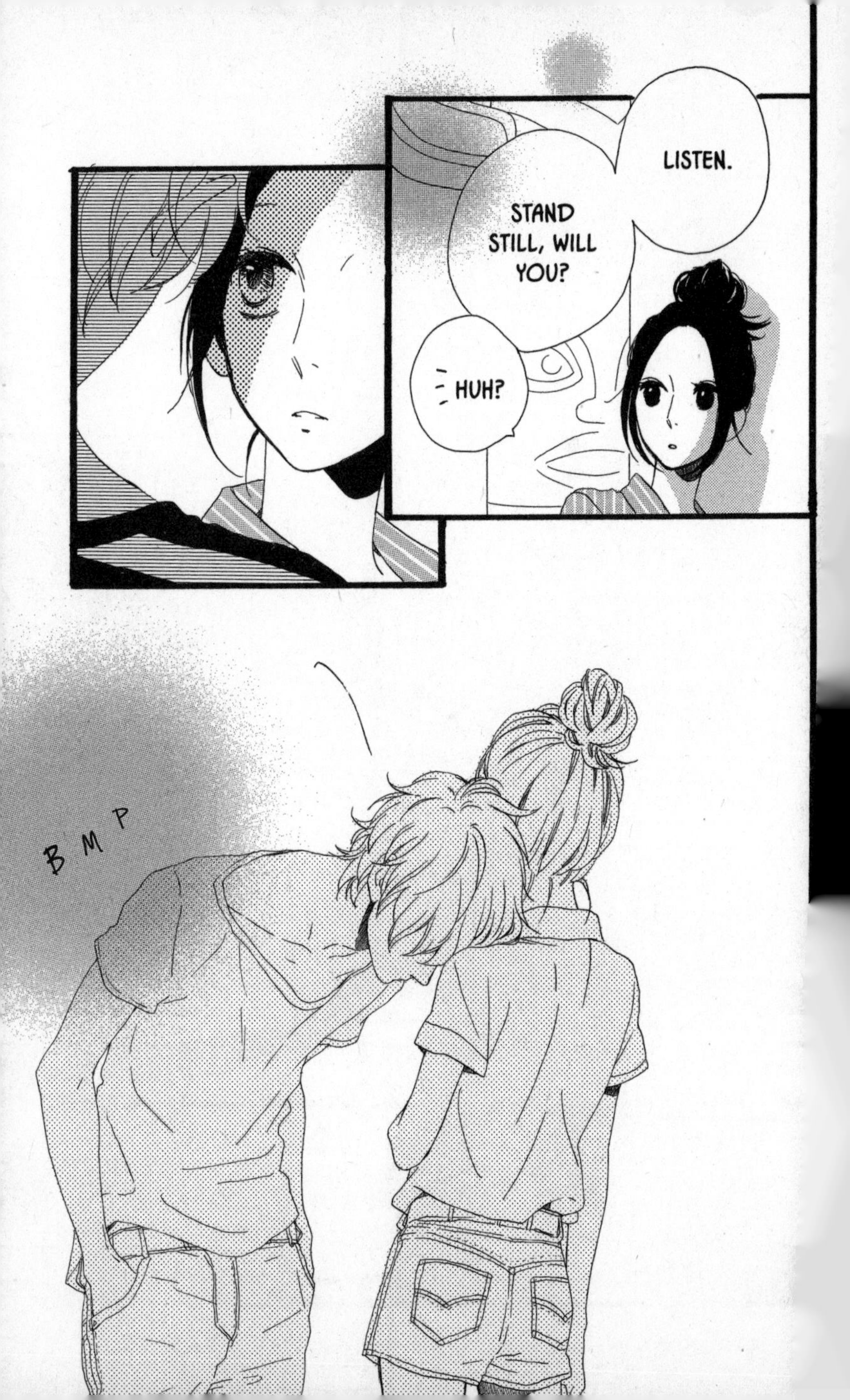
LISTEN.
STAND STILL, WILL YOU?
HUH?
BMP

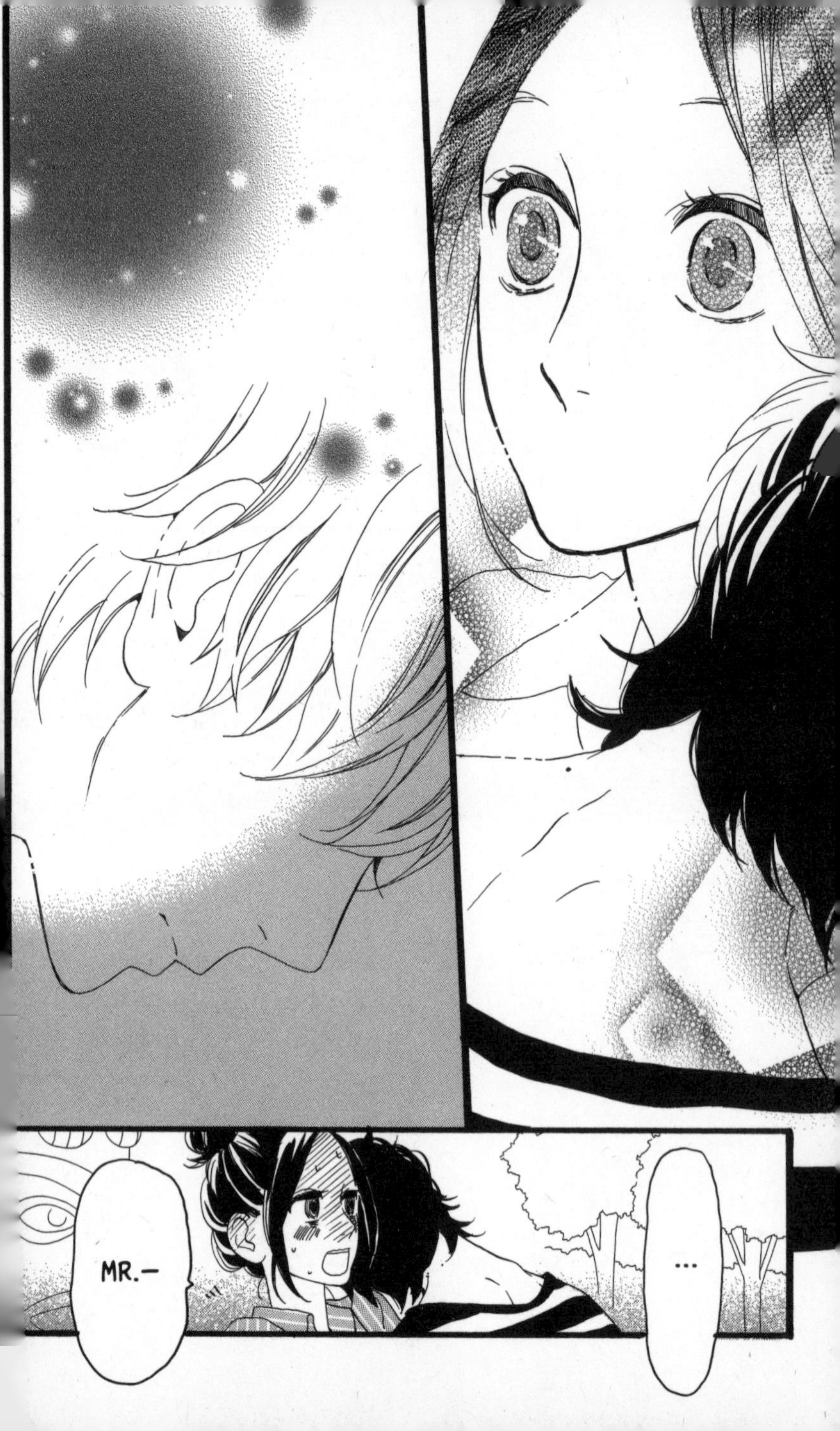

...
MR.–

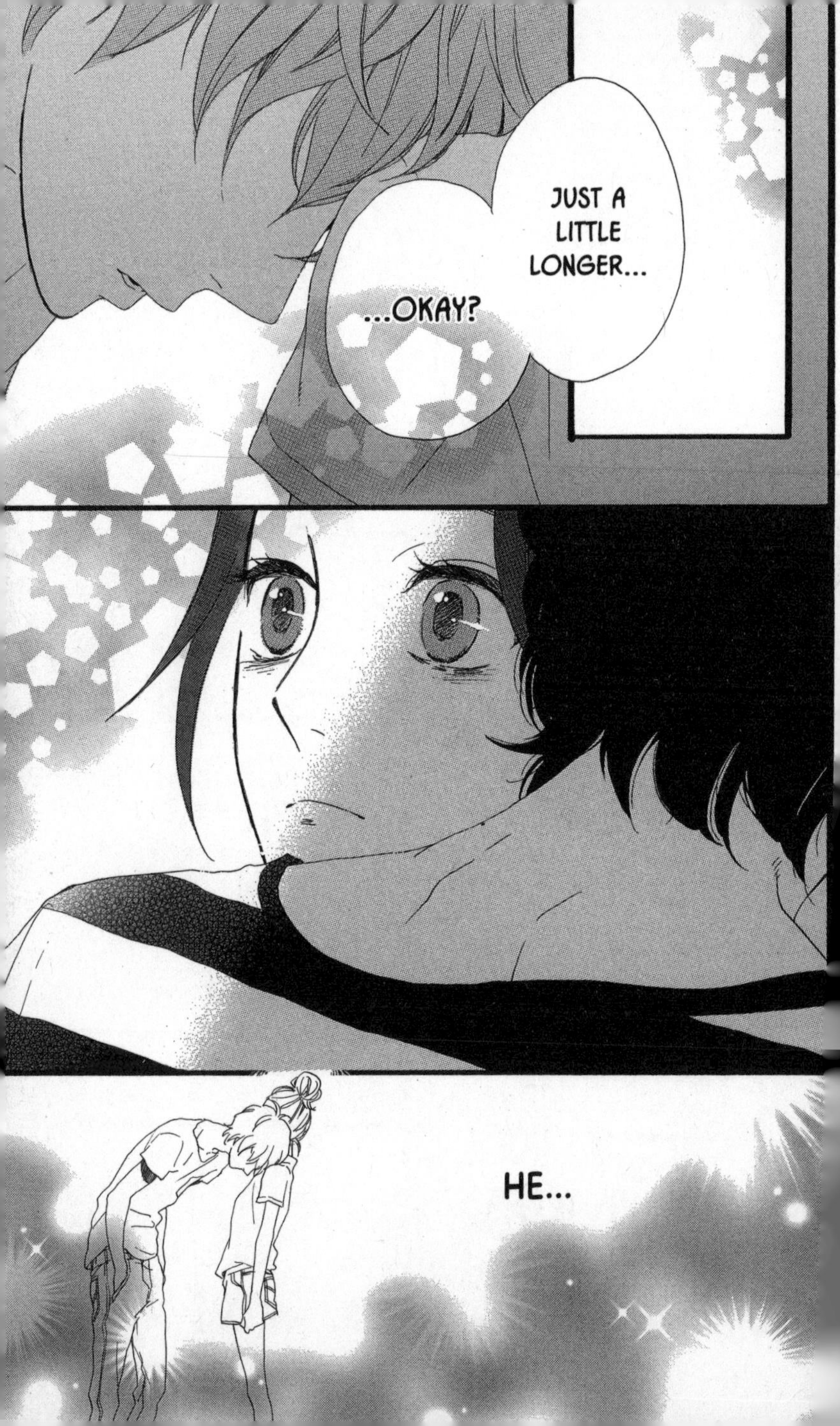
JUST A LITTLE LONGER...
...OKAY?
HE...

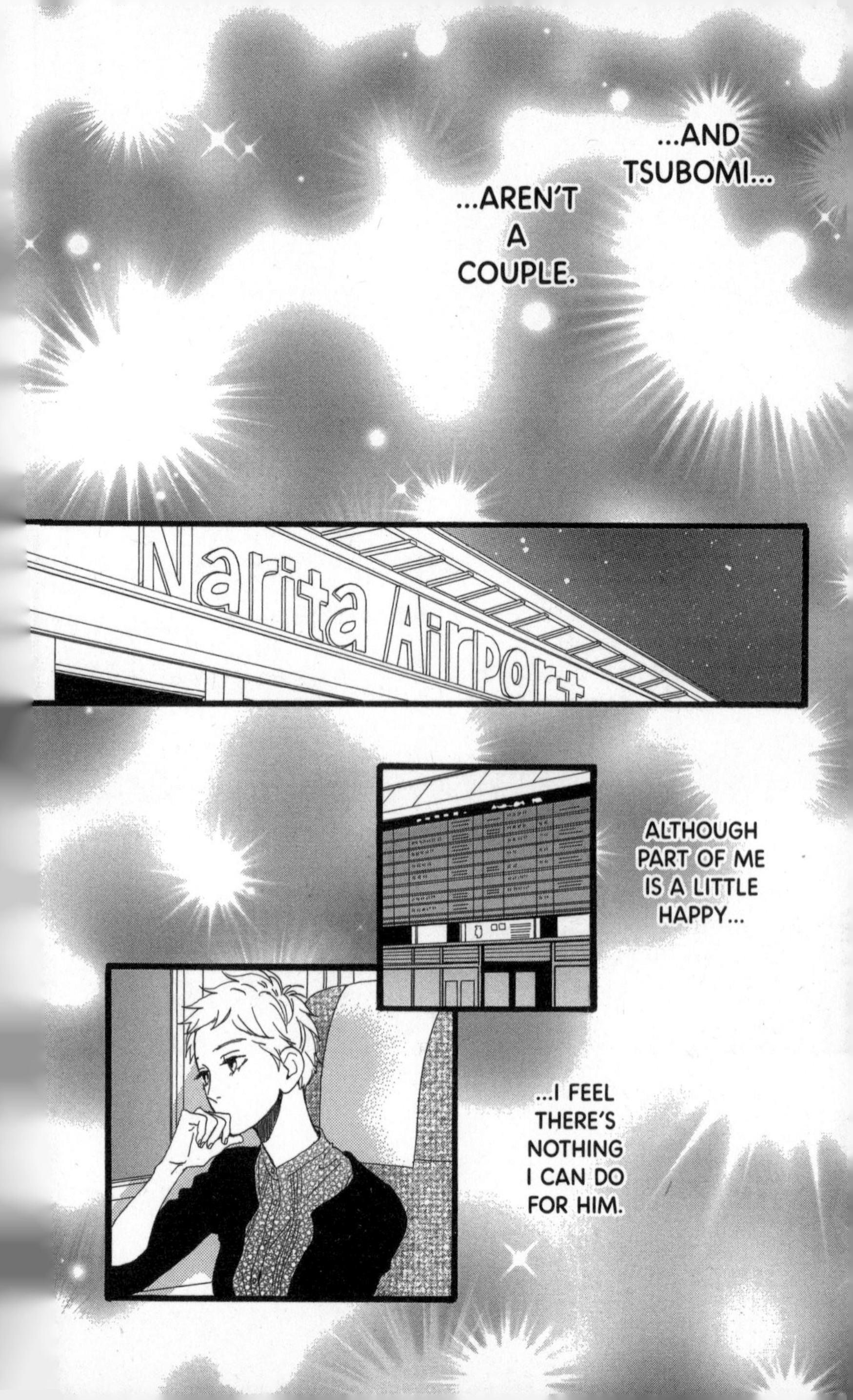
...AND TSUBOMI...
...AREN'T A COUPLE.
Narita Airport
ALTHOUGH PART OF ME IS A LITTLE HAPPY...
...I FEEL THERE'S NOTHING I CAN DO FOR HIM.

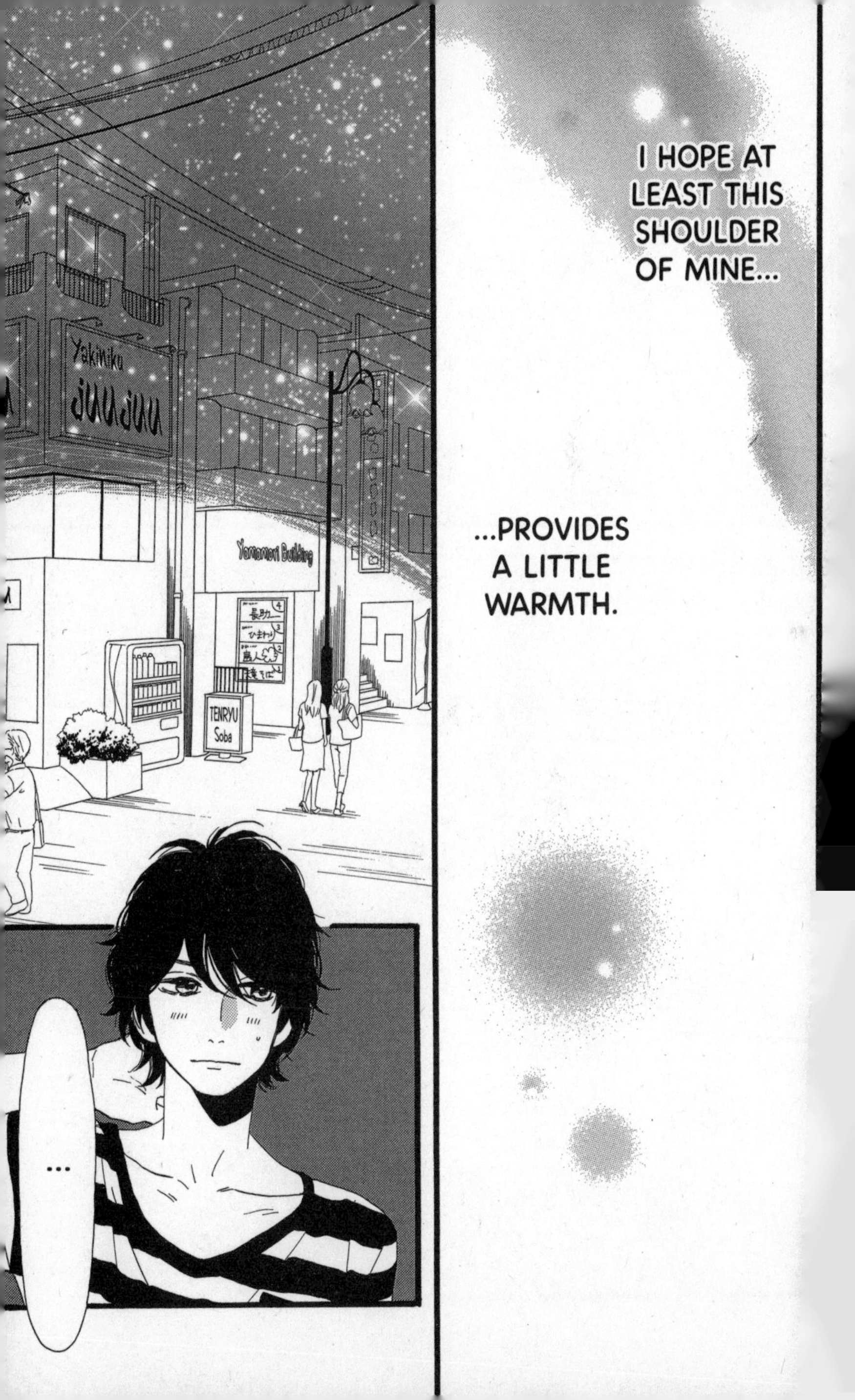
I HOPE AT LEAST THIS SHOULDER OF MINE...
...PROVIDES A LITTLE WARMTH.
Yakiniku
JUUJUU
Yamamori Building
長助
ひまわり
TENRYU Soba
...

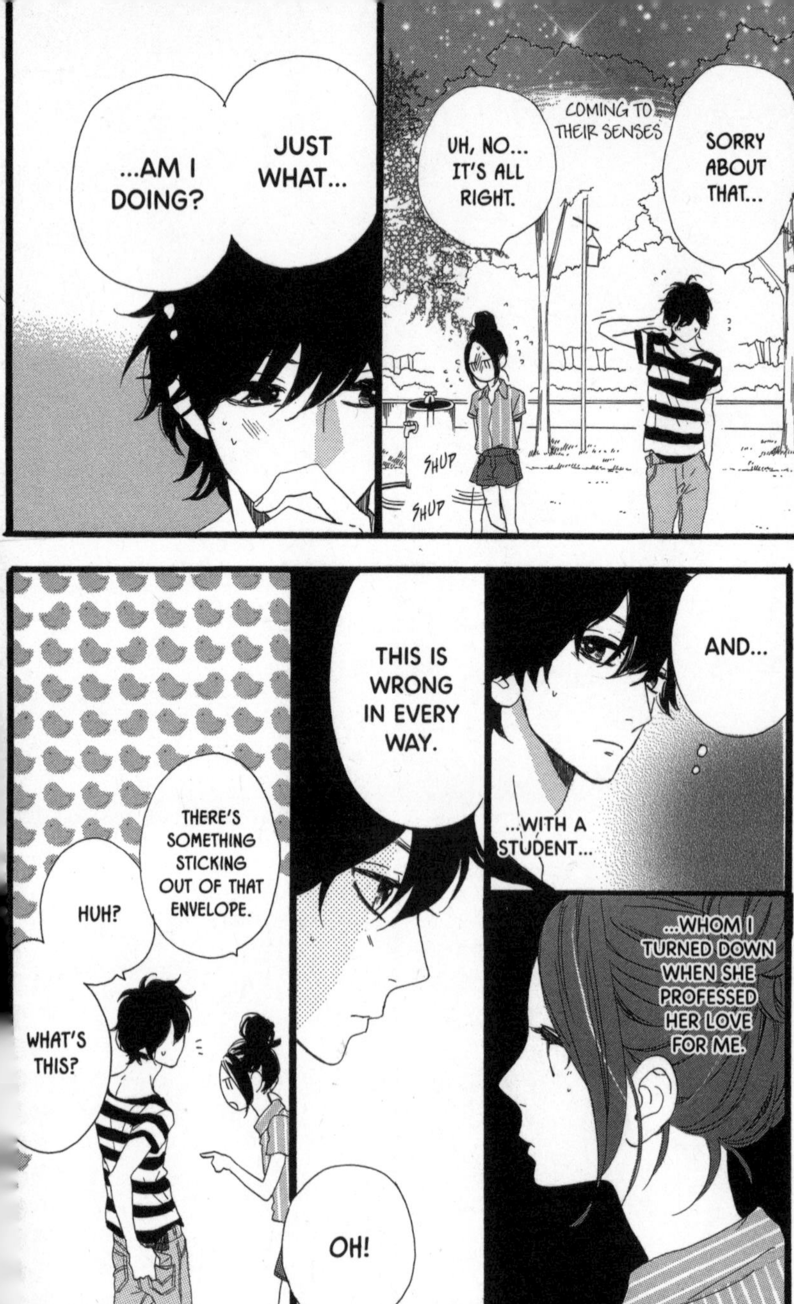
SORRY ABOUT THAT...
COMING TO THEIR SENSES
UH, NO... IT'S ALL RIGHT.
SHUP
SHUP
JUST WHAT...
...AM I DOING?
AND...
...WITH A STUDENT...
...WHOM I TURNED DOWN WHEN SHE PROFESSED HER LOVE FOR ME.
THIS IS WRONG IN EVERY WAY.
THERE'S SOMETHING STICKING OUT OF THAT ENVELOPE.
HUH?
WHAT'S THIS?
OH!

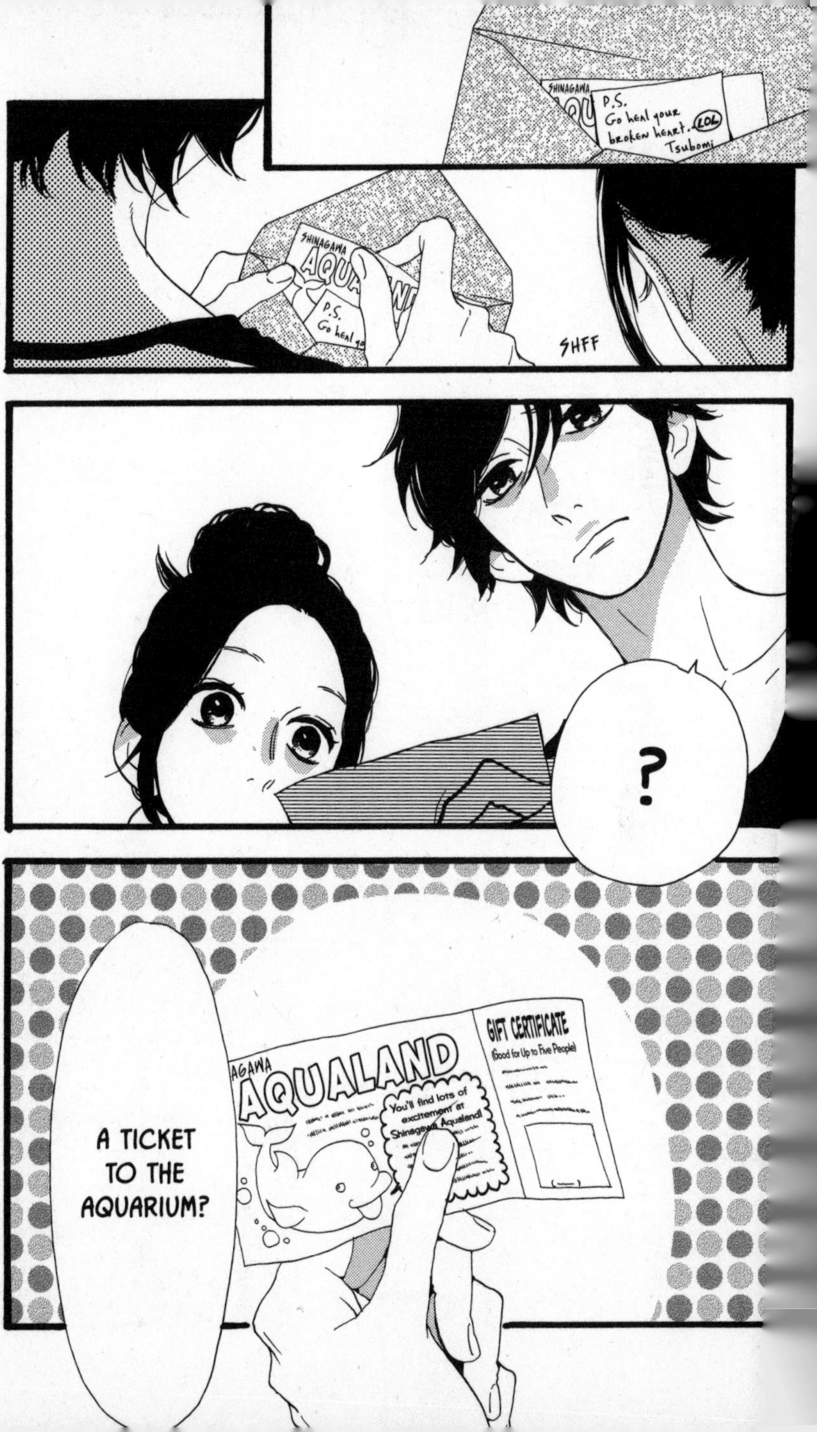
SHINAGAWA AQU
P.S.
Go heal your broken heart. LOL
Tsubomi
SHINAGAWA AQUA
P.S.
SHFF
?
AGAWA AQUALAND
You'll find lots of excitement at Shinagawa Aqualand!
GIFT CERTIFICATE
(Good for Up to Five People)
A TICKET TO THE AQUARIUM?

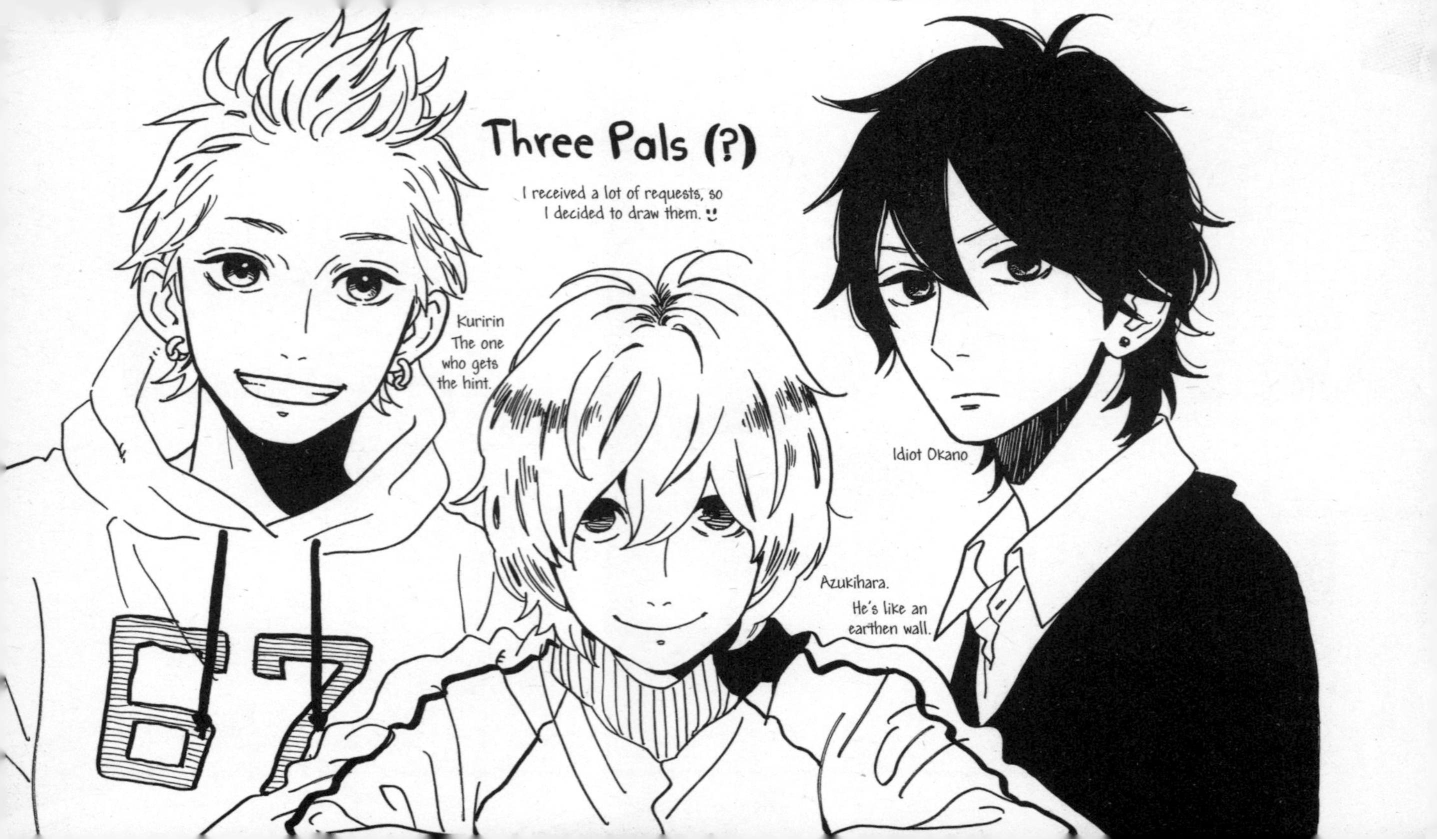
Three Pals (?)
I received a lot of requests, so I decided to draw them.
Kuririn The one who gets the hint.
Idiot Okano
Azukihara. He's like an earthen wall.
67

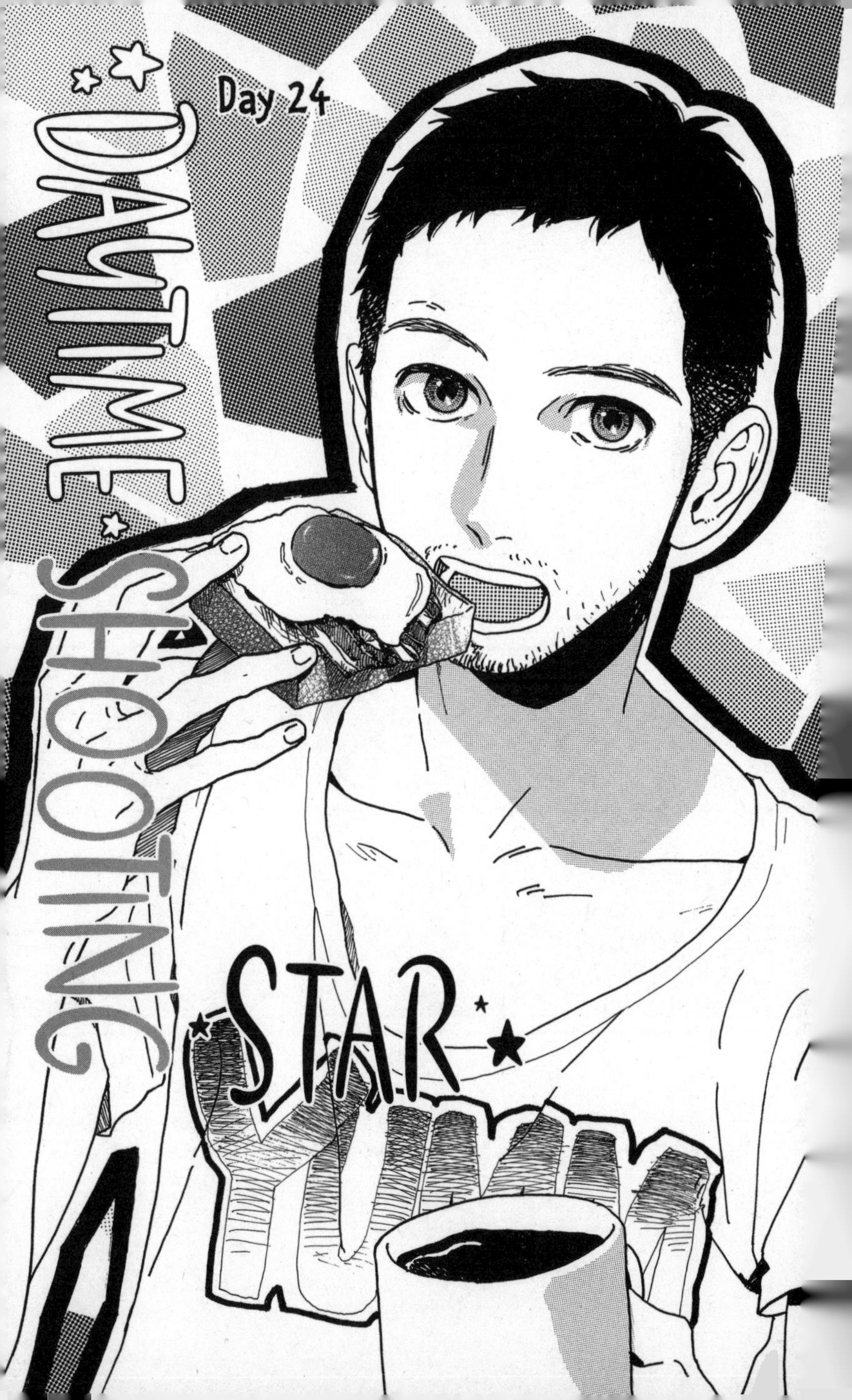
Day 24
DAYTIME SHOOTING STAR

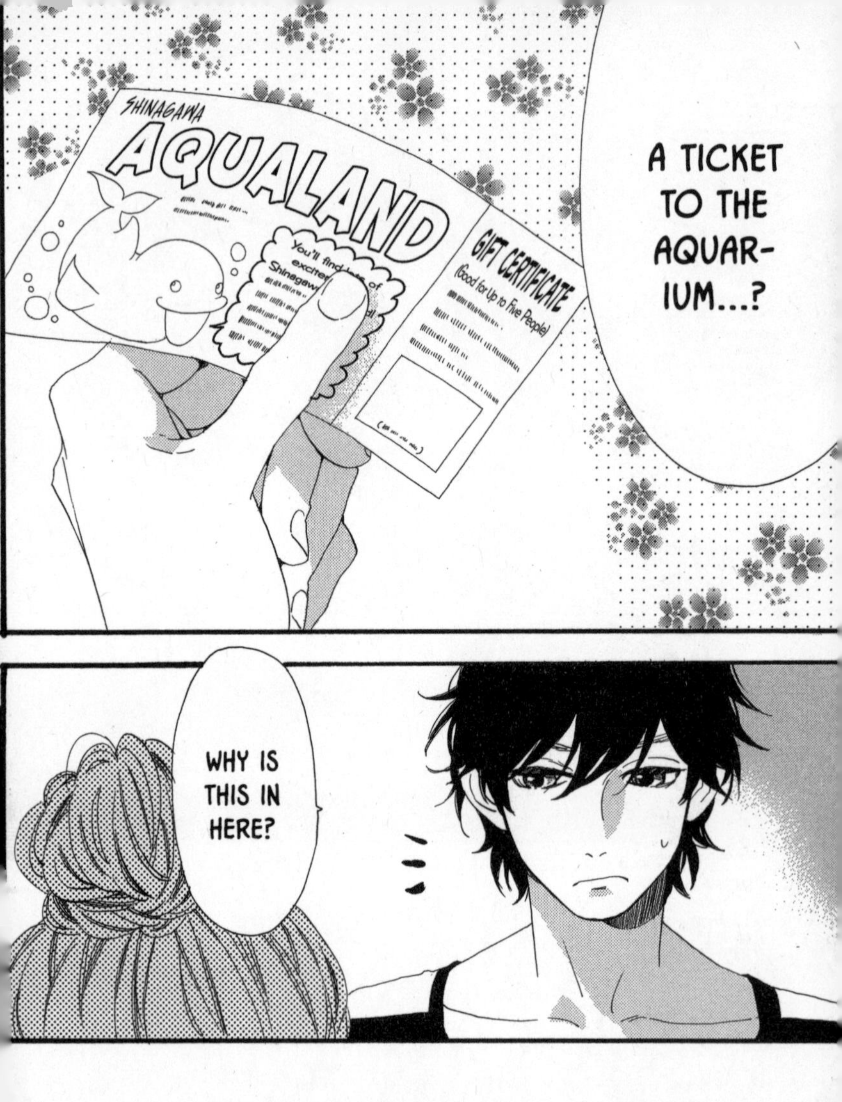
SHINAGAWA AQUALAND
GIFT CERTIFICATE (Good for Up to Five People)
A TICKET TO THE AQUARIUM...?
WHY IS THIS IN HERE?

Suzume, Talking to Herself

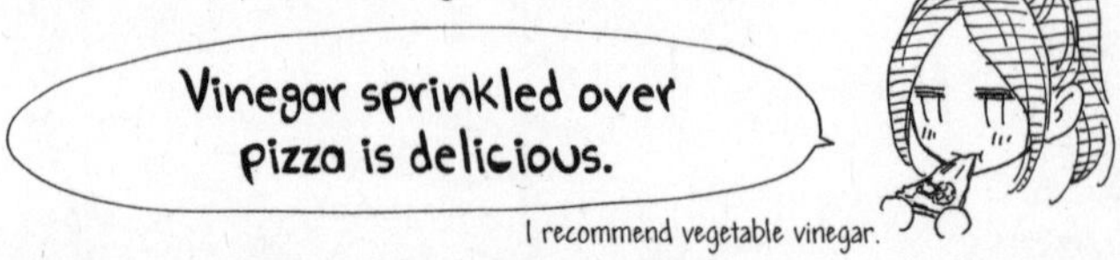
Vinegar sprinkled over pizza is delicious.

I recommend vegetable vinegar.

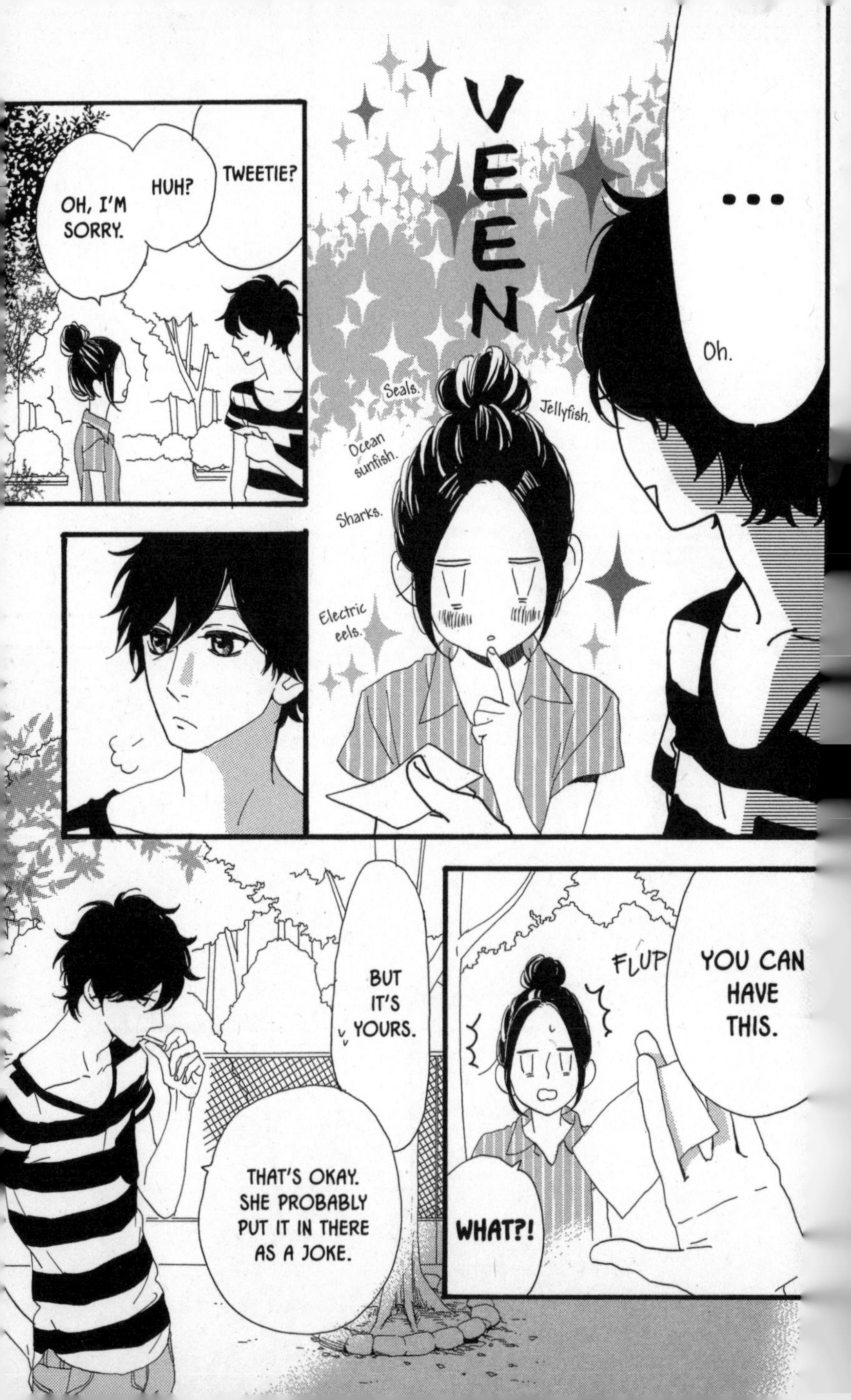
...
Oh.
VEEN
Jellyfish.
Seals.
Ocean sunfish.
Sharks.
Electric eels.
TWEETIE?
HUH?
OH, I'M SORRY.
YOU CAN HAVE THIS.
FLUP
WHAT?!
BUT IT'S YOURS.
THAT'S OKAY. SHE PROBABLY PUT IT IN THERE AS A JOKE.

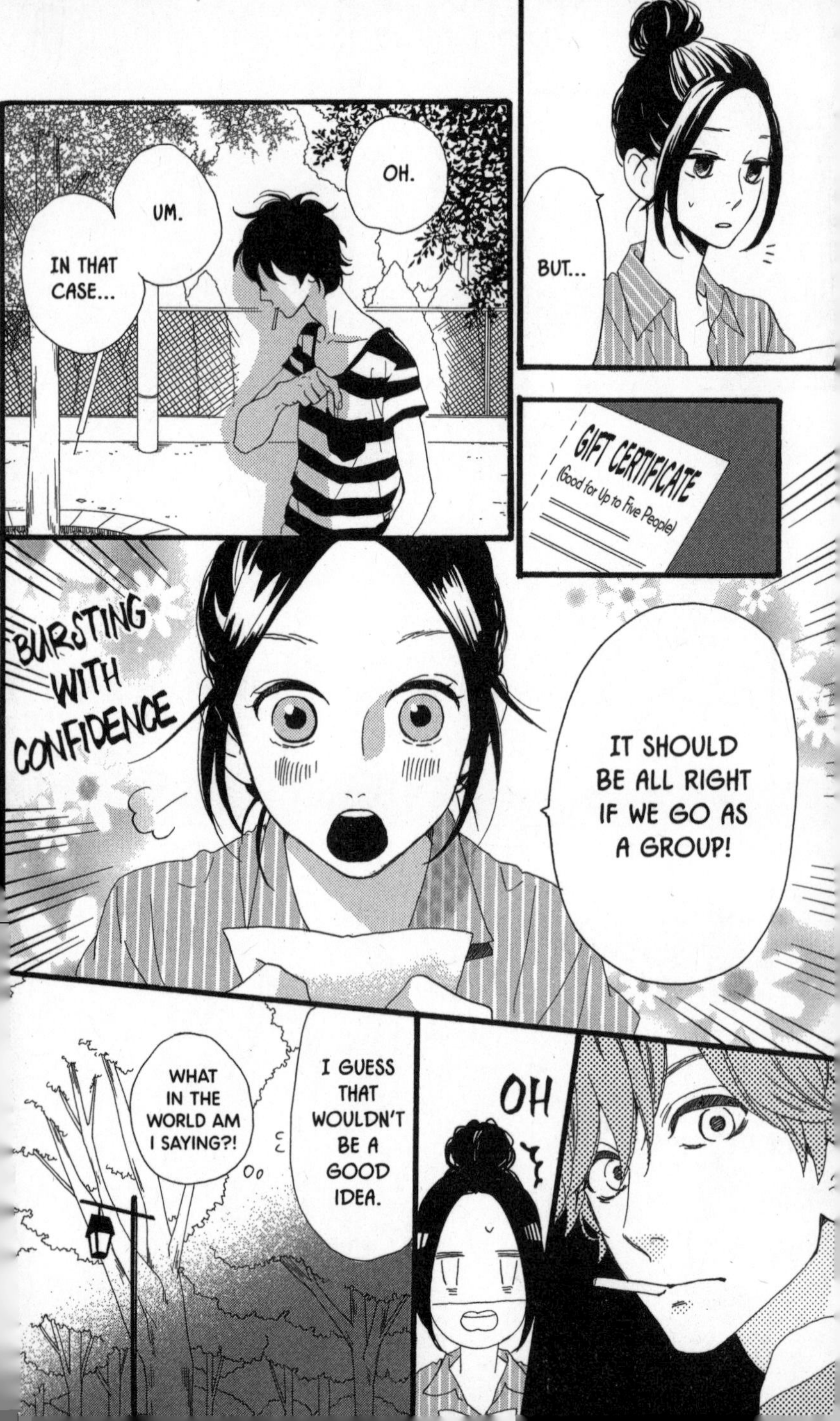
BUT...
GIFT CERTIFICATE
(Good for Up to Five People)
OH.
UM.
IN THAT CASE...
IT SHOULD BE ALL RIGHT IF WE GO AS A GROUP!
BURSTING WITH CONFIDENCE
OH
I GUESS THAT WOULDN'T BE A GOOD IDEA.
WHAT IN THE WORLD AM I SAYING?!

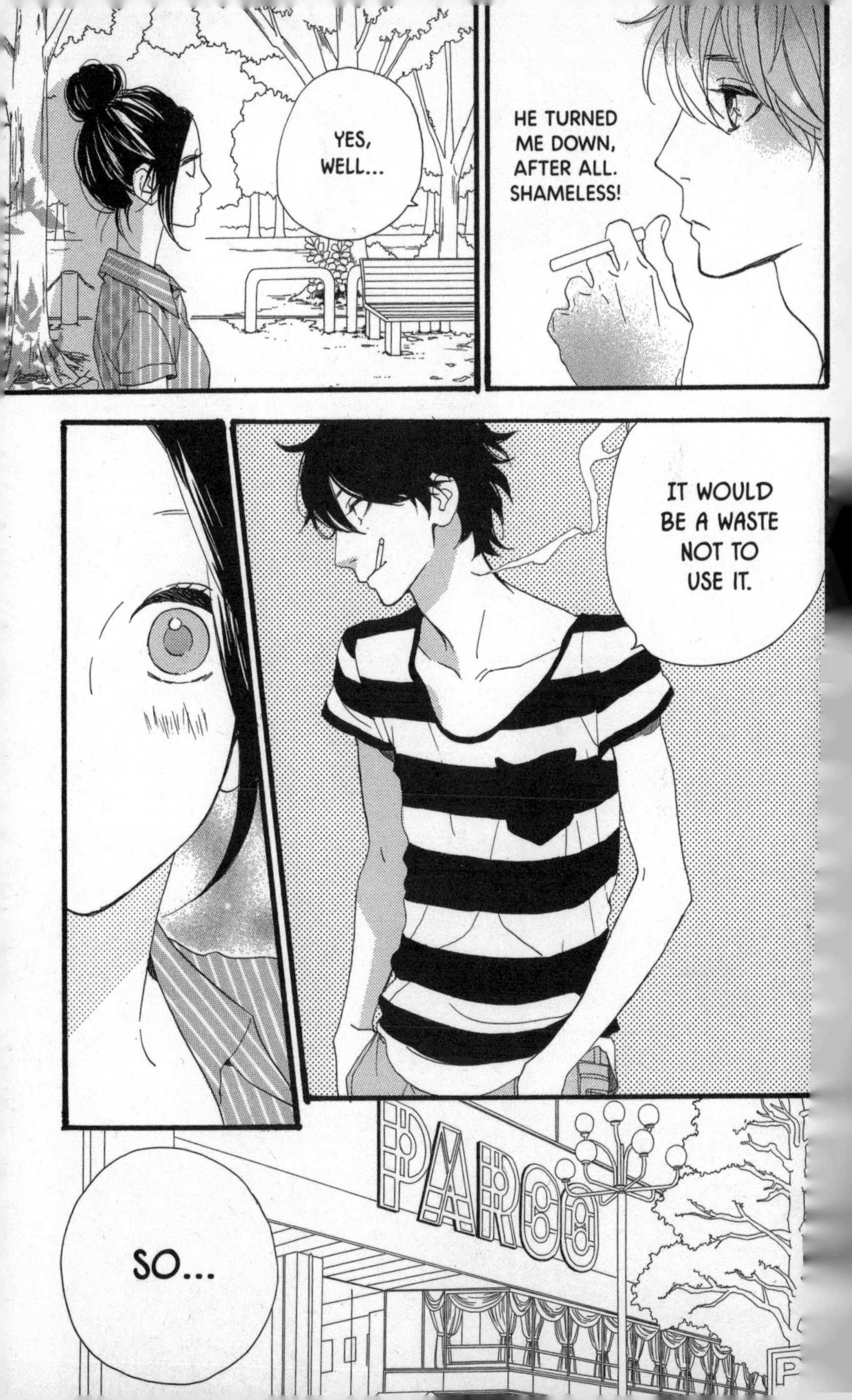
HE TURNED ME DOWN, AFTER ALL. SHAMELESS!
YES, WELL...
IT WOULD BE A WASTE NOT TO USE IT.
PARCO
SO...

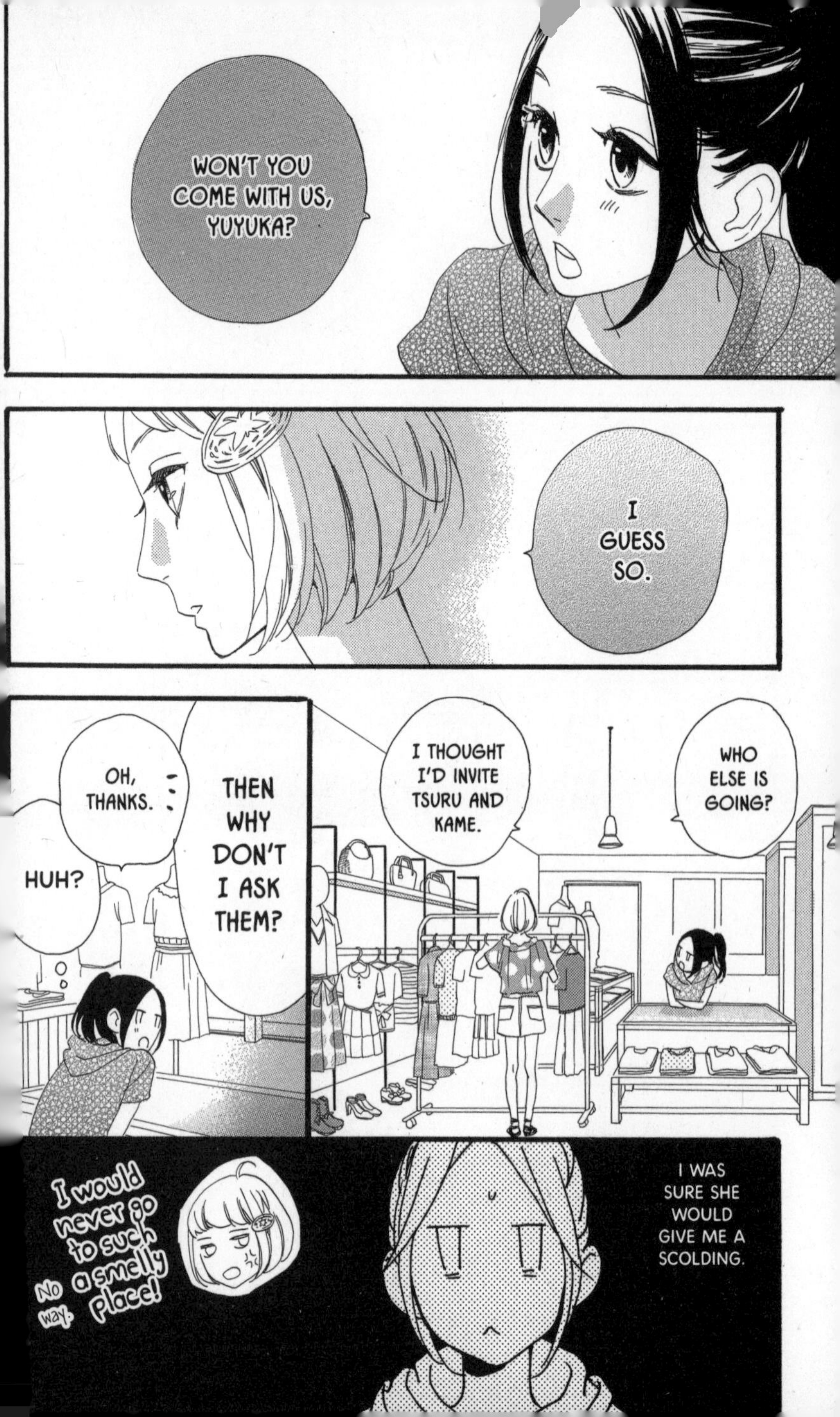

WON'T YOU COME WITH US, YUYUKA?
I GUESS SO.
WHO ELSE IS GOING?
I THOUGHT I'D INVITE TSURU AND KAME.
THEN WHY DON'T I ASK THEM?
OH, THANKS.
HUH?
I WAS SURE SHE WOULD GIVE ME A SCOLDING.
I would never go to such a smelly place!
No way.

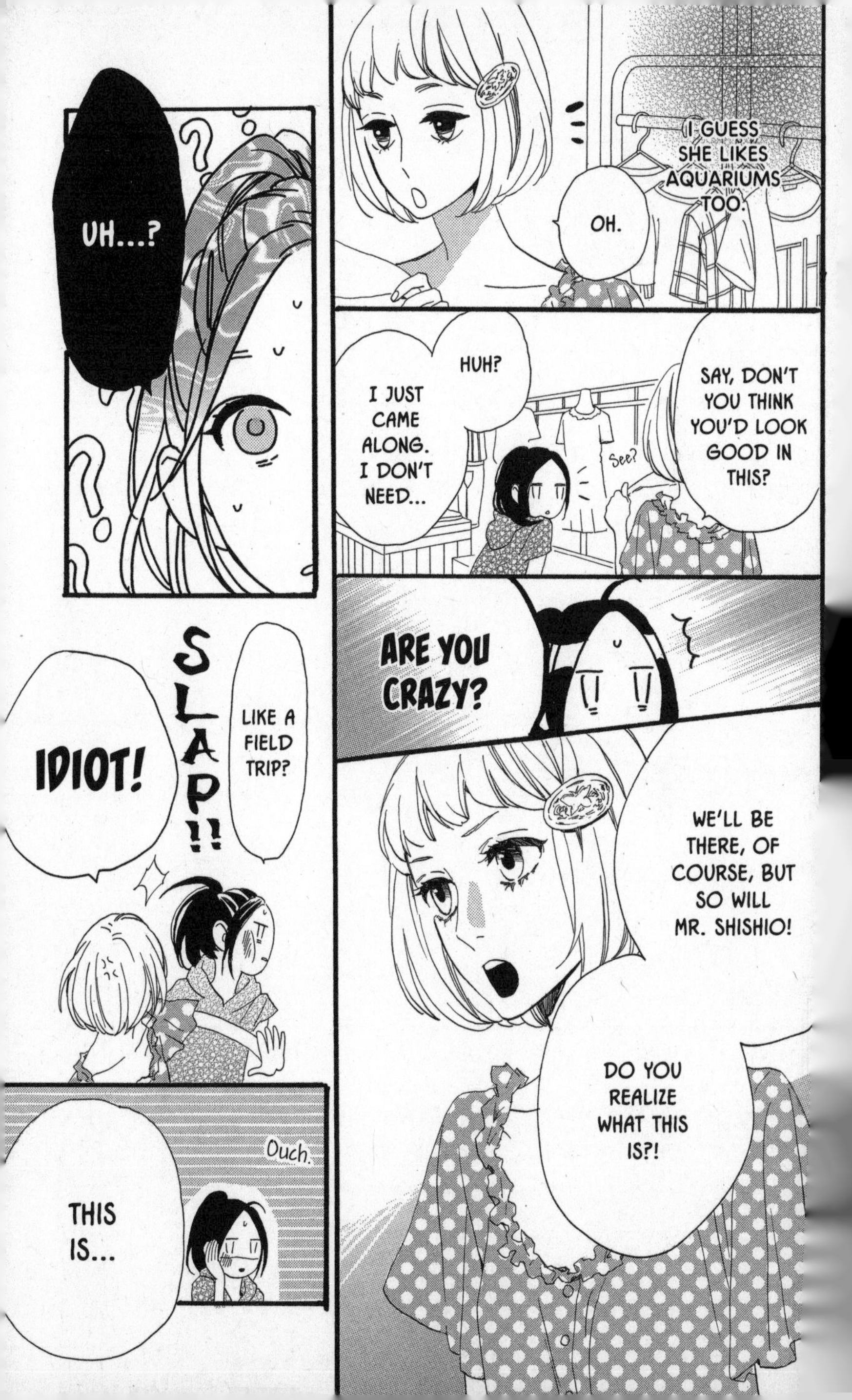
I GUESS SHE LIKES AQUARIUMS TOO.
OH.
SAY, DON'T YOU THINK YOU'D LOOK GOOD IN THIS?
See?
HUH?
I JUST CAME ALONG. I DON'T NEED...
ARE YOU CRAZY?
WE'LL BE THERE, OF COURSE, BUT SO WILL MR. SHISHIO!
DO YOU REALIZE WHAT THIS IS?!
UH...?
LIKE A FIELD TRIP?
SLAP!!
IDIOT!
Ouch.
THIS IS...

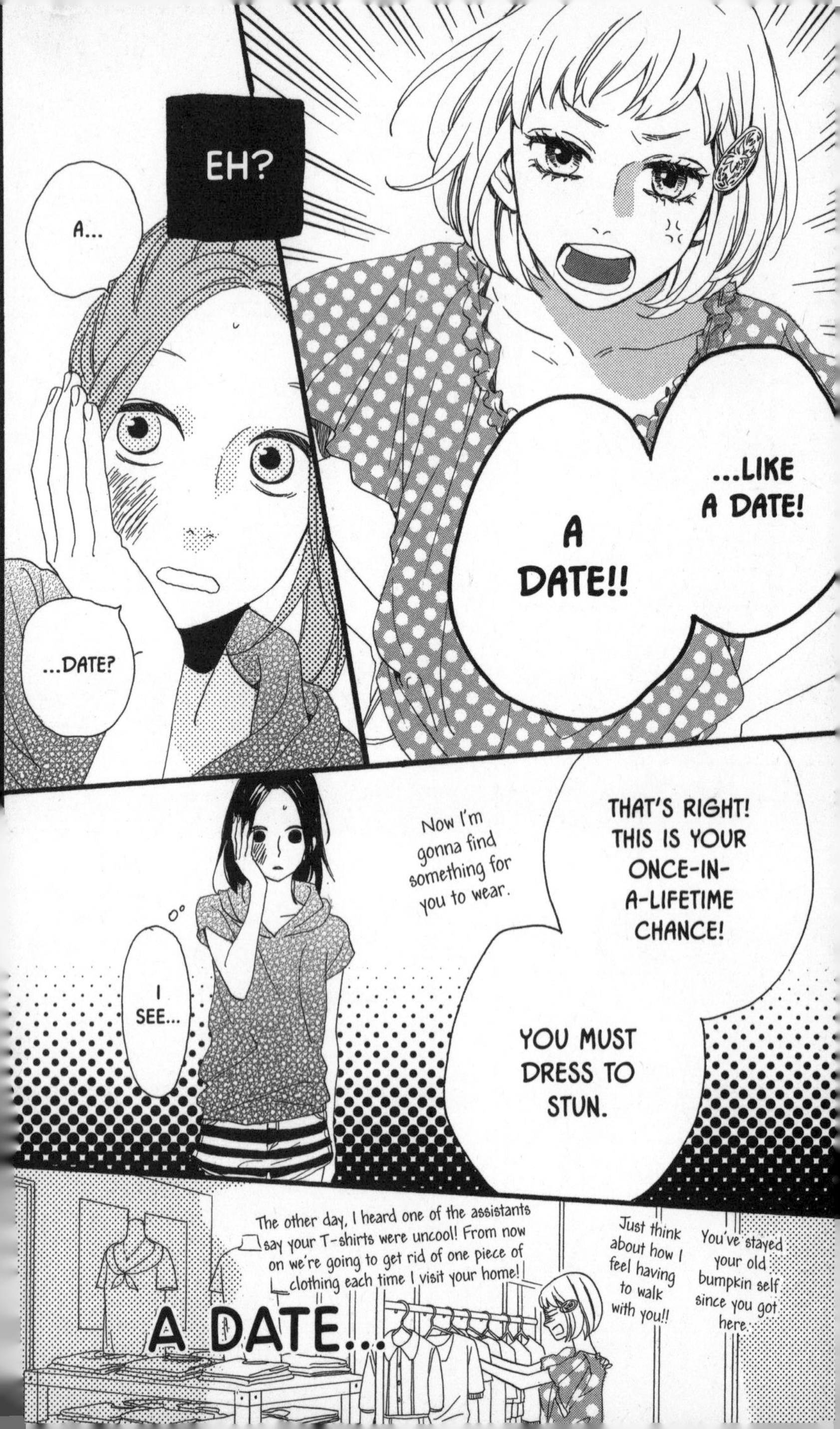
...LIKE A DATE!
A DATE!!
EH?
A...
...DATE?
THAT'S RIGHT! THIS IS YOUR ONCE-IN-A-LIFETIME CHANCE!
YOU MUST DRESS TO STUN.
Now I'm gonna find something for you to wear.
I SEE...
You've stayed your old bumpkin self since you got here.
Just think about how I feel having to walk with you!!
The other day, I heard one of the assistants say your T-shirts were uncool! From now on we're going to get rid of one piece of clothing each time I visit your home!
A DATE...

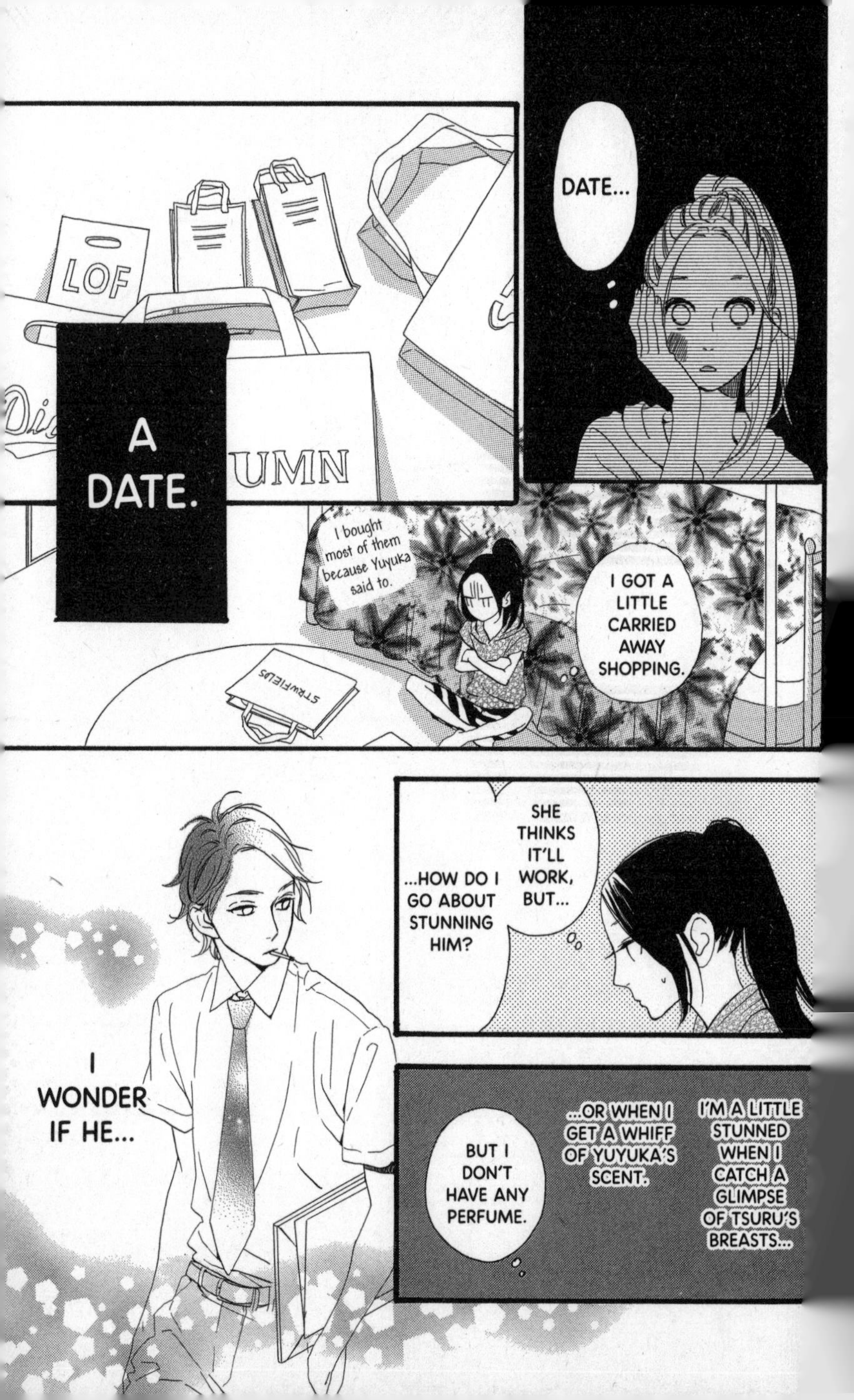
DATE...
A DATE.
LOF
UMN
I GOT A LITTLE CARRIED AWAY SHOPPING.
I bought most of them because Yuyuka said to.
STRWFIELDS
SHE THINKS IT'LL WORK, BUT...
...HOW DO I GO ABOUT STUNNING HIM?
I'M A LITTLE STUNNED WHEN I CATCH A GLIMPSE OF TSURU'S BREASTS...
...OR WHEN I GET A WHIFF OF YUYUKA'S SCENT.
BUT I DON'T HAVE ANY PERFUME.
I WONDER IF HE...

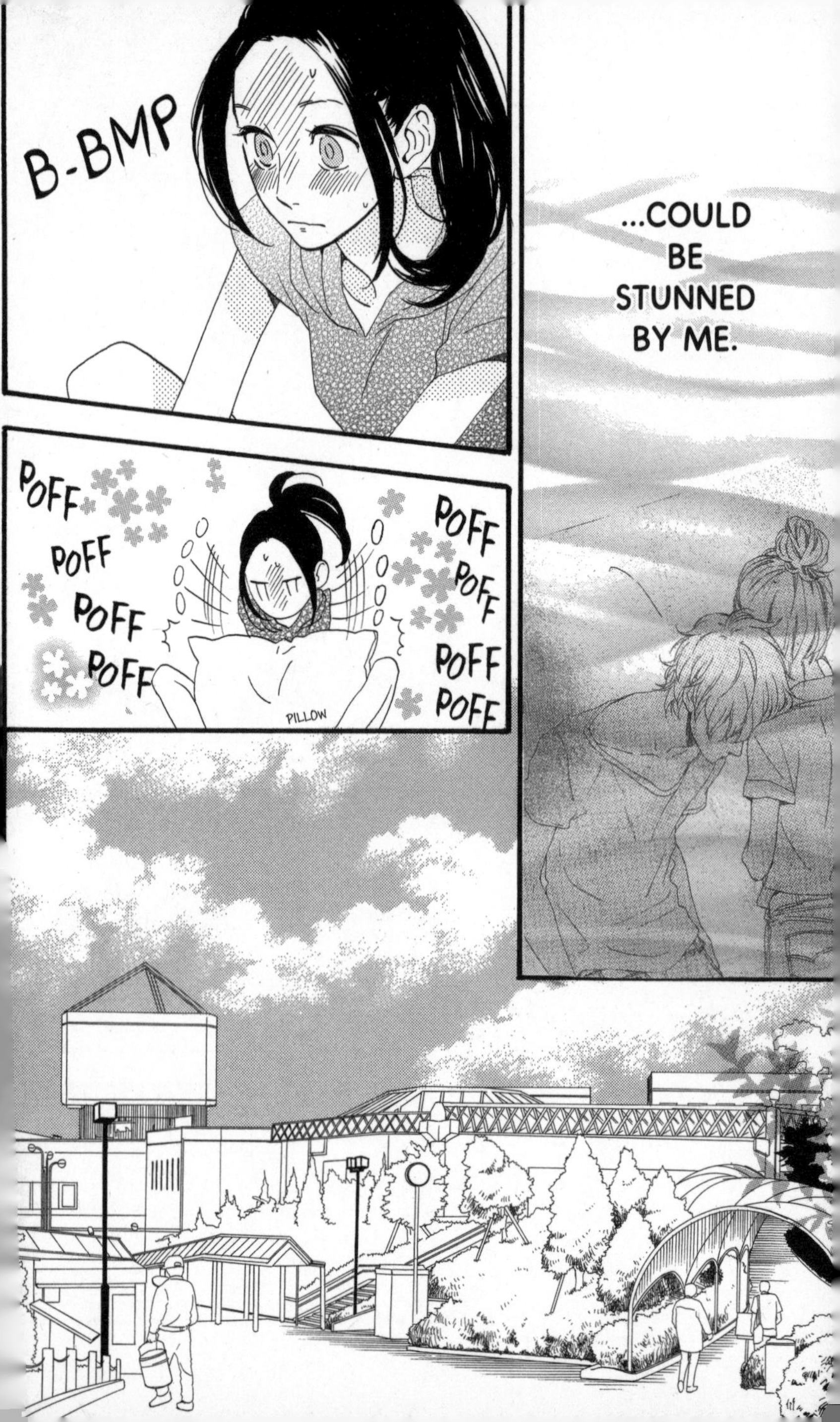
...COULD BE STUNNED BY ME.
B-BMP
POFF
POFF
POFF
POFF
POFF
POFF
POFF
POFF
PILLOW

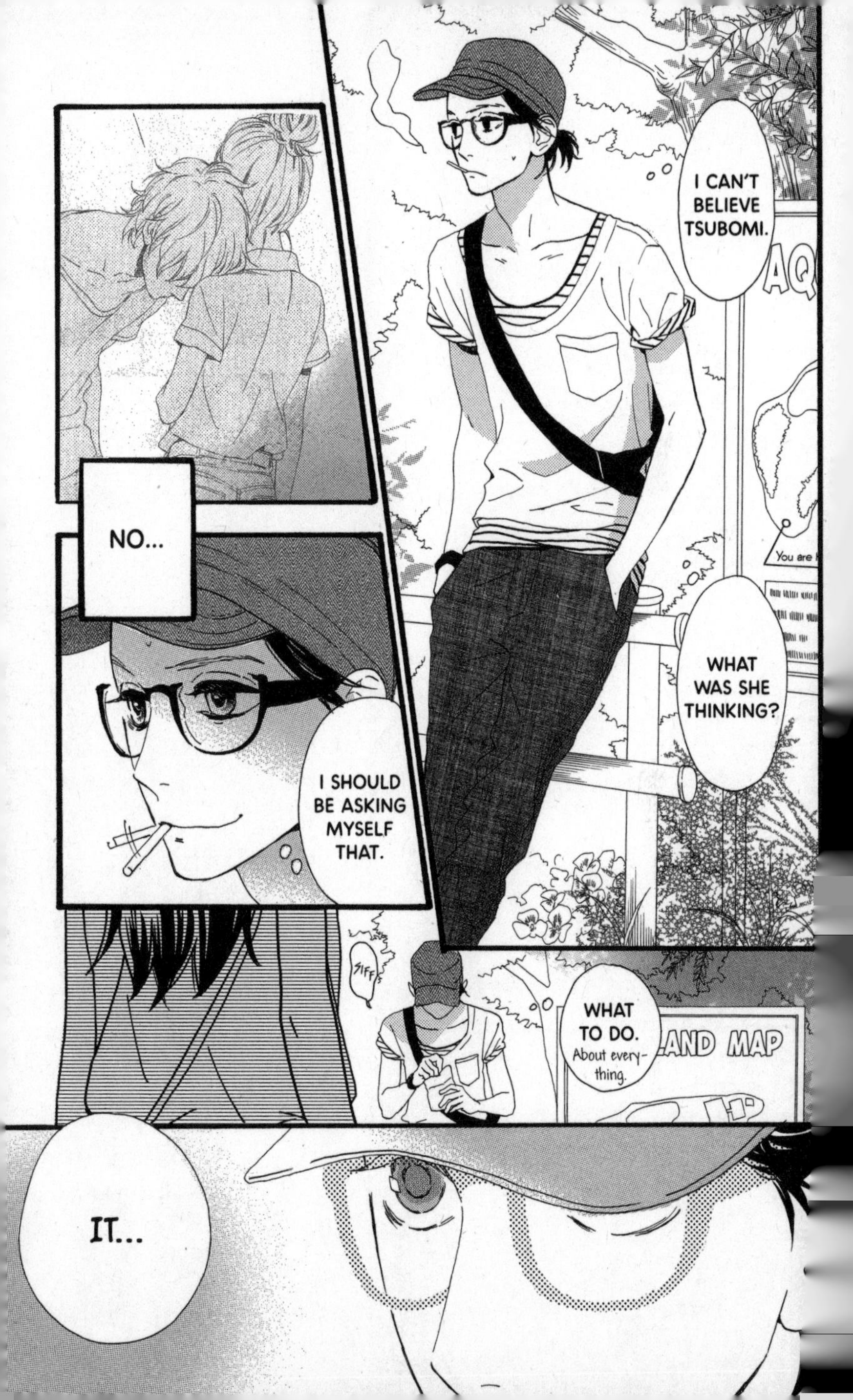
I CAN'T BELIEVE TSUBOMI.
WHAT WAS SHE THINKING?
NO...
I SHOULD BE ASKING MYSELF THAT.
WHAT TO DO. About every-thing.
SIFF
LAND MAP
IT...

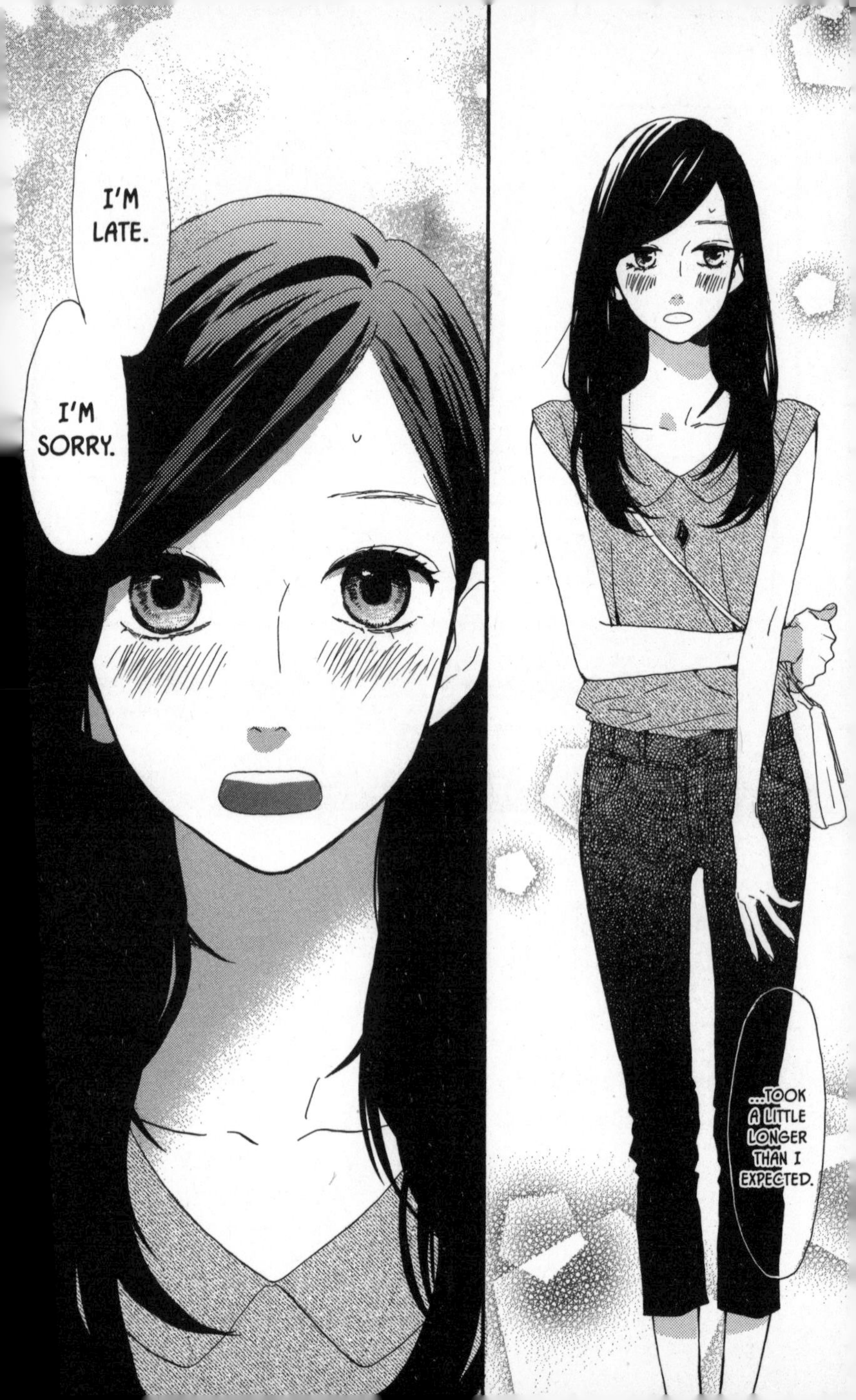
...TOOK A LITTLE LONGER THAN I EXPECTED.
I'M LATE.
I'M SORRY.

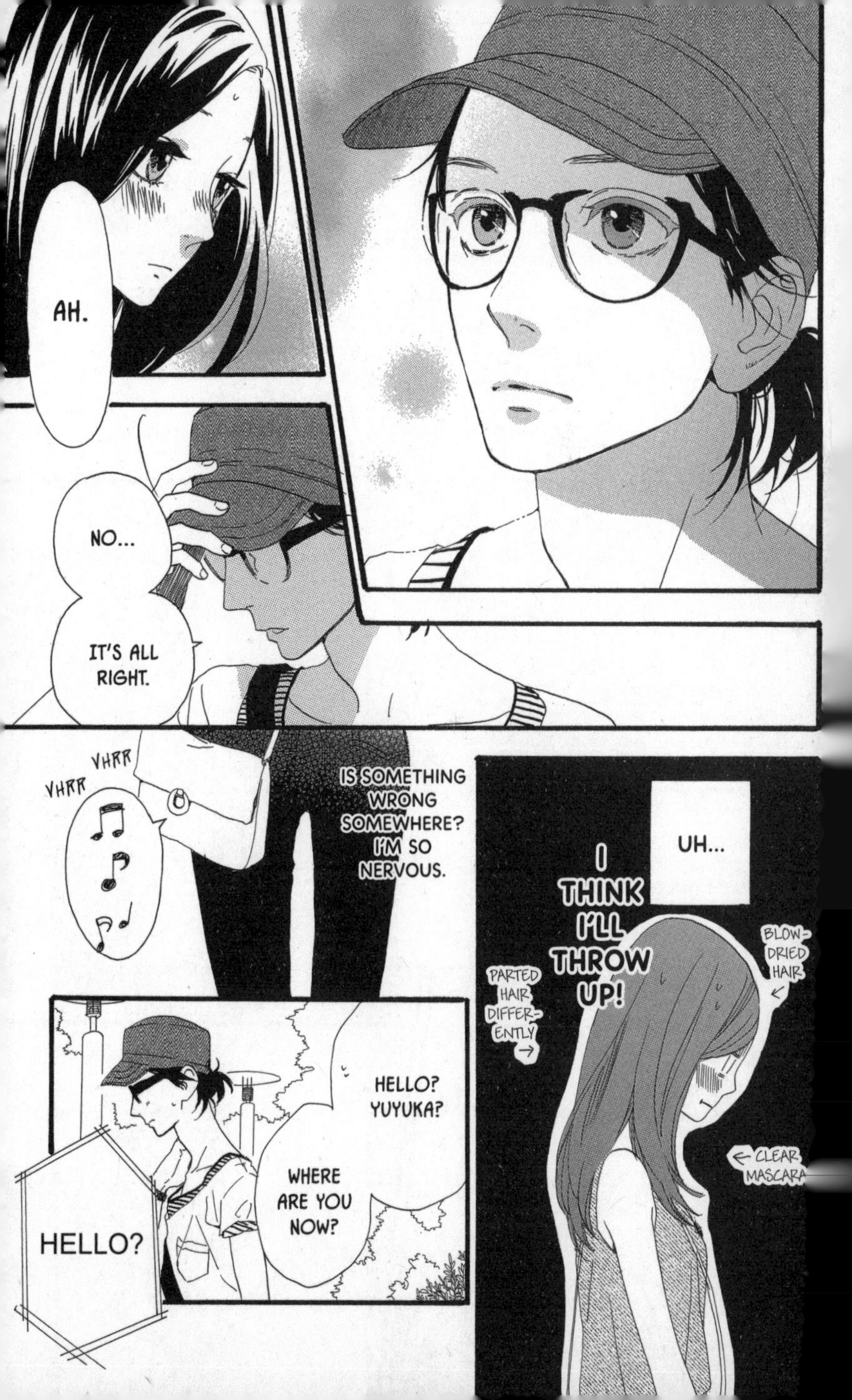
AH.
NO...
IT'S ALL RIGHT.
UH...
I THINK I'LL THROW UP!
BLOW-DRIED HAIR
PARTED HAIR DIFFERENTLY
CLEAR MASCARA
IS SOMETHING WRONG SOMEWHERE? I'M SO NERVOUS.
VHRR
VHRR
HELLO? YUYUKA?
WHERE ARE YOU NOW?
HELLO?

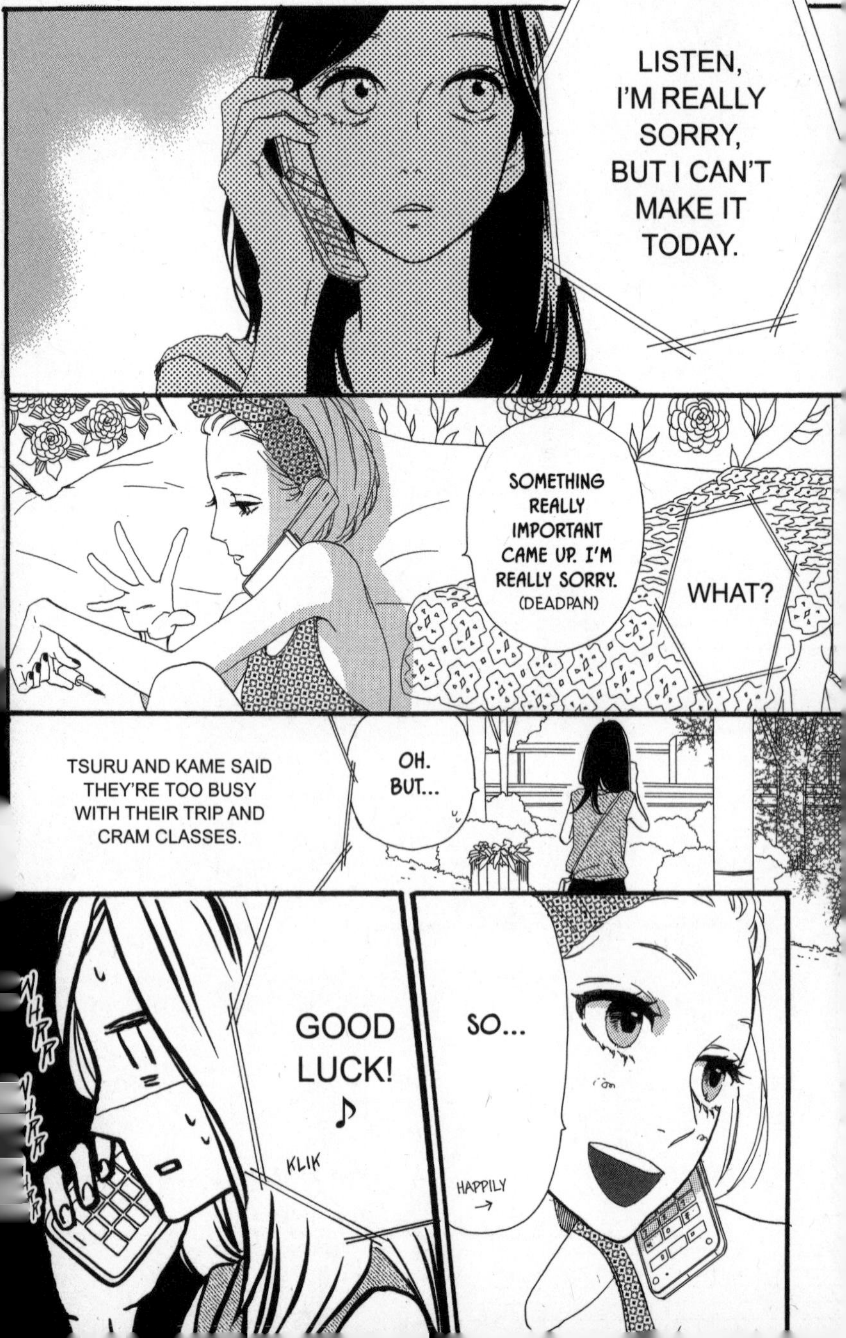
LISTEN, I'M REALLY SORRY, BUT I CAN'T MAKE IT TODAY.
WHAT?
SOMETHING REALLY IMPORTANT CAME UP. I'M REALLY SORRY.
(DEADPAN)
OH. BUT...
TSURU AND KAME SAID THEY'RE TOO BUSY WITH THEIR TRIP AND CRAM CLASSES.
SO...
HAPPILY →
GOOD LUCK! ♪
KLIK
WHRR
WHRR

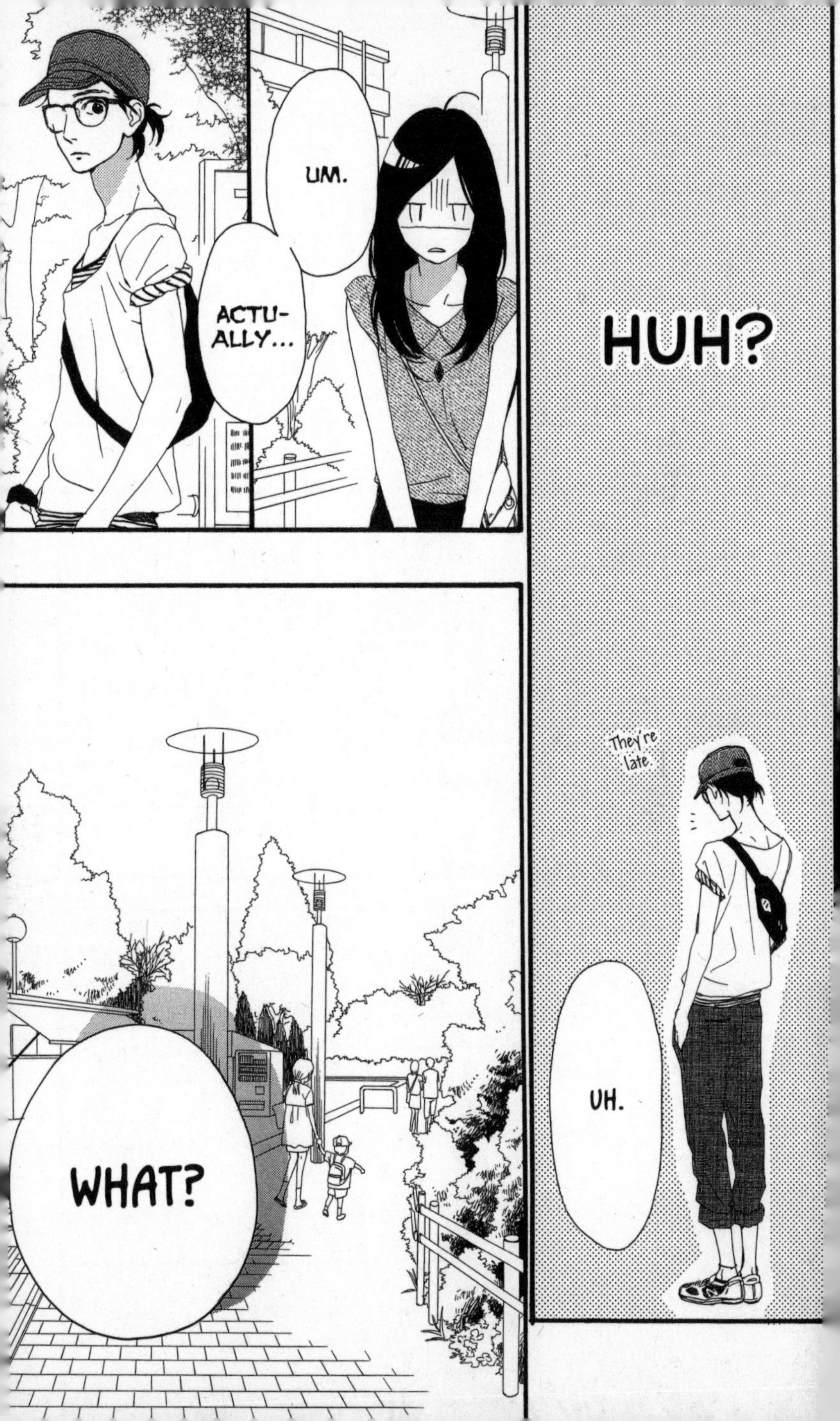
HUH?
They're late.
UH.
UM.
ACTU-ALLY...
WHAT?

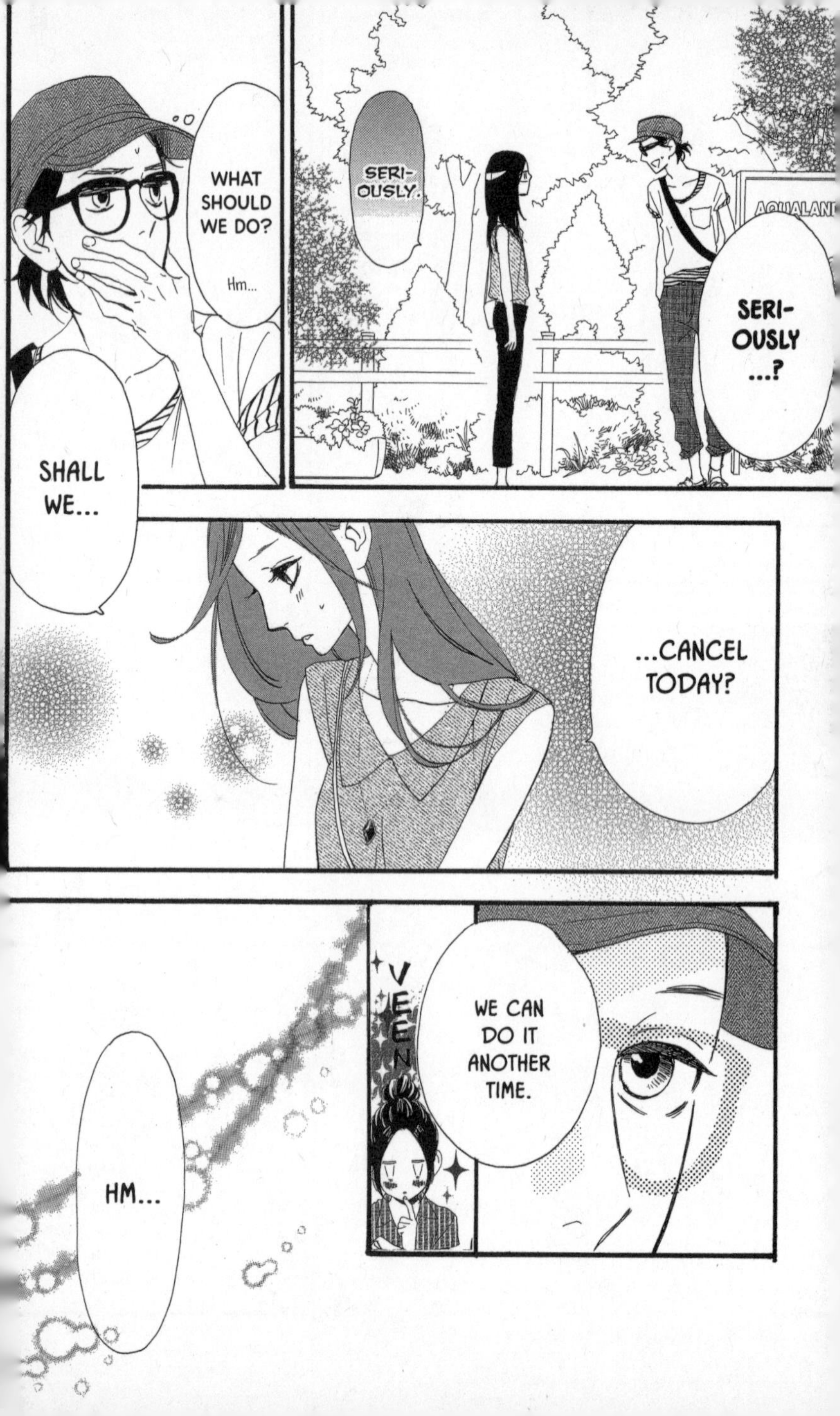
AQUALAN
SERI-OUSLY ...?
SERI-OUSLY.
WHAT SHOULD WE DO?
Hm...
SHALL WE...
...CANCEL TODAY?
WE CAN DO IT ANOTHER TIME.
VEEN
HM...

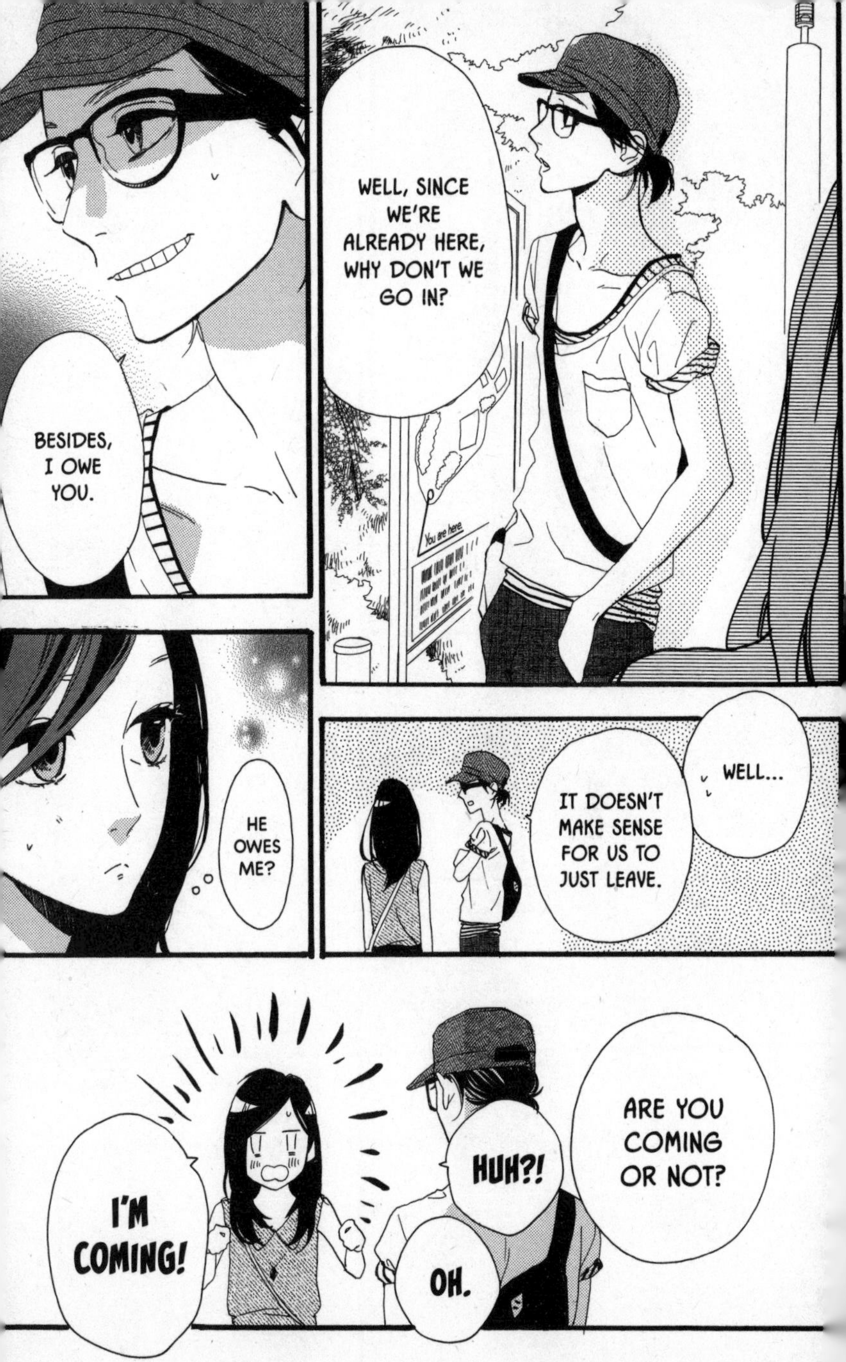

WELL, SINCE WE'RE ALREADY HERE, WHY DON'T WE GO IN?
You are here.
BESIDES, I OWE YOU.
WELL...
IT DOESN'T MAKE SENSE FOR US TO JUST LEAVE.
HE OWES ME?
ARE YOU COMING OR NOT?
HUH?!
OH.
I'M COMING!

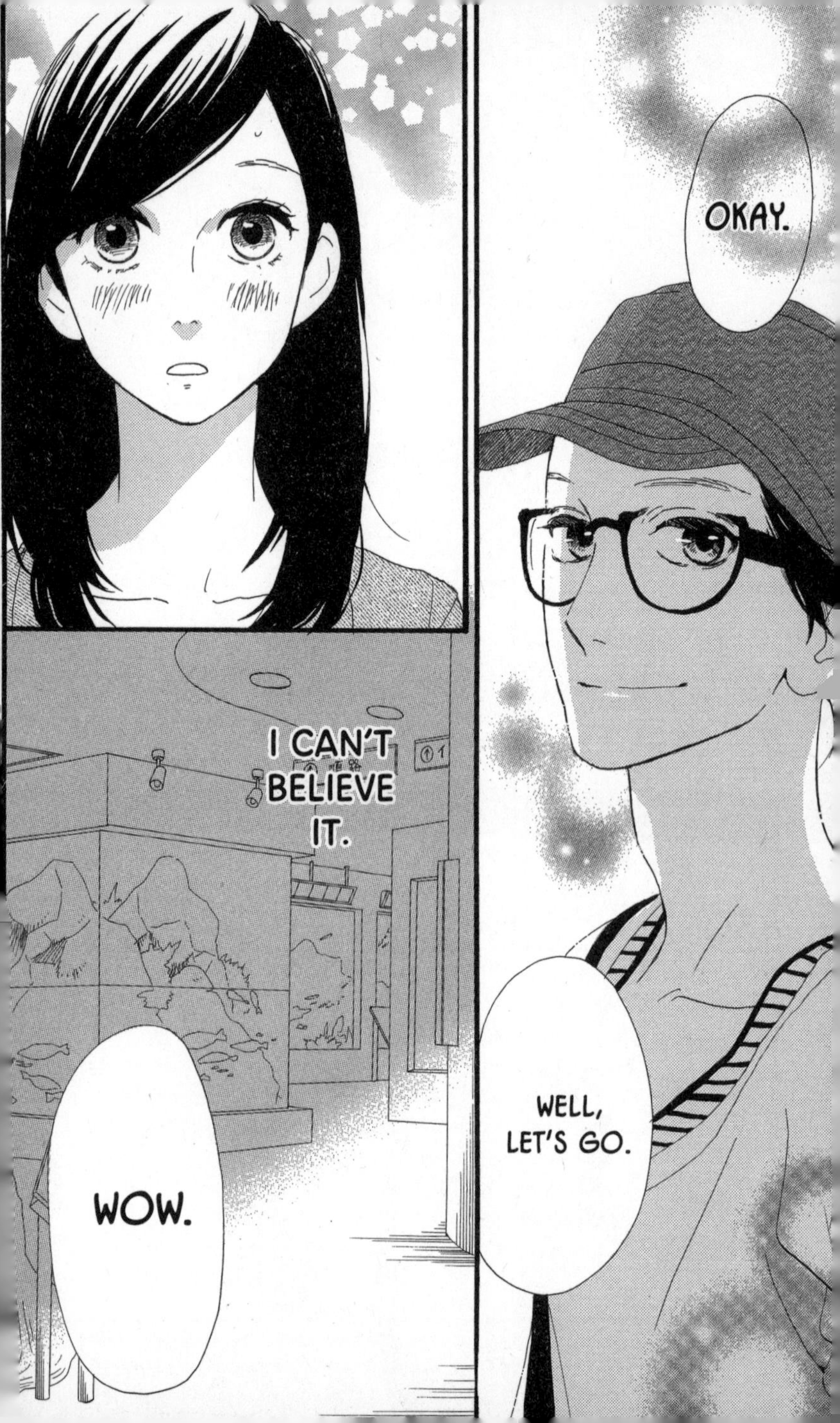
OKAY.
WELL, LET'S GO.
I CAN'T BELIEVE IT.
WOW.

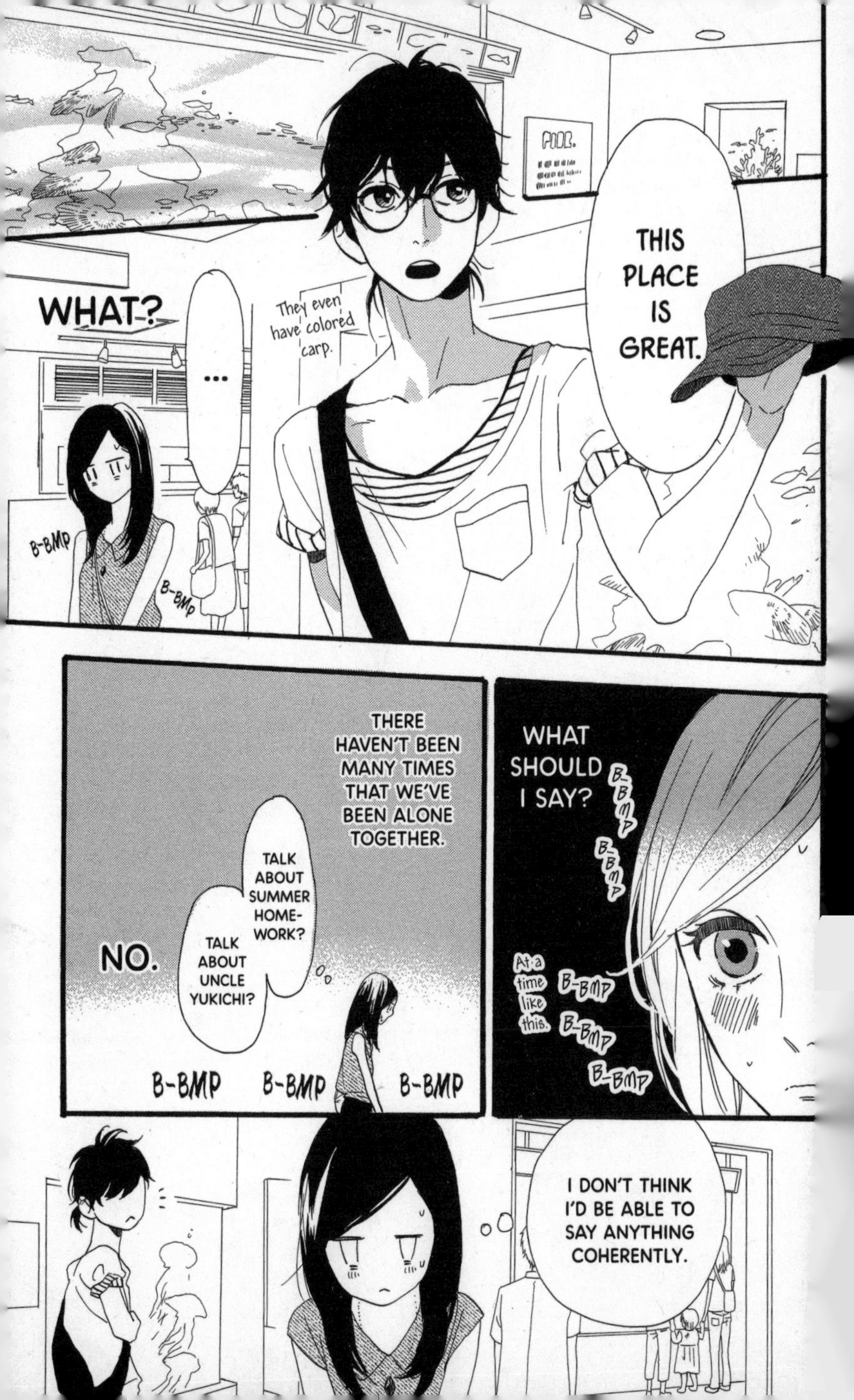
THIS PLACE IS GREAT.
They even have colored carp.
...
WHAT?
B-BMP
B-BMP
WHAT SHOULD I SAY?
B-BMP
B-BMP
At a time like this.
B-BMP
B-BMP
B-BMP
THERE HAVEN'T BEEN MANY TIMES THAT WE'VE BEEN ALONE TOGETHER.
TALK ABOUT SUMMER HOME-WORK?
TALK ABOUT UNCLE YUKICHI?
NO.
B-BMP
B-BMP
B-BMP
I DON'T THINK I'D BE ABLE TO SAY ANYTHING COHERENTLY.

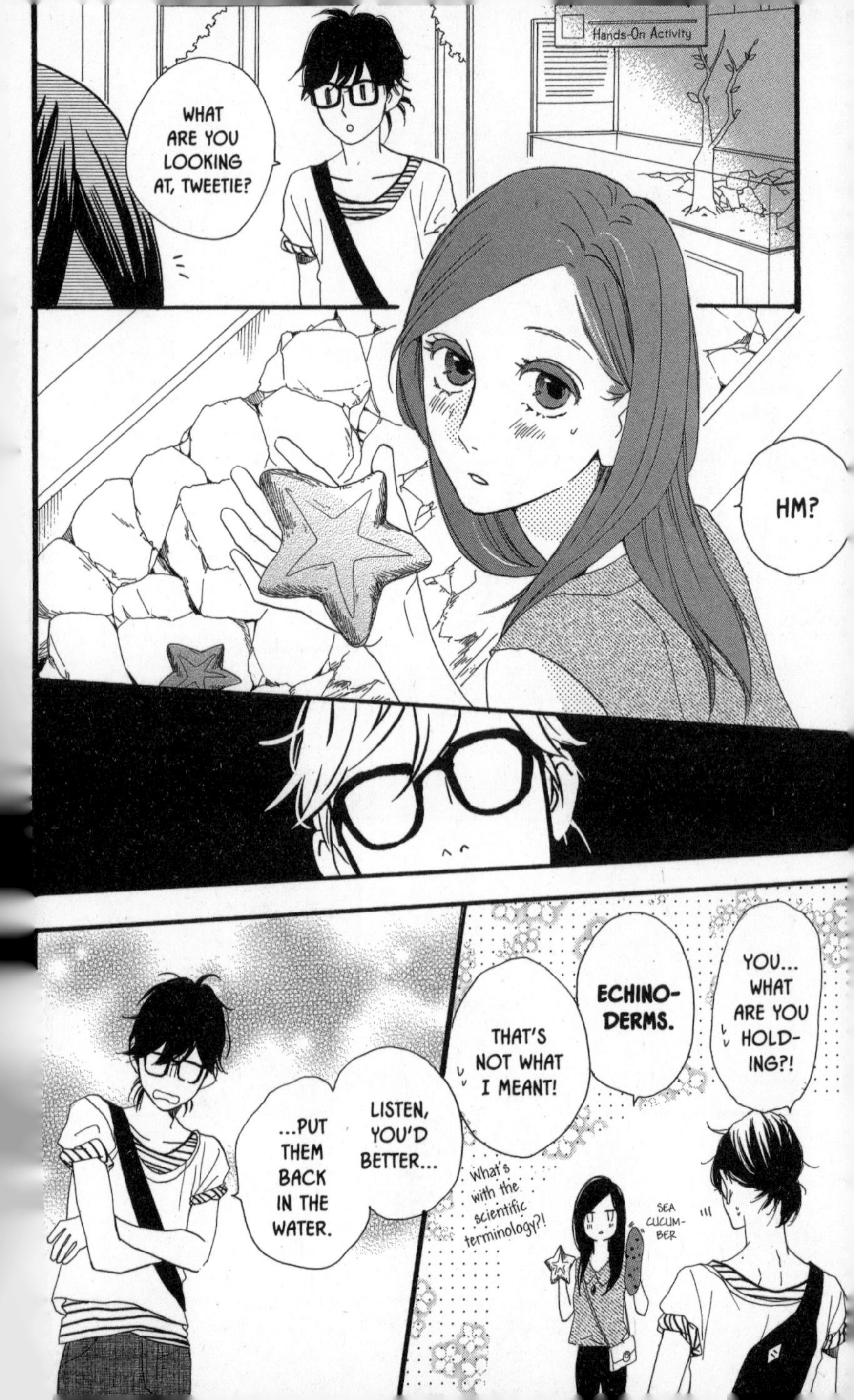
Hands-On Activity
WHAT ARE YOU LOOKING AT, TWEETIE?
HM?
YOU... WHAT ARE YOU HOLDING?!
ECHINO-DERMS.
THAT'S NOT WHAT I MEANT!
What's with the scientific terminology?!
SEA CUCUM-BER
LISTEN, YOU'D BETTER...
...PUT THEM BACK IN THE WATER.

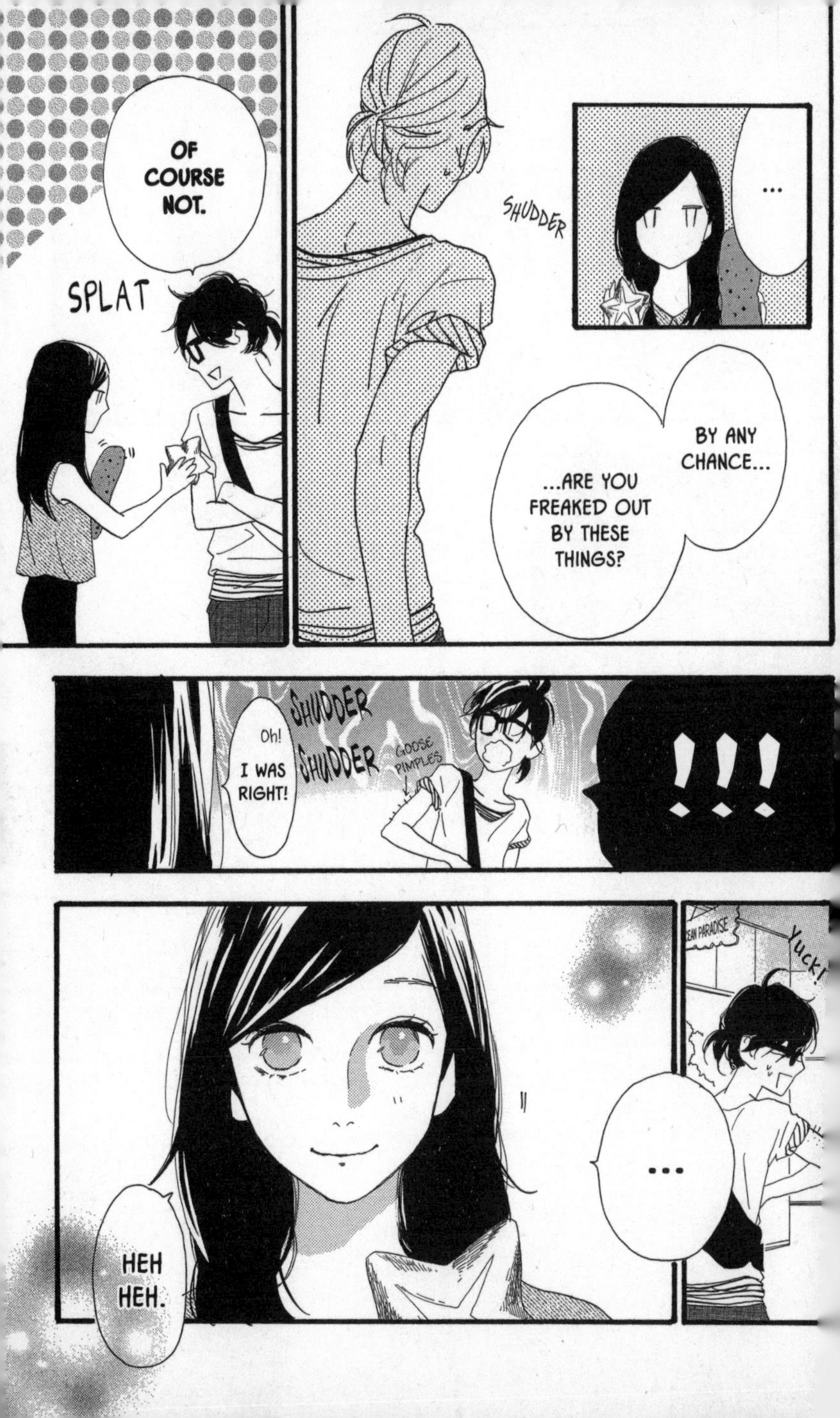
SHUDDER
...
BY ANY CHANCE...
...ARE YOU FREAKED OUT BY THESE THINGS?
OF COURSE NOT.
SPLAT
!!!
GOOSE PIMPLES
SHUDDER SHUDDER
Oh! I WAS RIGHT!
EAN PARADISE
YUCK!
...
HEH HEH.

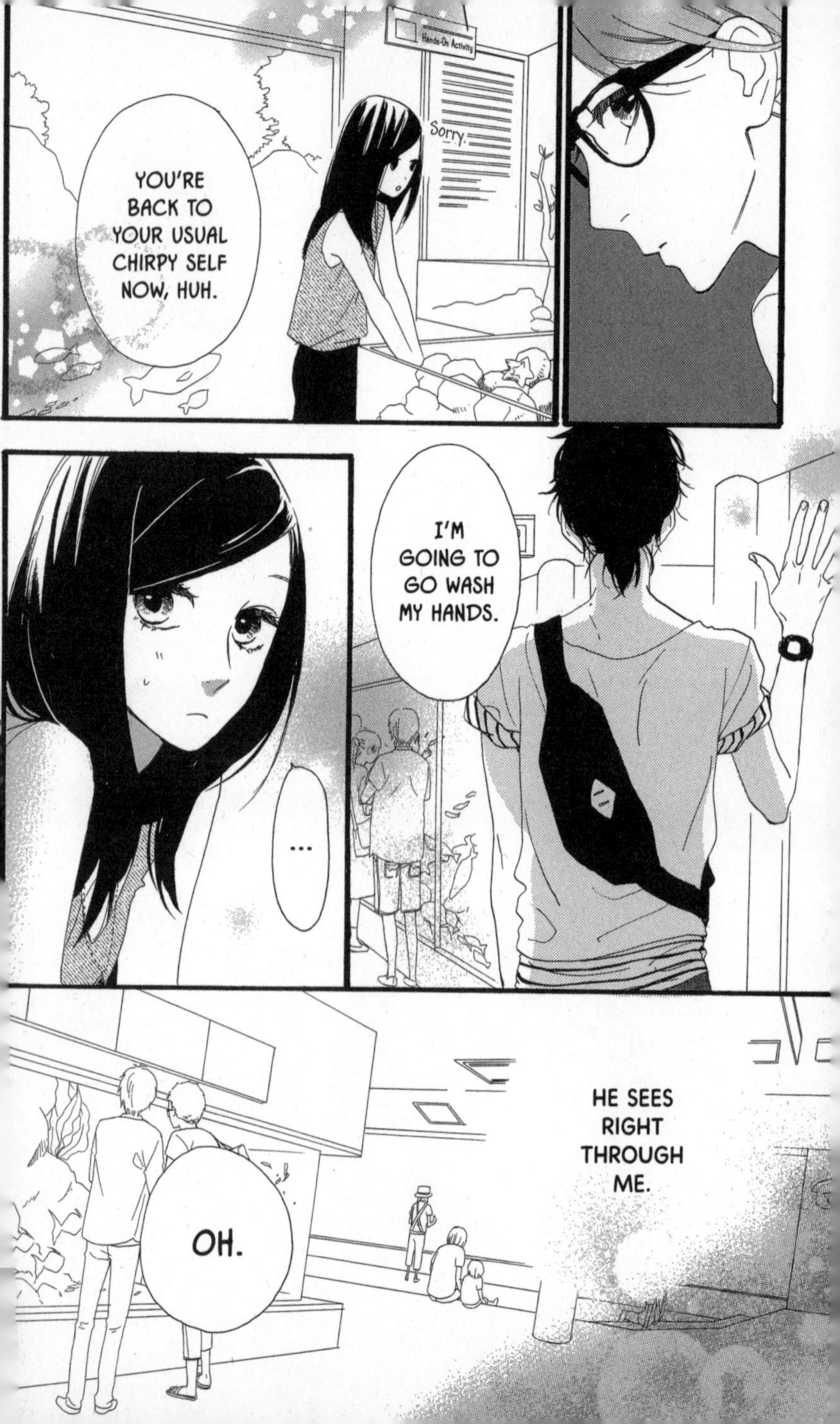
Hands-On Activity
Sorry.
YOU'RE BACK TO YOUR USUAL CHIRPY SELF NOW, HUH.
I'M GOING TO GO WASH MY HANDS.
...
HE SEES RIGHT THROUGH ME.
OH.

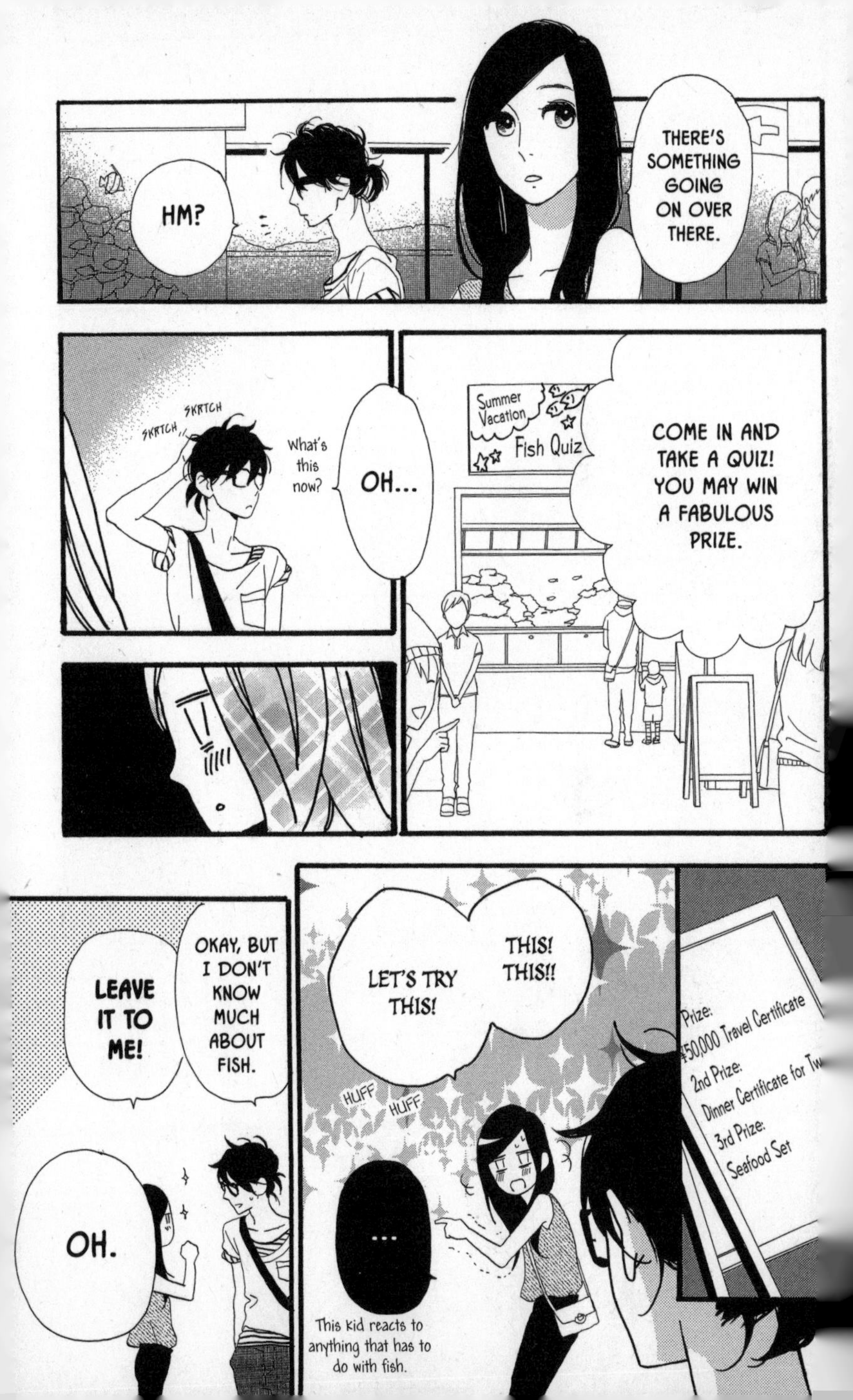
THERE'S SOMETHING GOING ON OVER THERE.
HM?
Summer Vacation
Fish Quiz
COME IN AND TAKE A QUIZ! YOU MAY WIN A FABULOUS PRIZE.
OH...
What's this now?
SKRTCH
SKRTCH
Prize:
¥50,000 Travel Certificate
2nd Prize:
Dinner Certificate for Tw
3rd Prize:
Seafood Set
THIS! THIS!!
LET'S TRY THIS!
HUFF
HUFF
...
This kid reacts to anything that has to do with fish.
OKAY, BUT I DON'T KNOW MUCH ABOUT FISH.
LEAVE IT TO ME!
OH.

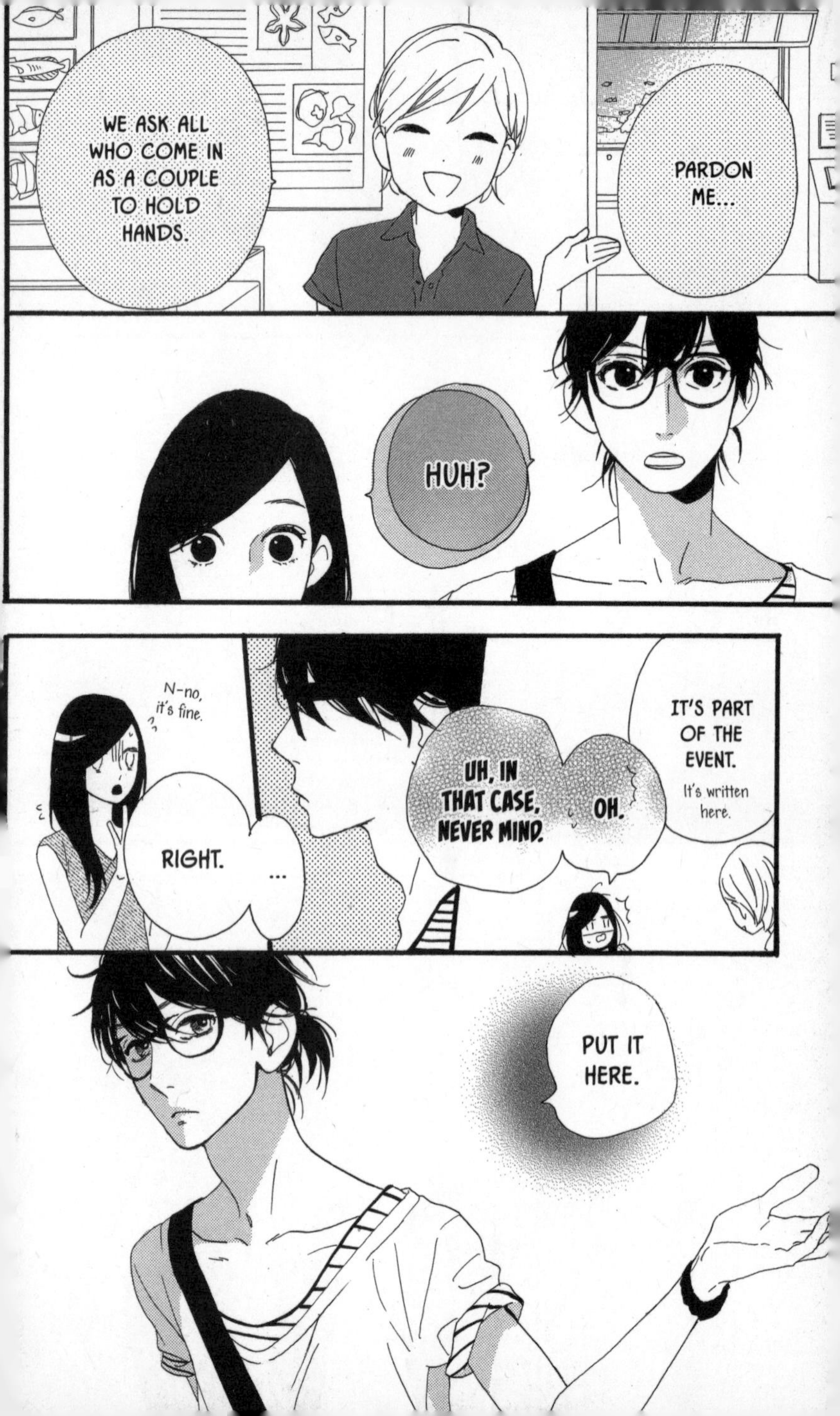
PARDON ME...
WE ASK ALL WHO COME IN AS A COUPLE TO HOLD HANDS.
HUH?
IT'S PART OF THE EVENT.
It's written here.
OH.
UH, IN THAT CASE, NEVER MIND.
N-no, it's fine.
...
RIGHT.
PUT IT HERE.

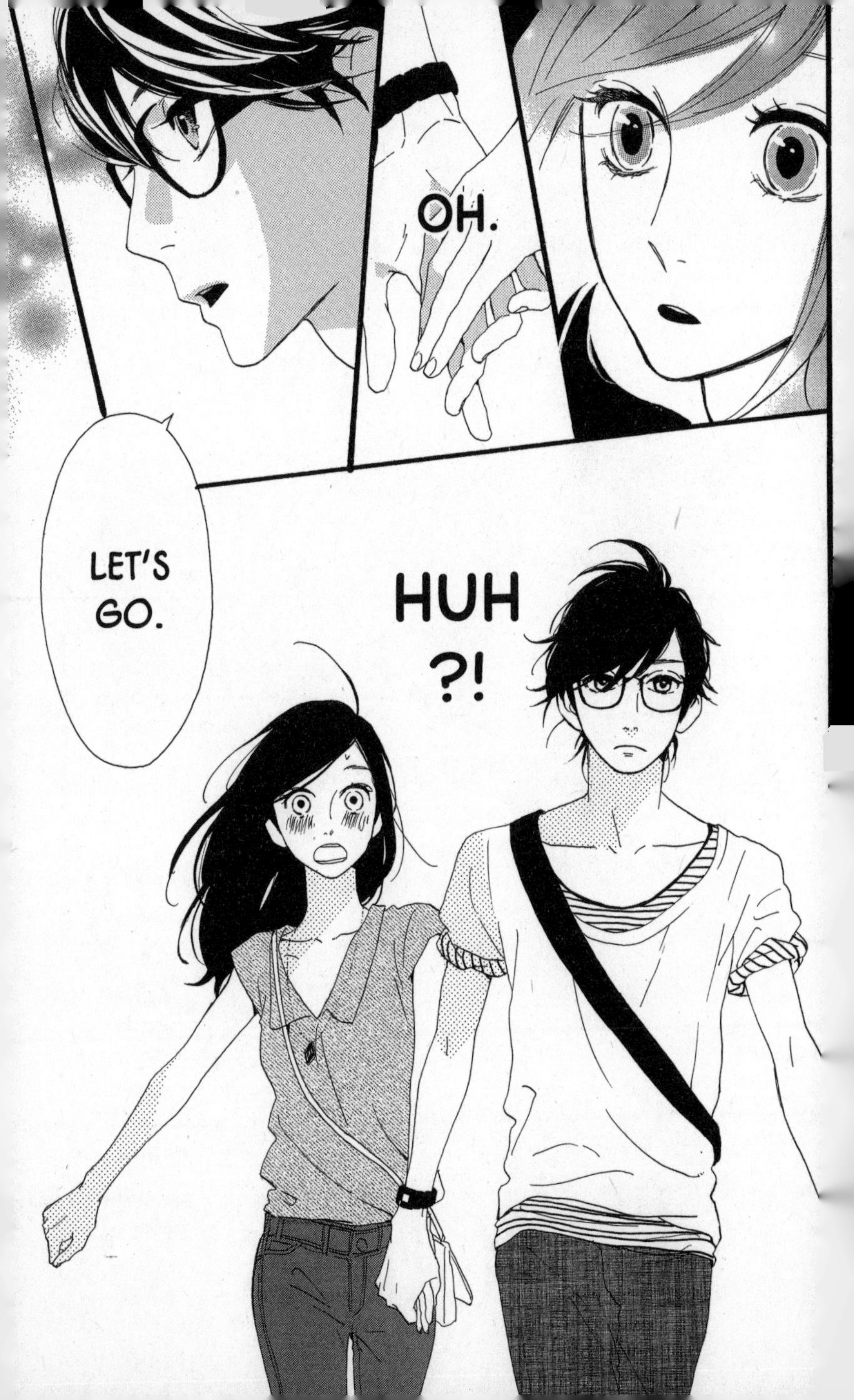
OH.
HUH ?!
LET'S GO.

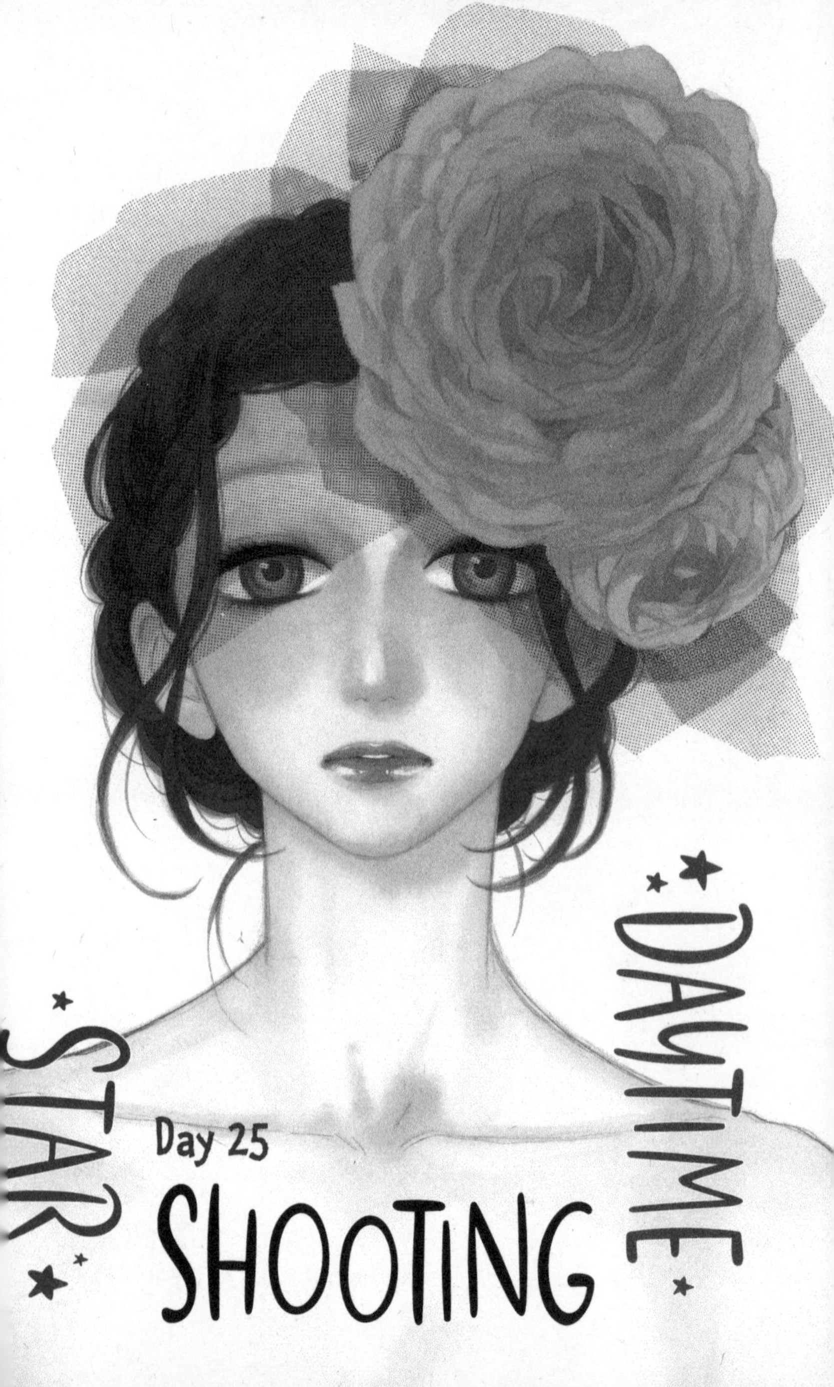
Day 25
Daytime Shooting Star

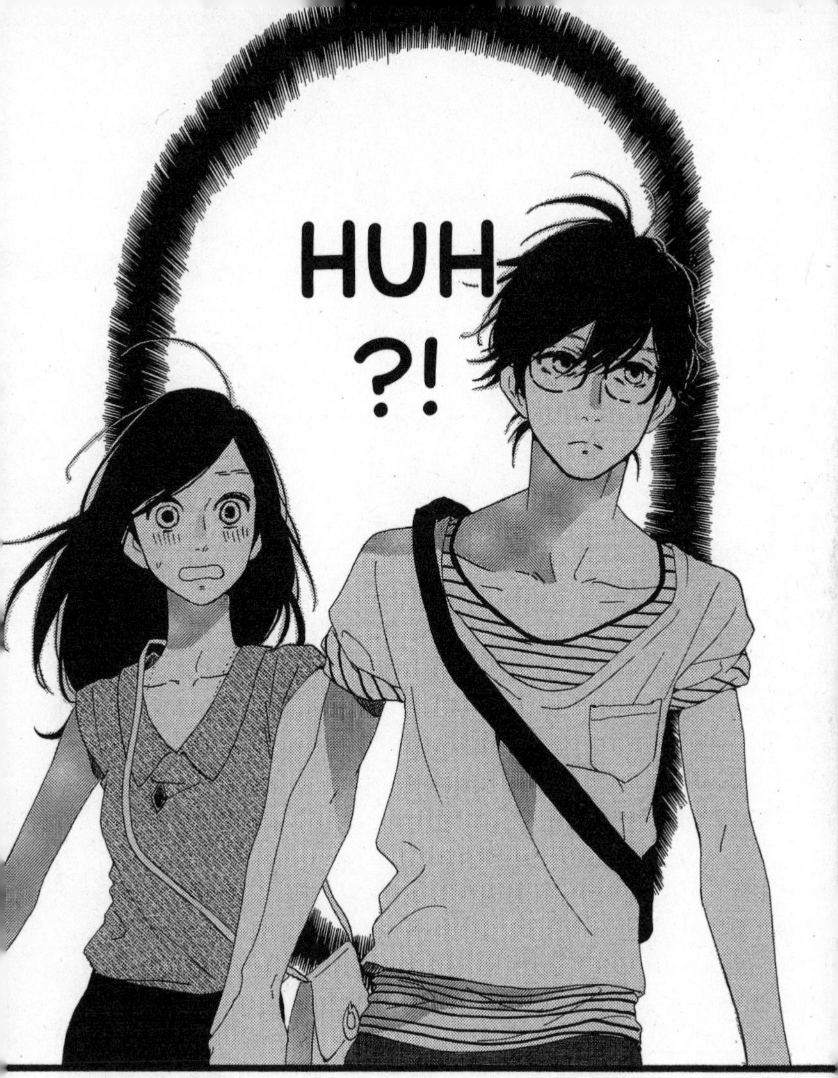
HUH ?!

Shishio, Talking to Himself

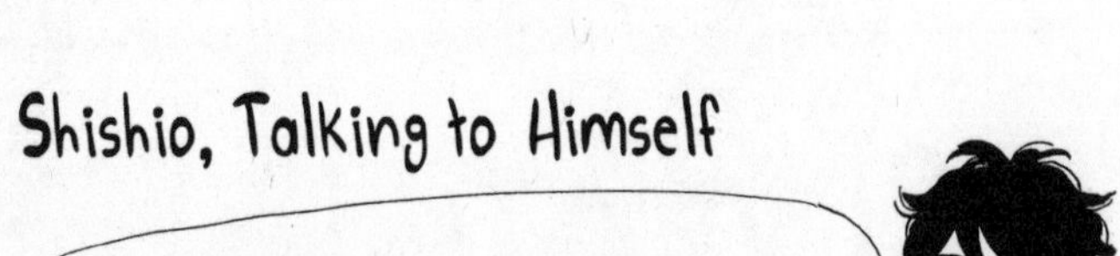
Time flies once you're over 20.

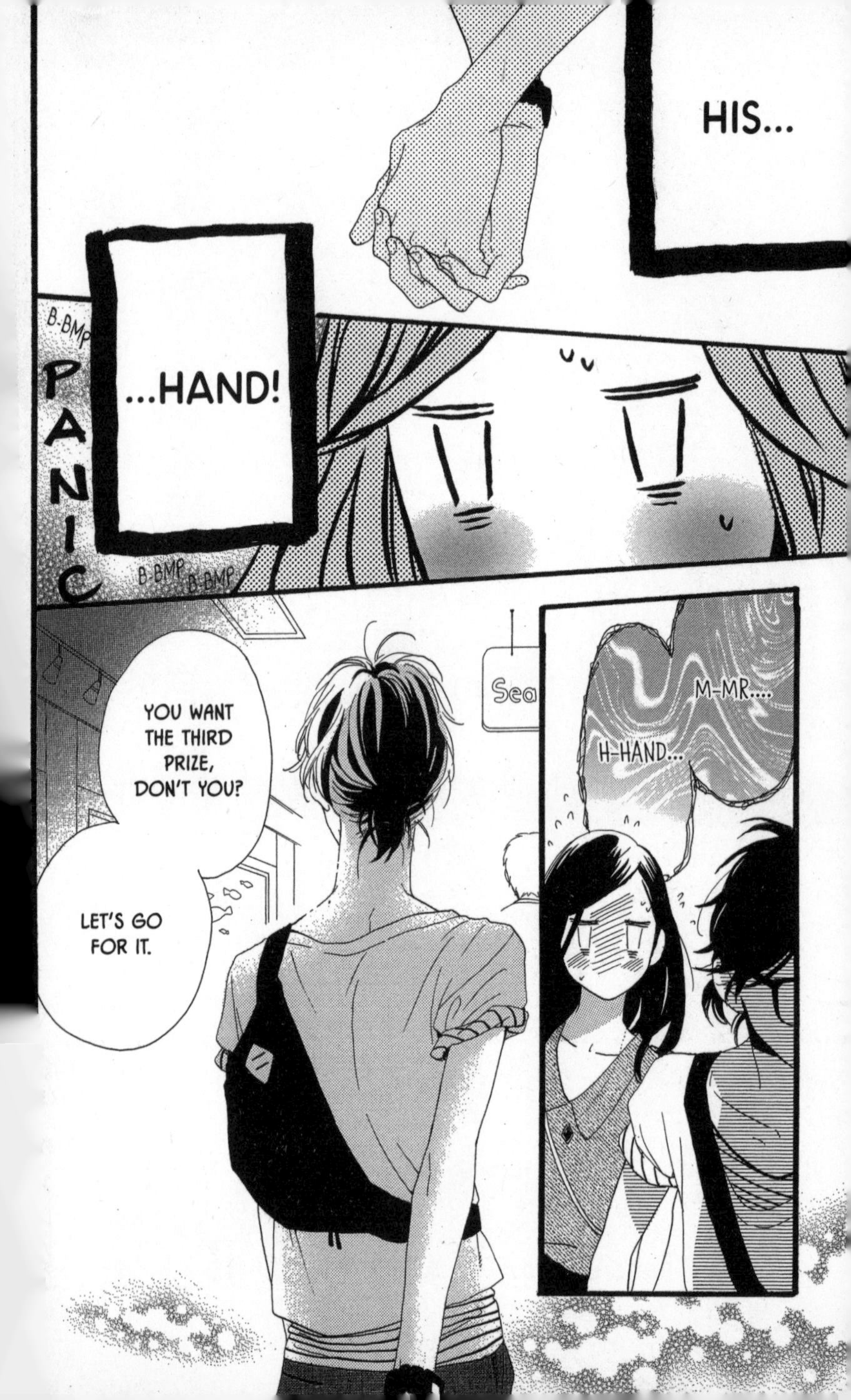
HIS...
...HAND!
B-BMP
PANIC
B-BMP B-BMP
M-MR....
H-HAND...
Sea
YOU WANT THE THIRD PRIZE, DON'T YOU?
LET'S GO FOR IT.

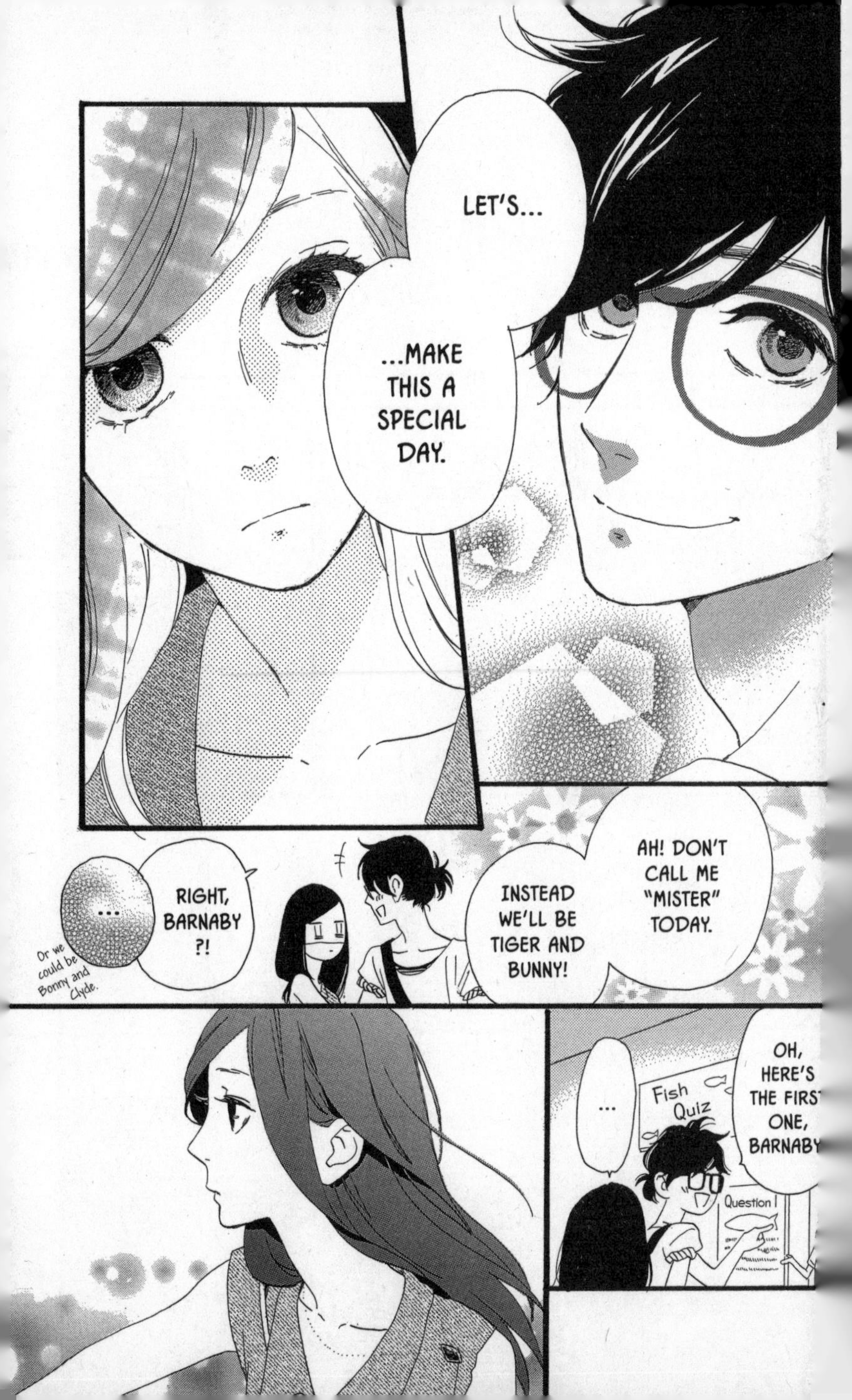
LET'S...
...MAKE THIS A SPECIAL DAY.
AH! DON'T CALL ME "MISTER" TODAY.
INSTEAD WE'LL BE TIGER AND BUNNY!
RIGHT, BARNABY ?!
...
Or we could be Bonny and Clyde.
OH, HERE'S THE FIRST ONE, BARNABY
Fish Quiz
Question 1
...

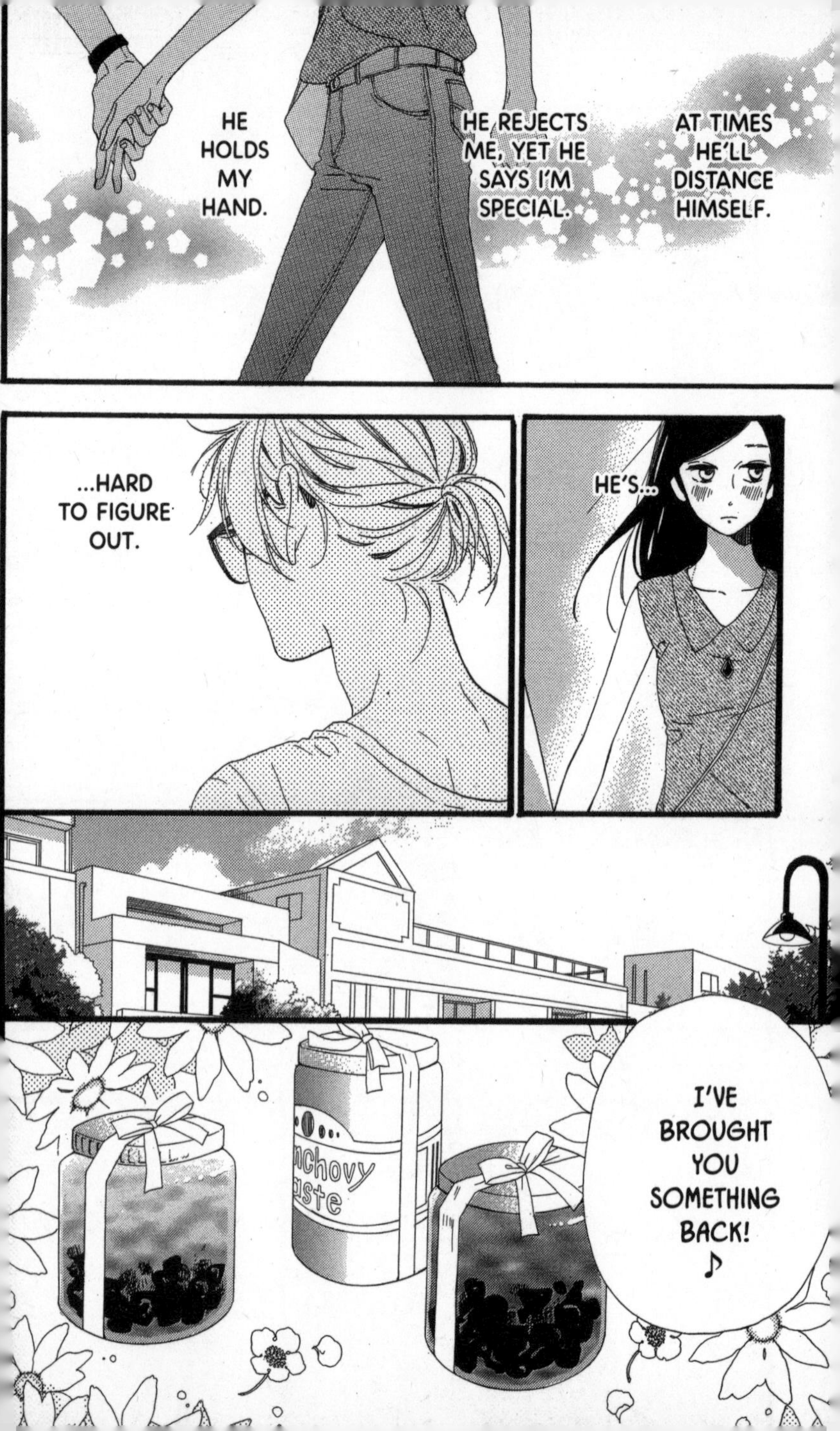
AT TIMES HE'LL DISTANCE HIMSELF.
HE REJECTS ME, YET HE SAYS I'M SPECIAL.
HE HOLDS MY HAND.
HE'S...
...HARD TO FIGURE OUT.
I'VE BROUGHT YOU SOMETHING BACK! ♪

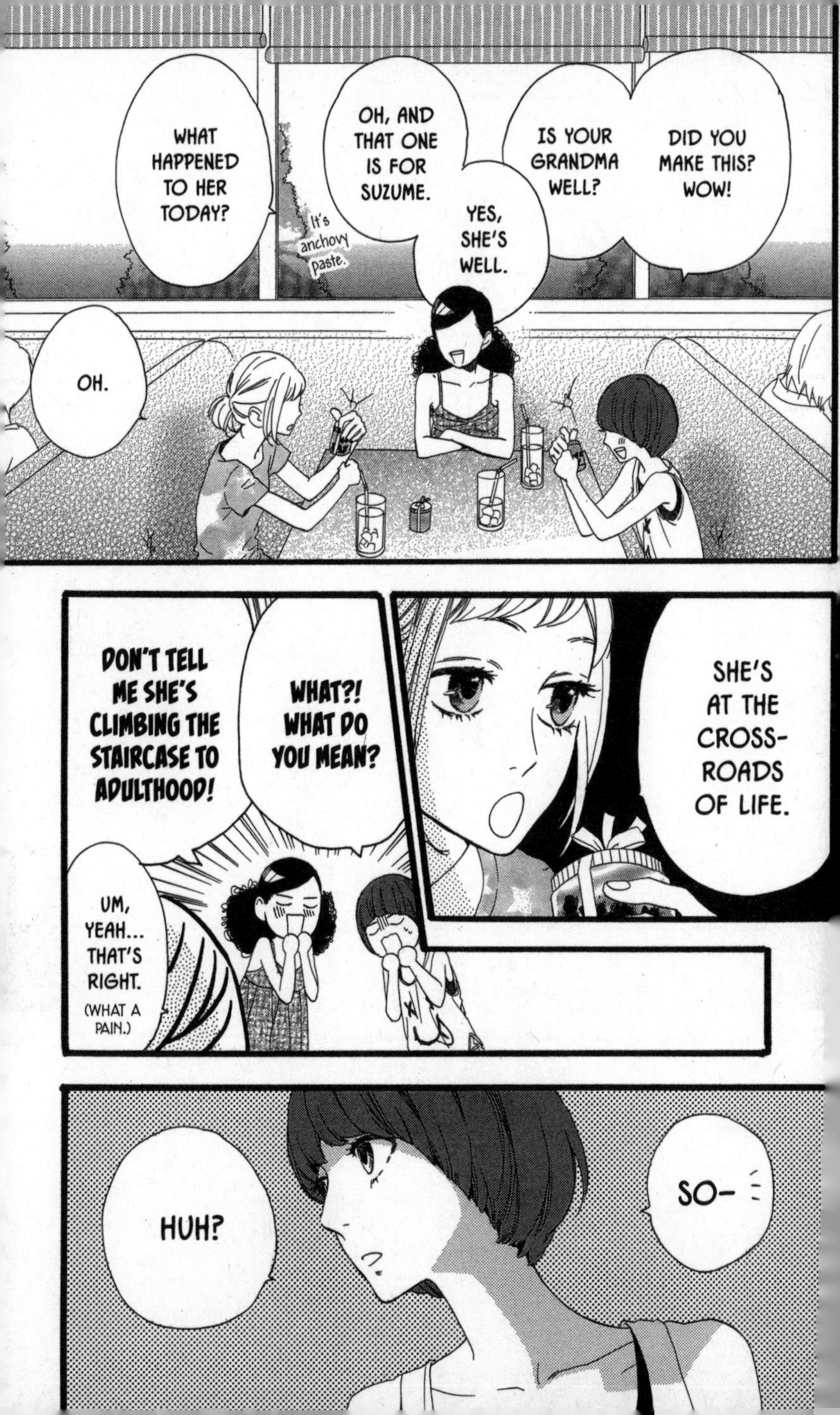
DID YOU MAKE THIS? WOW!
IS YOUR GRANDMA WELL?
YES, SHE'S WELL.
OH, AND THAT ONE IS FOR SUZUME.
It's anchovy paste.
WHAT HAPPENED TO HER TODAY?
OH.
SHE'S AT THE CROSS-ROADS OF LIFE.
WHAT?! WHAT DO YOU MEAN?
DON'T TELL ME SHE'S CLIMBING THE STAIRCASE TO ADULTHOOD!
UM, YEAH... THAT'S RIGHT.
(WHAT A PAIN.)
SO-
HUH?

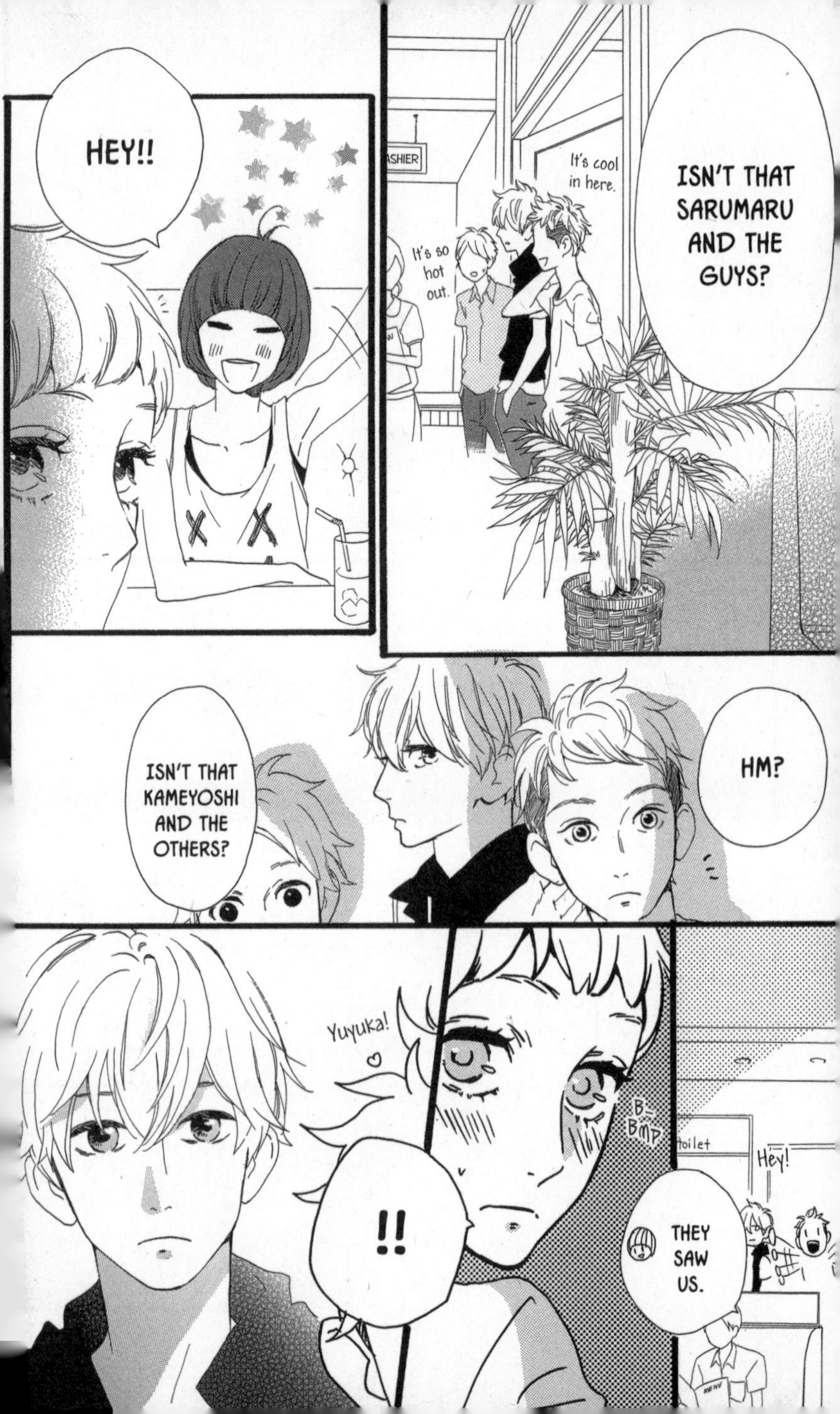
ISN'T THAT SARUMARU AND THE GUYS?
It's cool in here.
It's so hot out.
HEY!!
HM?
ISN'T THAT KAMEYOSHI AND THE OTHERS?
toilet
Hey!
THEY SAW US.
B-BMP
Yuyuka!
!!

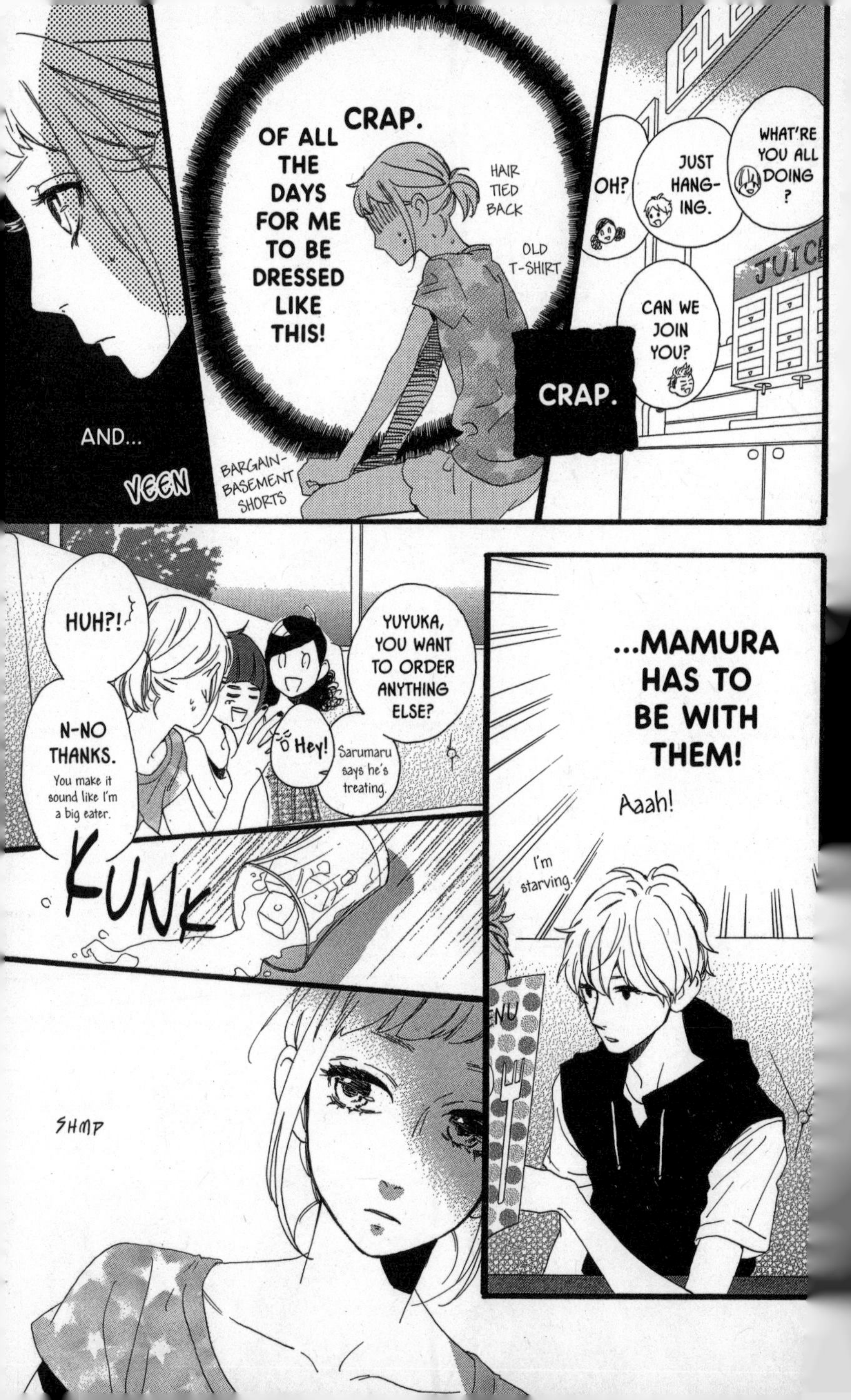
WHAT'RE YOU ALL DOING?
JUST HANG-ING.
OH?
CAN WE JOIN YOU?
CRAP.
CRAP.
OF ALL THE DAYS FOR ME TO BE DRESSED LIKE THIS!
HAIR TIED BACK
OLD T-SHIRT
BARGAIN-BASEMENT SHORTS
AND...
VEEN
...MAMURA HAS TO BE WITH THEM!
Aaah!
I'm starving.
YUYUKA, YOU WANT TO ORDER ANYTHING ELSE?
Sarumaru says he's treating.
Hey!
HUH?!
N-NO THANKS.
You make it sound like I'm a big eater.
KUNK
SHMP

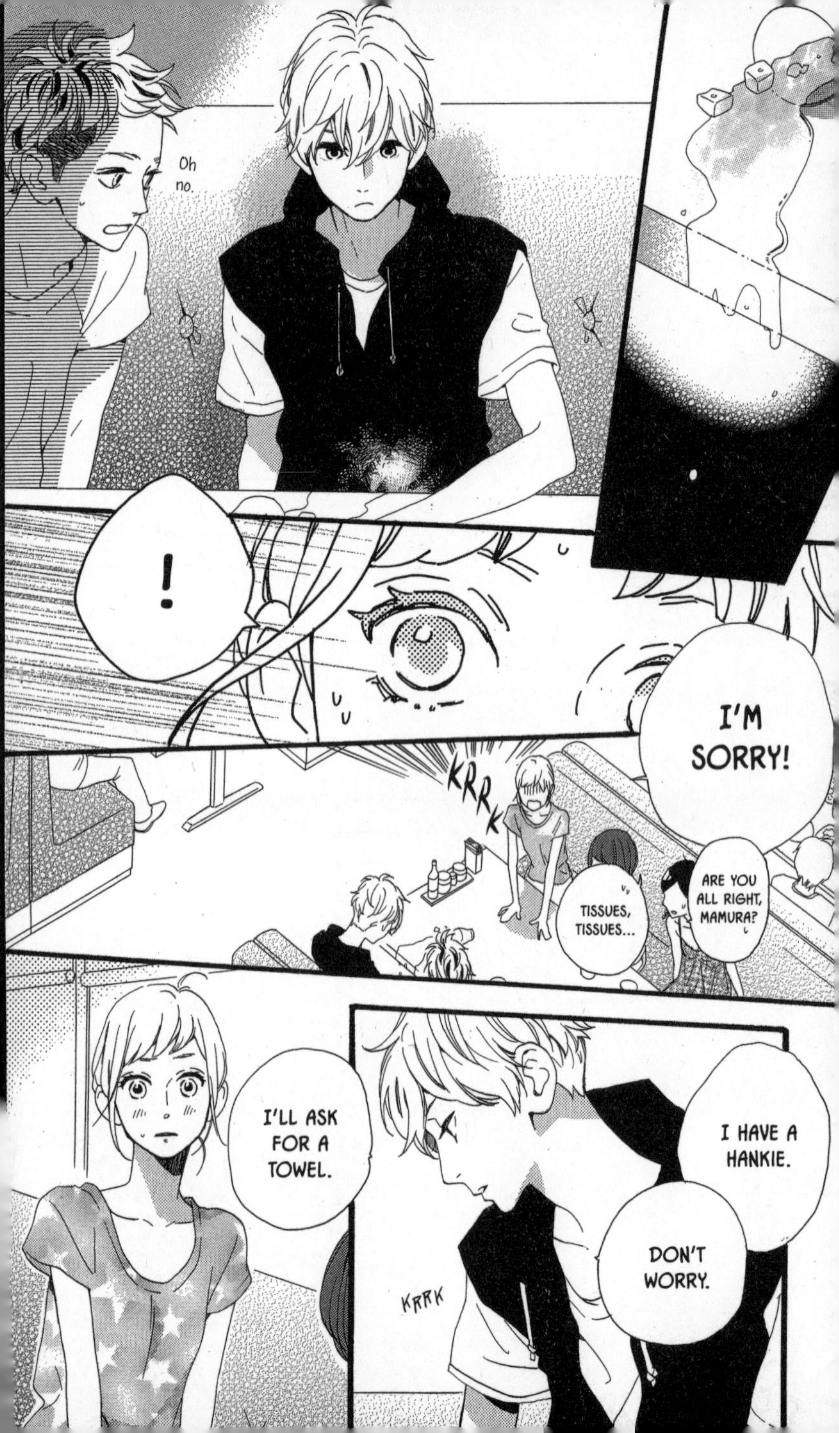
Oh no.
!
I'M SORRY!
KRRK
ARE YOU ALL RIGHT, MAMURA?
TISSUES, TISSUES...
I HAVE A HANKIE.
DON'T WORRY.
KRRK
I'LL ASK FOR A TOWEL.

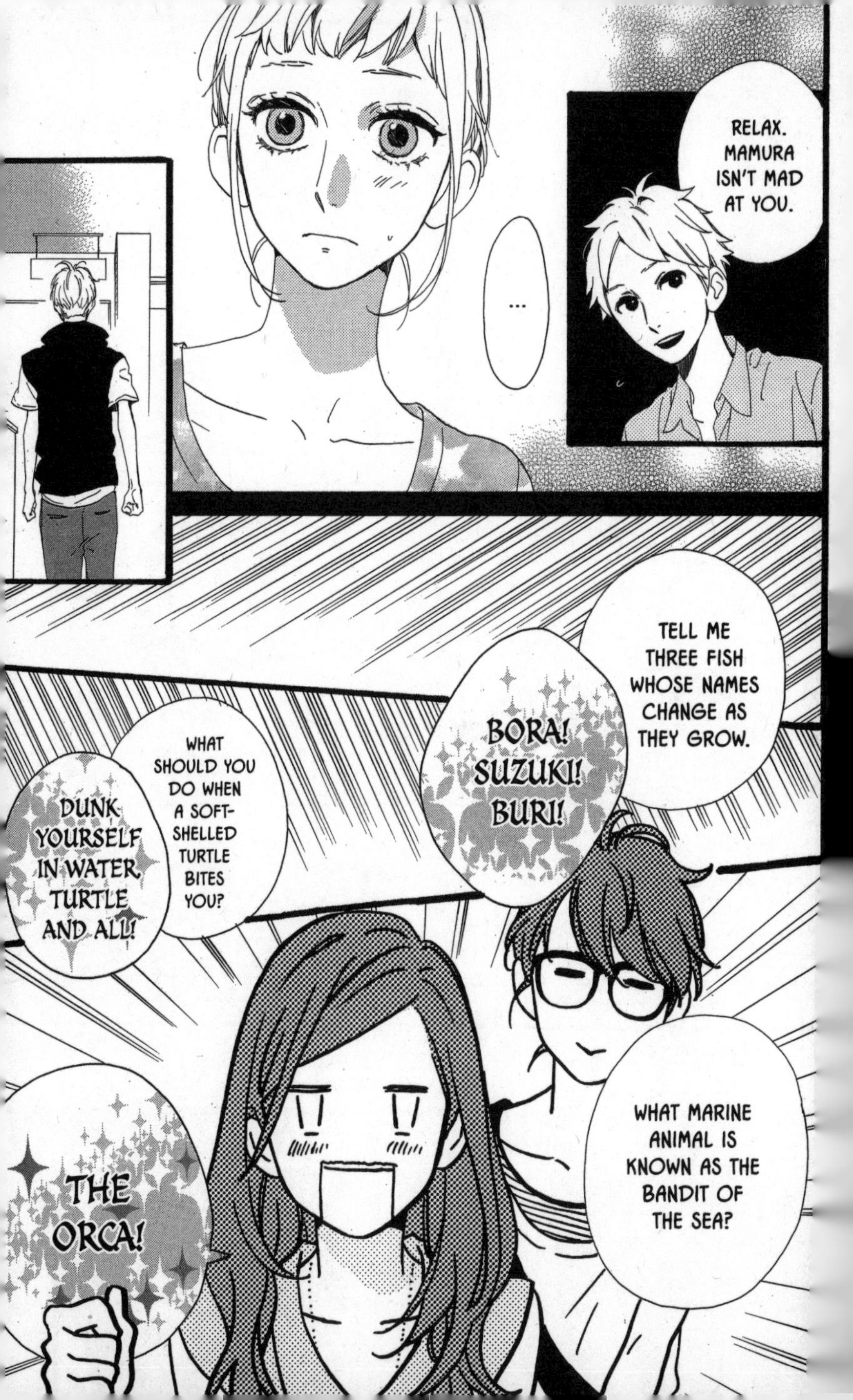
RELAX. MAMURA ISN'T MAD AT YOU.
...
TELL ME THREE FISH WHOSE NAMES CHANGE AS THEY GROW.
BORA! SUZUKI! BURI!
WHAT SHOULD YOU DO WHEN A SOFT-SHELLED TURTLE BITES YOU?
DUNK YOURSELF IN WATER, TURTLE AND ALL!
WHAT MARINE ANIMAL IS KNOWN AS THE BANDIT OF THE SEA?
THE ORCA!

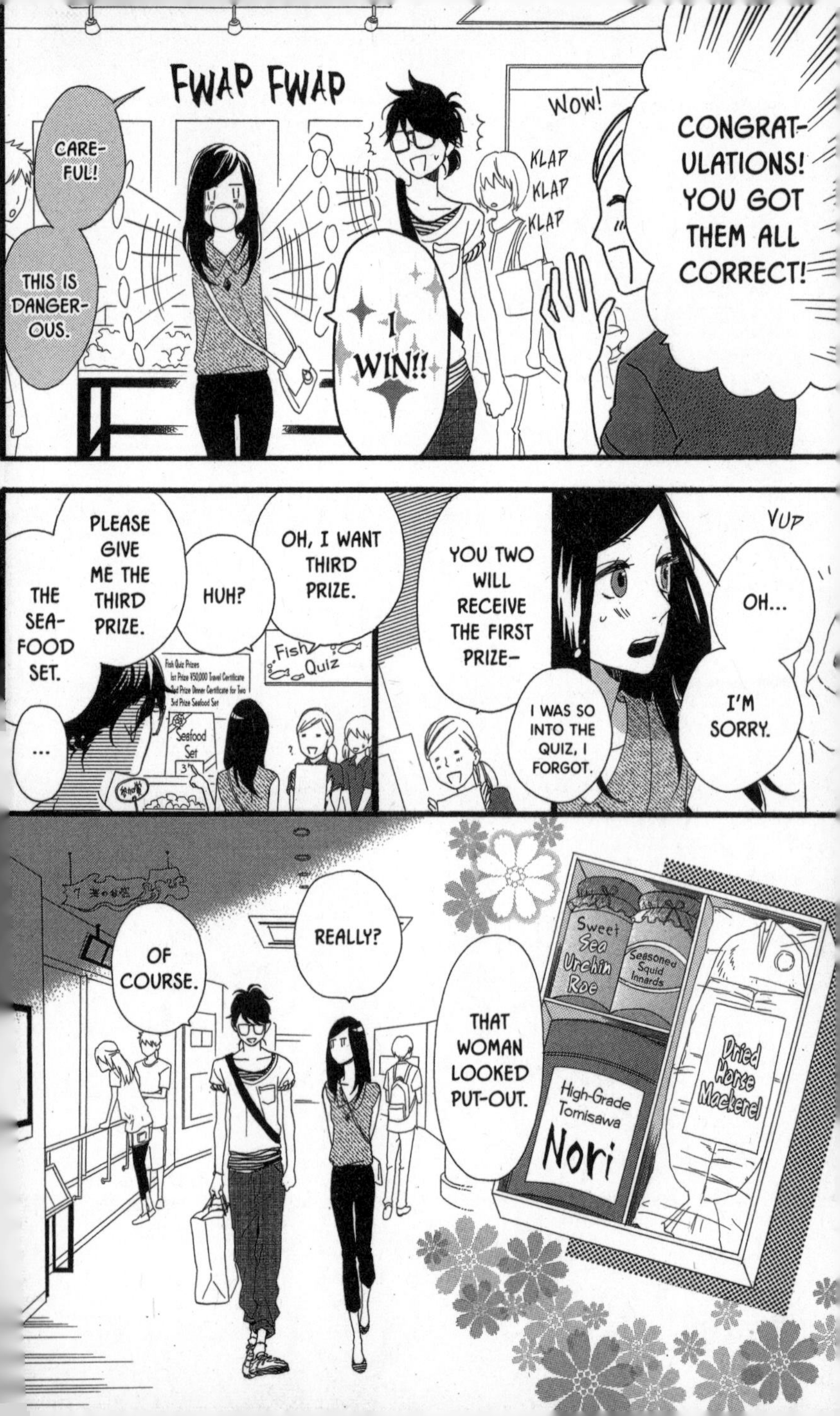
CONGRAT-ULATIONS! YOU GOT THEM ALL CORRECT!
WOW!
KLAP KLAP KLAP
I WIN!!
FWAP FWAP
CARE-FUL!
THIS IS DANGER-OUS.
VUP
OH...
I'M SORRY.
I WAS SO INTO THE QUIZ, I FORGOT.
YOU TWO WILL RECEIVE THE FIRST PRIZE—
OH, I WANT THIRD PRIZE.
Fish Quiz
HUH?
PLEASE GIVE ME THE THIRD PRIZE.
THE SEA-FOOD SET.
Fish Quiz Prizes
1st Prize ¥50,000 Travel Certificate
2nd Prize Dinner Certificate for Two
3rd Prize Seafood Set
Seafood Set
...
Sweet Sea Urchin Roe
Seasoned Squid Innards
Dried Horse Mackerel
High-Grade Tomisawa Nori
THAT WOMAN LOOKED PUT-OUT.
REALLY?
OF COURSE.

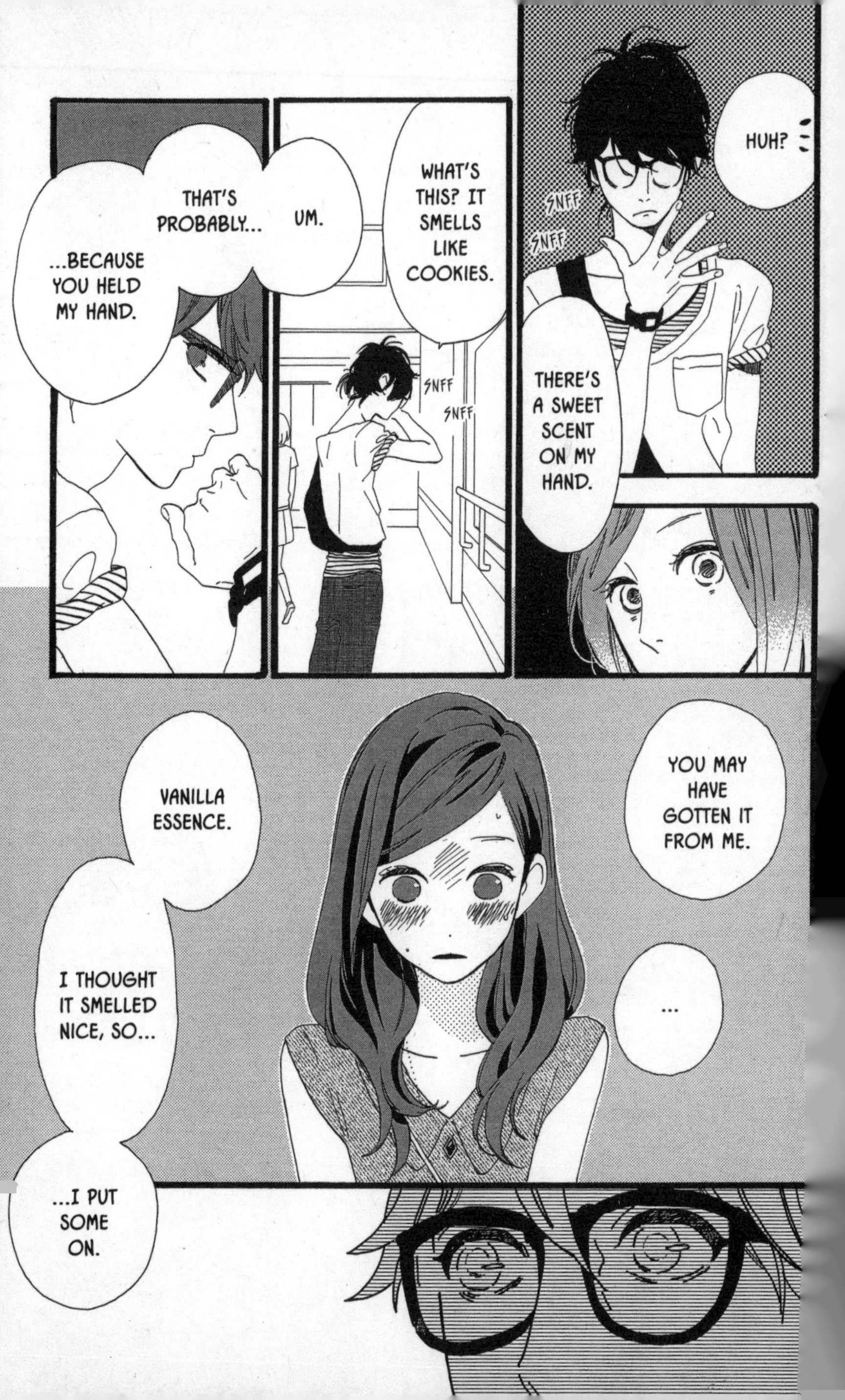

SNFF
SNFF
HUH?
THERE'S A SWEET SCENT ON MY HAND.
WHAT'S THIS? IT SMELLS LIKE COOKIES.
SNFF
SNFF
UM.
THAT'S PROBABLY...
...BECAUSE YOU HELD MY HAND.
YOU MAY HAVE GOTTEN IT FROM ME.
...
VANILLA ESSENCE.
I THOUGHT IT SMELLED NICE, SO...
...I PUT SOME ON.

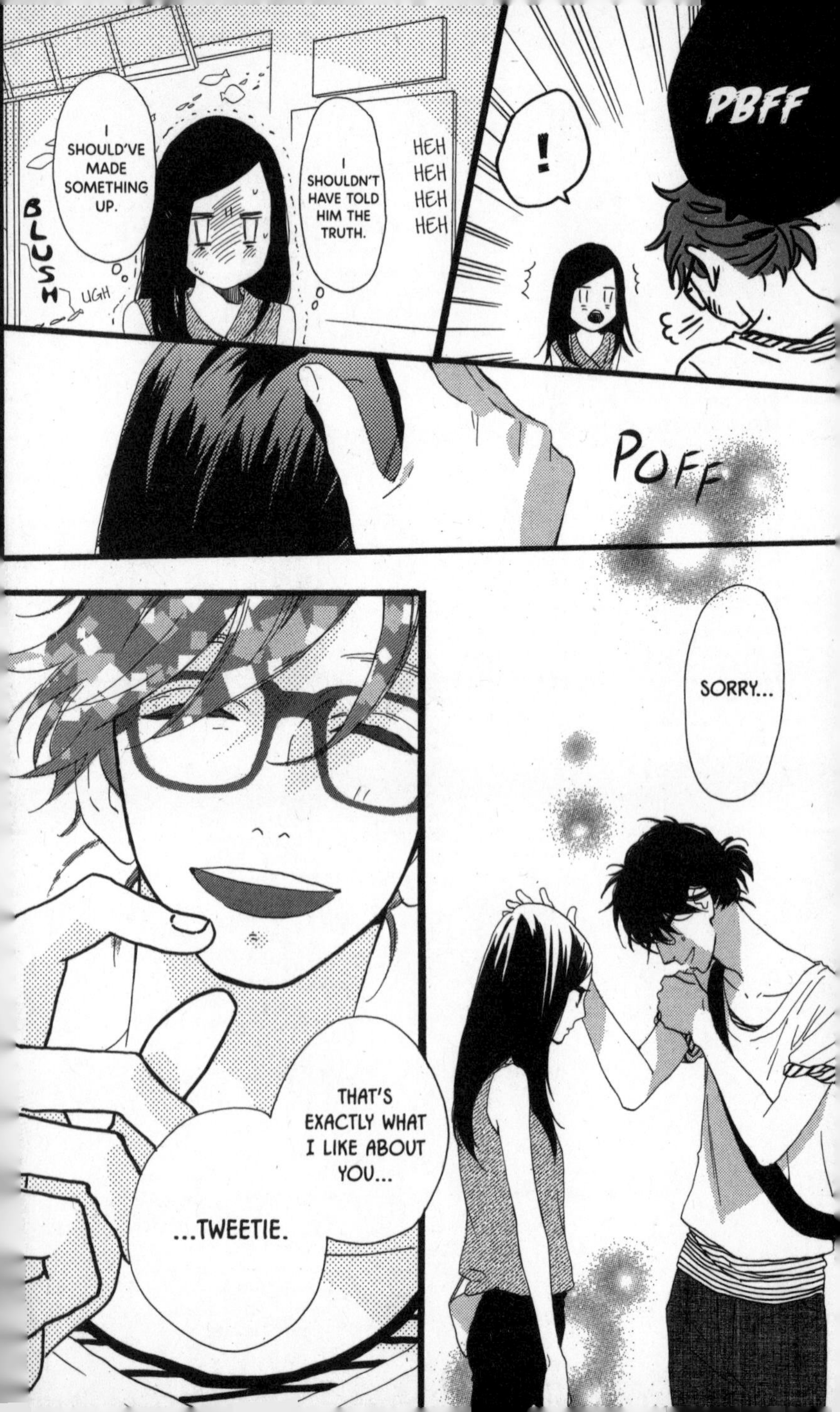
!
PBFF
I SHOULDN'T HAVE TOLD HIM THE TRUTH.
HEH HEH HEH HEH
I SHOULD'VE MADE SOMETHING UP.
BLUSH
UGH
POFF
SORRY...
THAT'S EXACTLY WHAT I LIKE ABOUT YOU...
...TWEETIE.

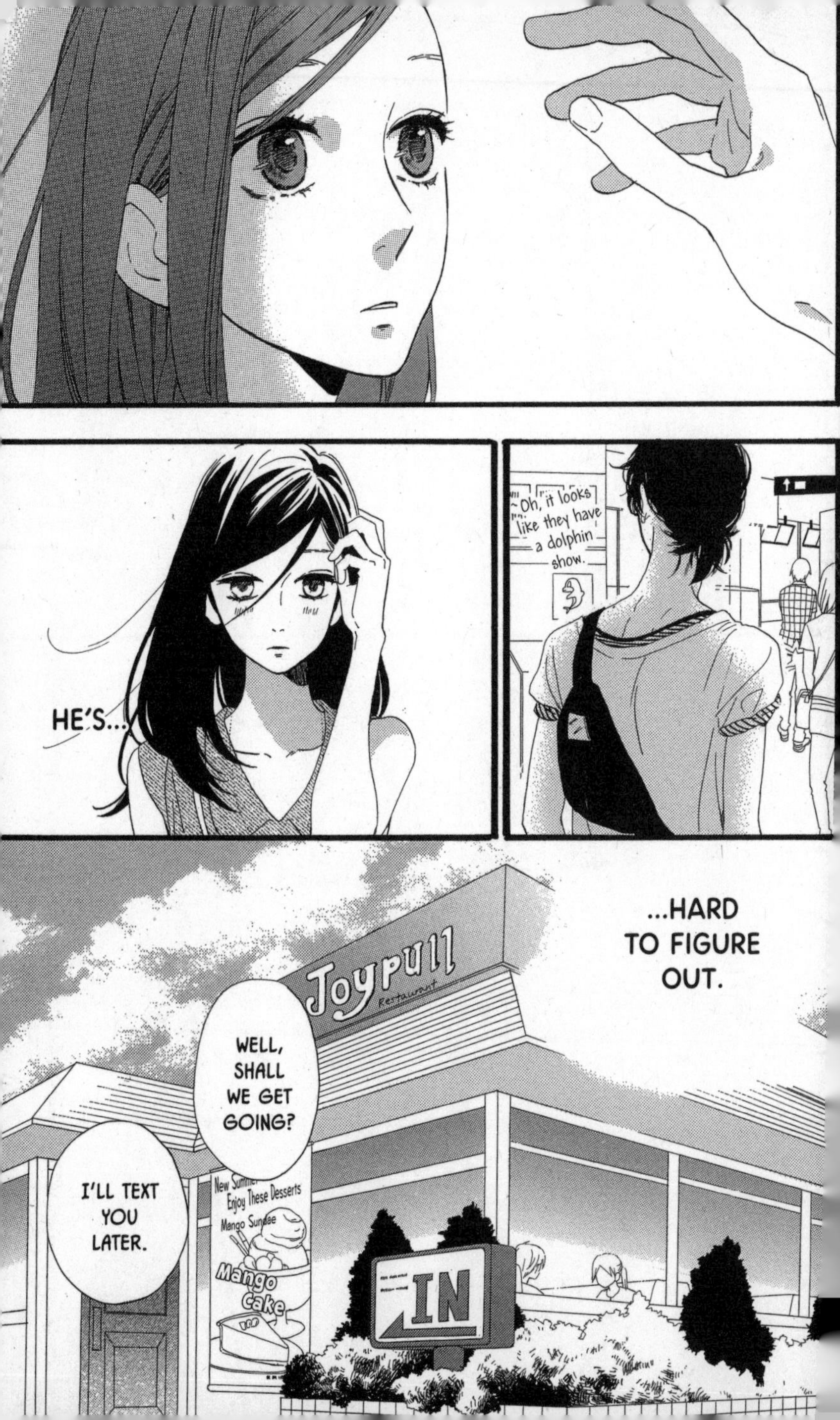
~Oh, it looks like they have a dolphin show.
HE'S...
...HARD TO FIGURE OUT.
Joypull
Restaurant
WELL, SHALL WE GET GOING?
I'LL TEXT YOU LATER.
Enjoy These Desserts
Mango Sundae
Mango cake
IN

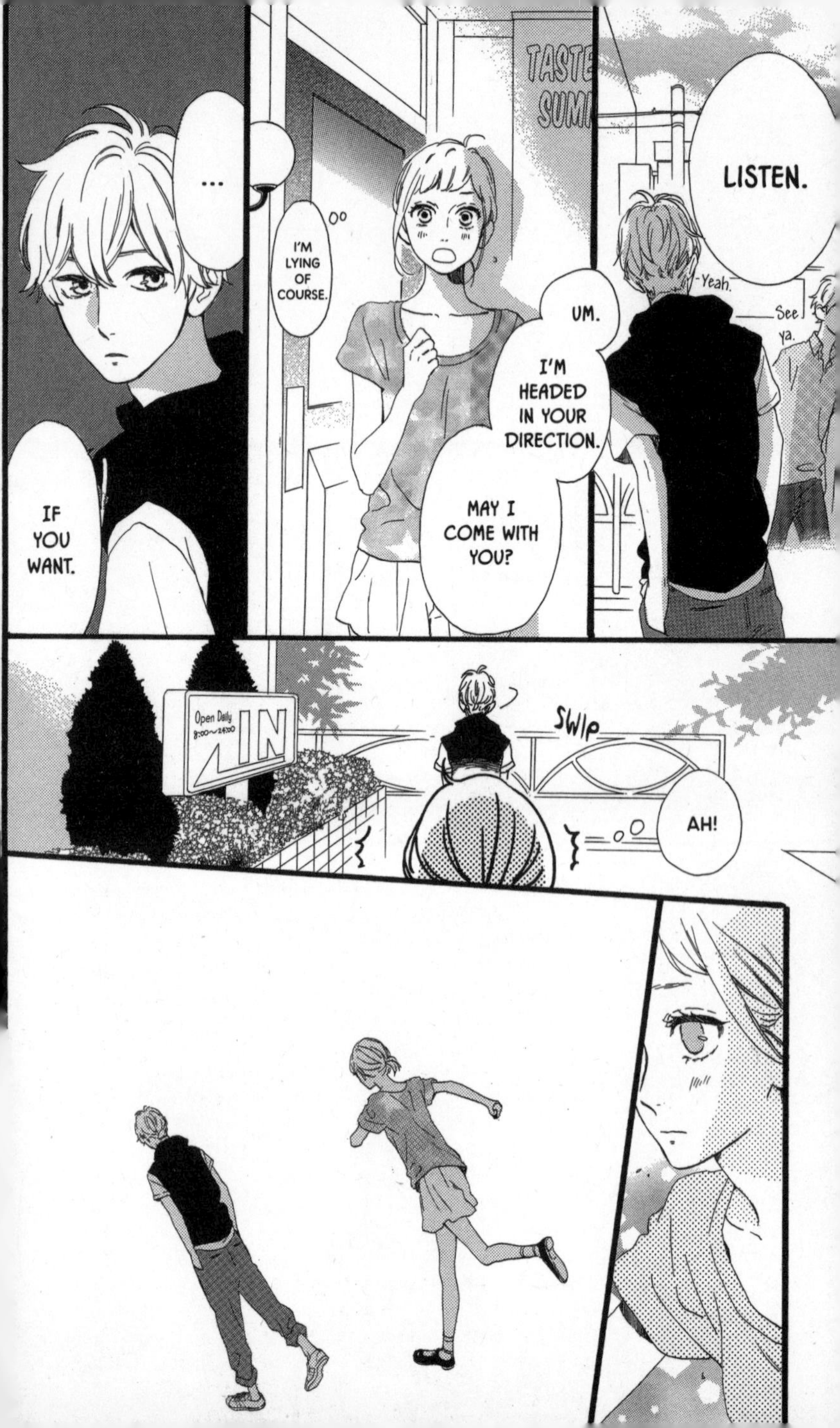

LISTEN.
-Yeah.
See ya.
UM.
I'M HEADED IN YOUR DIRECTION.
MAY I COME WITH YOU?
I'M LYING OF COURSE.
...
IF YOU WANT.
SWIP
AH!
Open Daily 8:00~24:00
IN

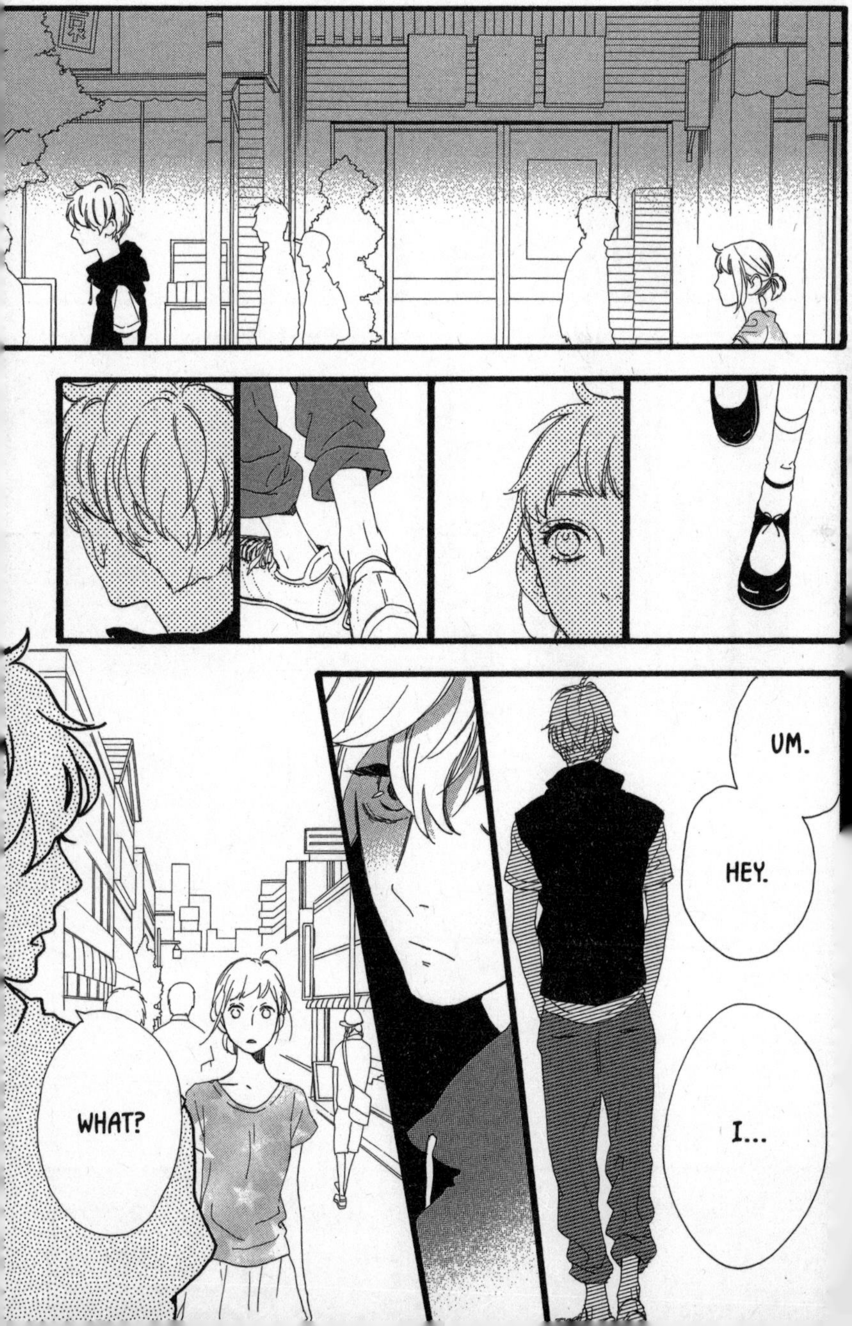
UM.
HEY.
I...
WHAT?

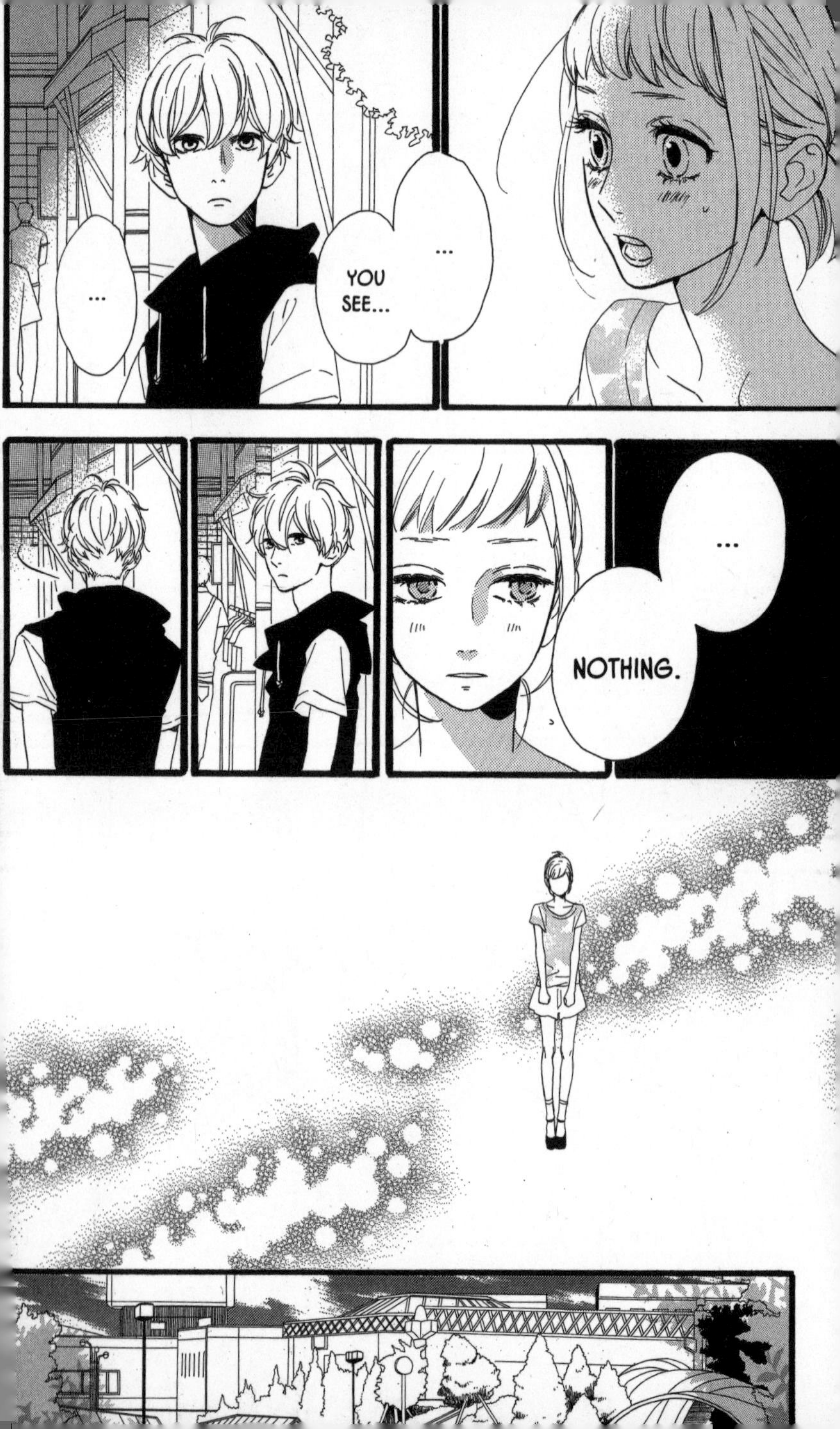
...
YOU SEE...
...
...
NOTHING.

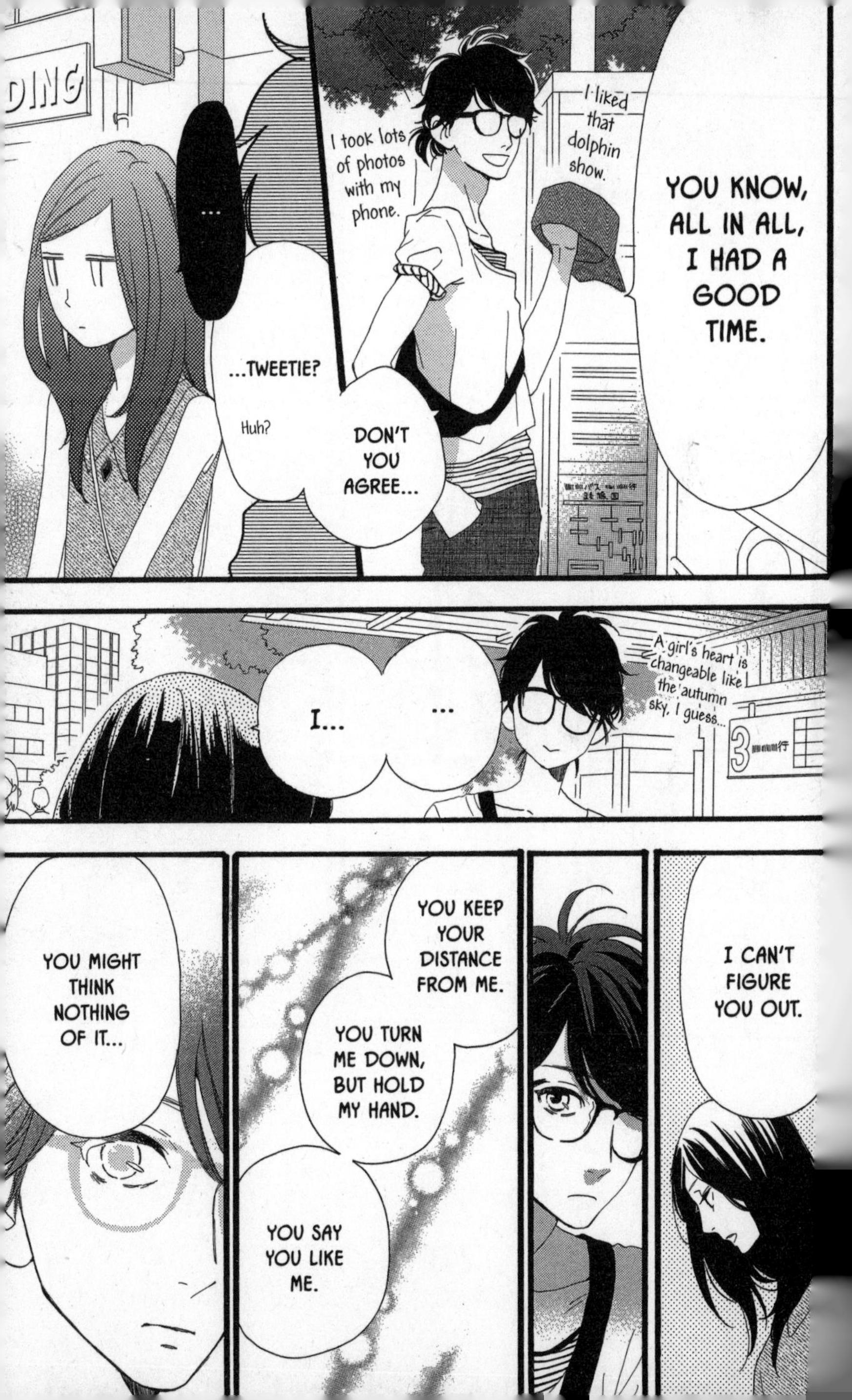
YOU KNOW, ALL IN ALL, I HAD A GOOD TIME.
I liked that dolphin show.
I took lots of photos with my phone.
DON'T YOU AGREE...
...
...TWEETIE?
Huh?
A girl's heart is changeable like the autumn sky, I guess...
...
I...
I CAN'T FIGURE YOU OUT.
YOU KEEP YOUR DISTANCE FROM ME.
YOU TURN ME DOWN, BUT HOLD MY HAND.
YOU SAY YOU LIKE ME.
YOU MIGHT THINK NOTHING OF IT...

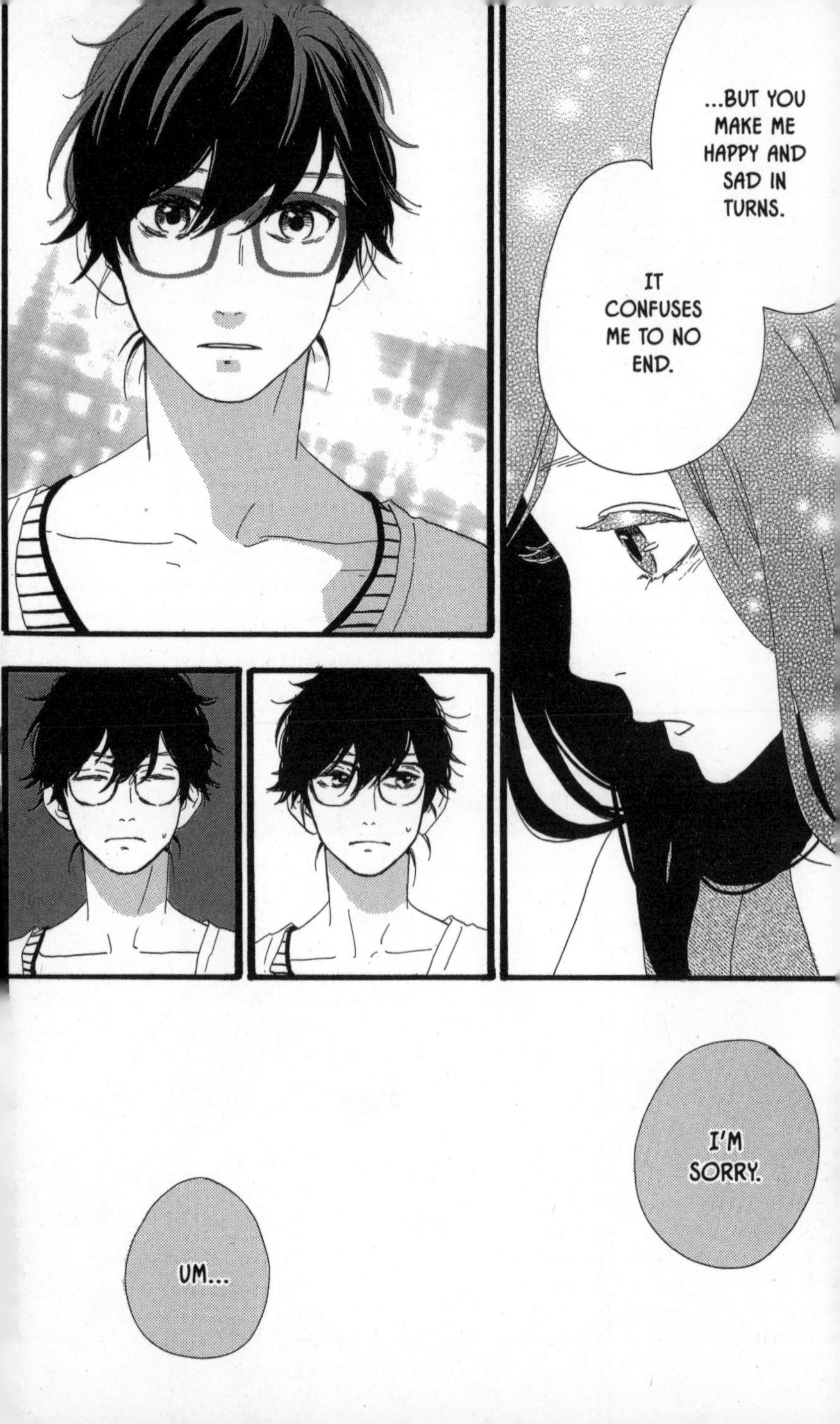
...BUT YOU MAKE ME HAPPY AND SAD IN TURNS.
IT CONFUSES ME TO NO END.
I'M SORRY.
UM...

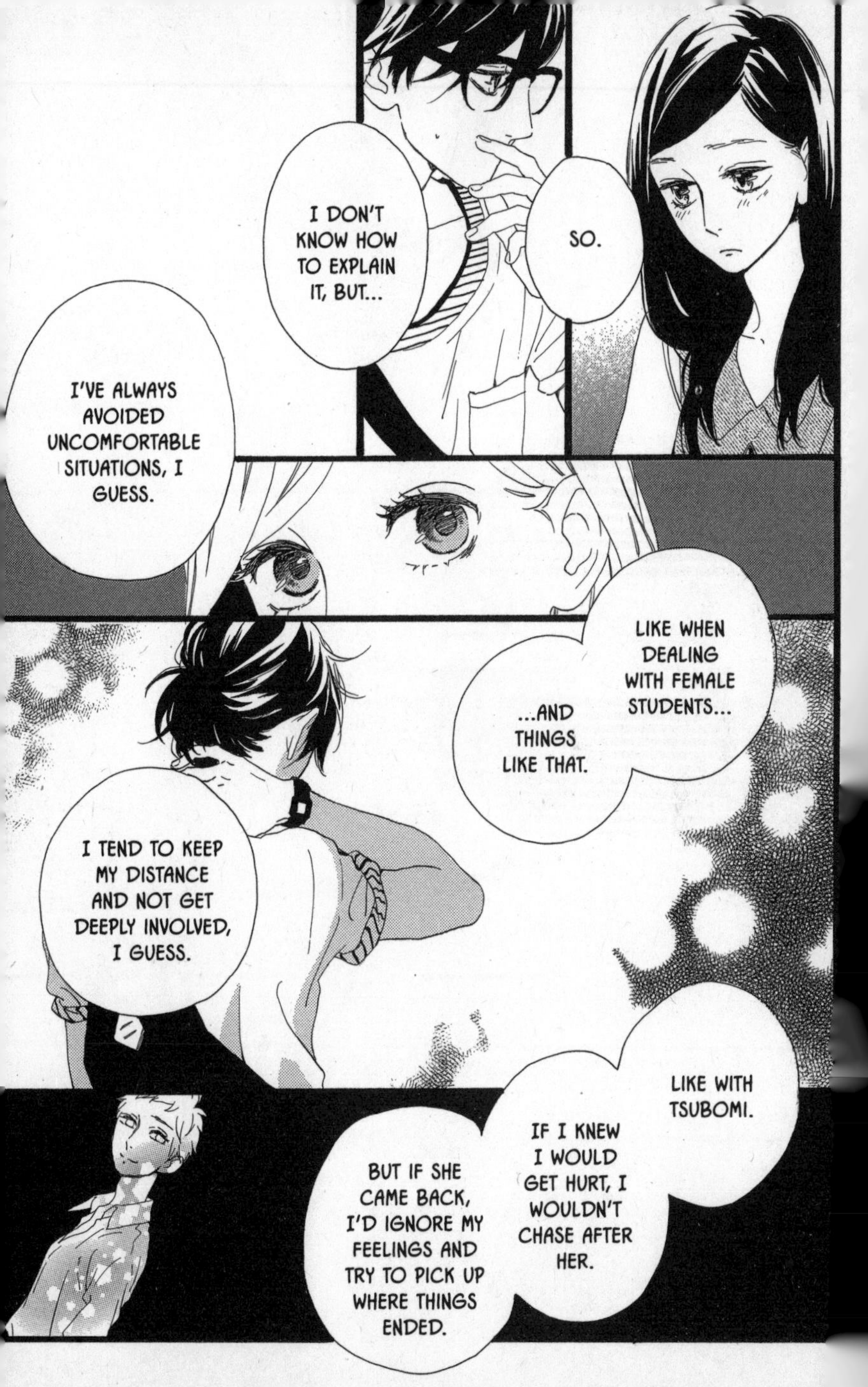
SO.
I DON'T KNOW HOW TO EXPLAIN IT, BUT...
I'VE ALWAYS AVOIDED UNCOMFORTABLE SITUATIONS, I GUESS.
LIKE WHEN DEALING WITH FEMALE STUDENTS...
...AND THINGS LIKE THAT.
I TEND TO KEEP MY DISTANCE AND NOT GET DEEPLY INVOLVED, I GUESS.
LIKE WITH TSUBOMI.
IF I KNEW I WOULD GET HURT, I WOULDN'T CHASE AFTER HER.
BUT IF SHE CAME BACK, I'D IGNORE MY FEELINGS AND TRY TO PICK UP WHERE THINGS ENDED.

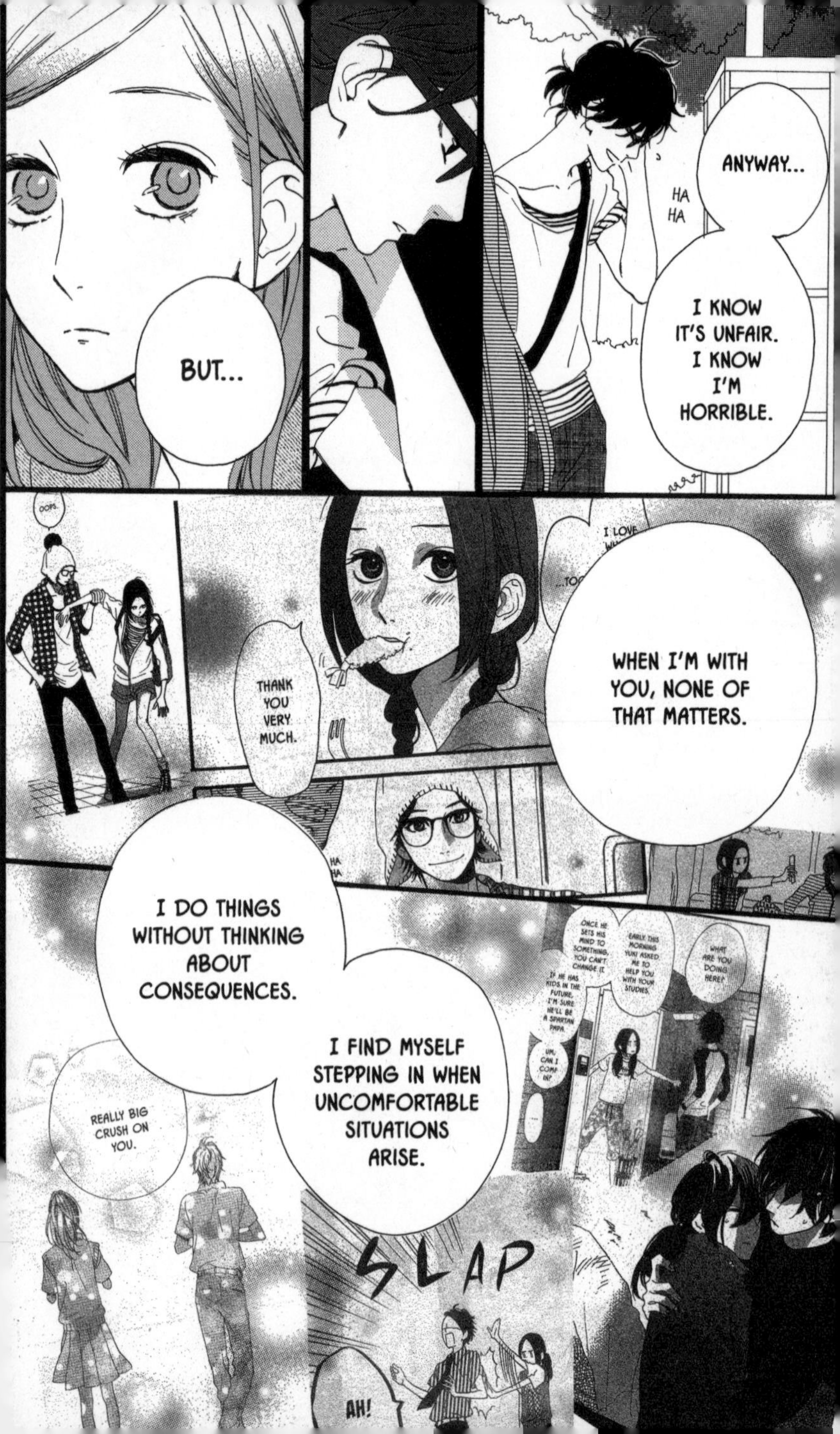

ANYWAY...
HA HA
I KNOW IT'S UNFAIR. I KNOW I'M HORRIBLE.
BUT...
WHEN I'M WITH YOU, NONE OF THAT MATTERS.
I LOVE
THANK YOU VERY MUCH.
HA HA
OOPS.
I DO THINGS WITHOUT THINKING ABOUT CONSEQUENCES.
I FIND MYSELF STEPPING IN WHEN UNCOMFORTABLE SITUATIONS ARISE.
WHAT ARE YOU DOING HERE?
EARLY THIS MORNING YUKI ASKED ME TO HELP YOU WITH YOUR STUDIES.
ONCE HE SETS HIS MIND TO SOMETHING, YOU CAN'T CHANGE IT.
IF HE HAS KIDS IN THE FUTURE, I'M SURE HE'LL BE A SPARTAN PAPA.
UM, CAN I COME IN?
...
SLAP
AH!
REALLY BIG CRUSH ON YOU.

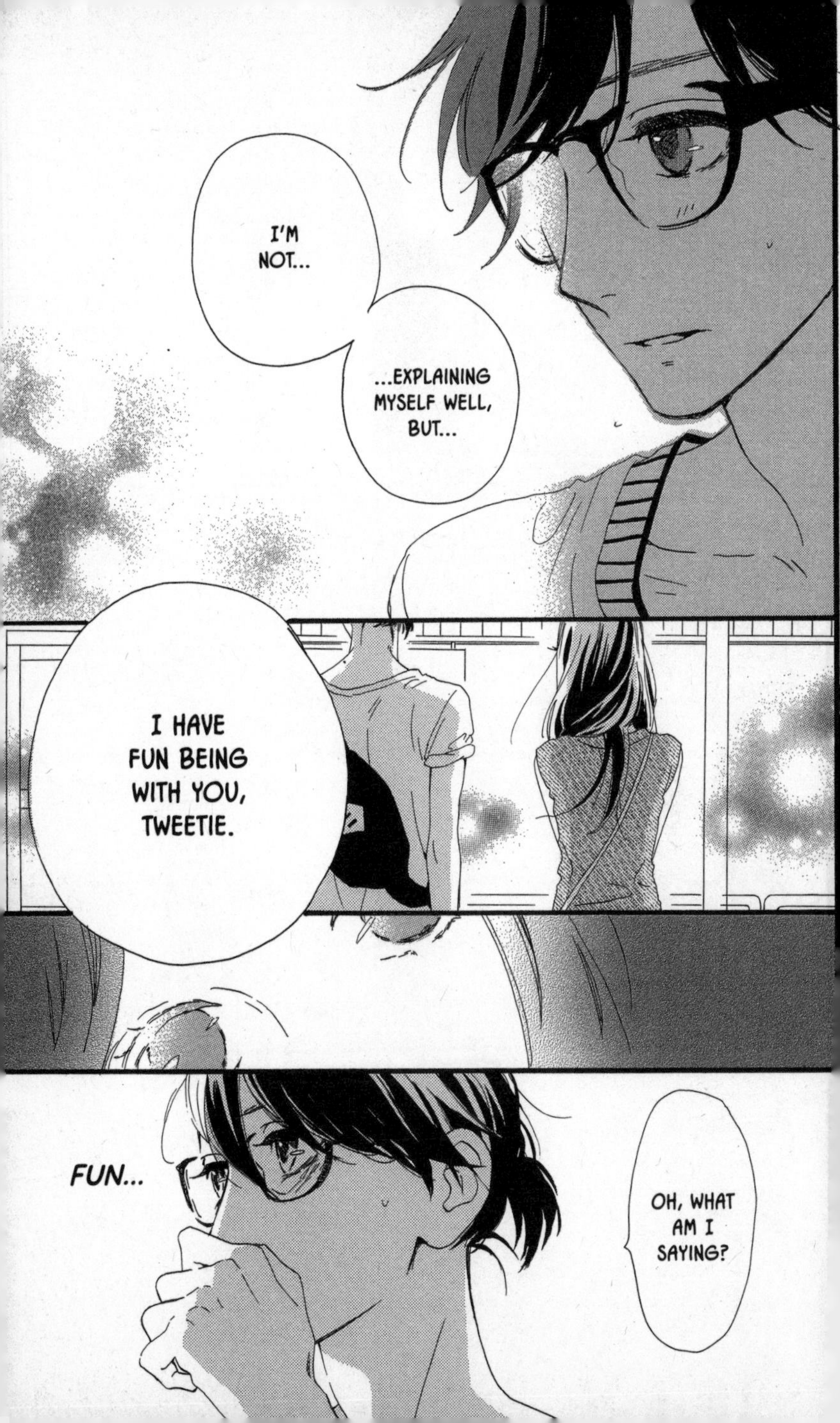
I'M NOT...
...EXPLAINING MYSELF WELL, BUT...
I HAVE FUN BEING WITH YOU, TWEETIE.
OH, WHAT AM I SAYING?
FUN...

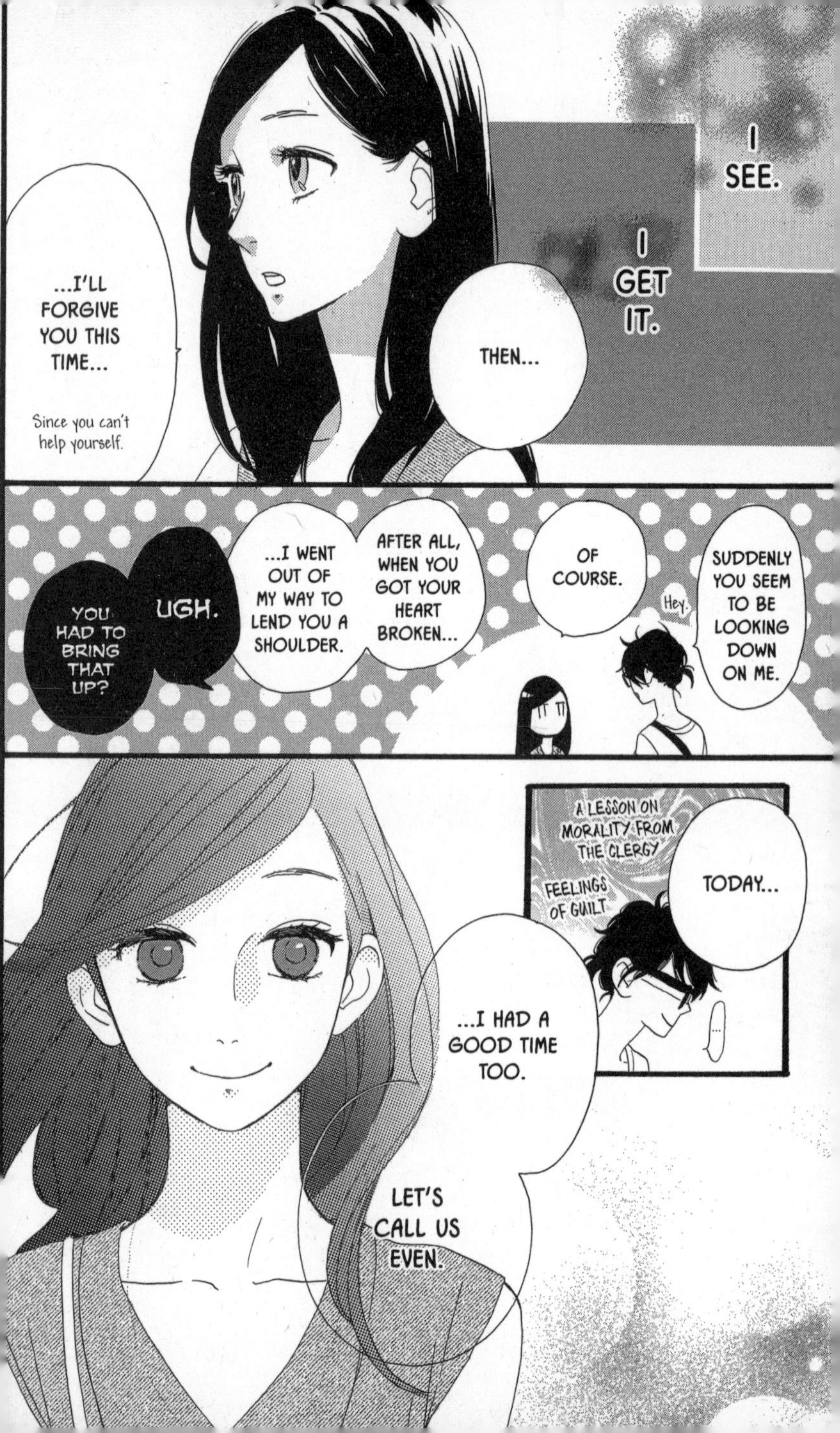
I SEE.
I GET IT.
THEN...
...I'LL FORGIVE YOU THIS TIME...
Since you can't help yourself.
Hey.
SUDDENLY YOU SEEM TO BE LOOKING DOWN ON ME.
OF COURSE.
AFTER ALL, WHEN YOU GOT YOUR HEART BROKEN...
...I WENT OUT OF MY WAY TO LEND YOU A SHOULDER.
UGH.
YOU HAD TO BRING THAT UP?
A LESSON ON MORALITY FROM THE CLERGY
FEELINGS OF GUILT
TODAY...
...
...I HAD A GOOD TIME TOO.
LET'S CALL US EVEN.

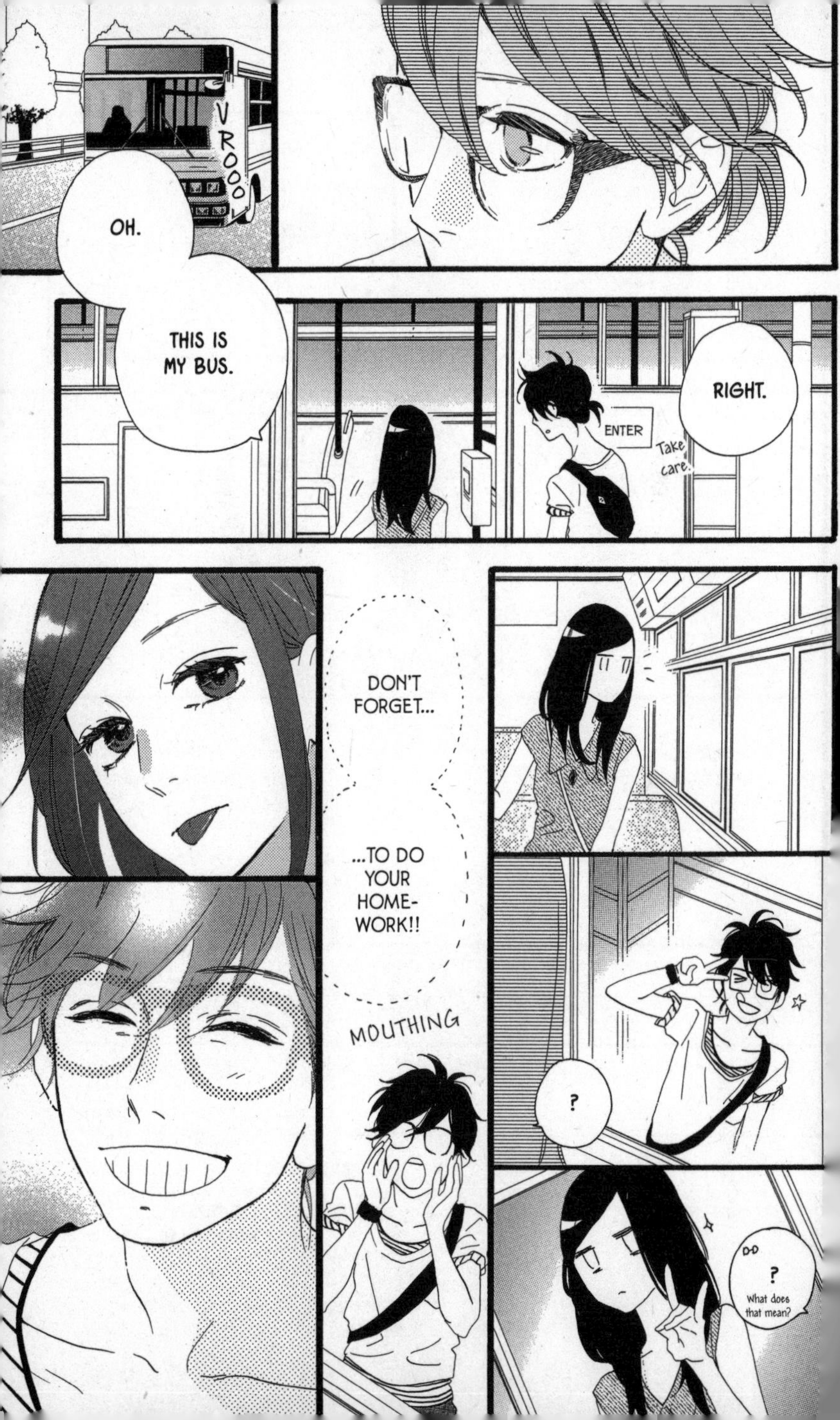
VROOO
OH.
THIS IS MY BUS.
ENTER
RIGHT.
Take care.
?
?
What does that mean?
DON'T FORGET...
...TO DO YOUR HOME-WORK!!
MOUTHING

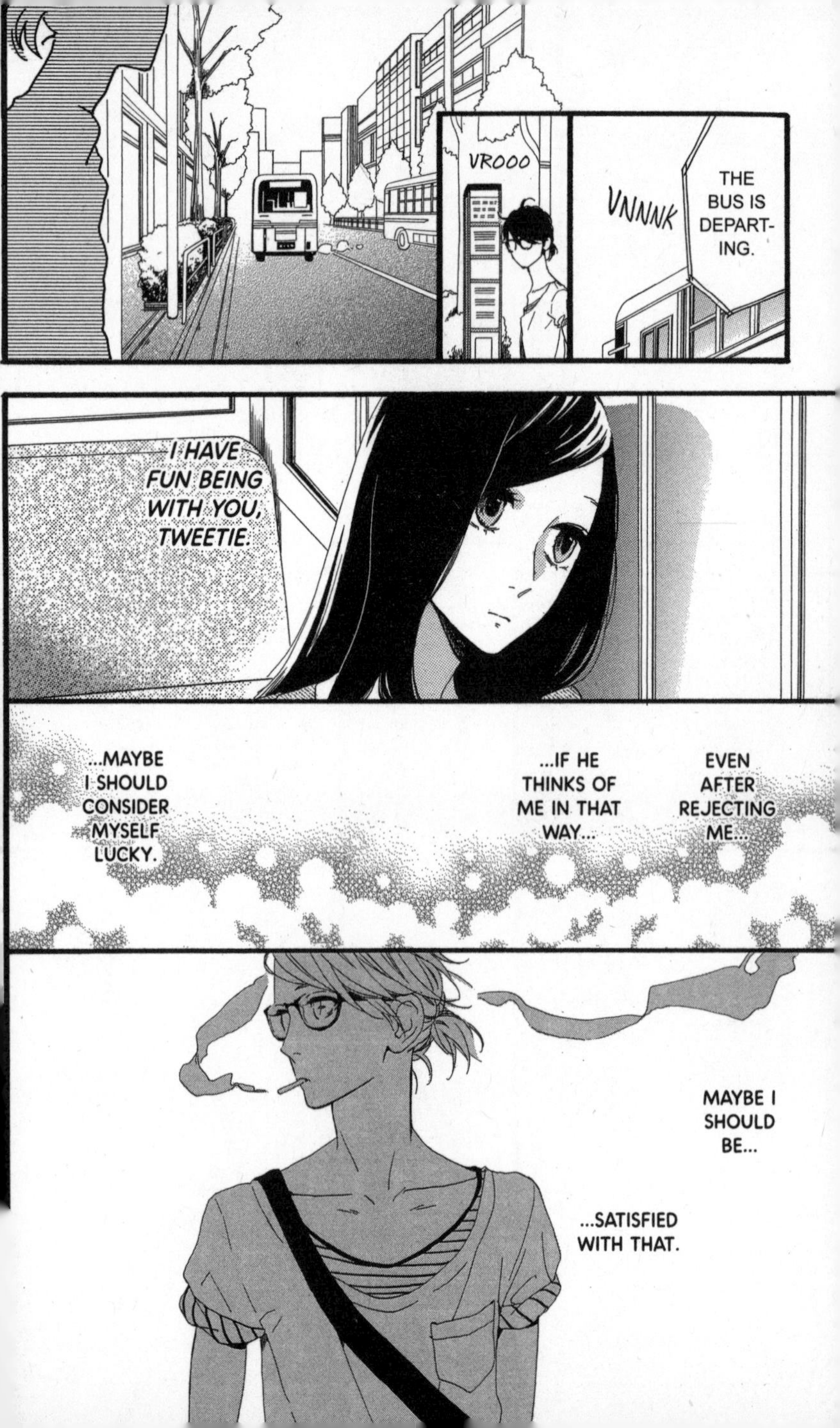
THE BUS IS DEPART-ING.
VNNNK
VROOO
I HAVE FUN BEING WITH YOU, TWEETIE.
EVEN AFTER REJECTING ME...
...IF HE THINKS OF ME IN THAT WAY...
...MAYBE I SHOULD CONSIDER MYSELF LUCKY.
MAYBE I SHOULD BE...
...SATISFIED WITH THAT.

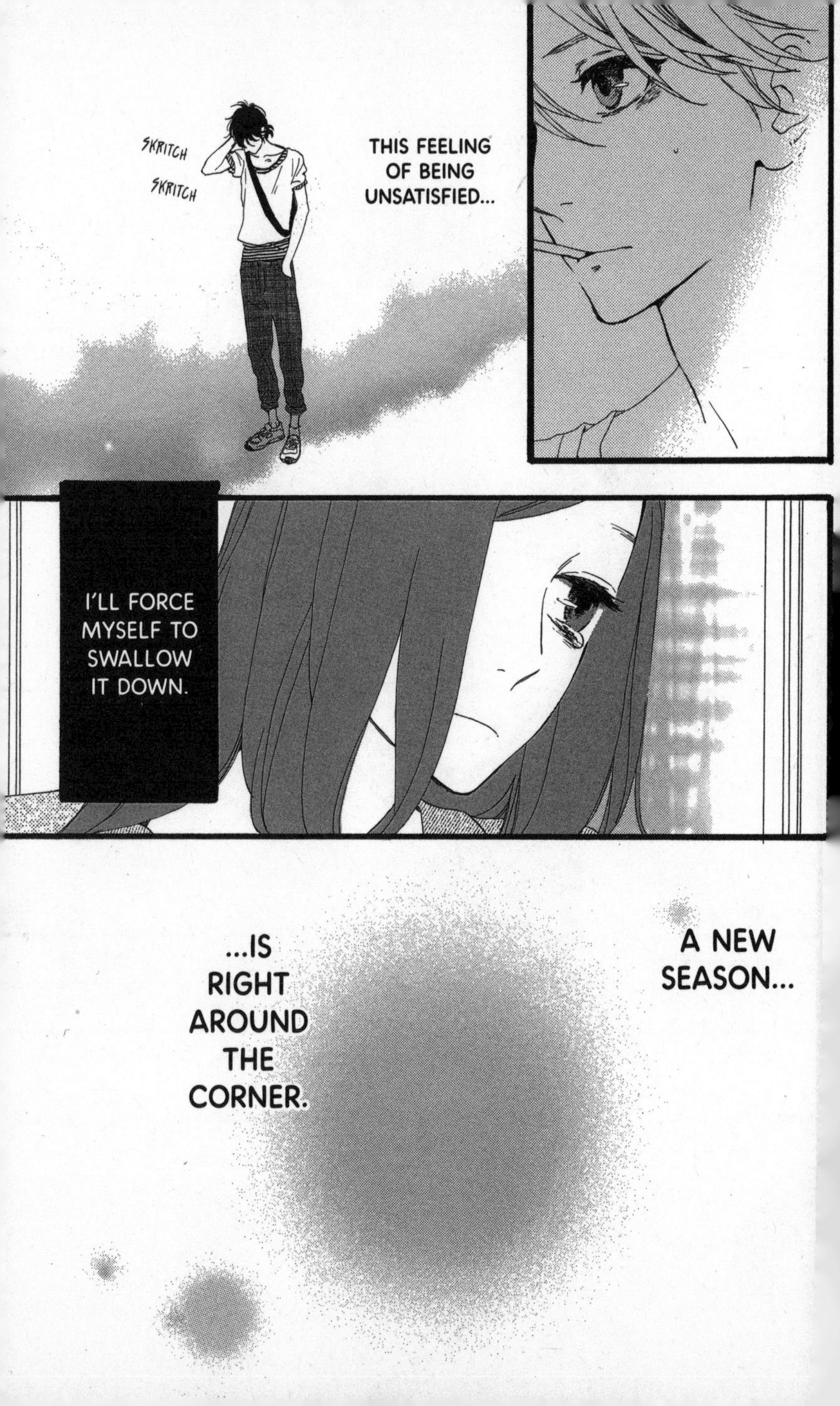
THIS FEELING OF BEING UNSATISFIED...
SKRITCH
SKRITCH
I'LL FORCE MYSELF TO SWALLOW IT DOWN.
A NEW SEASON...
...IS RIGHT AROUND THE CORNER.

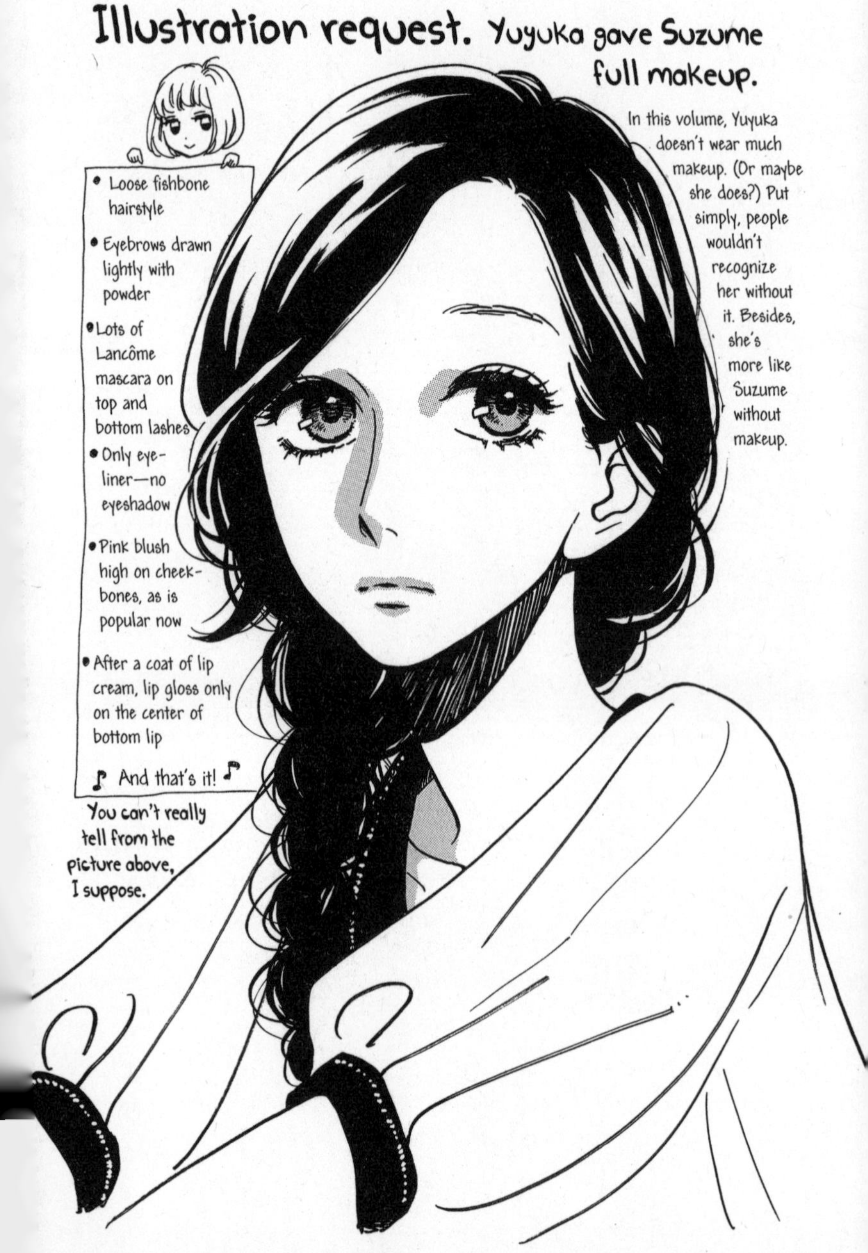
Illustration request. Yuyuka gave Suzume full makeup.
• Loose fishbone hairstyle
• Eyebrows drawn lightly with powder
• Lots of Lancôme mascara on top and bottom lashes
• Only eye-liner—no eyeshadow
• Pink blush high on cheek-bones, as is popular now
• After a coat of lip cream, lip gloss only on the center of bottom lip
♪ And that's it! ♪
You can't really tell from the picture above, I suppose.
In this volume, Yuyuka doesn't wear much makeup. (Or maybe she does?) Put simply, people wouldn't recognize her without it. Besides, she's more like Suzume without makeup.

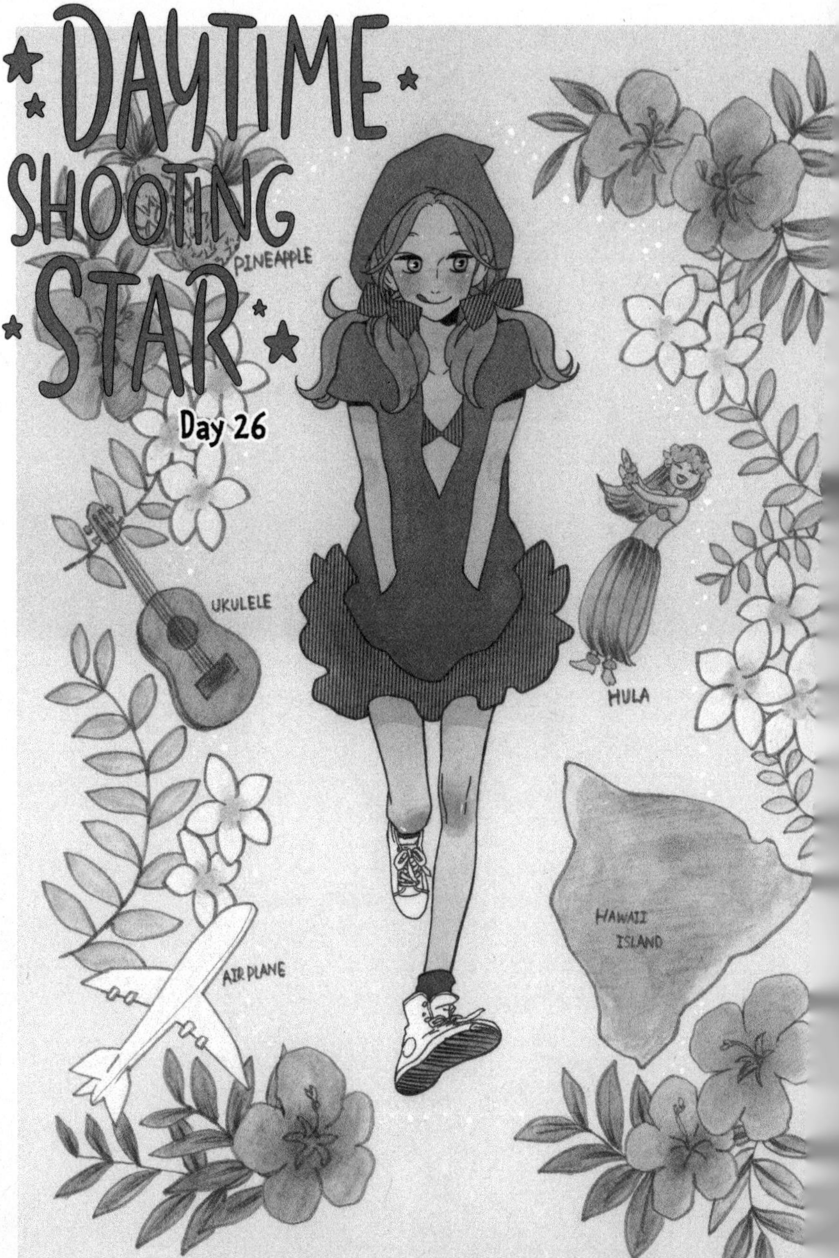
DAYTIME
SHOOTING
STAR
Day 26
PINEAPPLE
UKULELE
HULA
HAWAII ISLAND
AIRPLANE

Mamura's Everyday Life Part 2

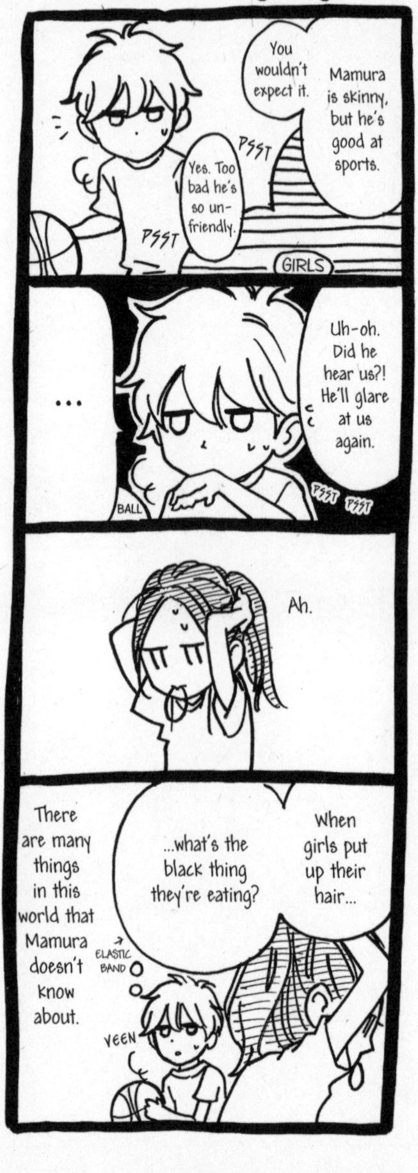
Mamura is skinny, but he's good at sports.
You wouldn't expect it.
PSST
Yes. Too bad he's so un-friendly.
PSST
GIRLS
Uh-oh. Did he hear us?! He'll glare at us again.
PSST PSST
...
BALL
Ah.
When girls put up their hair...
...what's the black thing they're eating?
ELASTIC BAND
There are many things in this world that Mamura doesn't know about.
VEEN

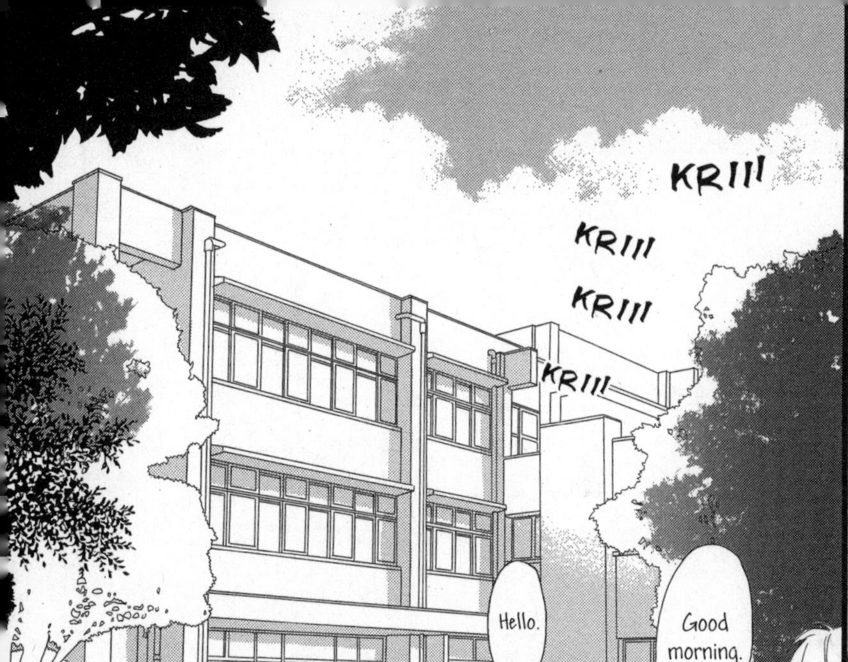
KRIII
KRIII
KRIII
KRIII
Good morning.
Hello.
Hey, what's up?
KRIII

Yuyuka, Talking to Herself

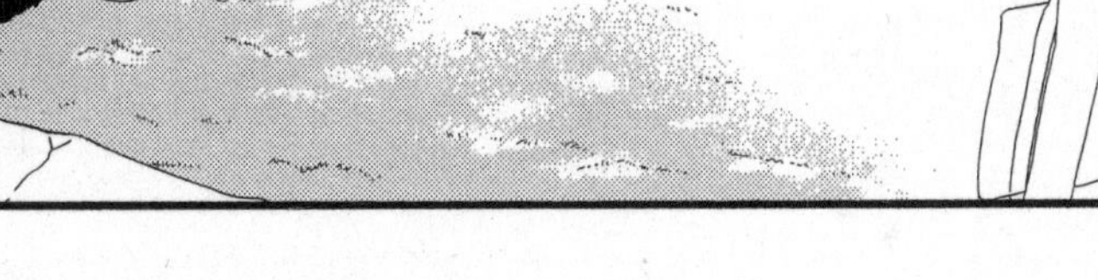
If you put on false eyelashes before any lotion, they will stay on better, you know.

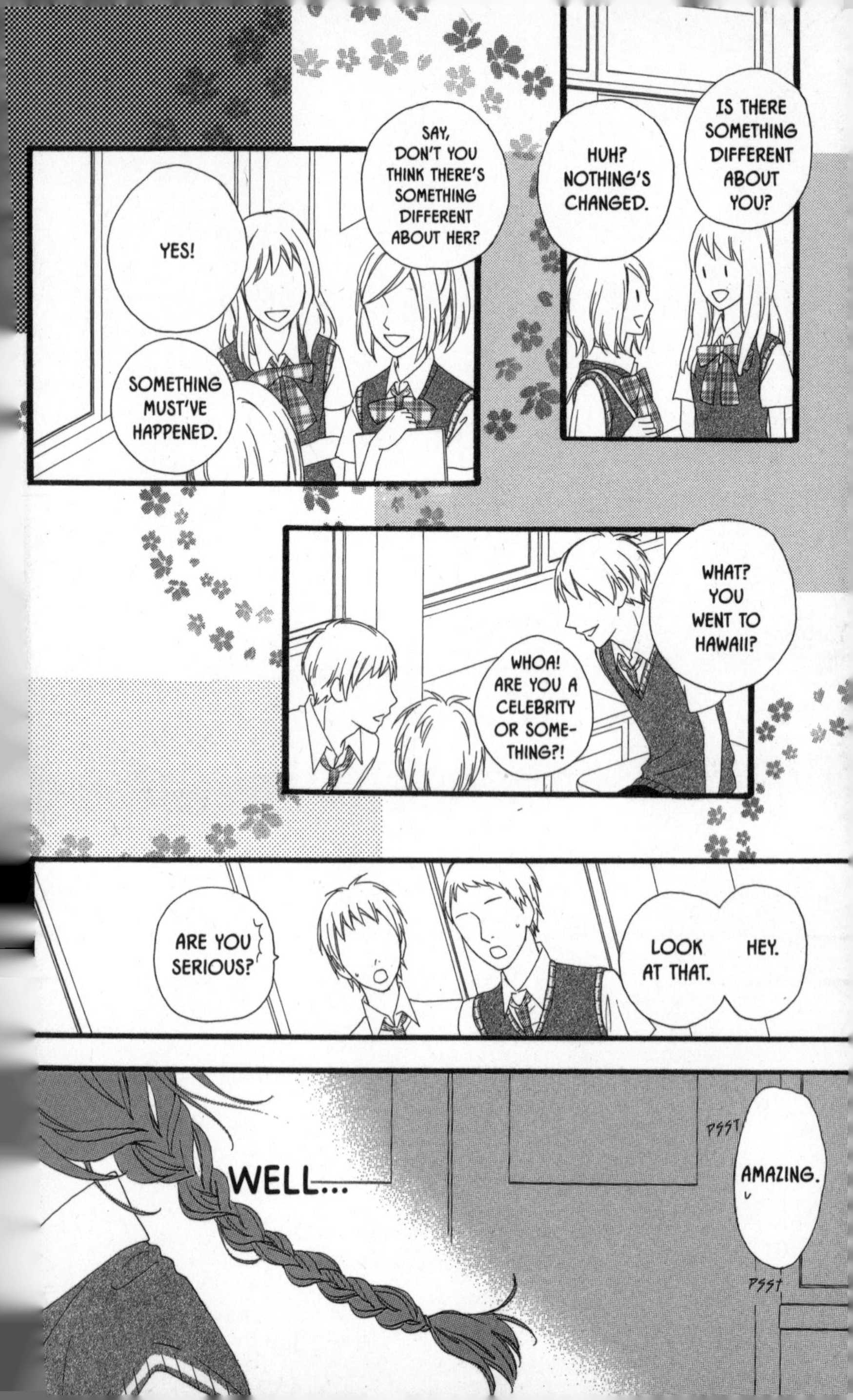
IS THERE SOMETHING DIFFERENT ABOUT YOU?
HUH? NOTHING'S CHANGED.
SAY, DON'T YOU THINK THERE'S SOMETHING DIFFERENT ABOUT HER?
YES!
SOMETHING MUST'VE HAPPENED.
WHAT? YOU WENT TO HAWAII?
WHOA! ARE YOU A CELEBRITY OR SOME-THING?!
HEY.
LOOK AT THAT.
ARE YOU SERIOUS?
PSST
AMAZING.
PSST
WELL...

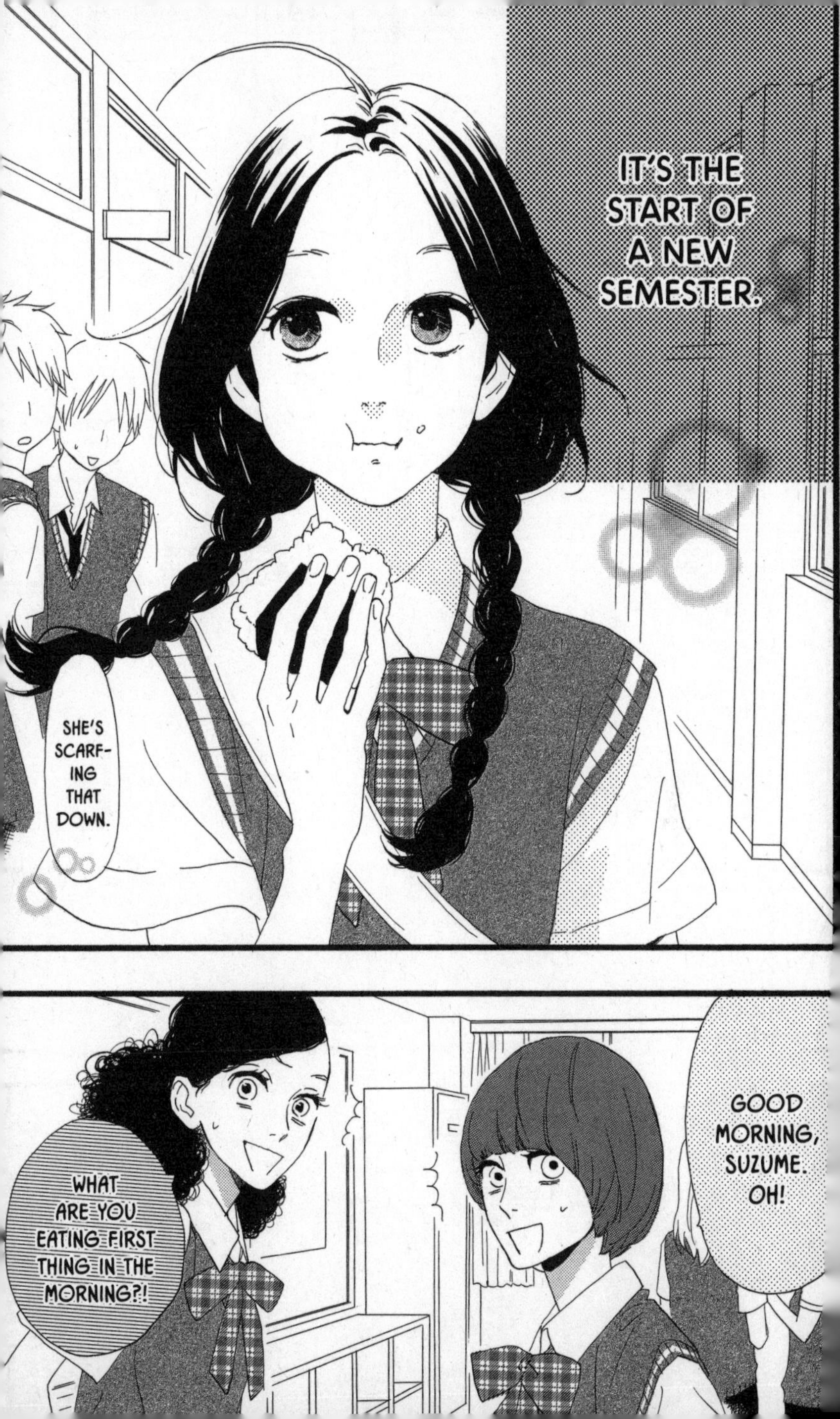
IT'S THE START OF A NEW SEMESTER.
SHE'S SCARF-ING THAT DOWN.
GOOD MORNING, SUZUME. OH!
WHAT ARE YOU EATING FIRST THING IN THE MORNING?!

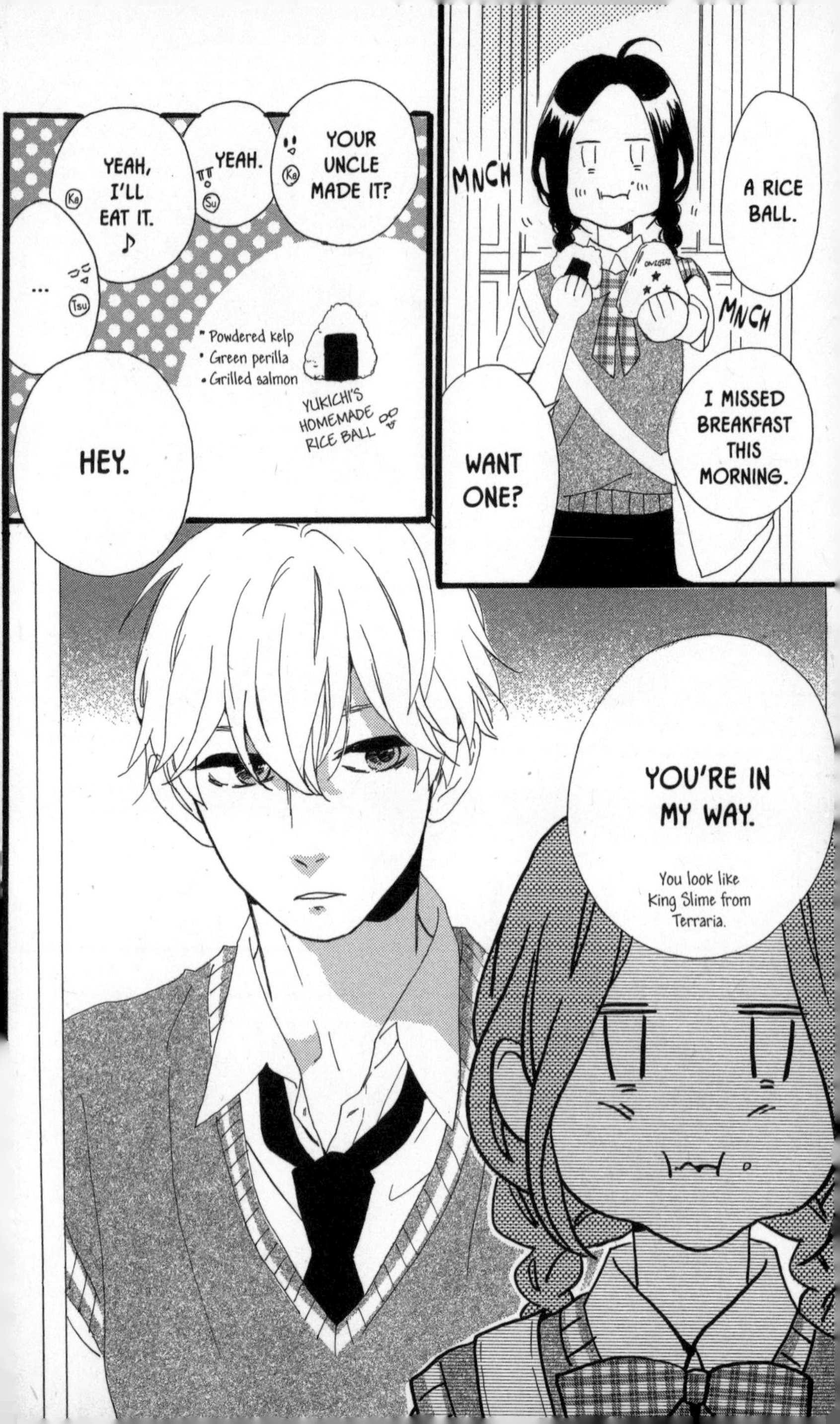
A RICE BALL.
MNCH
MNCH
I MISSED BREAKFAST THIS MORNING.
WANT ONE?
YOUR UNCLE MADE IT?
YEAH.
YEAH, I'LL EAT IT. ♪
...
• Powdered kelp
• Green perilla
• Grilled salmon
YUKICHI'S HOMEMADE RICE BALL
HEY.
YOU'RE IN MY WAY.
You look like King Slime from Terraria.

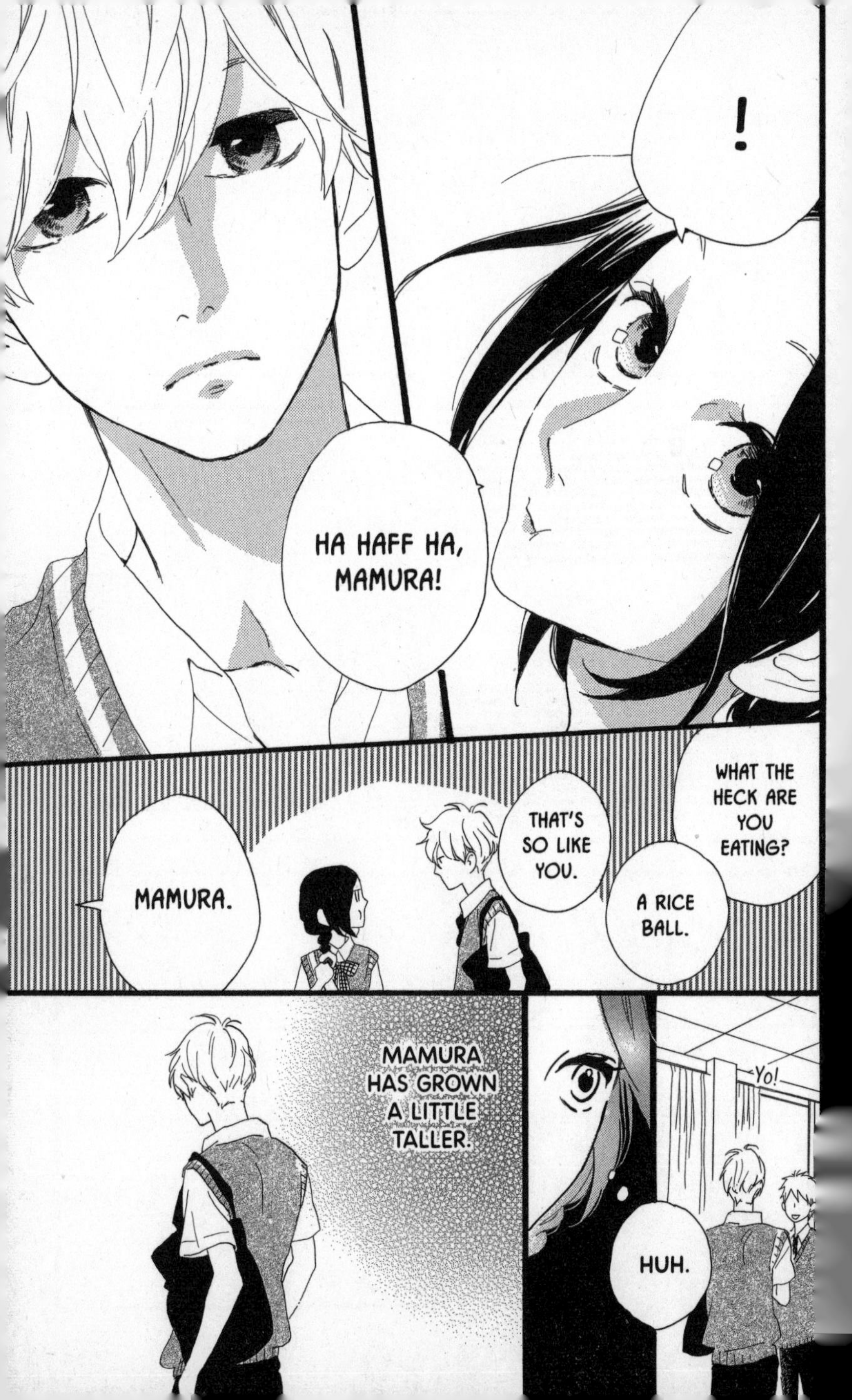
!
HA HAFF HA, MAMURA!
WHAT THE HECK ARE YOU EATING?
A RICE BALL.
THAT'S SO LIKE YOU.
MAMURA.
Yo!
HUH.
MAMURA HAS GROWN A LITTLE TALLER.

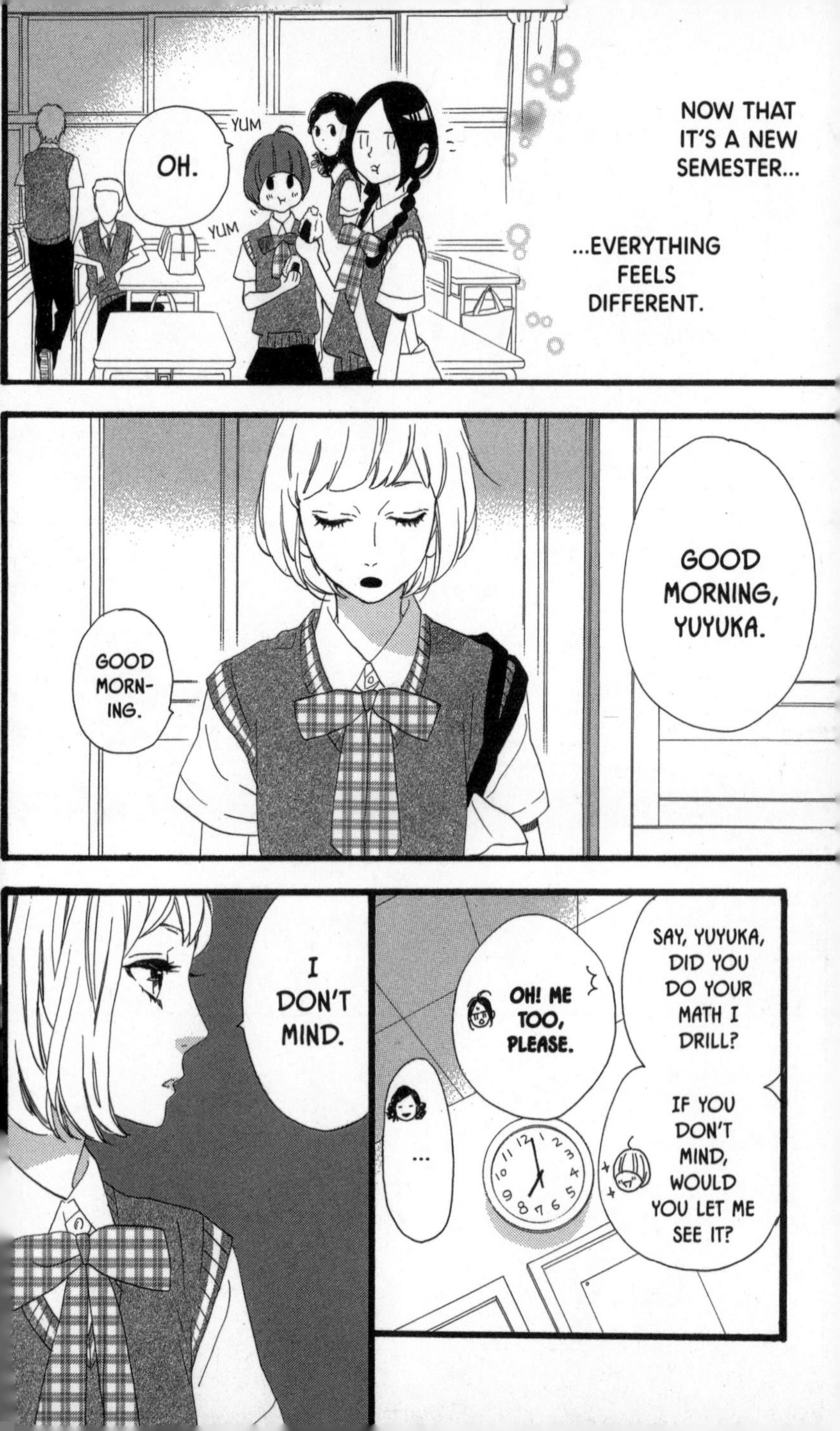
NOW THAT IT'S A NEW SEMESTER...
...EVERYTHING FEELS DIFFERENT.
YUM
OH.
YUM
GOOD MORNING, YUYUKA.
GOOD MORN-ING.
SAY, YUYUKA, DID YOU DO YOUR MATH I DRILL?
IF YOU DON'T MIND, WOULD YOU LET ME SEE IT?
OH! ME TOO, PLEASE.
...
I DON'T MIND.

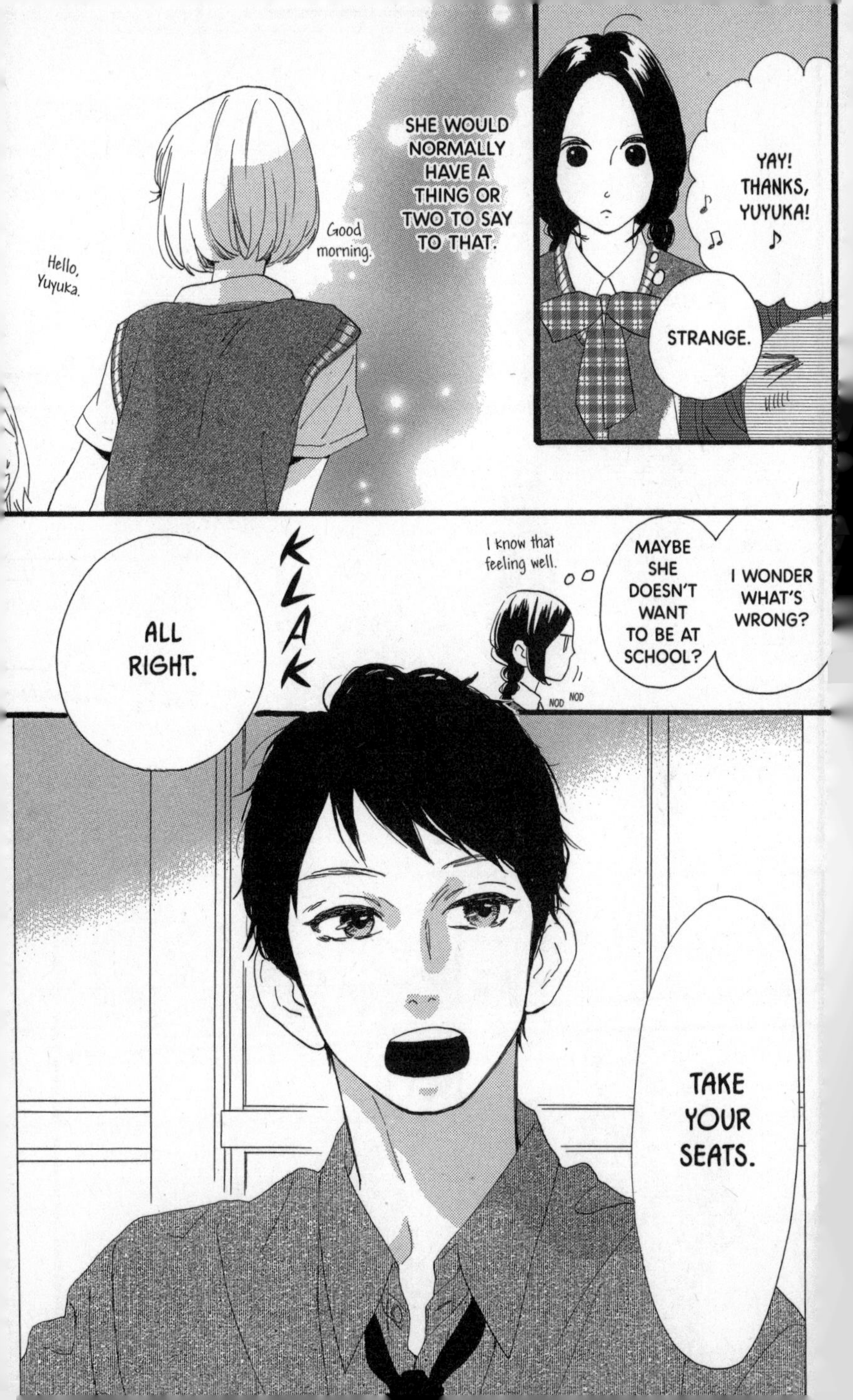
YAY! THANKS, YUYUKA! ♪ ♫ ♪
STRANGE.
SHE WOULD NORMALLY HAVE A THING OR TWO TO SAY TO THAT.
Good morning.
Hello, Yuyuka.
I WONDER WHAT'S WRONG?
MAYBE SHE DOESN'T WANT TO BE AT SCHOOL?
I know that feeling well.
NOD NOD
KLAK
ALL RIGHT.
TAKE YOUR SEATS.

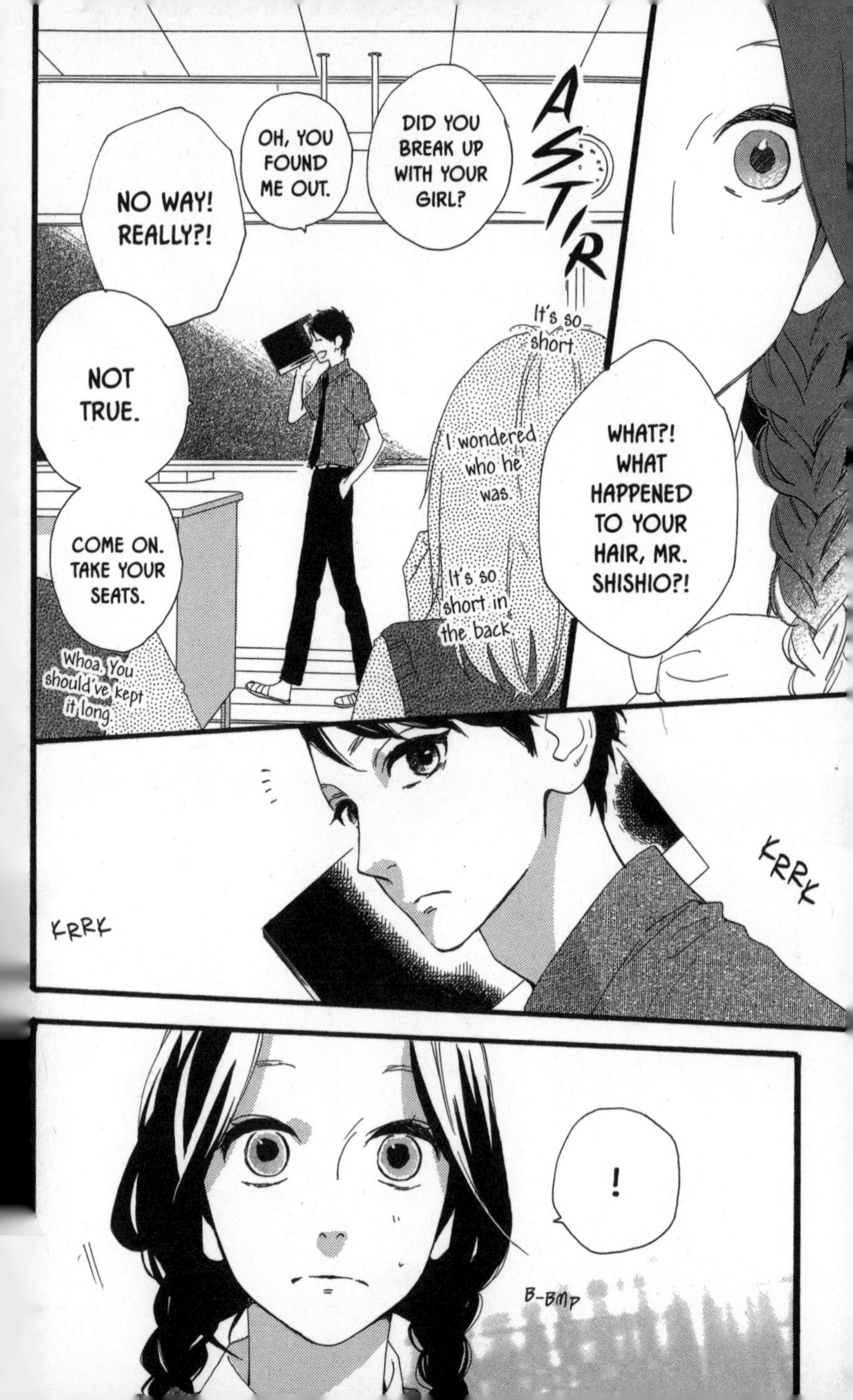
WHAT?! WHAT HAPPENED TO YOUR HAIR, MR. SHISHIO?!
ASTIR
It's so short
DID YOU BREAK UP WITH YOUR GIRL?
OH, YOU FOUND ME OUT.
NO WAY! REALLY?!
I wondered who he was.
It's so short in the back.
NOT TRUE.
COME ON. TAKE YOUR SEATS.
Whoa. You should've kept it long.
KRRK
KRRK
!
B-BMP

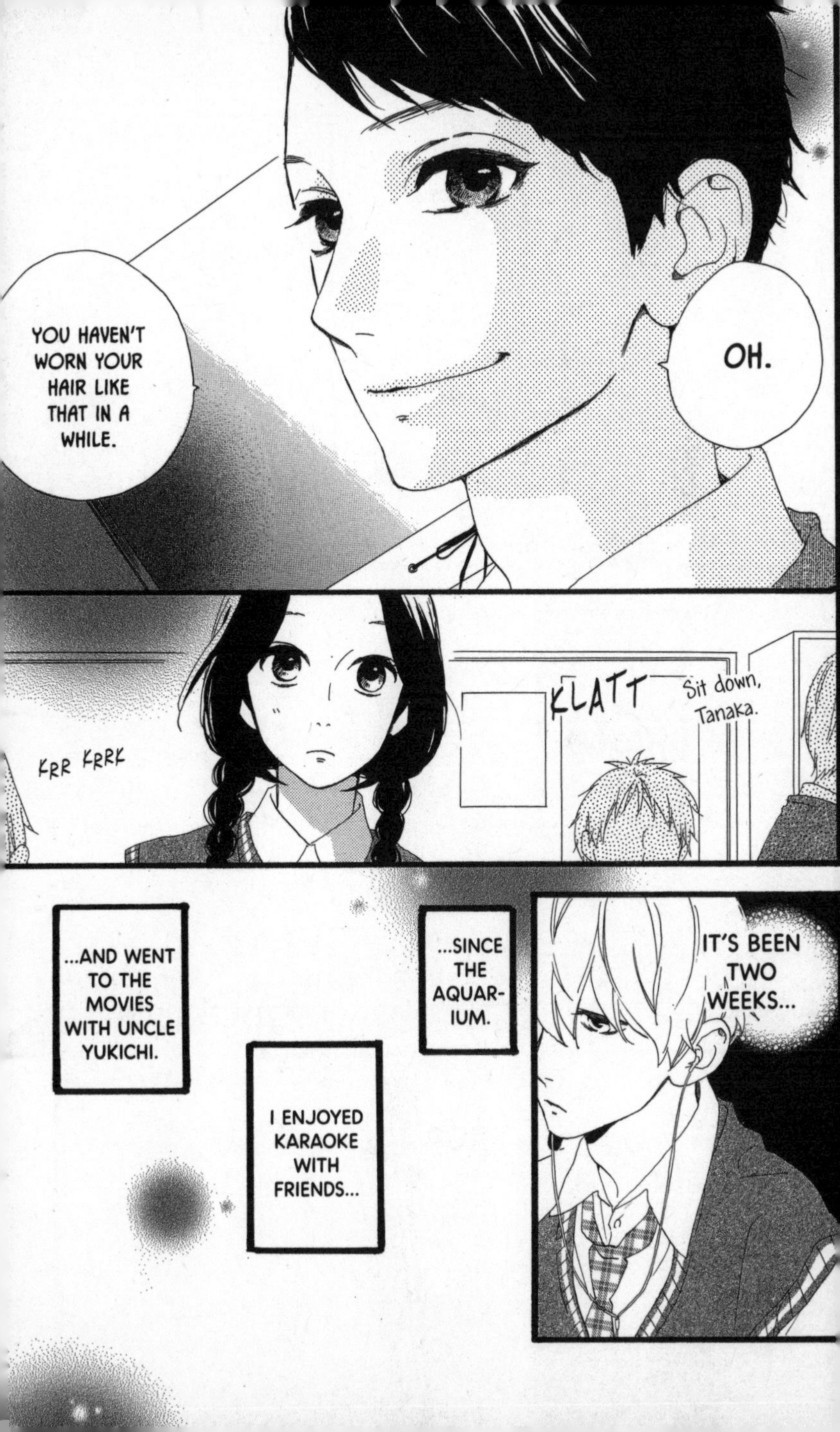
OH.
YOU HAVEN'T WORN YOUR HAIR LIKE THAT IN A WHILE.
Sit down, Tanaka.
KLATT
KRR KRRK
IT'S BEEN TWO WEEKS...
...SINCE THE AQUARIUM.
I ENJOYED KARAOKE WITH FRIENDS...
...AND WENT TO THE MOVIES WITH UNCLE YUKICHI.

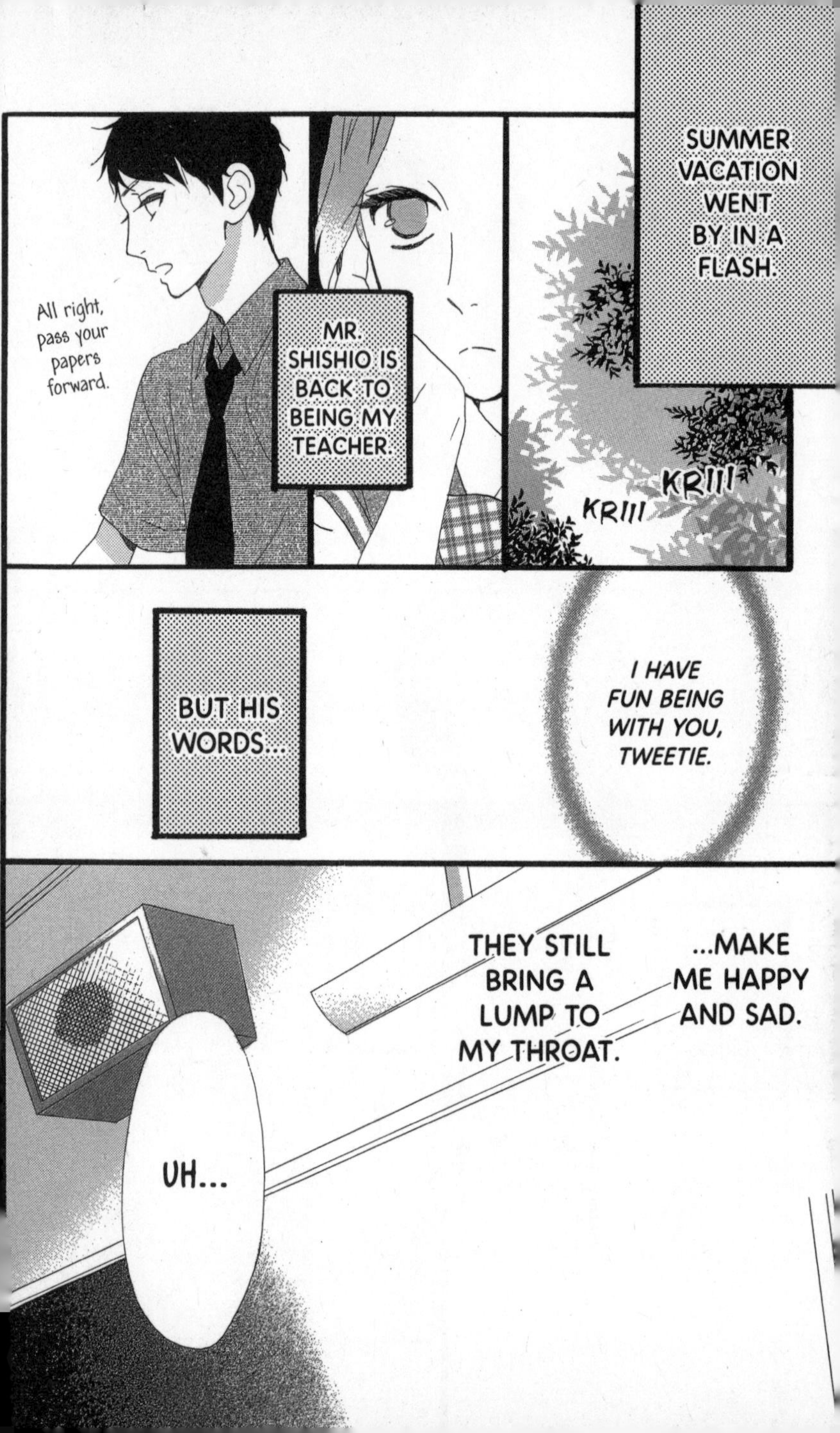

SUMMER VACATION WENT BY IN A FLASH.
KRIII
KRIII
MR. SHISHIO IS BACK TO BEING MY TEACHER.
All right, pass your papers forward.
I HAVE FUN BEING WITH YOU, TWEETIE.
BUT HIS WORDS...
...MAKE ME HAPPY AND SAD.
THEY STILL BRING A LUMP TO MY THROAT.
UH...

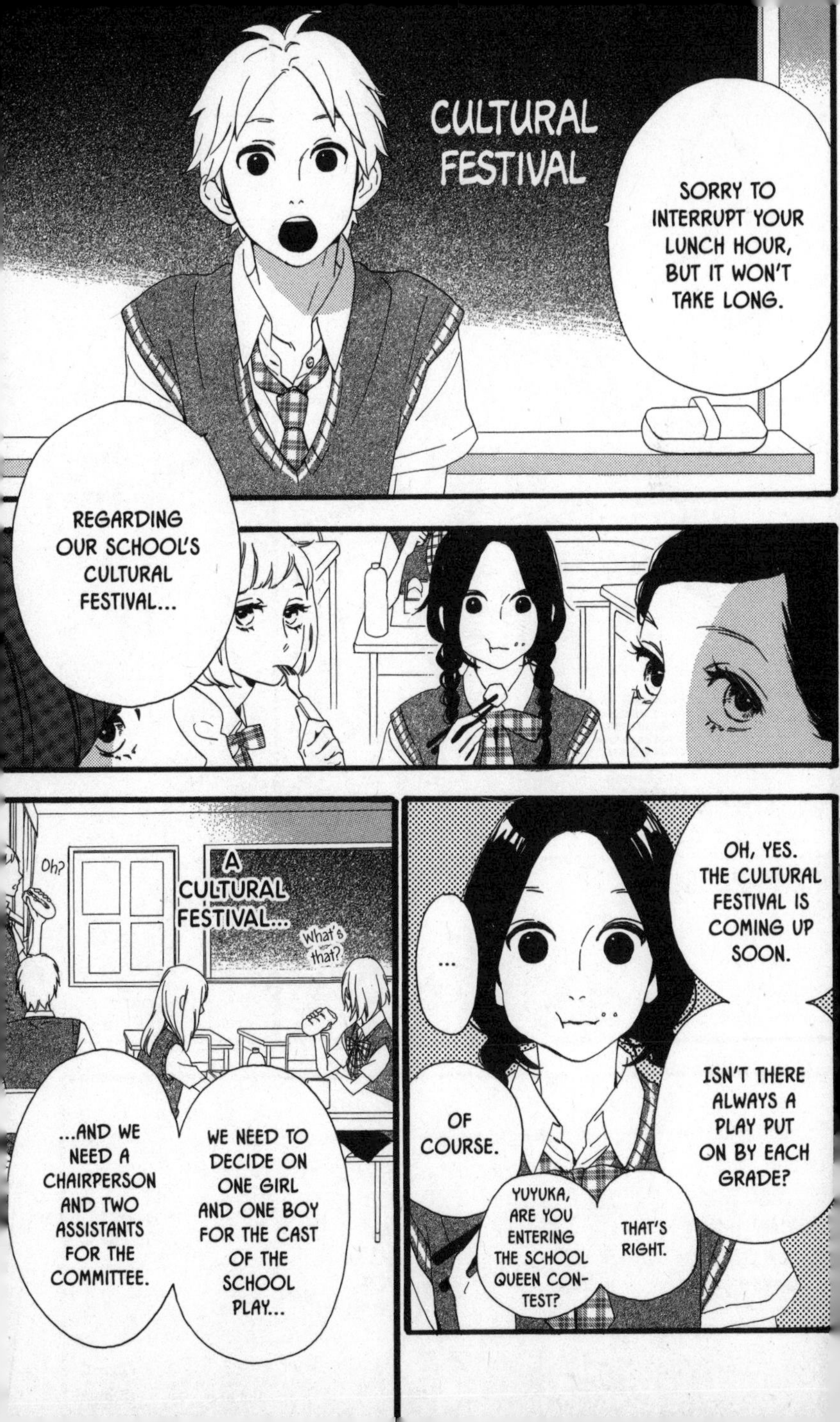
CULTURAL FESTIVAL
SORRY TO INTERRUPT YOUR LUNCH HOUR, BUT IT WON'T TAKE LONG.
REGARDING OUR SCHOOL'S CULTURAL FESTIVAL...
OH, YES. THE CULTURAL FESTIVAL IS COMING UP SOON.
...
ISN'T THERE ALWAYS A PLAY PUT ON BY EACH GRADE?
OF COURSE.
THAT'S RIGHT.
YUYUKA, ARE YOU ENTERING THE SCHOOL QUEEN CON-TEST?
A CULTURAL FESTIVAL...
What's that?
Oh?
WE NEED TO DECIDE ON ONE GIRL AND ONE BOY FOR THE CAST OF THE SCHOOL PLAY...
...AND WE NEED A CHAIRPERSON AND TWO ASSISTANTS FOR THE COMMITTEE.

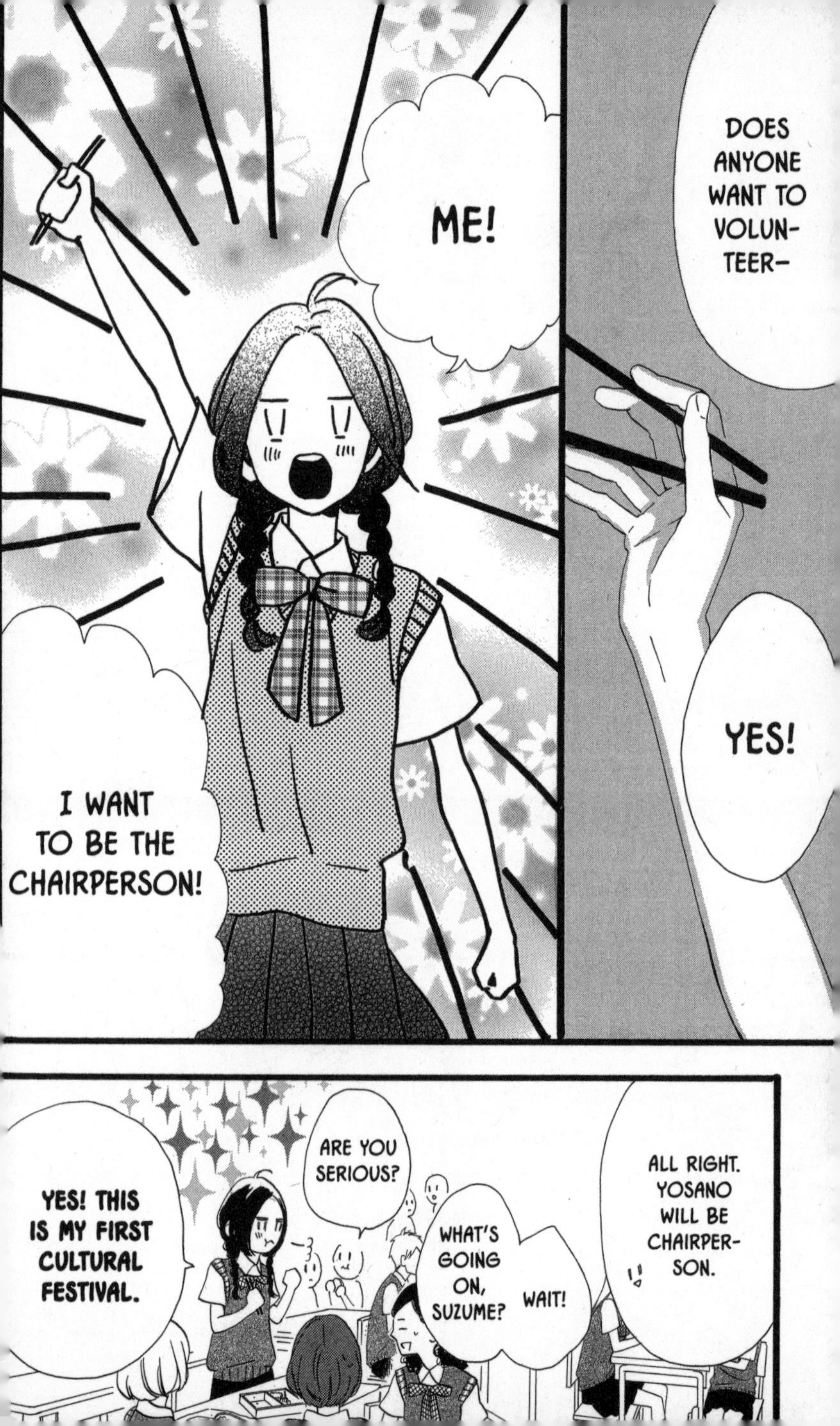
DOES ANYONE WANT TO VOLUN- TEER—
YES!
ME!
I WANT TO BE THE CHAIRPERSON!
ALL RIGHT. YOSANO WILL BE CHAIRPER- SON.
WAIT!
WHAT'S GOING ON, SUZUME?
ARE YOU SERIOUS?
YES! THIS IS MY FIRST CULTURAL FESTIVAL.

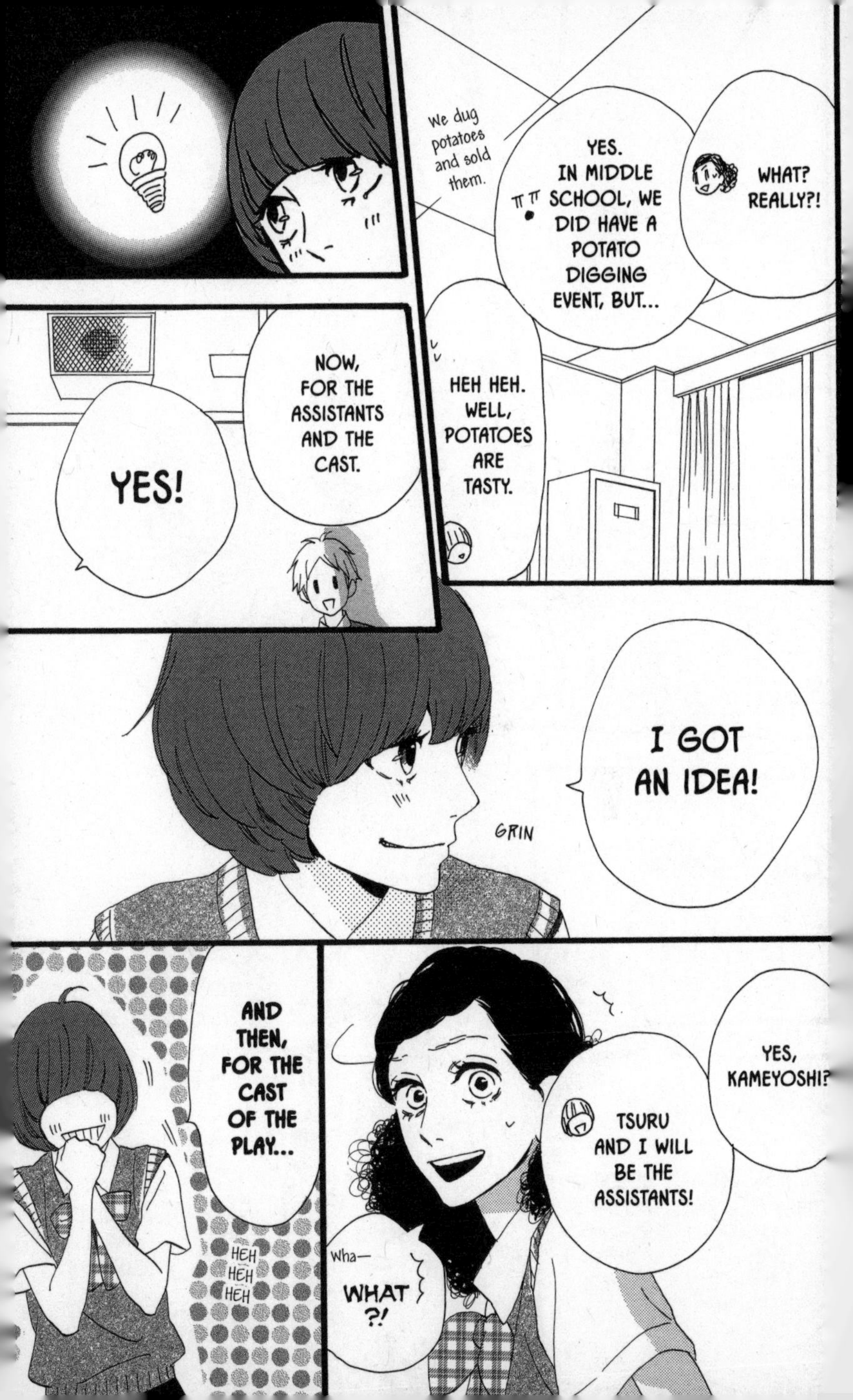
WHAT? REALLY?!
YES. IN MIDDLE SCHOOL, WE DID HAVE A POTATO DIGGING EVENT, BUT...
We dug potatoes and sold them.
HEH HEH. WELL, POTATOES ARE TASTY.
NOW, FOR THE ASSISTANTS AND THE CAST.
YES!
I GOT AN IDEA!
GRIN
YES, KAMEYOSHI?
TSURU AND I WILL BE THE ASSISTANTS!
Wha—
WHAT?!
AND THEN, FOR THE CAST OF THE PLAY...
HEH HEH HEH

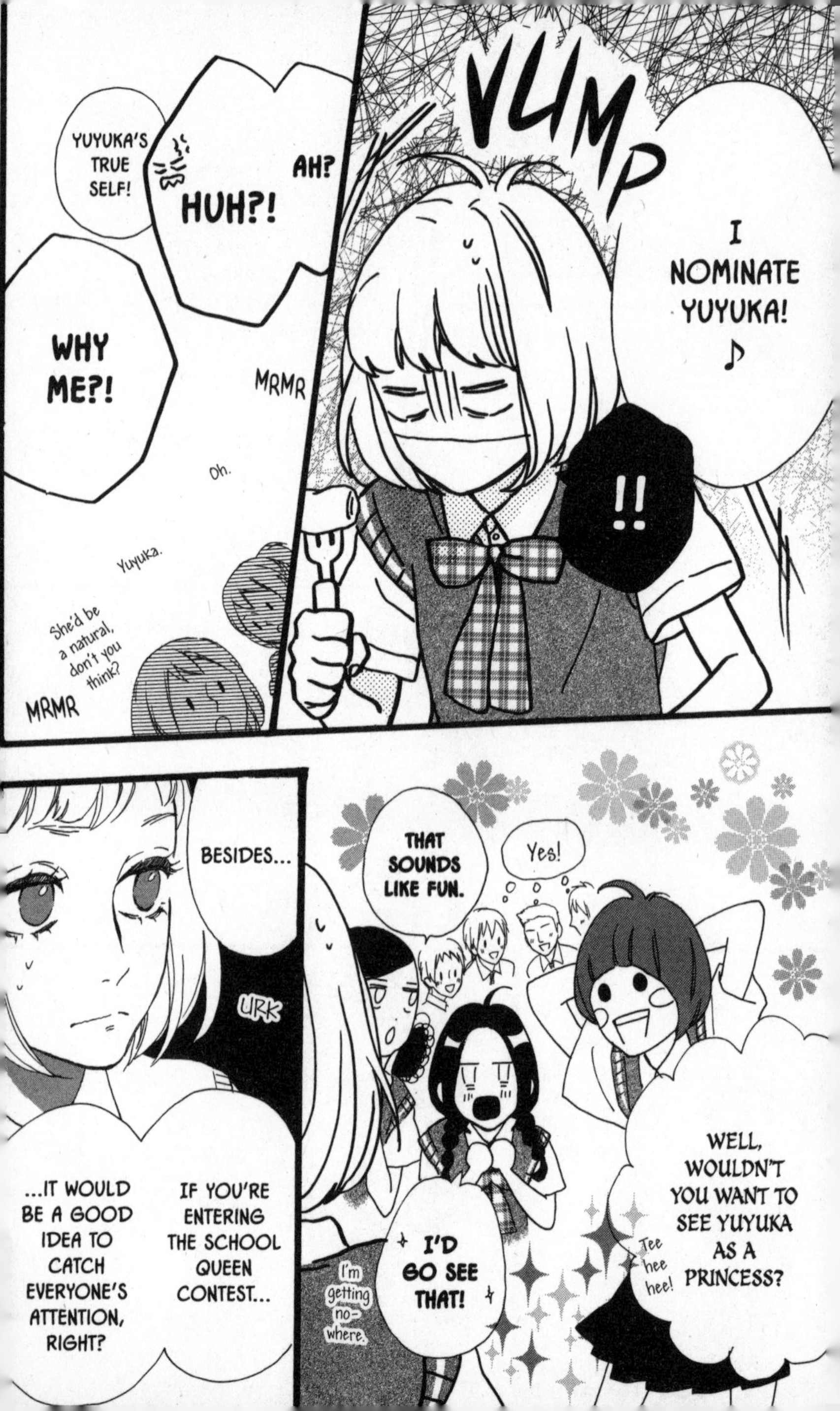
VUMP
I NOMINATE YUYUKA! ♪
!!
AH?
HUH?!
YUYUKA'S TRUE SELF!
WHY ME?!
MRMR
Oh.
Yuyuka.
She'd be a natural, don't you think?
MRMR
WELL, WOULDN'T YOU WANT TO SEE YUYUKA AS A PRINCESS?
Tee hee hee!
Yes!
THAT SOUNDS LIKE FUN.
I'D GO SEE THAT!
I'm getting no-where.
BESIDES...
URK
IF YOU'RE ENTERING THE SCHOOL QUEEN CONTEST...
...IT WOULD BE A GOOD IDEA TO CATCH EVERYONE'S ATTENTION, RIGHT?

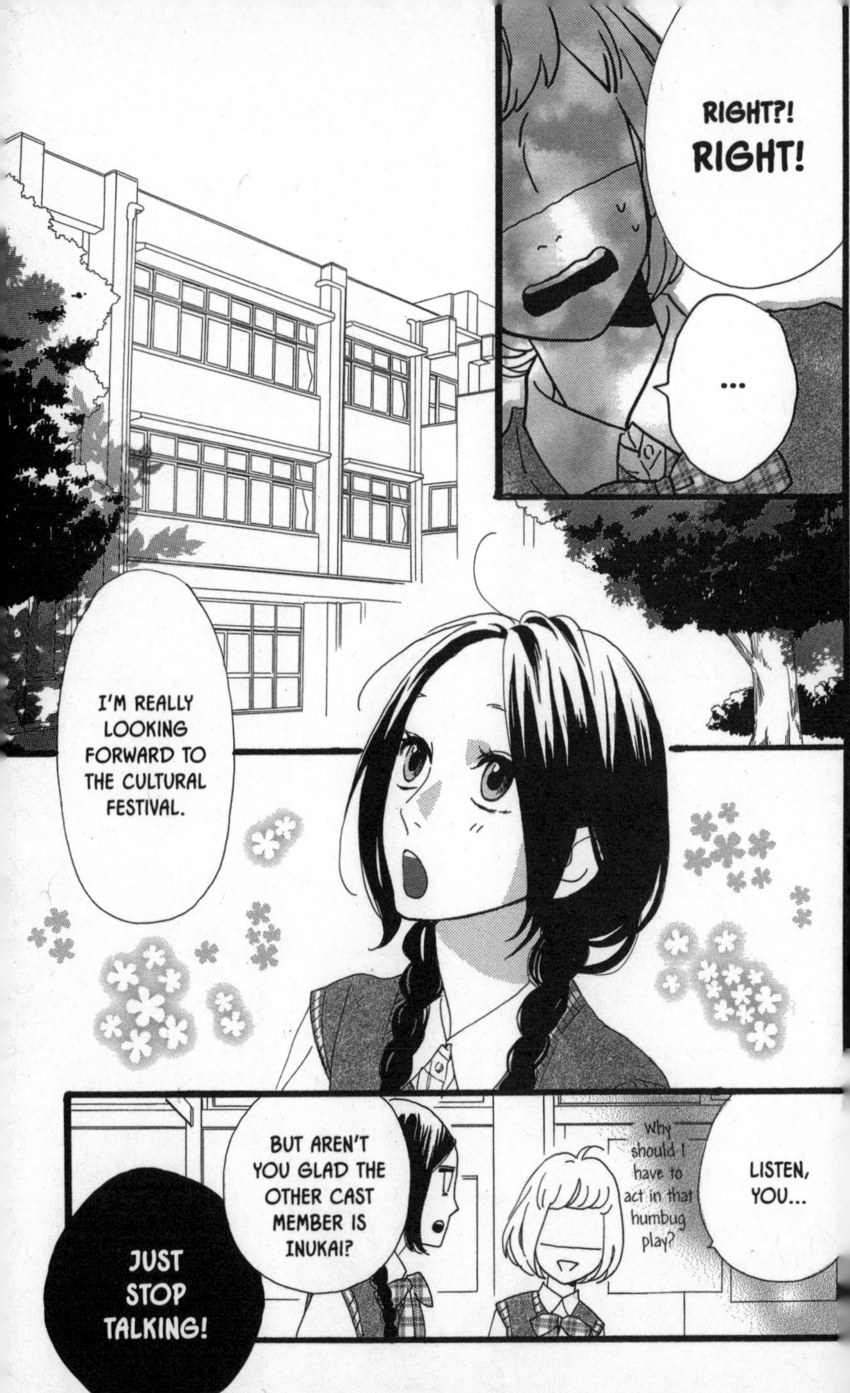
RIGHT?! RIGHT!
...
I'M REALLY LOOKING FORWARD TO THE CULTURAL FESTIVAL.
LISTEN, YOU...
Why should I have to act in that humbug play?
BUT AREN'T YOU GLAD THE OTHER CAST MEMBER IS INUKAI?
JUST STOP TALKING!

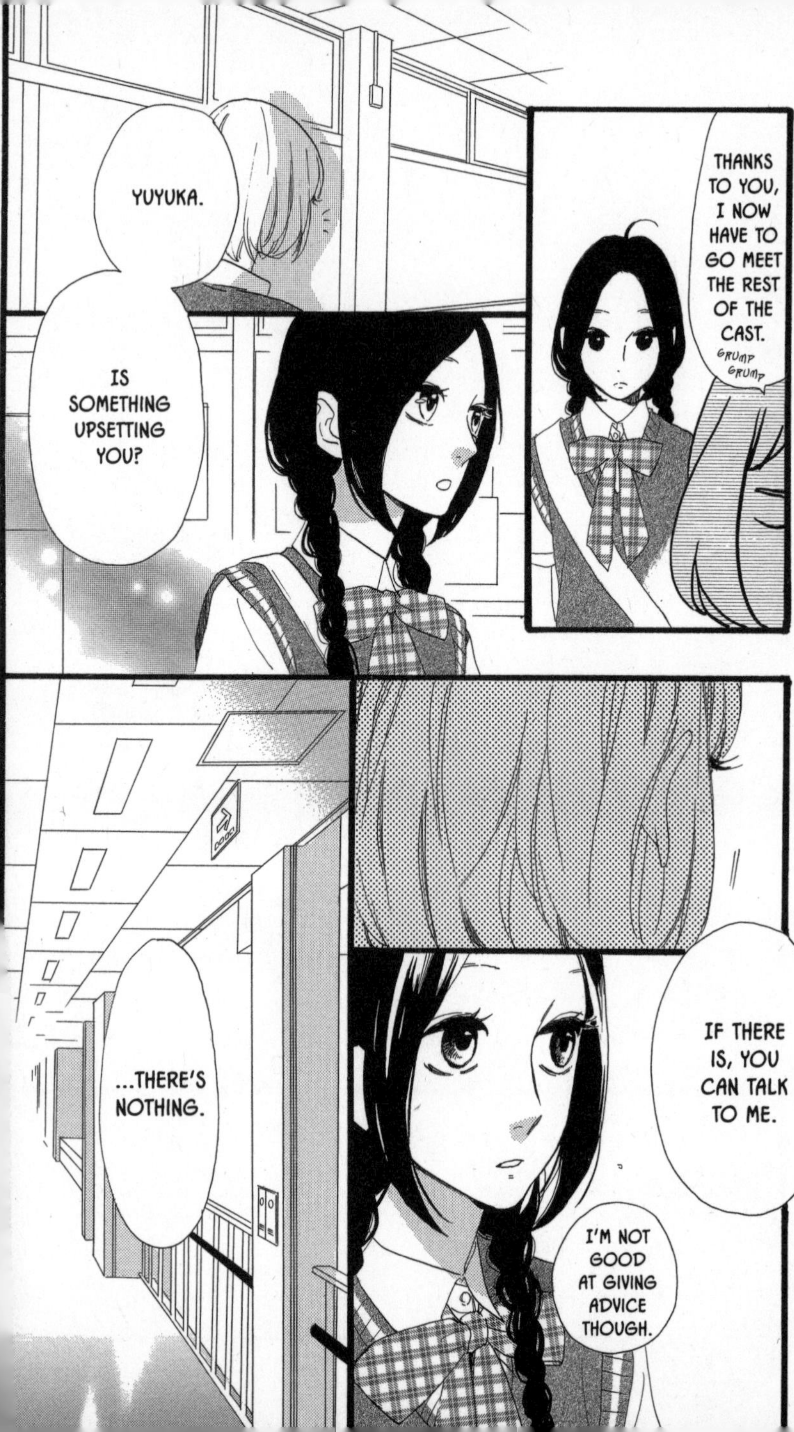
THANKS TO YOU, I NOW HAVE TO GO MEET THE REST OF THE CAST.
GRUMP GRUMP
YUYUKA.
IS SOMETHING UPSETTING YOU?
IF THERE IS, YOU CAN TALK TO ME.
I'M NOT GOOD AT GIVING ADVICE THOUGH.
...THERE'S NOTHING.

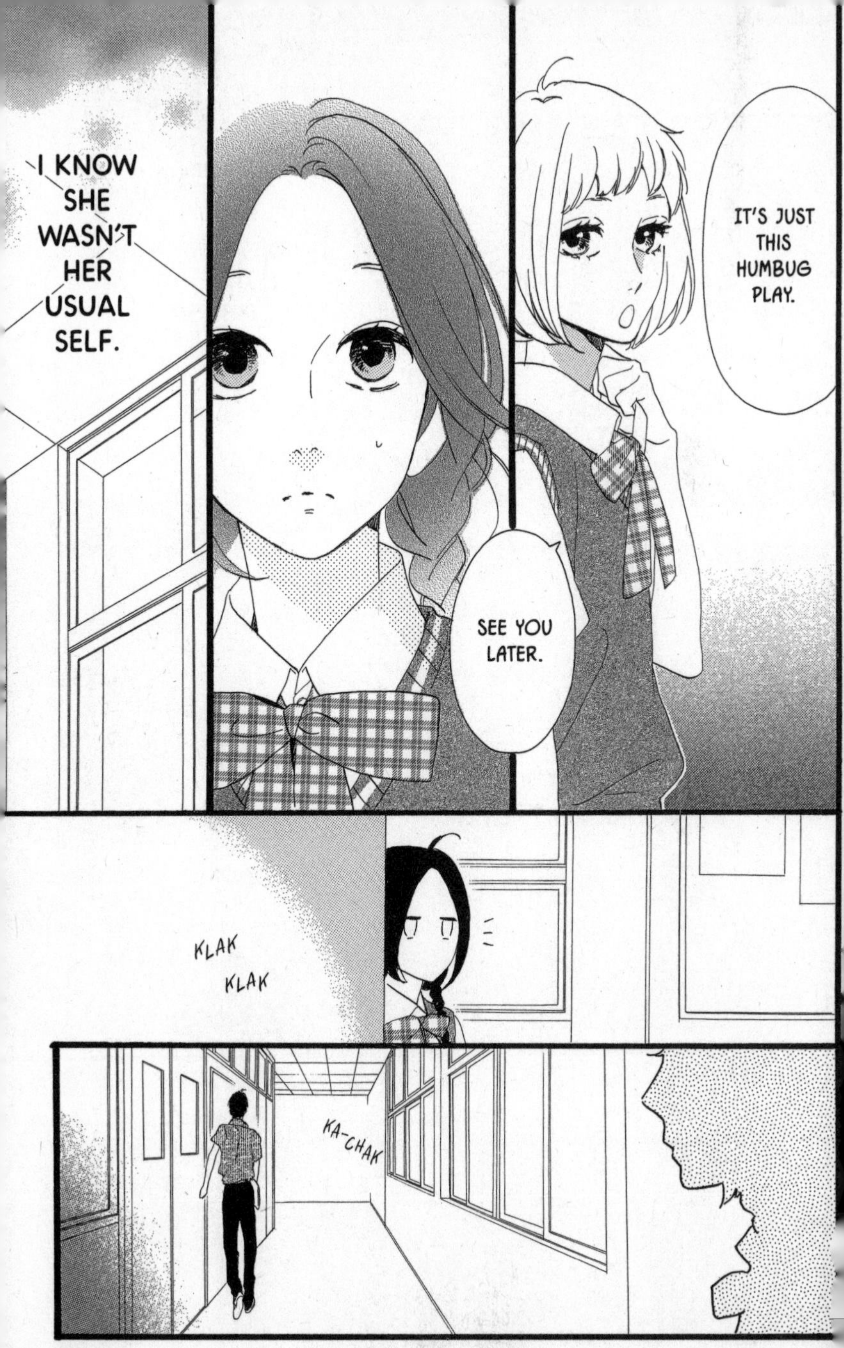
IT'S JUST THIS HUMBUG PLAY.
SEE YOU LATER.
I KNOW SHE WASN'T HER USUAL SELF.
KLAK KLAK
KA-CHAK

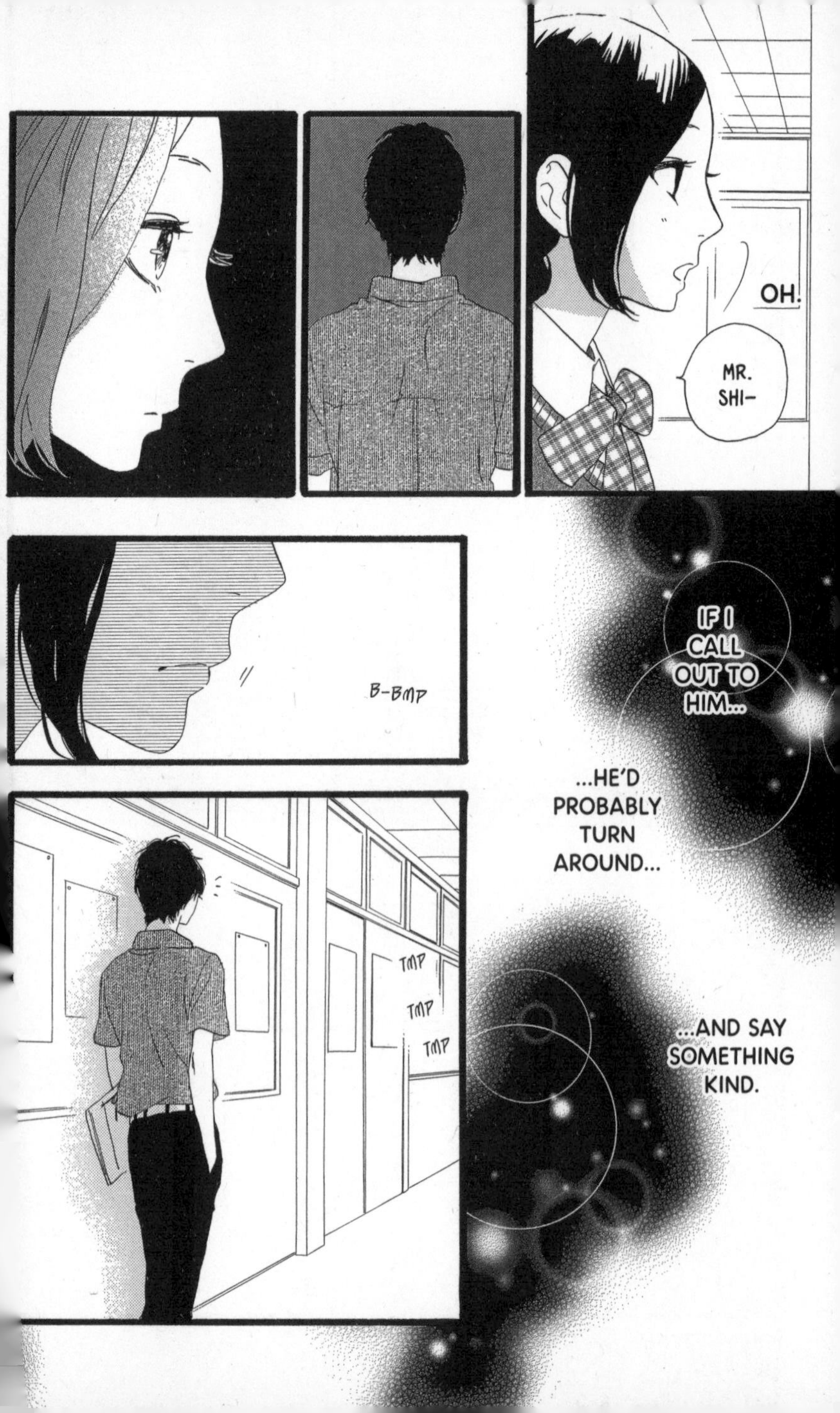
OH.
MR. SHI—
B-BMP
IF I CALL OUT TO HIM...
...HE'D PROBABLY TURN AROUND...
...AND SAY SOMETHING KIND.
TMP
TMP
TMP

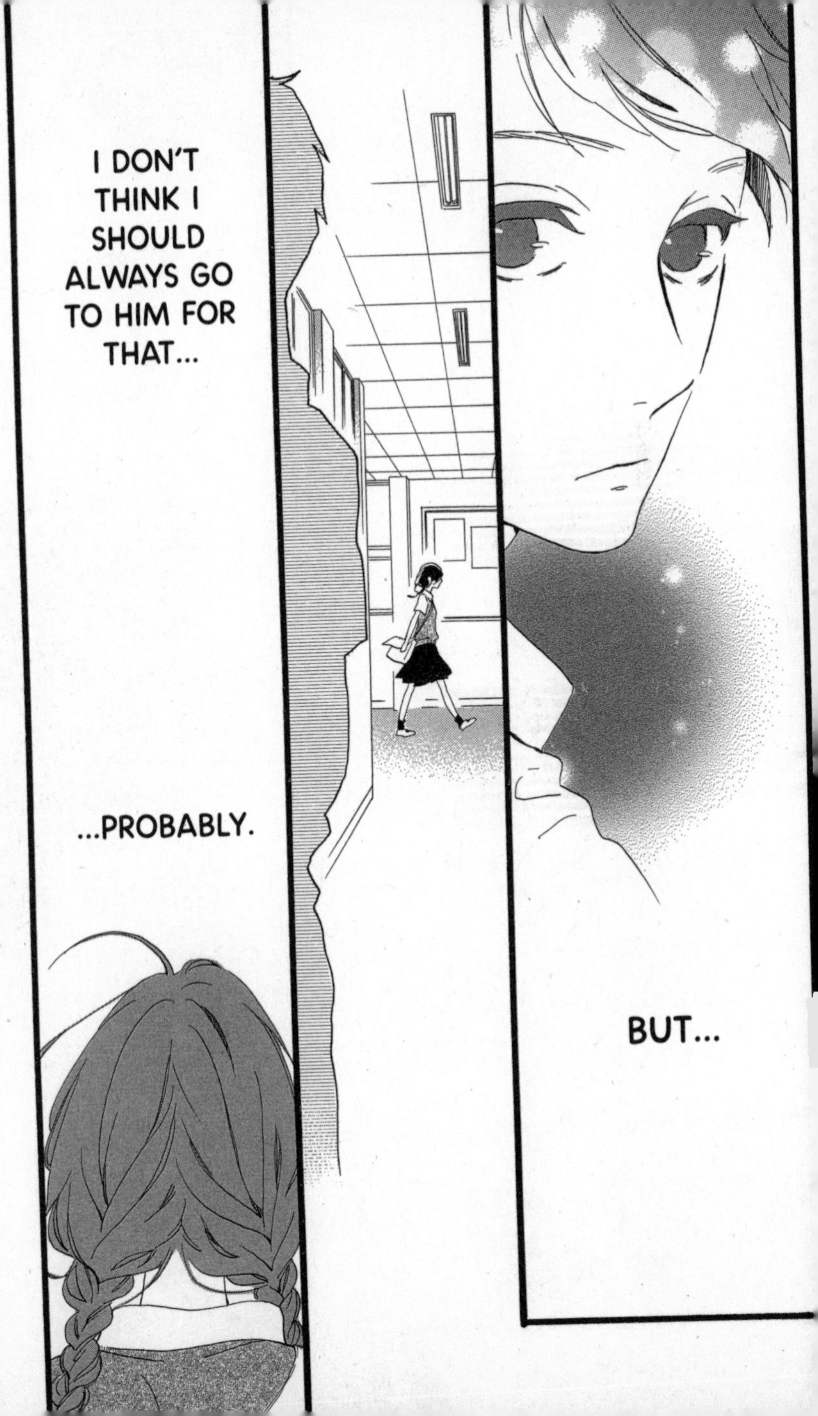
BUT...
I DON'T THINK I SHOULD ALWAYS GO TO HIM FOR THAT...
...PROBABLY.

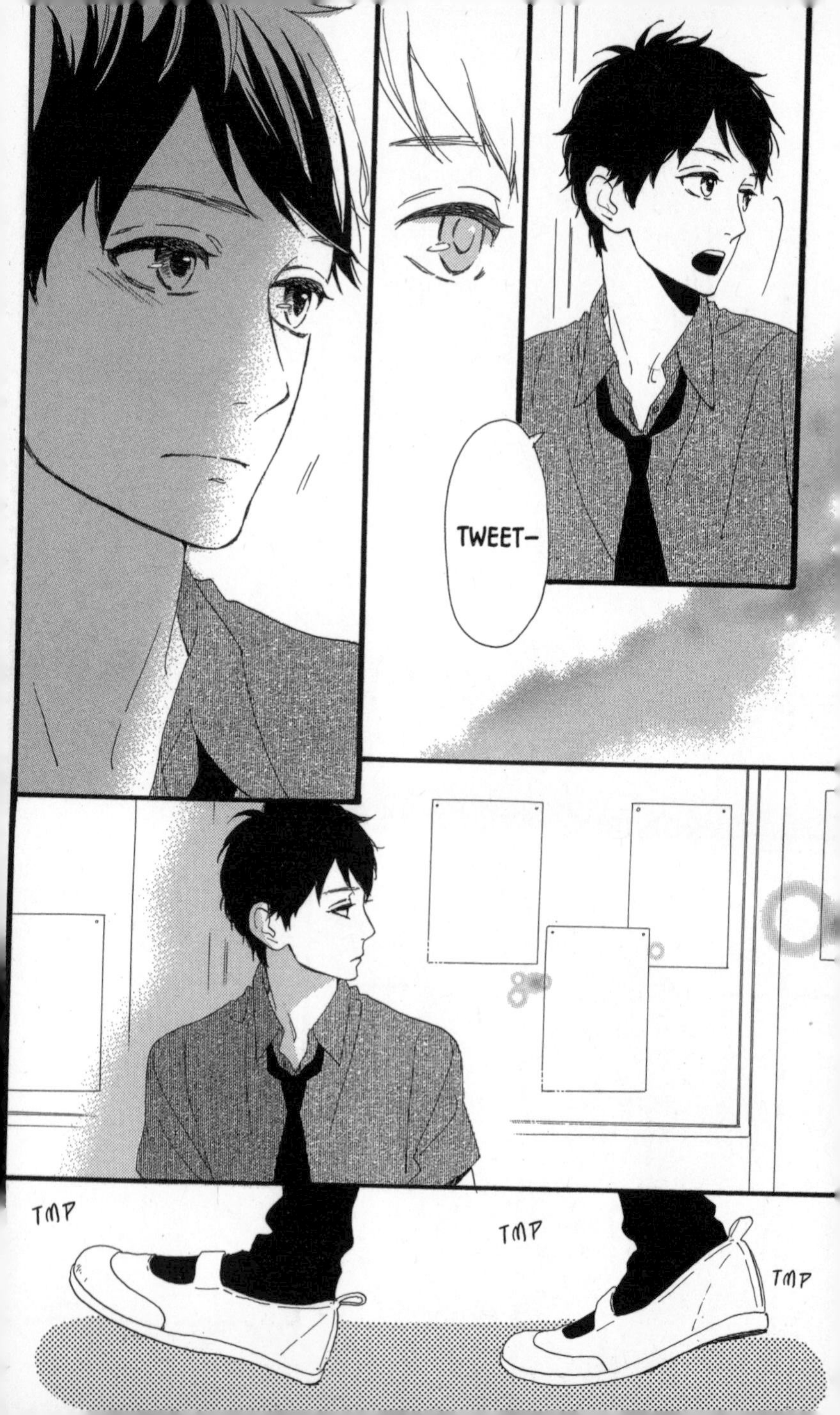
TWEET–
TMP
TMP
TMP

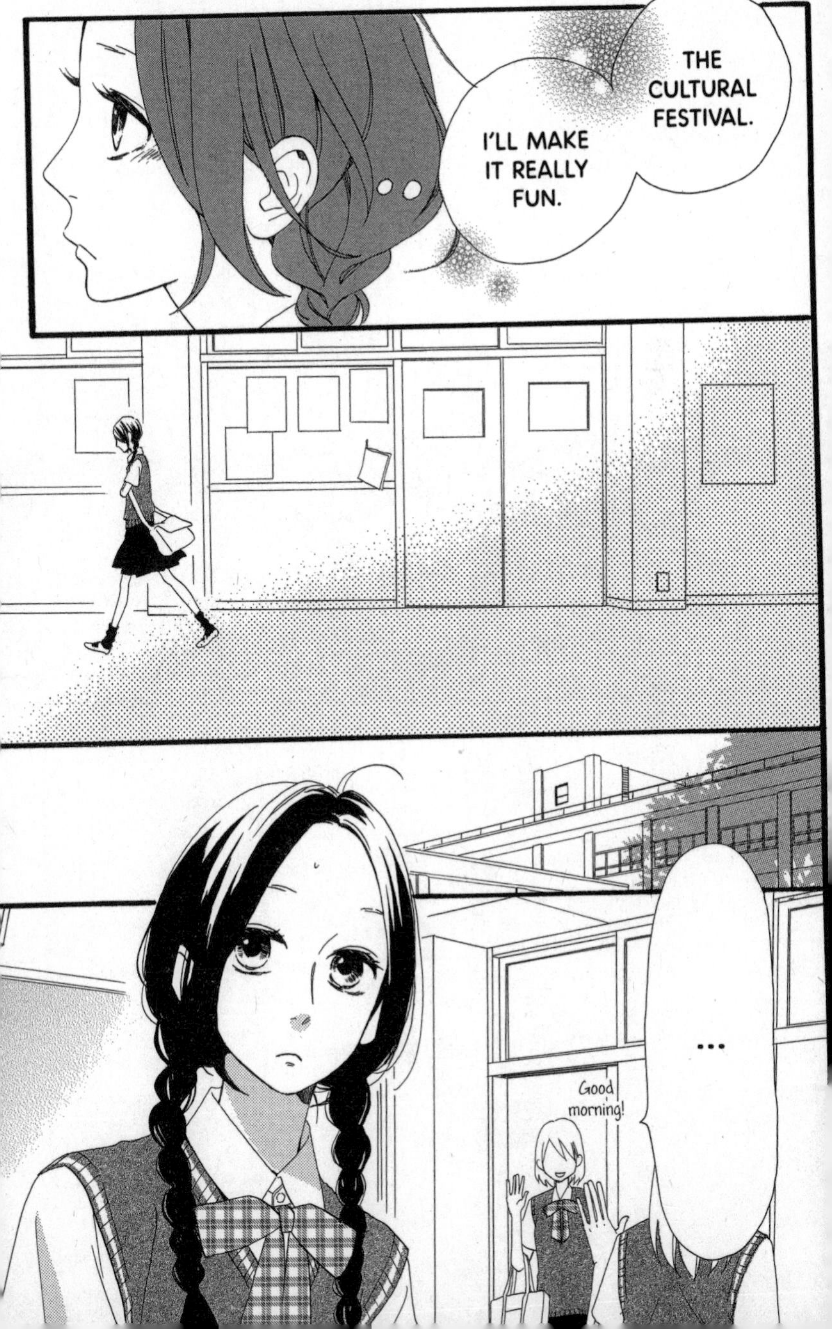
THE CULTURAL FESTIVAL.
I'LL MAKE IT REALLY FUN.
...
Good morning!

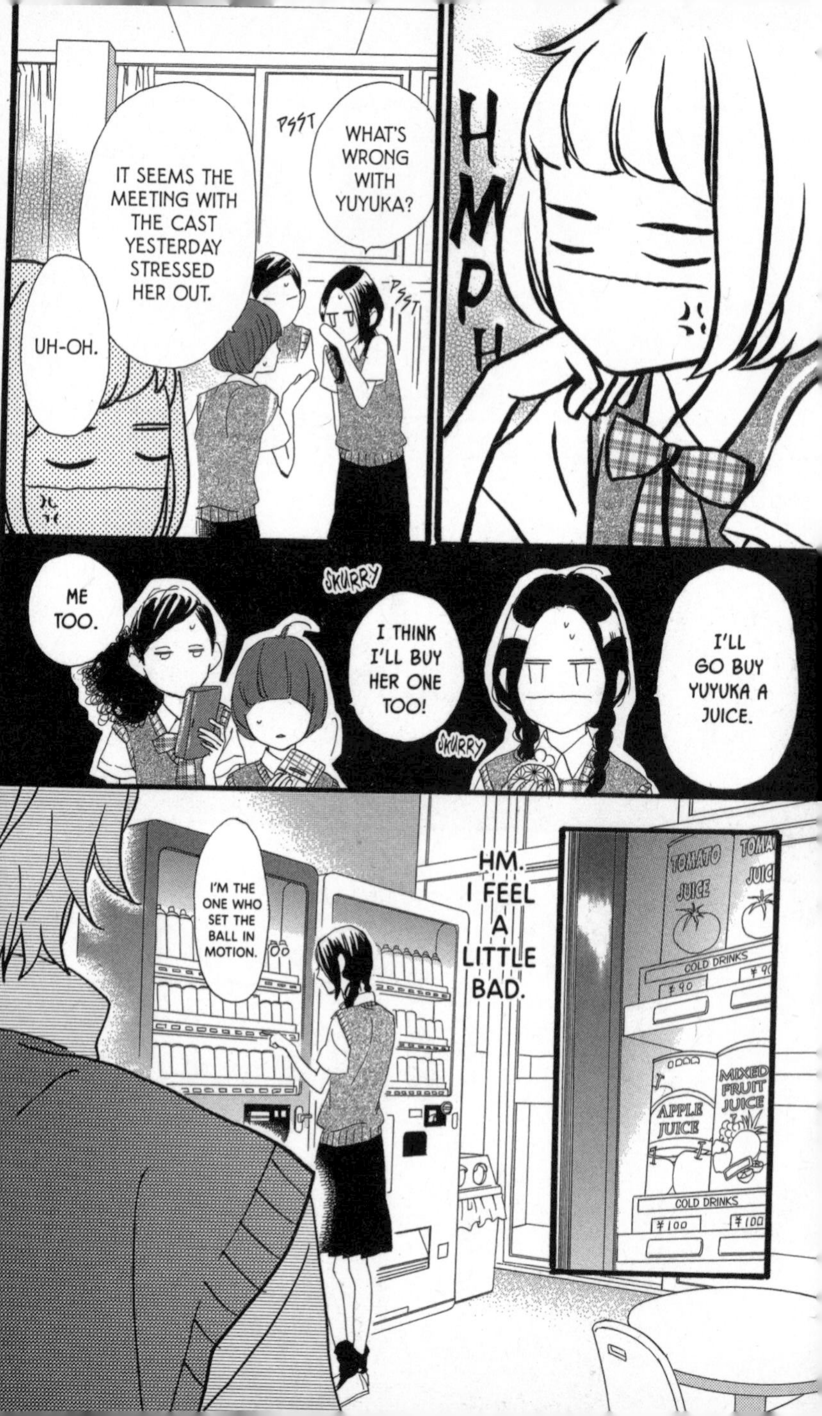
HMPH
PSST
WHAT'S WRONG WITH YUYUKA?
PSST
IT SEEMS THE MEETING WITH THE CAST YESTERDAY STRESSED HER OUT.
UH-OH.
I'LL GO BUY YUYUKA A JUICE.
SKURRY
I THINK I'LL BUY HER ONE TOO!
SKURRY
ME TOO.
TOMATO JUICE
COLD DRINKS
¥90
¥90
APPLE JUICE
MIXED FRUIT JUICE
COLD DRINKS
¥100
¥100
HM. I FEEL A LITTLE BAD.
I'M THE ONE WHO SET THE BALL IN MOTION.

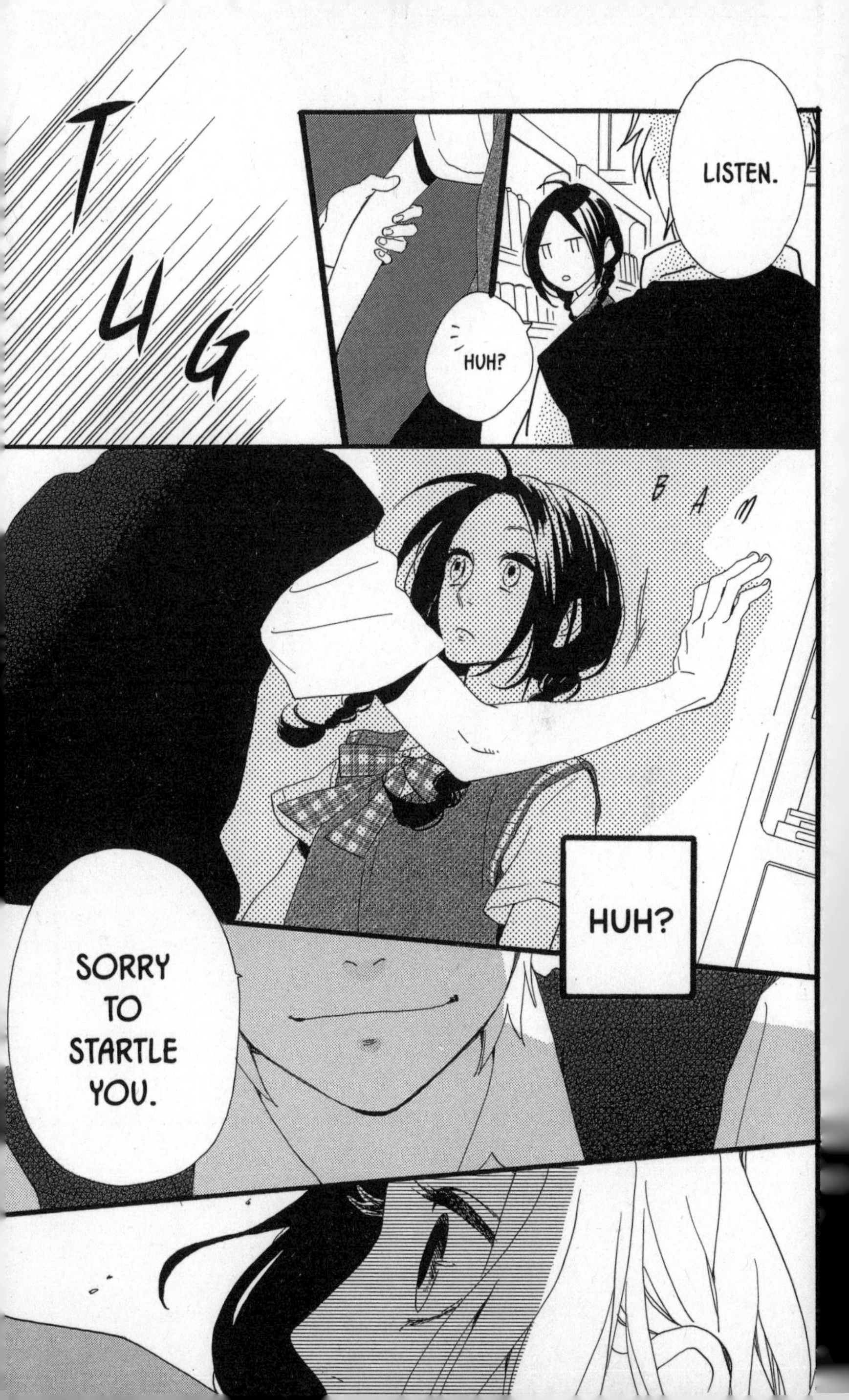
LISTEN.
HUH?
TUG
BAM
HUH?
SORRY TO STARTLE YOU.

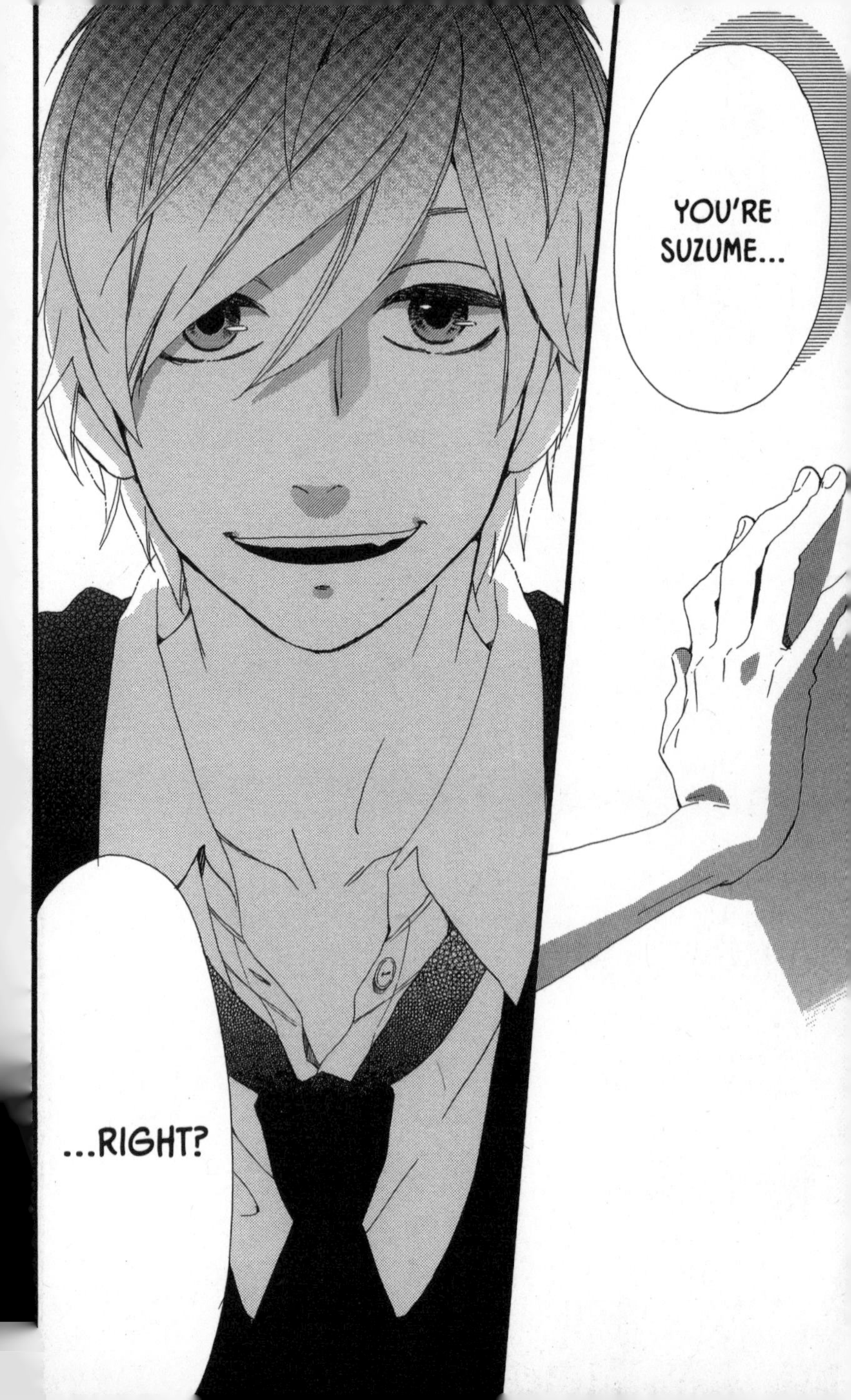
YOU'RE SUZUME...
...RIGHT?

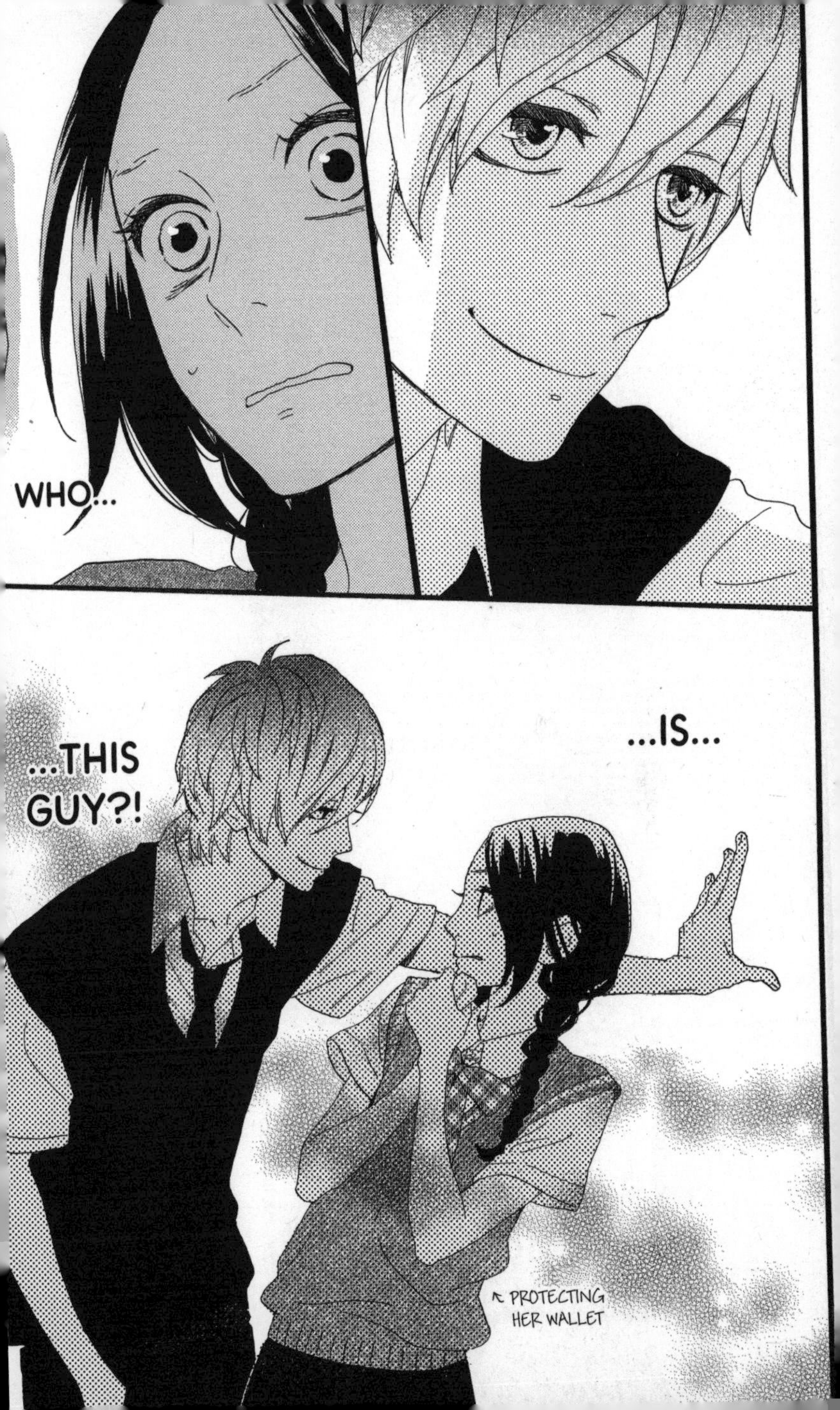
WHO...
...IS...
...THIS GUY?!
PROTECTING HER WALLET

What if Suzume and Yuyuka exchanged bodies?

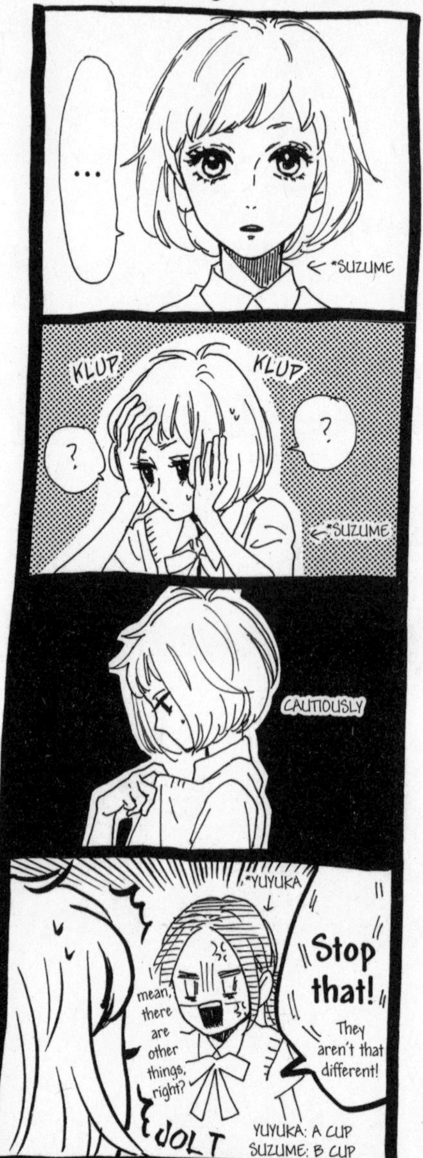
...
*SUZUME
KLUP
KLUP
?
?
*SUZUME
CAUTIOUSLY
*YUYUKA
Stop that!
They aren't that different!
I mean, there are other things, right?
JOLT
YUYUKA: A CUP
SUZUME: B CUP

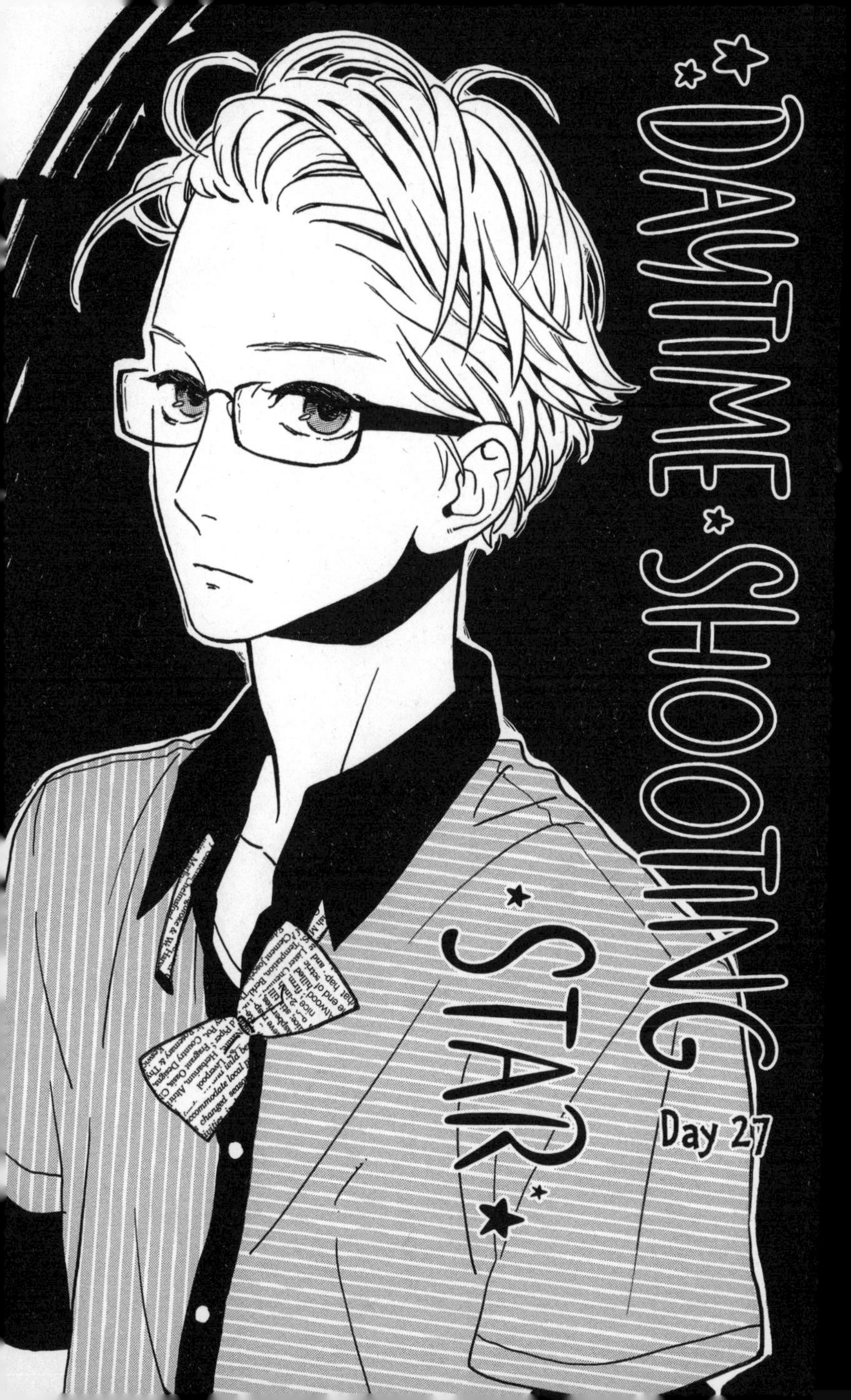
DAYTIME SHOOTING STAR
Day 27

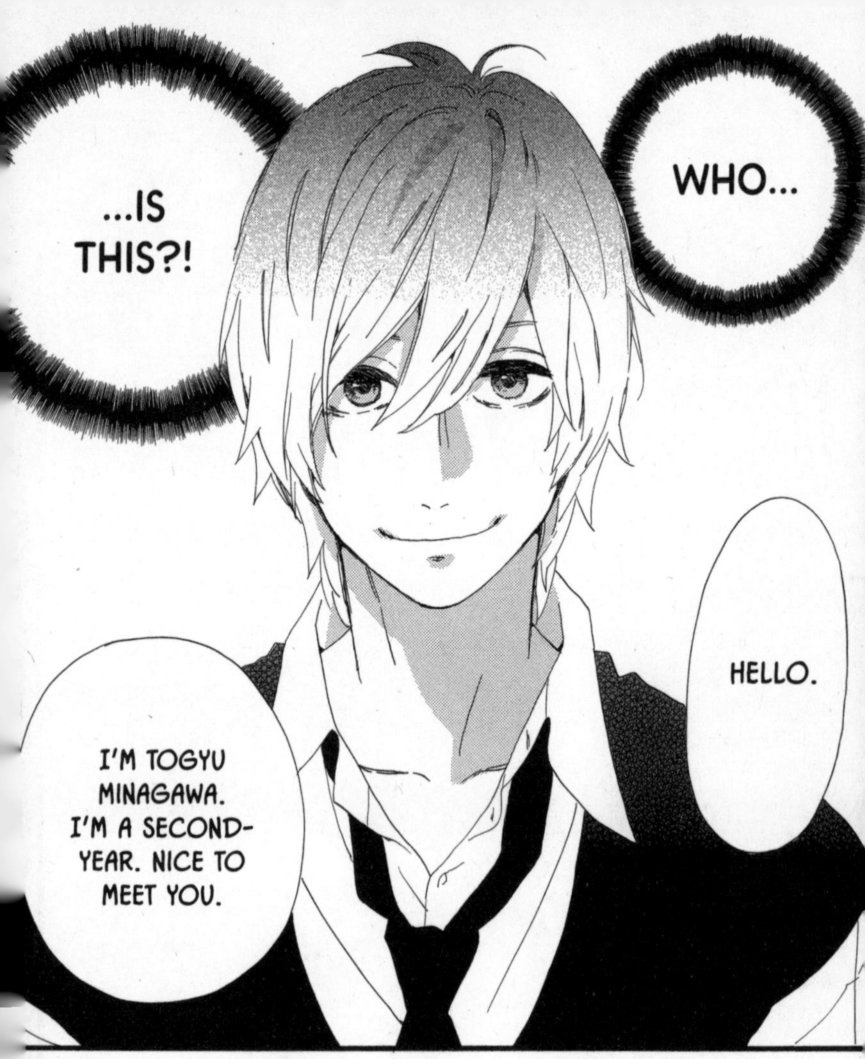
WHO...
...IS THIS?!
HELLO.
I'M TOGYU MINAGAWA. I'M A SECOND-YEAR. NICE TO MEET YOU.

Togyu Minagawa MOO MOO MOO

Birthday: November 3

Height: 5'8"

Weight: 133 lbs

Blood Type: B

① Yakiniku. Ice cream.

② Basketball.

③ Sometimes I'll suddenly feel lonely.

Gyu means "cow."

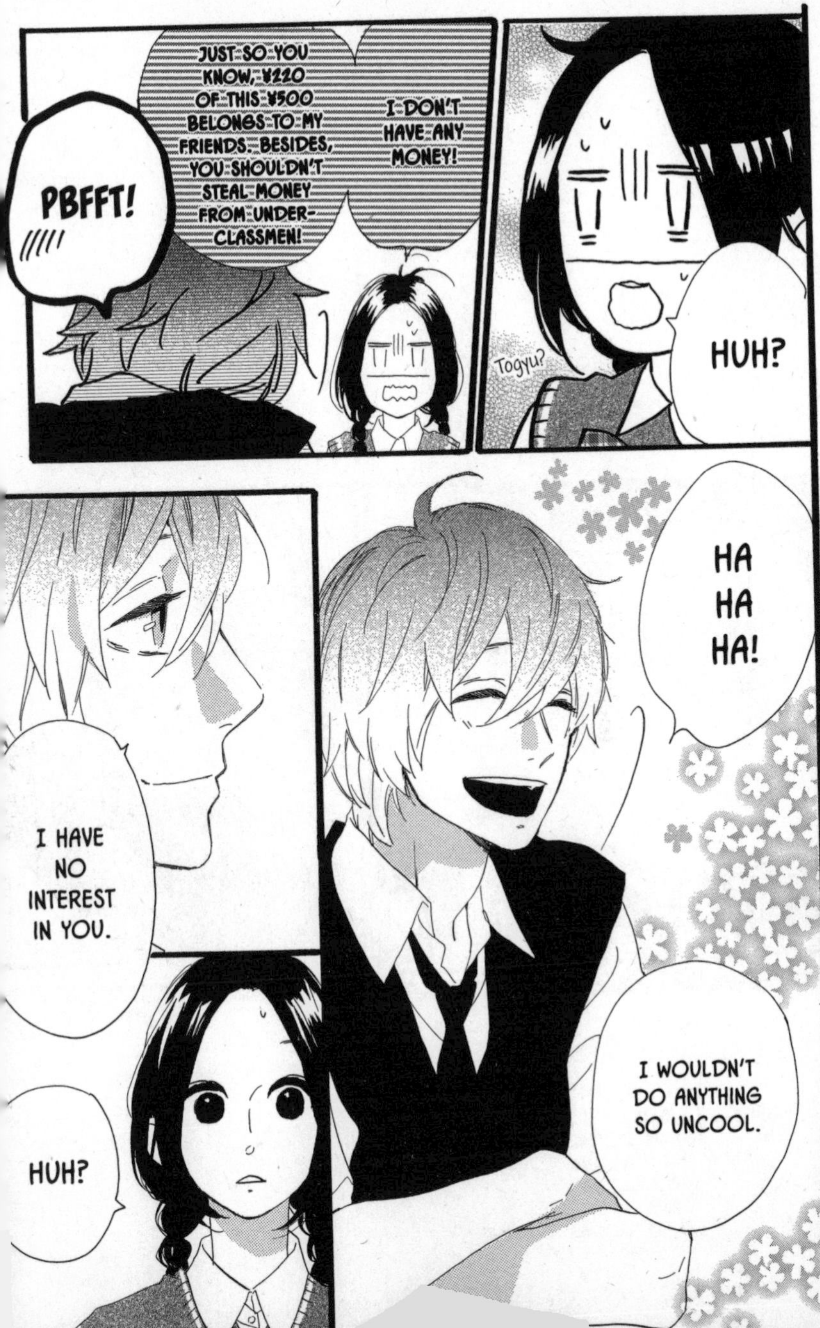
HUH?
Togyu?
I DON'T HAVE ANY MONEY!
JUST SO YOU KNOW, ¥220 OF THIS ¥500 BELONGS TO MY FRIENDS. BESIDES, YOU SHOULDN'T STEAL MONEY FROM UNDER-CLASSMEN!
PBFFT! /////
HA HA HA!
I WOULDN'T DO ANYTHING SO UNCOOL.
I HAVE NO INTEREST IN YOU.
HUH?

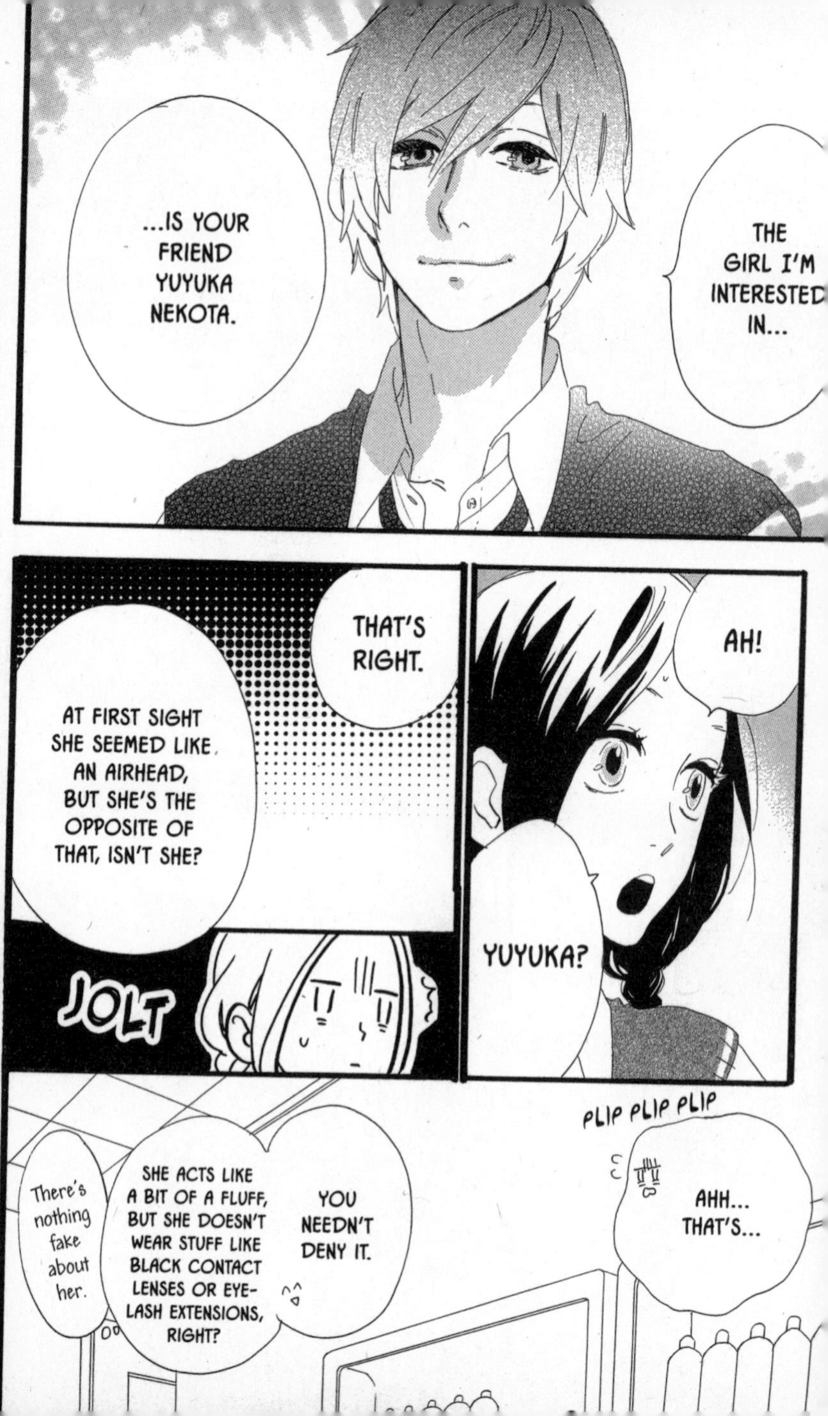
THE GIRL I'M INTERESTED IN...
...IS YOUR FRIEND YUYUKA NEKOTA.
AH!
YUYUKA?
THAT'S RIGHT.
AT FIRST SIGHT SHE SEEMED LIKE AN AIRHEAD, BUT SHE'S THE OPPOSITE OF THAT, ISN'T SHE?
JOLT
PLIP PLIP PLIP
AHH... THAT'S...
YOU NEEDN'T DENY IT.
SHE ACTS LIKE A BIT OF A FLUFF, BUT SHE DOESN'T WEAR STUFF LIKE BLACK CONTACT LENSES OR EYE-LASH EXTENSIONS, RIGHT?
There's nothing fake about her.

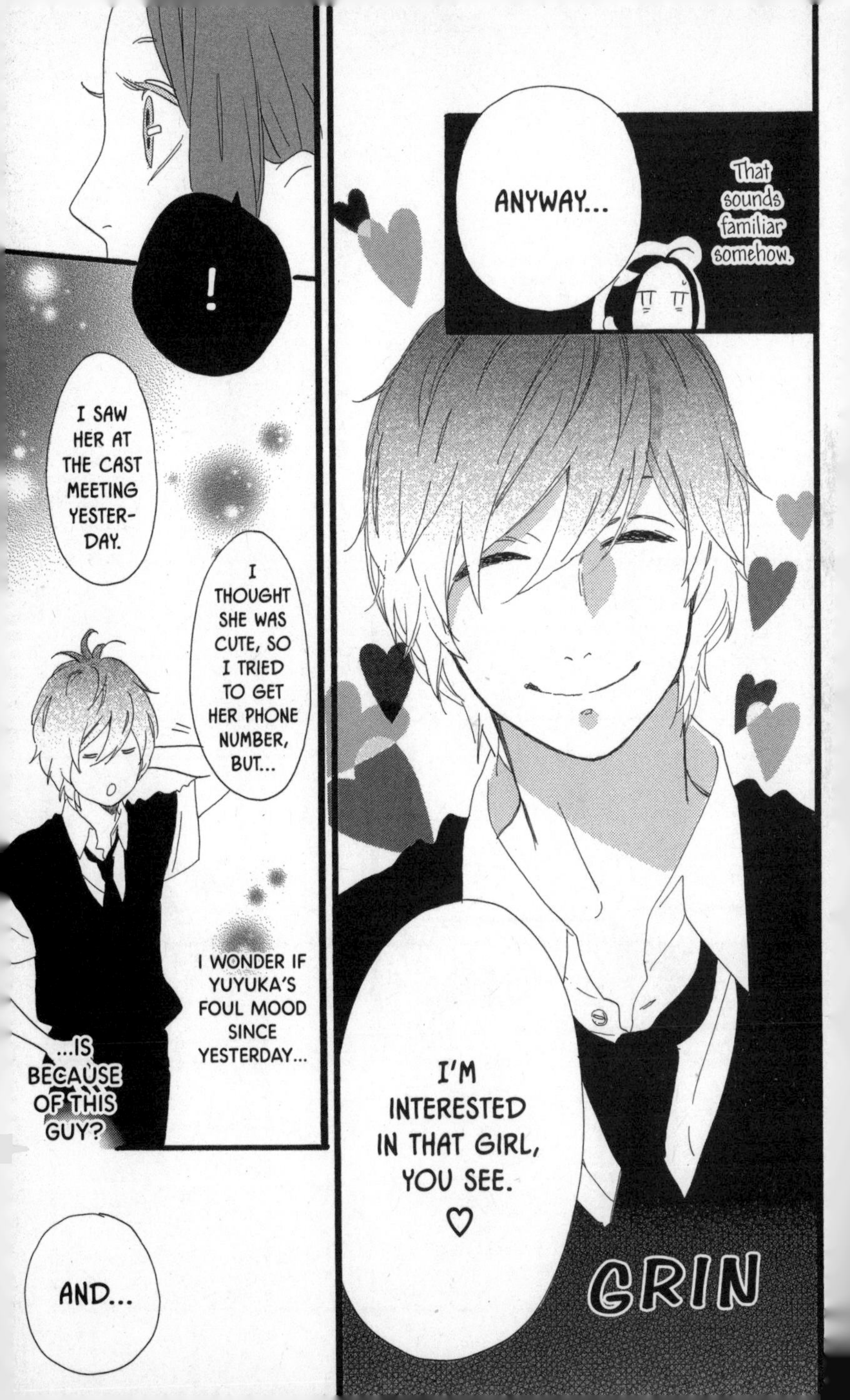
ANYWAY...
That sounds familiar somehow.
I'M INTERESTED IN THAT GIRL, YOU SEE. ♡
GRIN
!
I SAW HER AT THE CAST MEETING YESTER-DAY.
I THOUGHT SHE WAS CUTE, SO I TRIED TO GET HER PHONE NUMBER, BUT...
I WONDER IF YUYUKA'S FOUL MOOD SINCE YESTERDAY...
...IS BECAUSE OF THIS GUY?
AND...

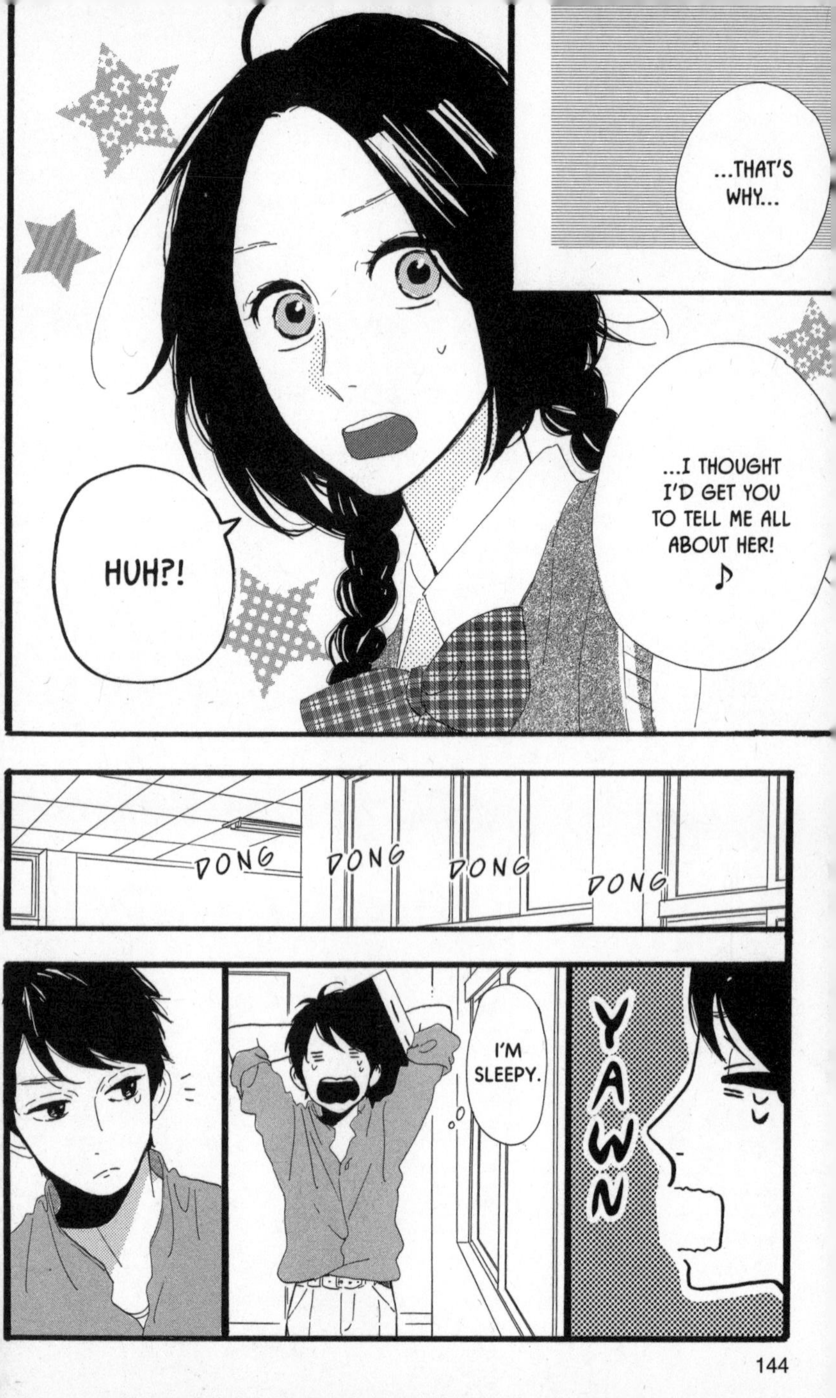
...THAT'S WHY...
...I THOUGHT I'D GET YOU TO TELL ME ALL ABOUT HER! ♪
HUH?!
DONG DONG DONG DONG
YAWN
I'M SLEEPY.

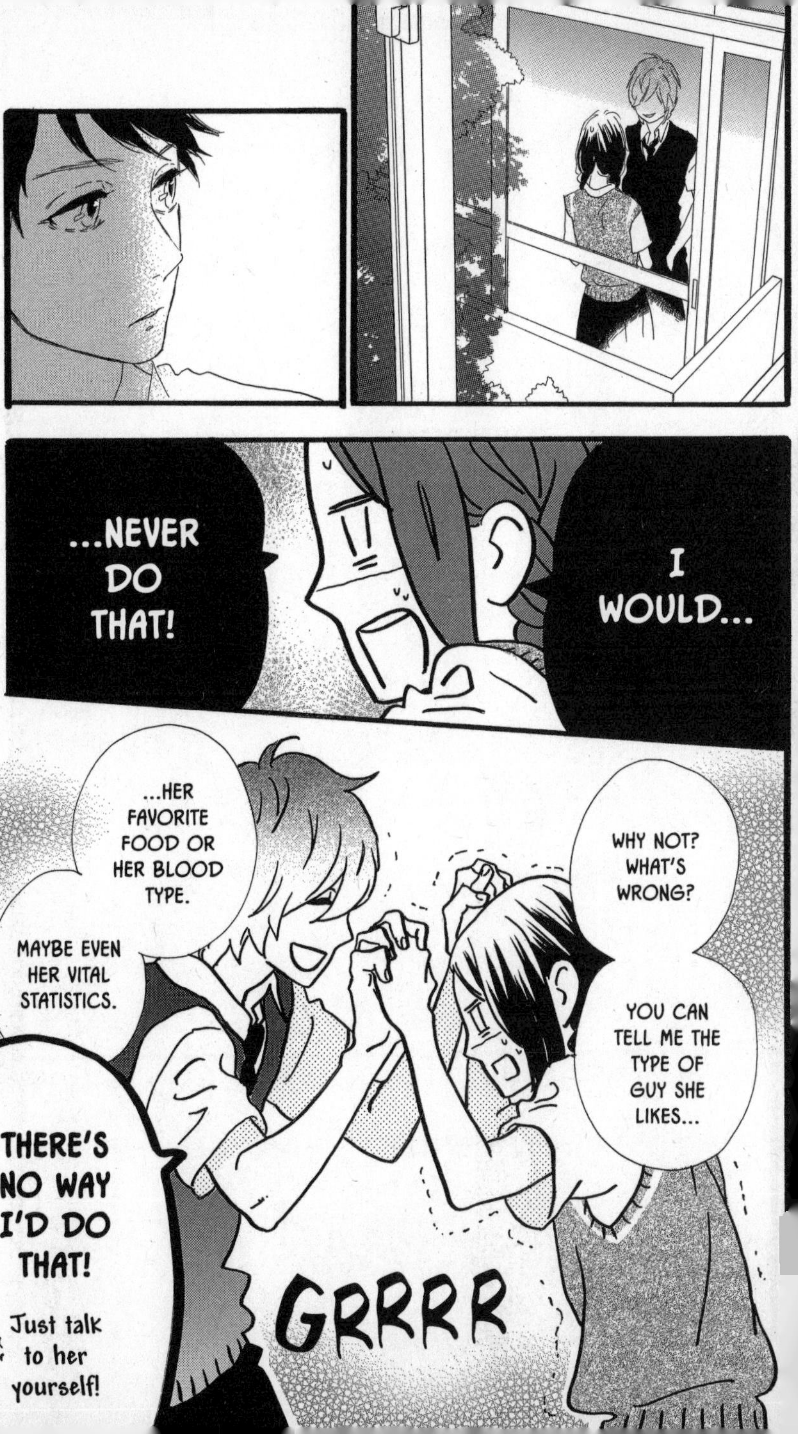
I WOULD...
...NEVER DO THAT!
WHY NOT? WHAT'S WRONG?
YOU CAN TELL ME THE TYPE OF GUY SHE LIKES...
...HER FAVORITE FOOD OR HER BLOOD TYPE.
MAYBE EVEN HER VITAL STATISTICS.
THERE'S NO WAY I'D DO THAT!
GRRRR
Just talk to her yourself!

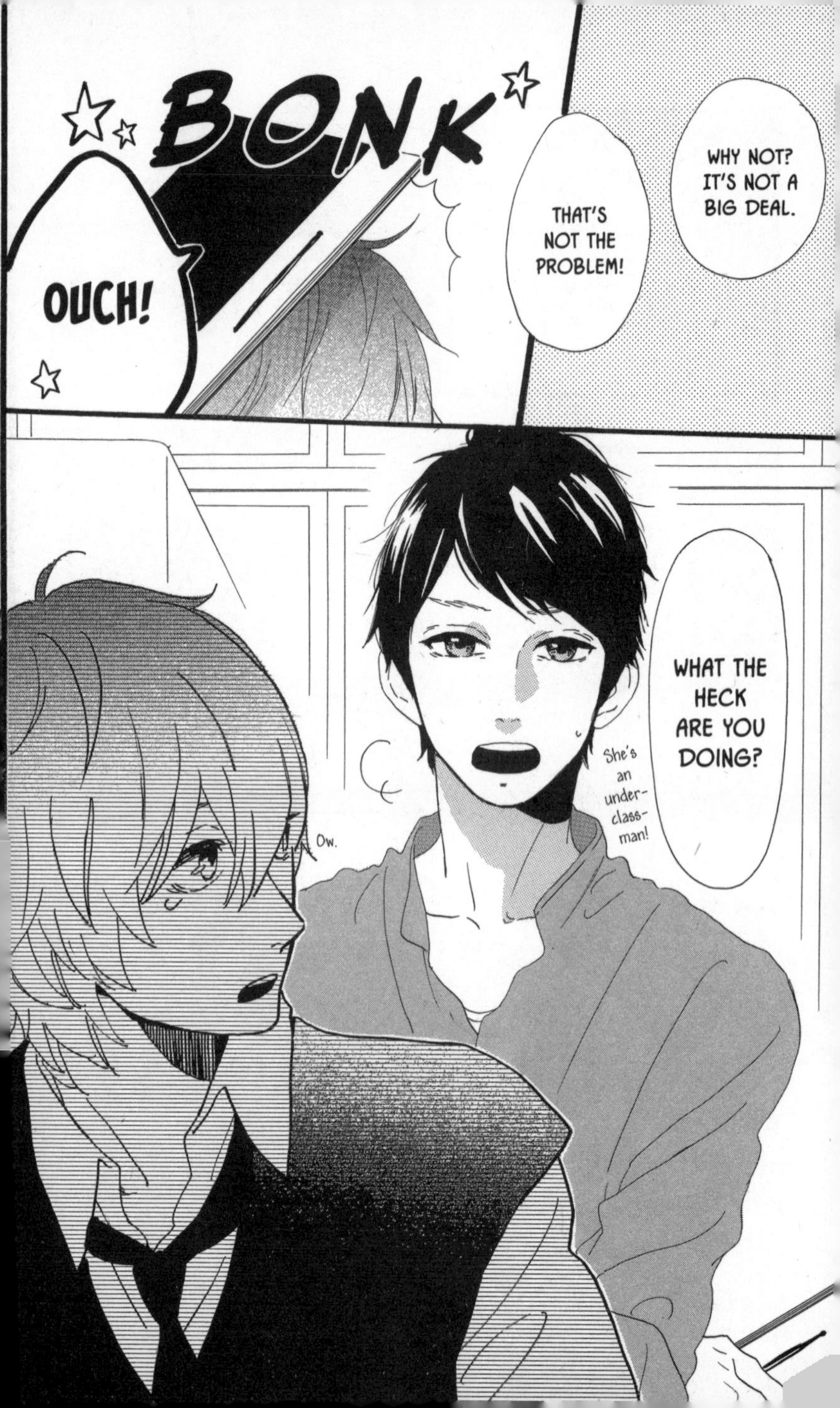
WHY NOT? IT'S NOT A BIG DEAL.
THAT'S NOT THE PROBLEM!
BONK
OUCH!
WHAT THE HECK ARE YOU DOING?
She's an under-class-man!
Ow.

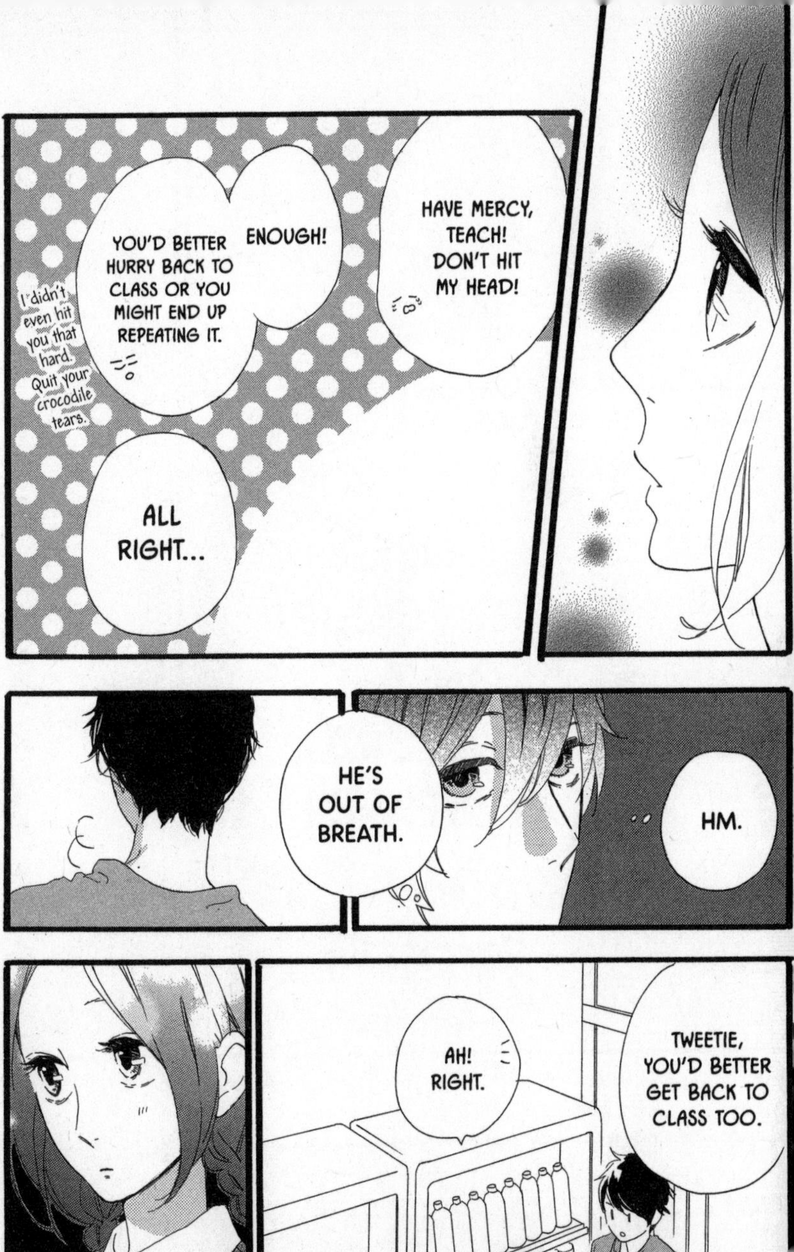
HAVE MERCY, TEACH! DON'T HIT MY HEAD!
ENOUGH!
YOU'D BETTER HURRY BACK TO CLASS OR YOU MIGHT END UP REPEATING IT.
I didn't even hit you that hard. Quit your crocodile tears.
ALL RIGHT...
HM.
HE'S OUT OF BREATH.
TWEETIE, YOU'D BETTER GET BACK TO CLASS TOO.
AH! RIGHT.

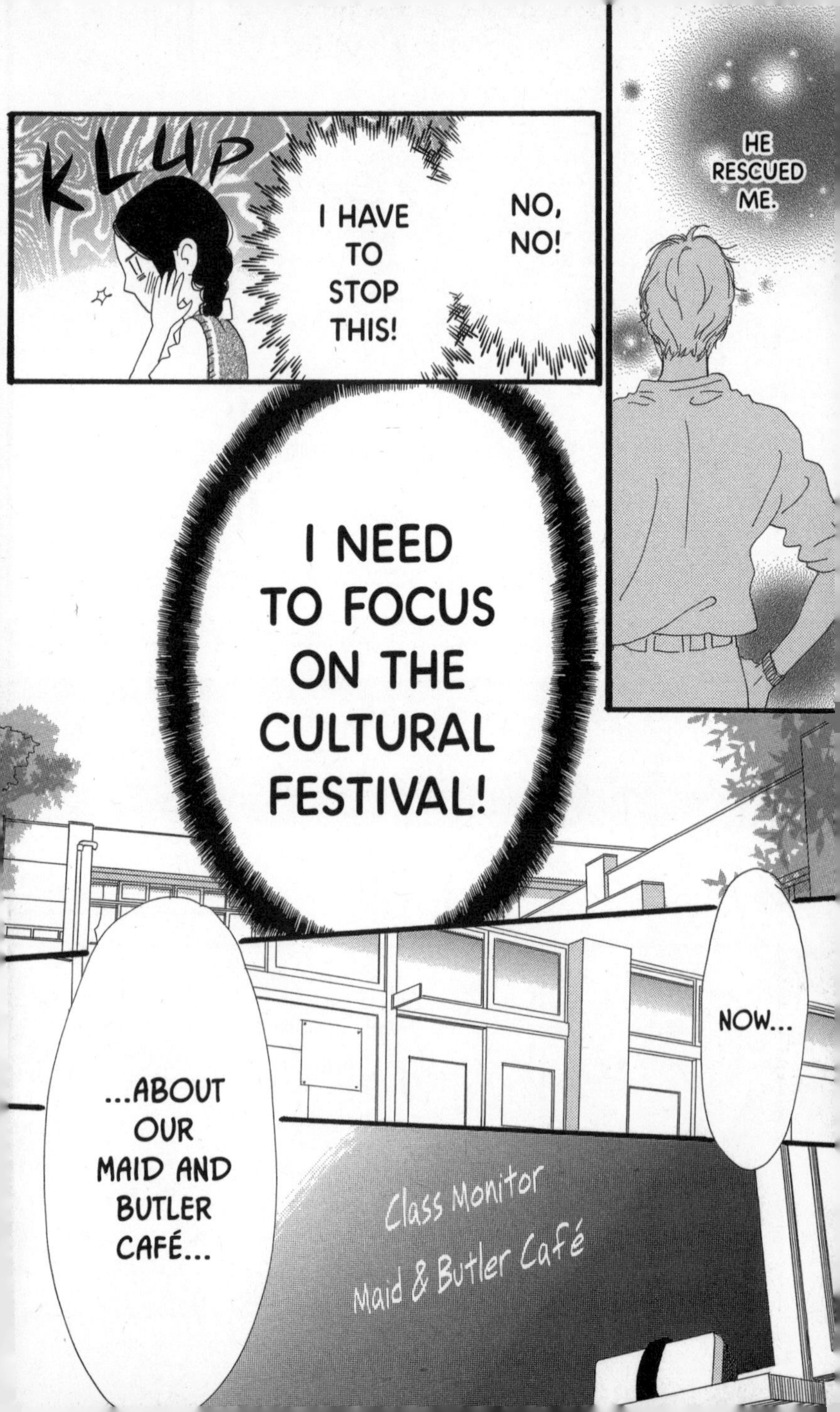
HE RESCUED ME.
KLUP
NO, NO!
I HAVE TO STOP THIS!
I NEED TO FOCUS ON THE CULTURAL FESTIVAL!
NOW...
...ABOUT OUR MAID AND BUTLER CAFÉ...
Class Monitor
Maid & Butler Café

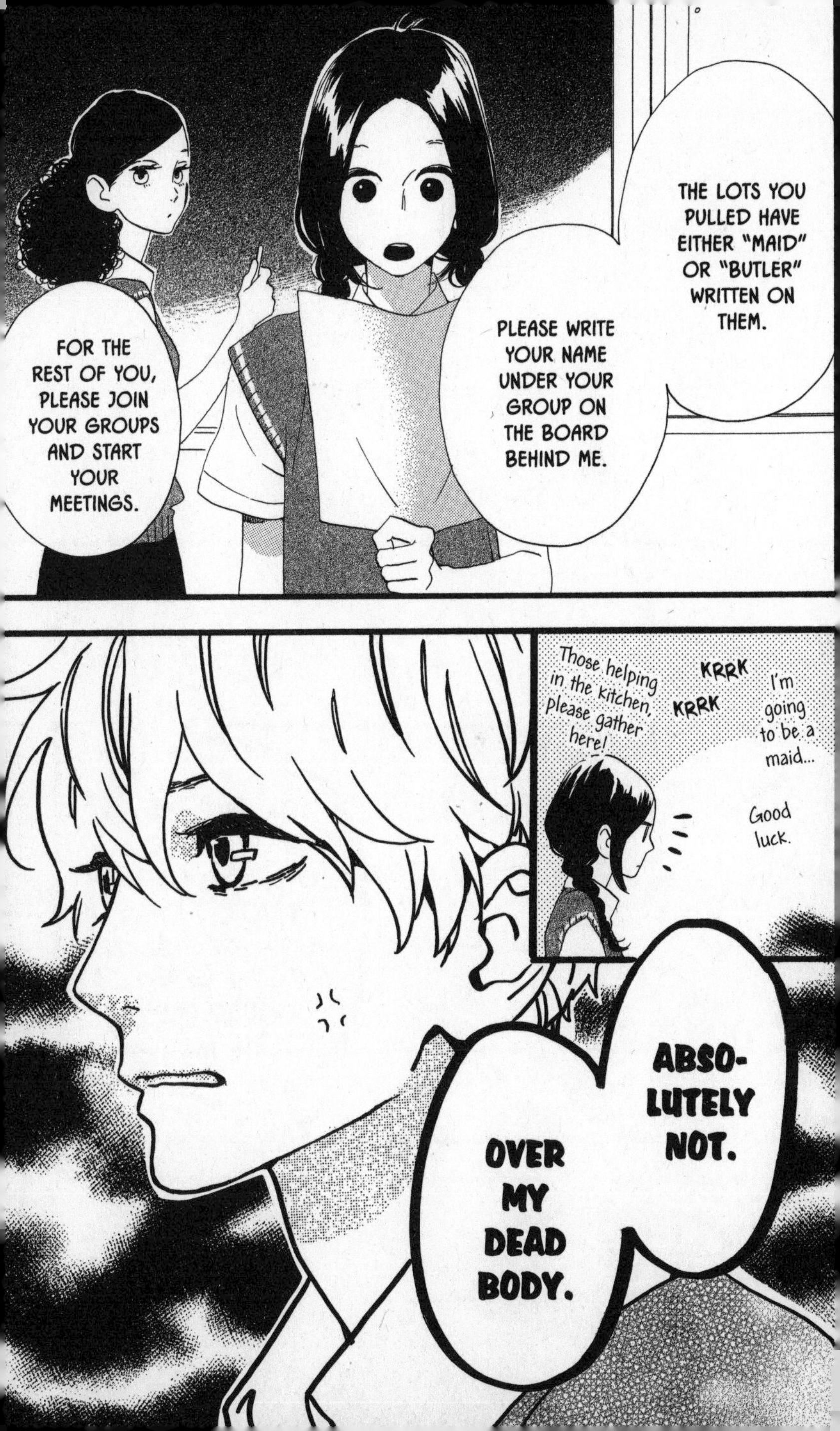
THE LOTS YOU PULLED HAVE EITHER "MAID" OR "BUTLER" WRITTEN ON THEM.
PLEASE WRITE YOUR NAME UNDER YOUR GROUP ON THE BOARD BEHIND ME.
FOR THE REST OF YOU, PLEASE JOIN YOUR GROUPS AND START YOUR MEETINGS.
I'm going to be a maid...
Good luck.
KRRK
KRRK
Those helping in the kitchen, please gather here!
ABSO-LUTELY NOT.
OVER MY DEAD BODY.

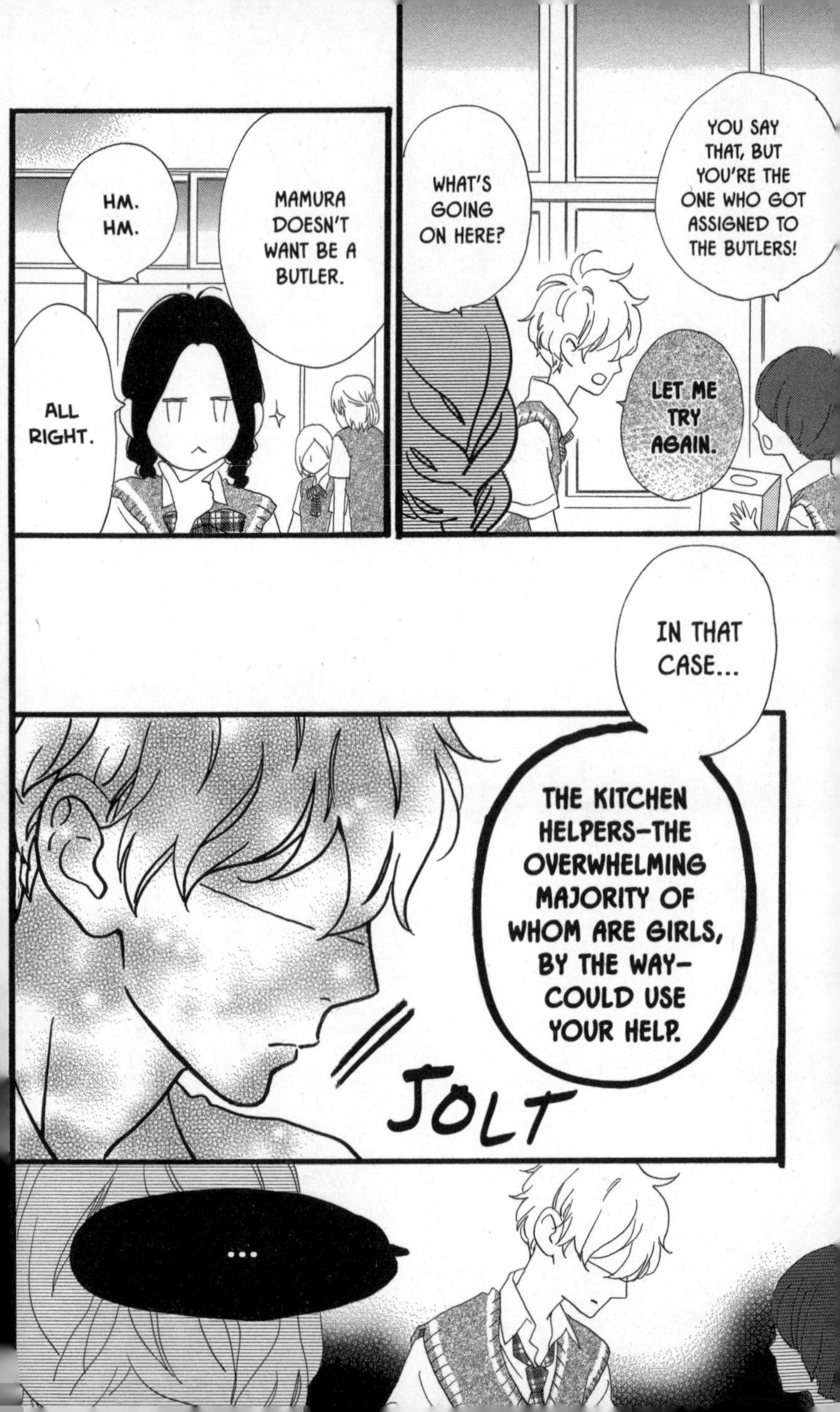
YOU SAY THAT, BUT YOU'RE THE ONE WHO GOT ASSIGNED TO THE BUTLERS!
WHAT'S GOING ON HERE?
LET ME TRY AGAIN.
MAMURA DOESN'T WANT BE A BUTLER.
HM. HM.
ALL RIGHT.
IN THAT CASE...
THE KITCHEN HELPERS—THE OVERWHELMING MAJORITY OF WHOM ARE GIRLS, BY THE WAY—COULD USE YOUR HELP.
JOLT
...

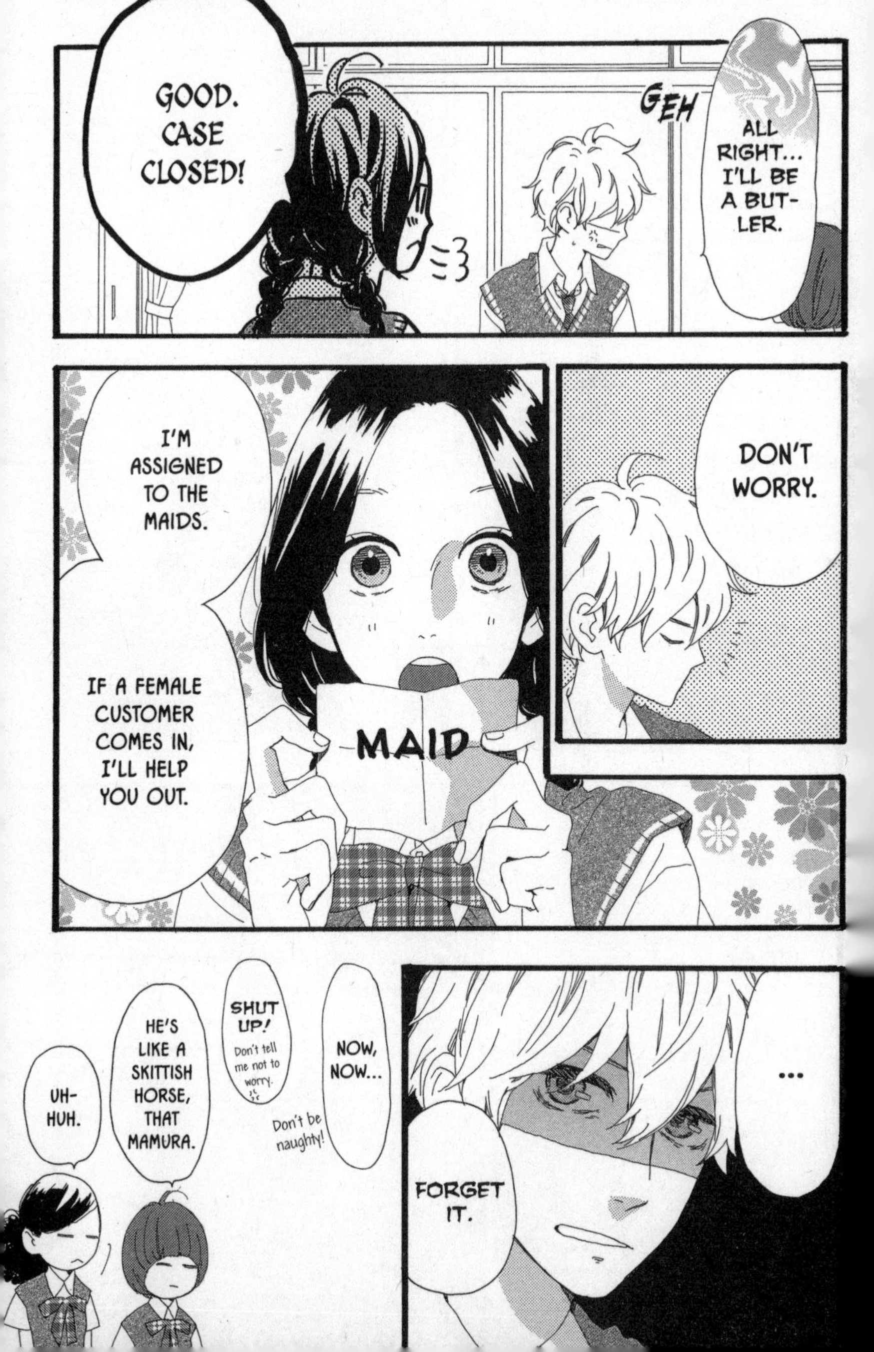
GEH
ALL RIGHT... I'LL BE A BUT- LER.
GOOD. CASE CLOSED!
DON'T WORRY.
I'M ASSIGNED TO THE MAIDS.
IF A FEMALE CUSTOMER COMES IN, I'LL HELP YOU OUT.
MAID
...
FORGET IT.
NOW, NOW...
Don't be naughty!
SHUT UP! Don't tell me not to worry.
HE'S LIKE A SKITTISH HORSE, THAT MAMURA.
UH-HUH.

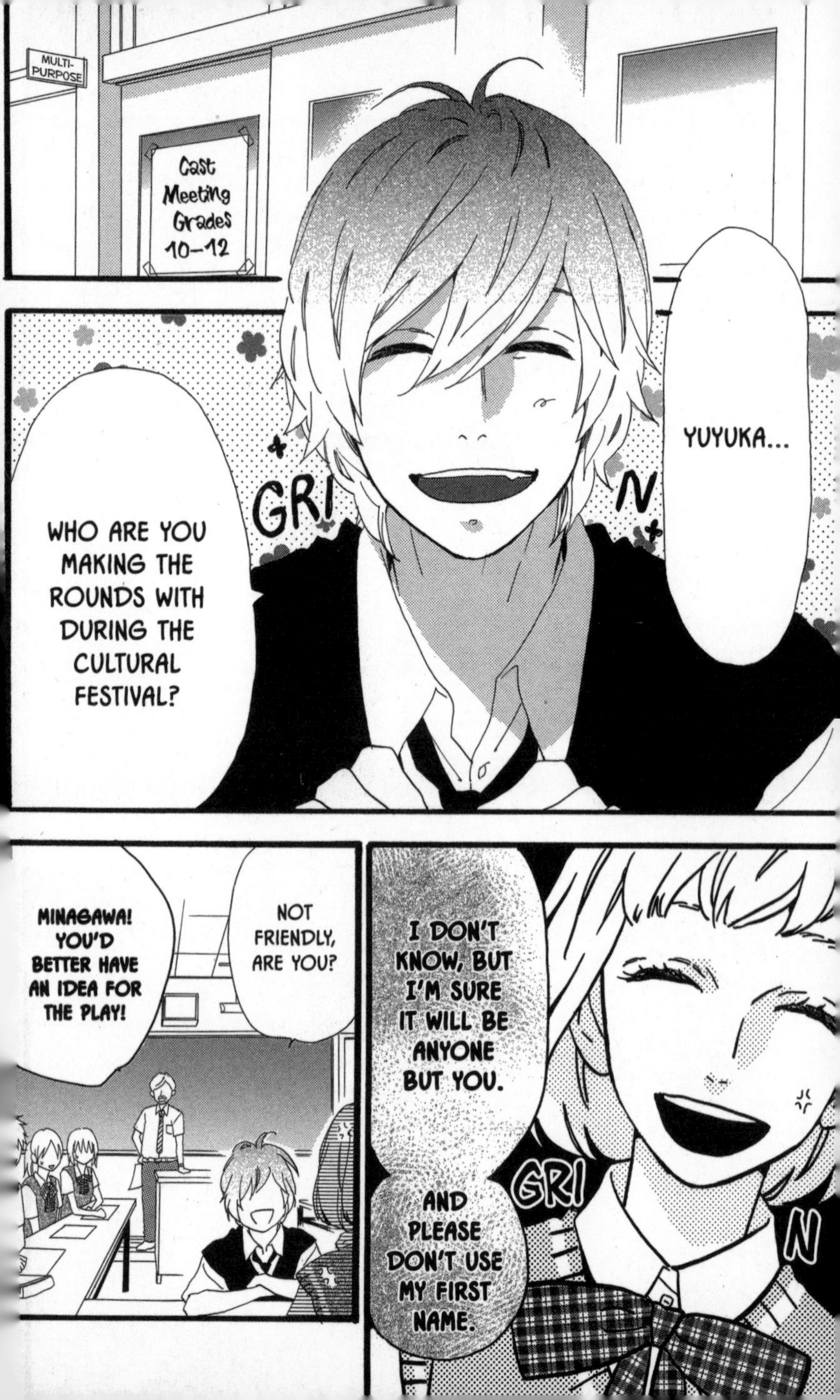
MULTI-PURPOSE
Cast Meeting Grades 10-12
YUYUKA...
GRIN
WHO ARE YOU MAKING THE ROUNDS WITH DURING THE CULTURAL FESTIVAL?
I DON'T KNOW, BUT I'M SURE IT WILL BE ANYONE BUT YOU.
AND PLEASE DON'T USE MY FIRST NAME.
GRIN
NOT FRIENDLY, ARE YOU?
MINAGAWA! YOU'D BETTER HAVE AN IDEA FOR THE PLAY!

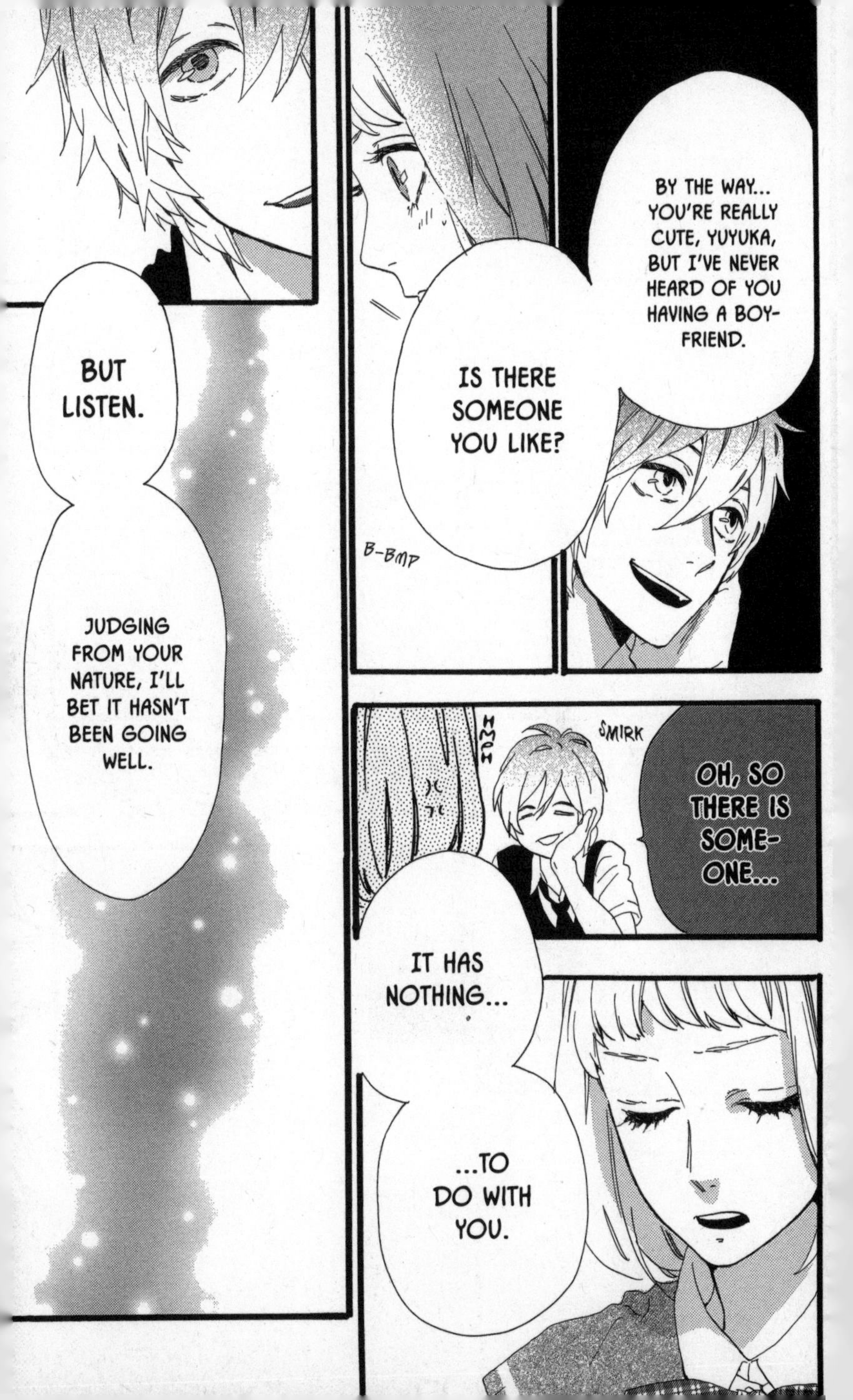
BY THE WAY... YOU'RE REALLY CUTE, YUYUKA, BUT I'VE NEVER HEARD OF YOU HAVING A BOY-FRIEND.
IS THERE SOMEONE YOU LIKE?
B-BMP
SMIRK
OH, SO THERE IS SOME-ONE...
HMPH
IT HAS NOTHING...
...TO DO WITH YOU.
BUT LISTEN.
JUDGING FROM YOUR NATURE, I'LL BET IT HASN'T BEEN GOING WELL.

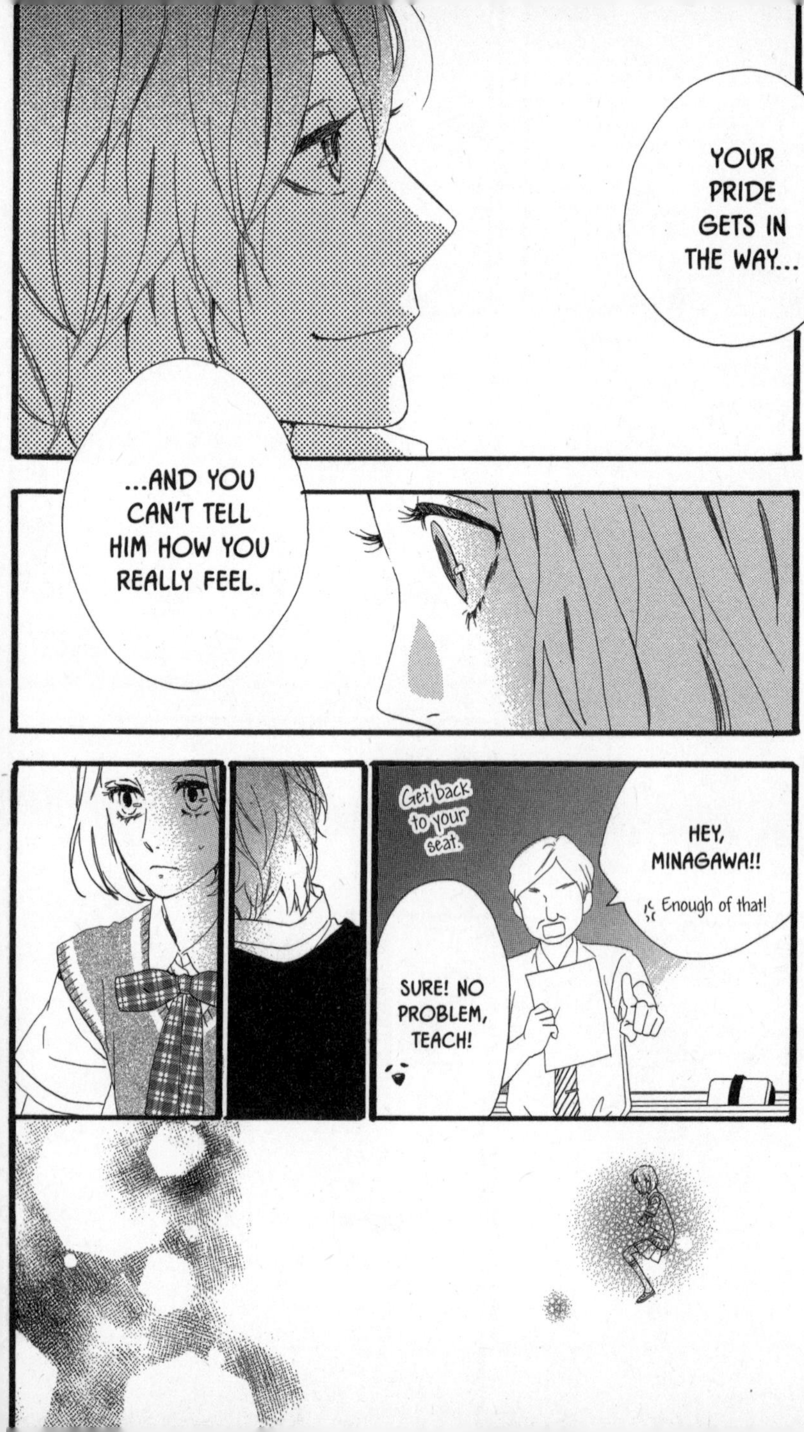
YOUR PRIDE GETS IN THE WAY...
...AND YOU CAN'T TELL HIM HOW YOU REALLY FEEL.
HEY, MINAGAWA!!
Enough of that!
Get back to your seat.
SURE! NO PROBLEM, TEACH!

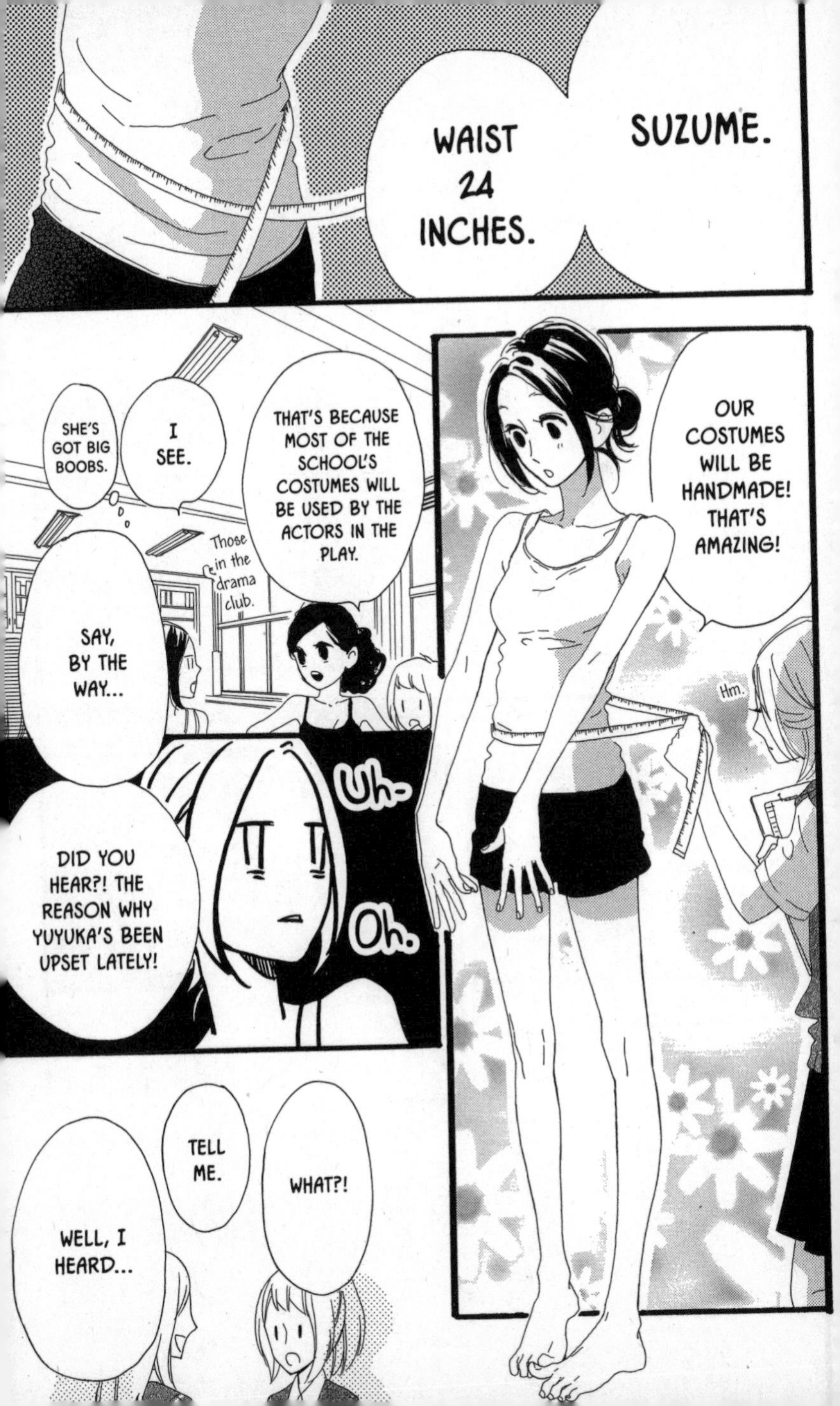
SUZUME.
WAIST 24 INCHES.
OUR COSTUMES WILL BE HANDMADE! THAT'S AMAZING!
Hm.
THAT'S BECAUSE MOST OF THE SCHOOL'S COSTUMES WILL BE USED BY THE ACTORS IN THE PLAY.
Those in the drama club.
I SEE.
SHE'S GOT BIG BOOBS.
SAY, BY THE WAY...
Uh-
Oh.
DID YOU HEAR?! THE REASON WHY YUYUKA'S BEEN UPSET LATELY!
WHAT?!
TELL ME.
WELL, I HEARD...

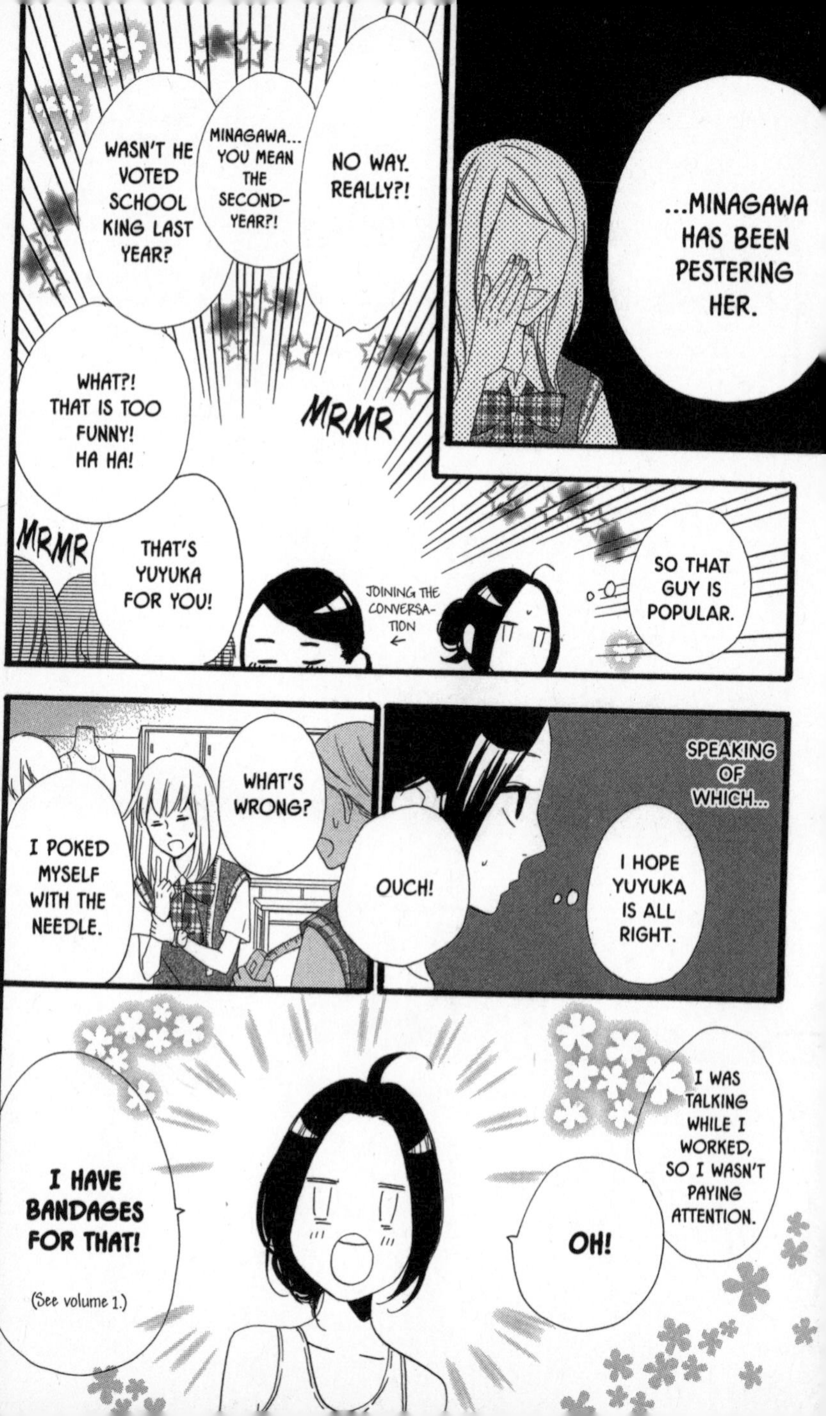
...MINAGAWA HAS BEEN PESTERING HER.
NO WAY. REALLY?!
MINAGAWA... YOU MEAN THE SECOND-YEAR?!
WASN'T HE VOTED SCHOOL KING LAST YEAR?
MRMR
WHAT?! THAT IS TOO FUNNY! HA HA!
SO THAT GUY IS POPULAR.
JOINING THE CONVERSA-TION
THAT'S YUYUKA FOR YOU!
MRMR
SPEAKING OF WHICH...
I HOPE YUYUKA IS ALL RIGHT.
OUCH!
WHAT'S WRONG?
I POKED MYSELF WITH THE NEEDLE.
I WAS TALKING WHILE I WORKED, SO I WASN'T PAYING ATTENTION.
OH!
I HAVE BANDAGES FOR THAT!
(See volume 1.)

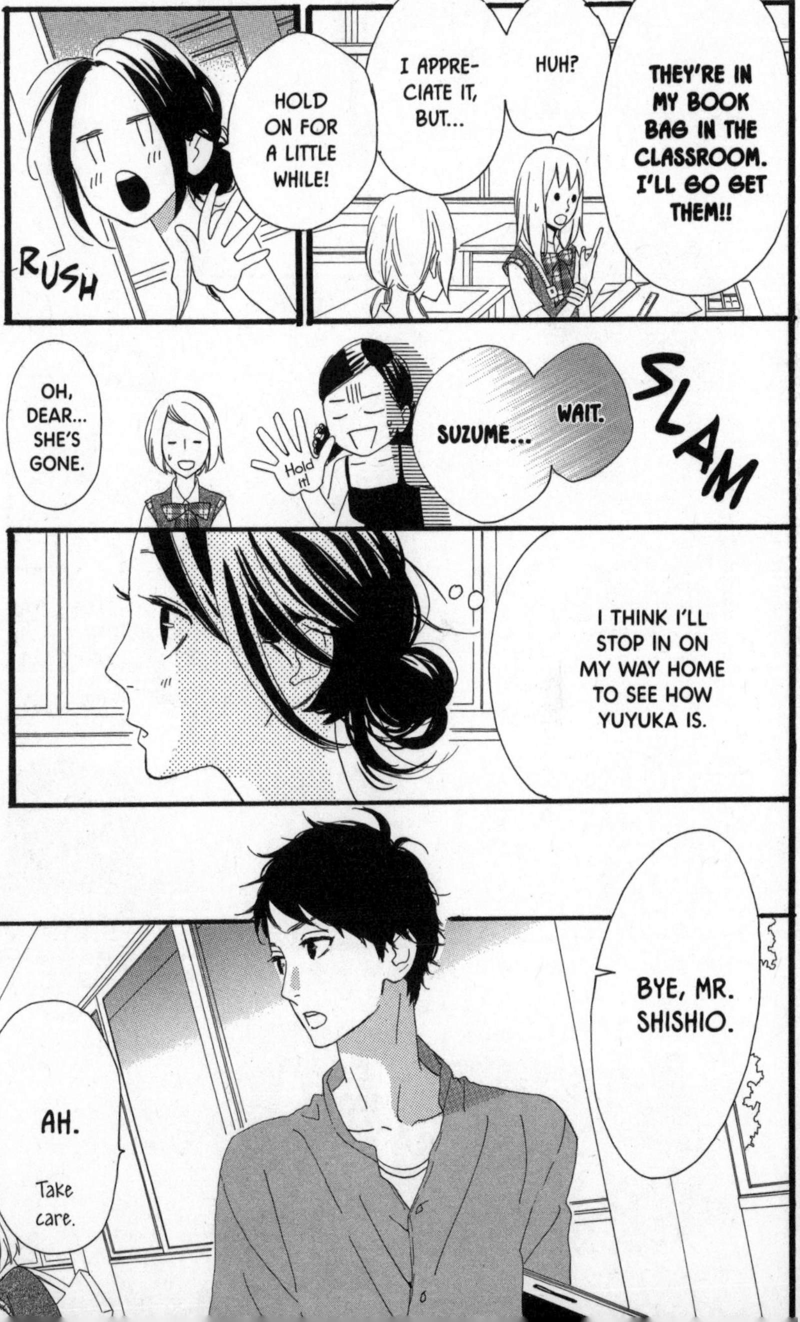
THEY'RE IN MY BOOK BAG IN THE CLASSROOM. I'LL GO GET THEM!!
HUH?
I APPRE-CIATE IT, BUT...
HOLD ON FOR A LITTLE WHILE!
RUSH
SLAM
SUZUME... WAIT.
Hold it!
OH, DEAR... SHE'S GONE.
I THINK I'LL STOP IN ON MY WAY HOME TO SEE HOW YUYUKA IS.
BYE, MR. SHISHIO.
AH.
Take care.

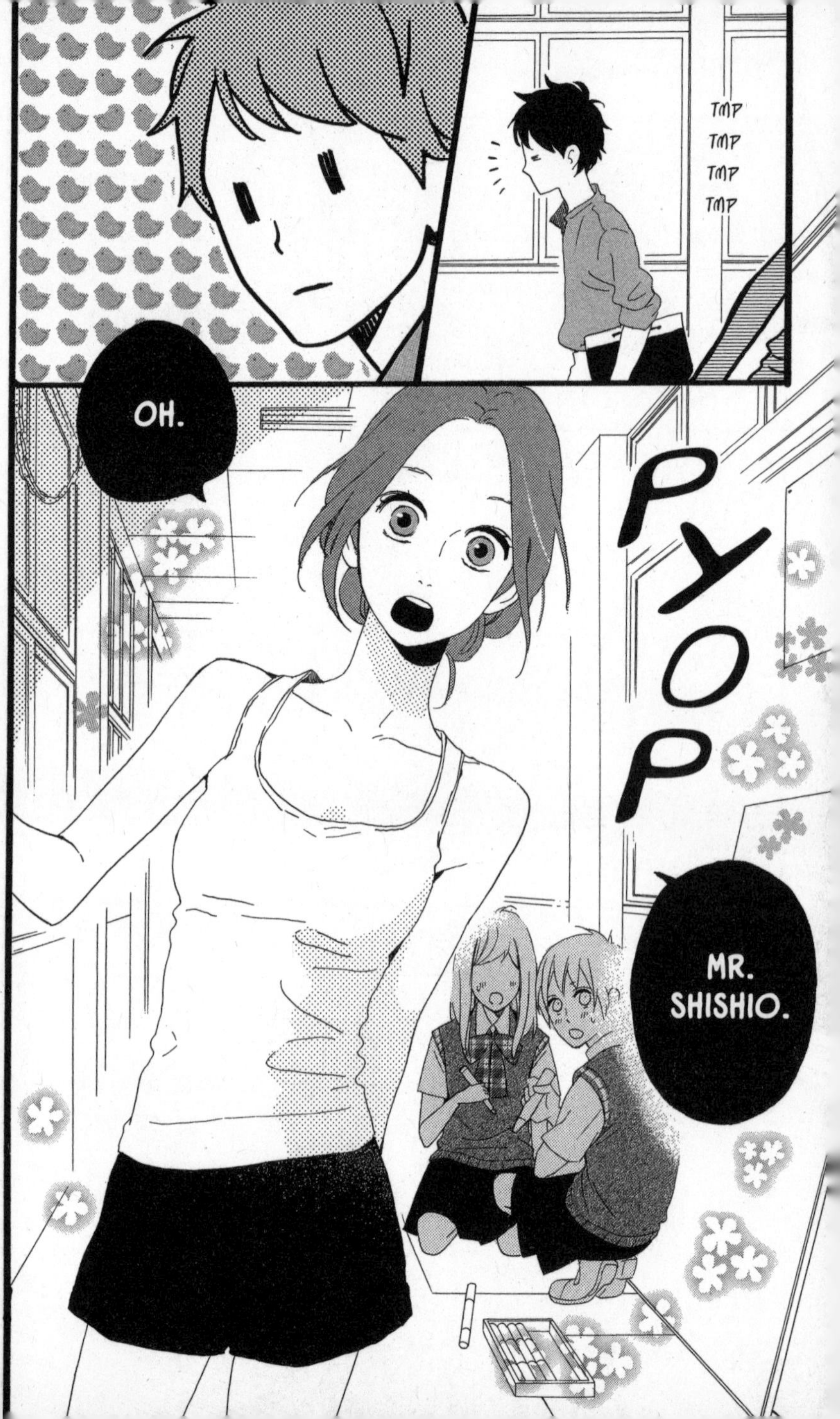
TMP
TMP
TMP
TMP
OH.
PYOP
MR. SHISHIO.

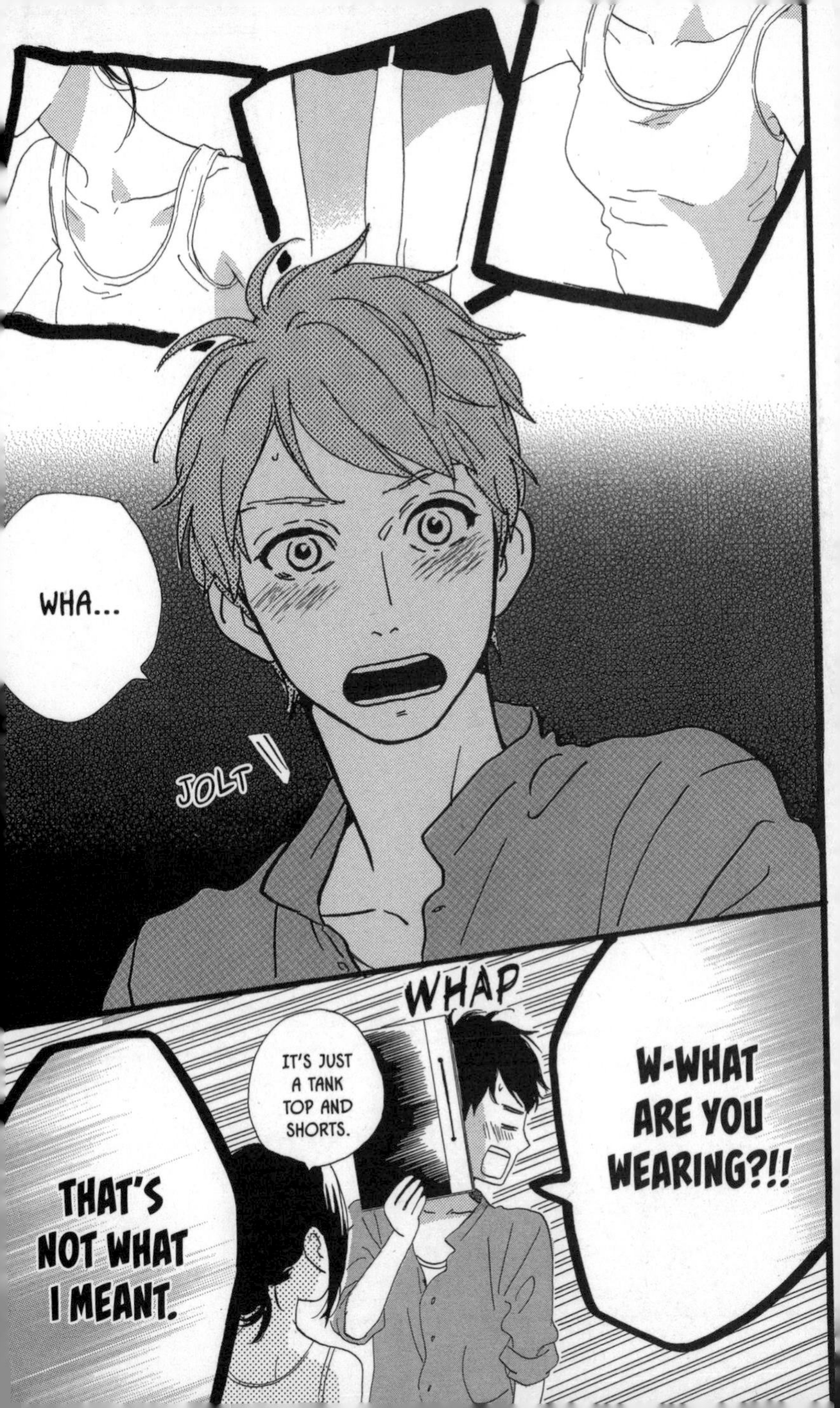
WHA...
JOLT
W-WHAT ARE YOU WEARING?!!
WHAP
IT'S JUST A TANK TOP AND SHORTS.
THAT'S NOT WHAT I MEANT.

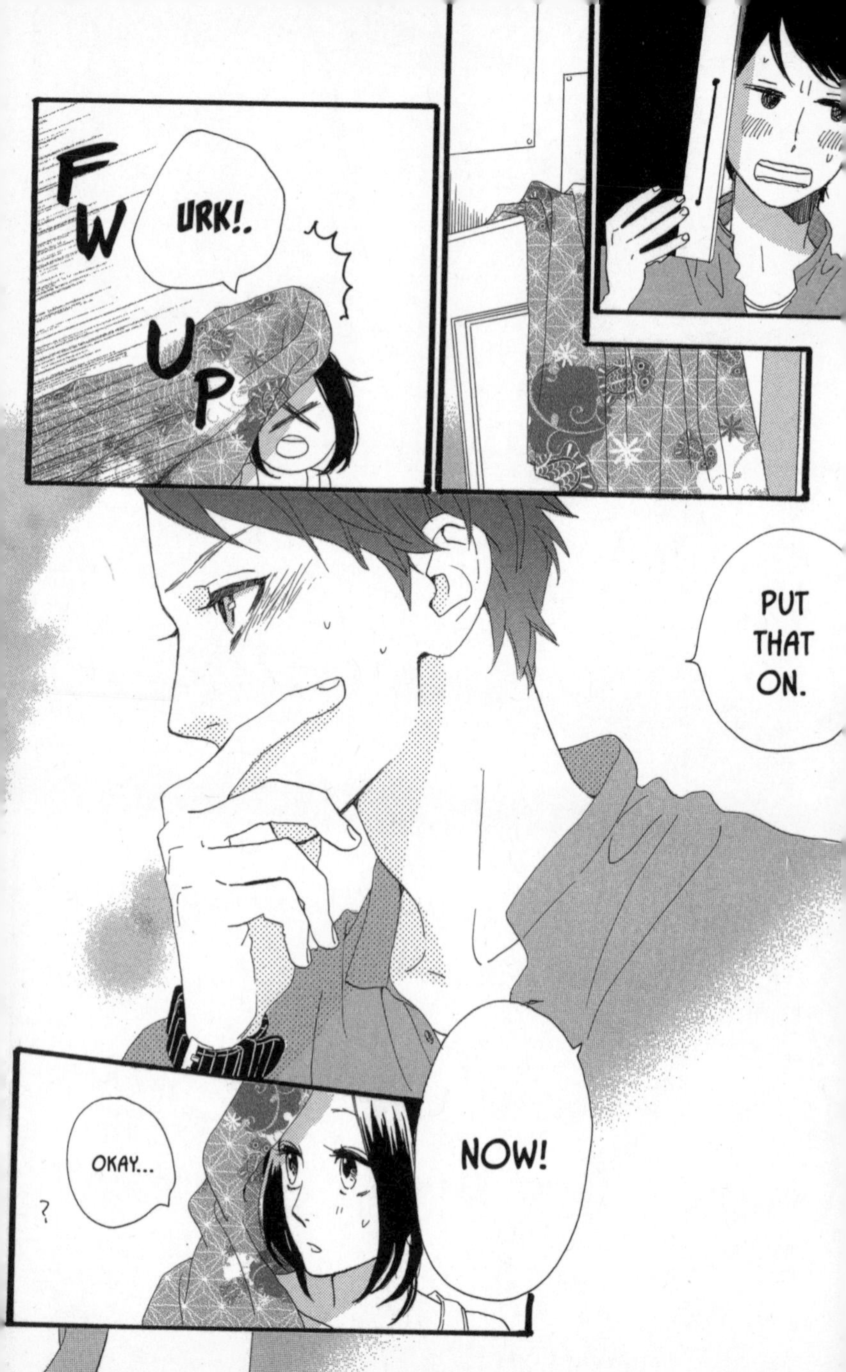
FWUP
URK!.
PUT THAT ON.
NOW!
OKAY...
?

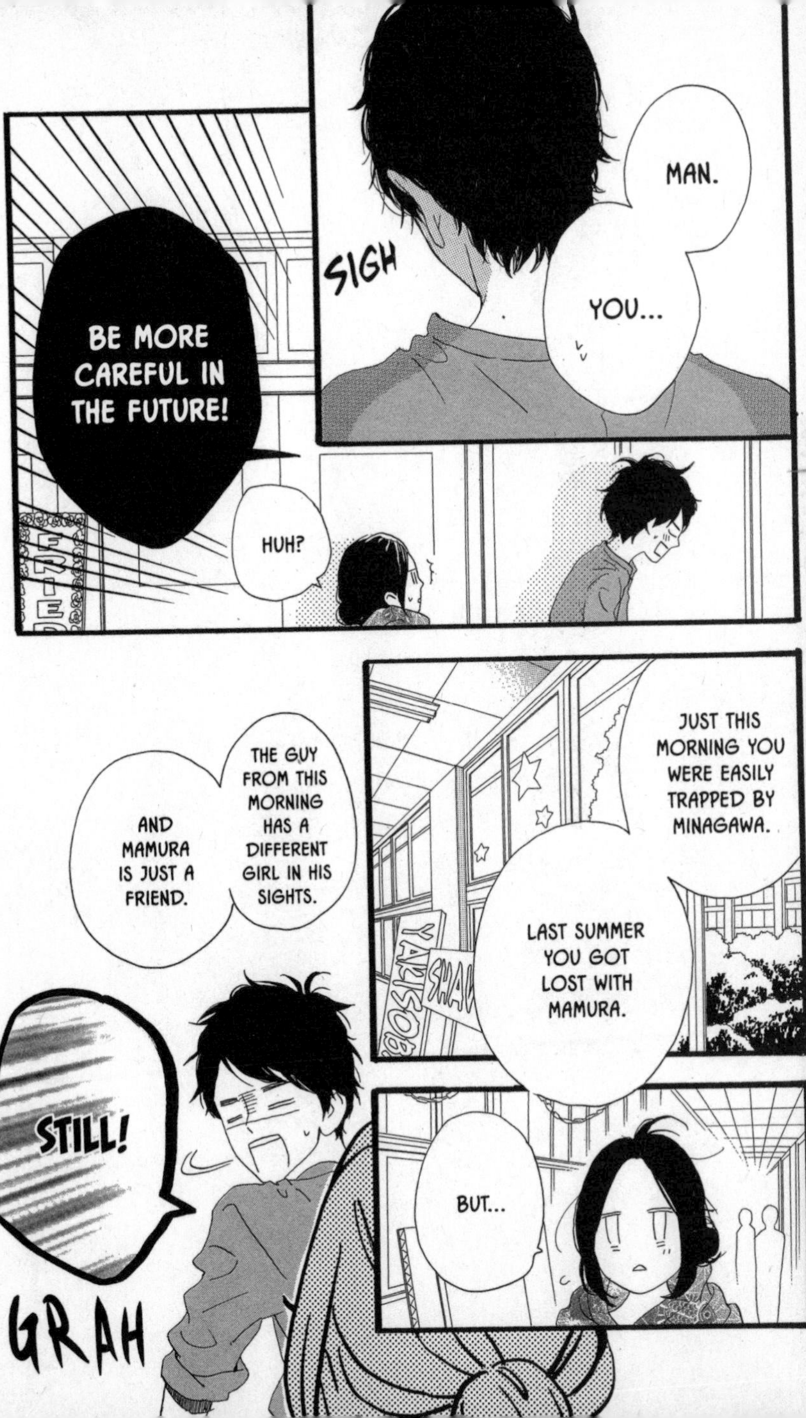
MAN.
YOU...
SIGH
BE MORE CAREFUL IN THE FUTURE!
HUH?
JUST THIS MORNING YOU WERE EASILY TRAPPED BY MINAGAWA.
LAST SUMMER YOU GOT LOST WITH MAMURA.
THE GUY FROM THIS MORNING HAS A DIFFERENT GIRL IN HIS SIGHTS.
AND MAMURA IS JUST A FRIEND.
BUT...
STILL!
GRAH

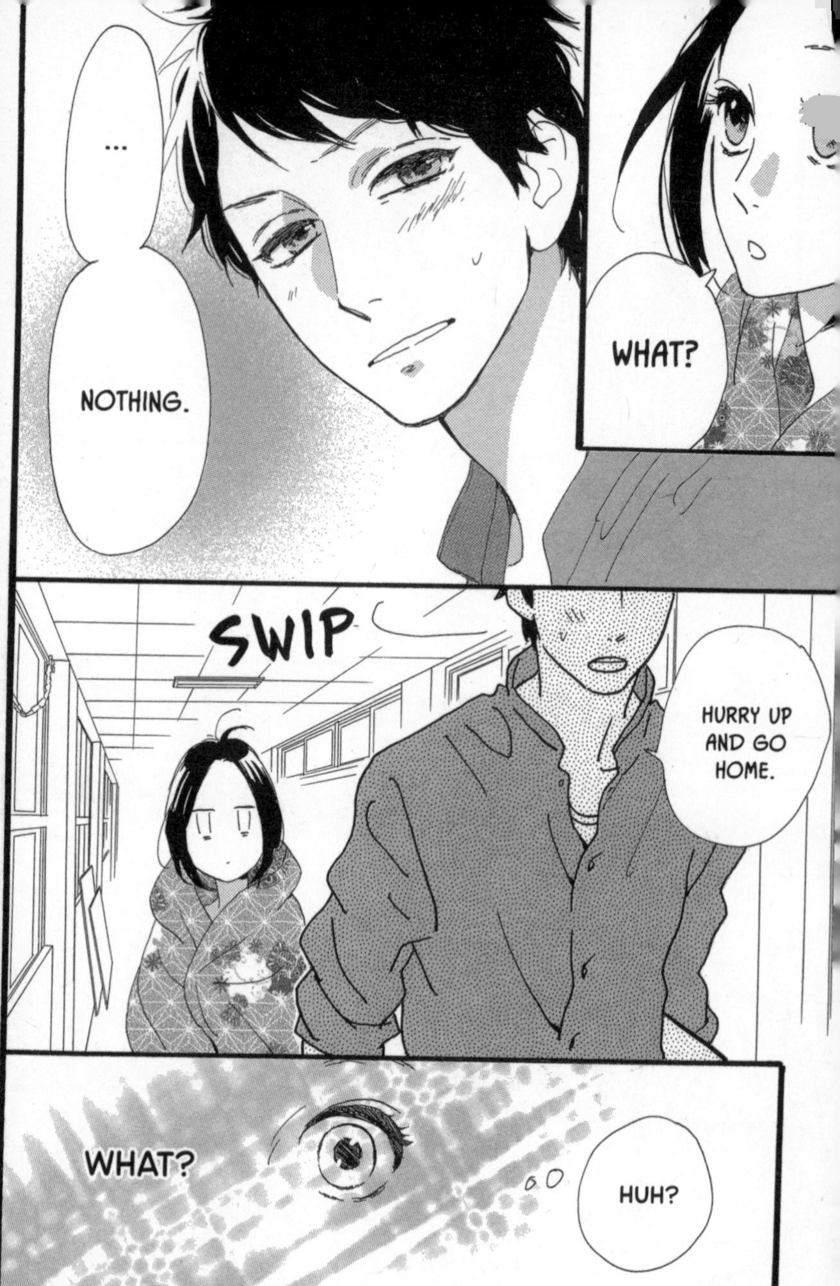
WHAT?
...
NOTHING.
HURRY UP AND GO HOME.
SWIP
HUH?
WHAT?

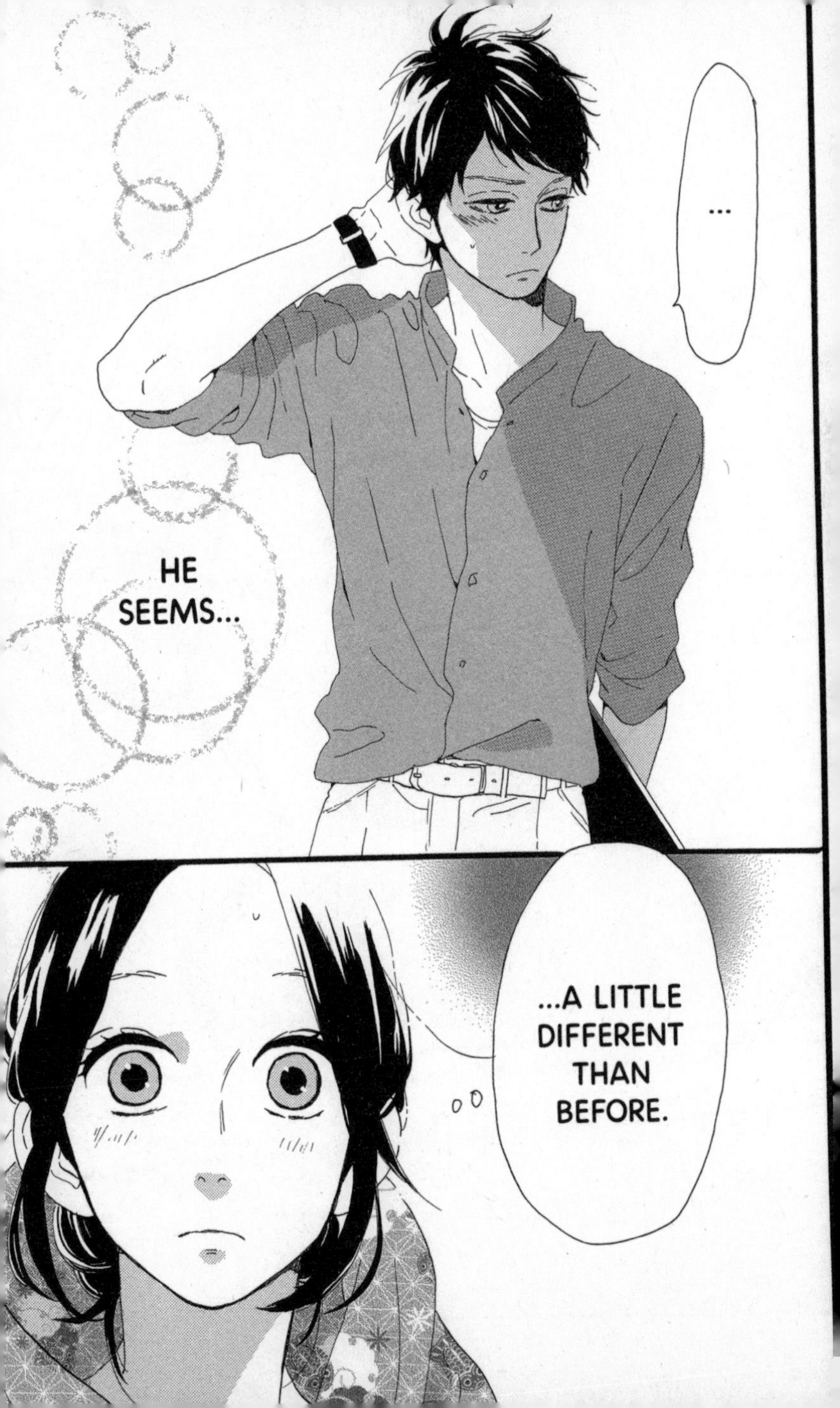
...
HE SEEMS...
...A LITTLE DIFFERENT THAN BEFORE.

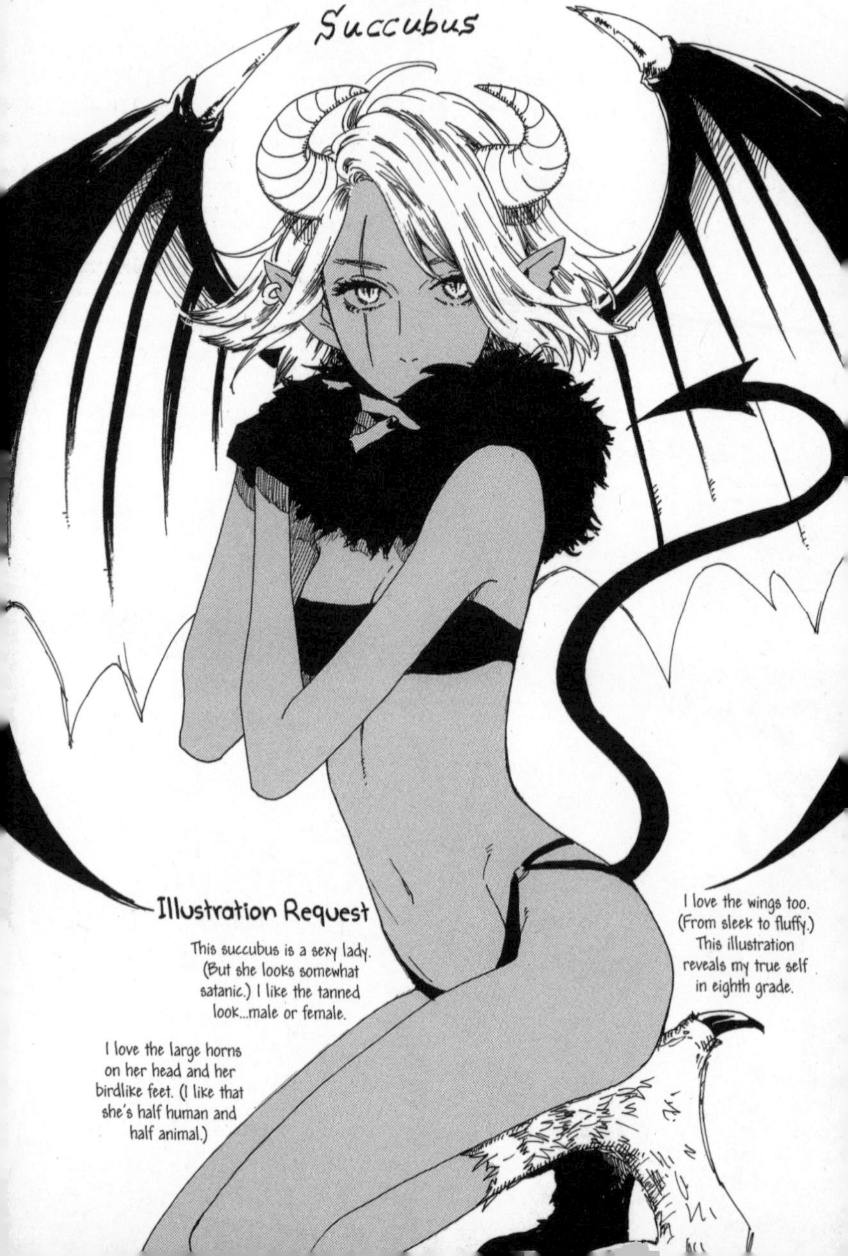

Succubus
Illustration Request
This succubus is a sexy lady. (But she looks somewhat satanic.) I like the tanned look...male or female.
I love the large horns on her head and her birdlike feet. (I like that she's half human and half animal.)
I love the wings too. (From sleek to fluffy.) This illustration reveals my true self in eighth grade.

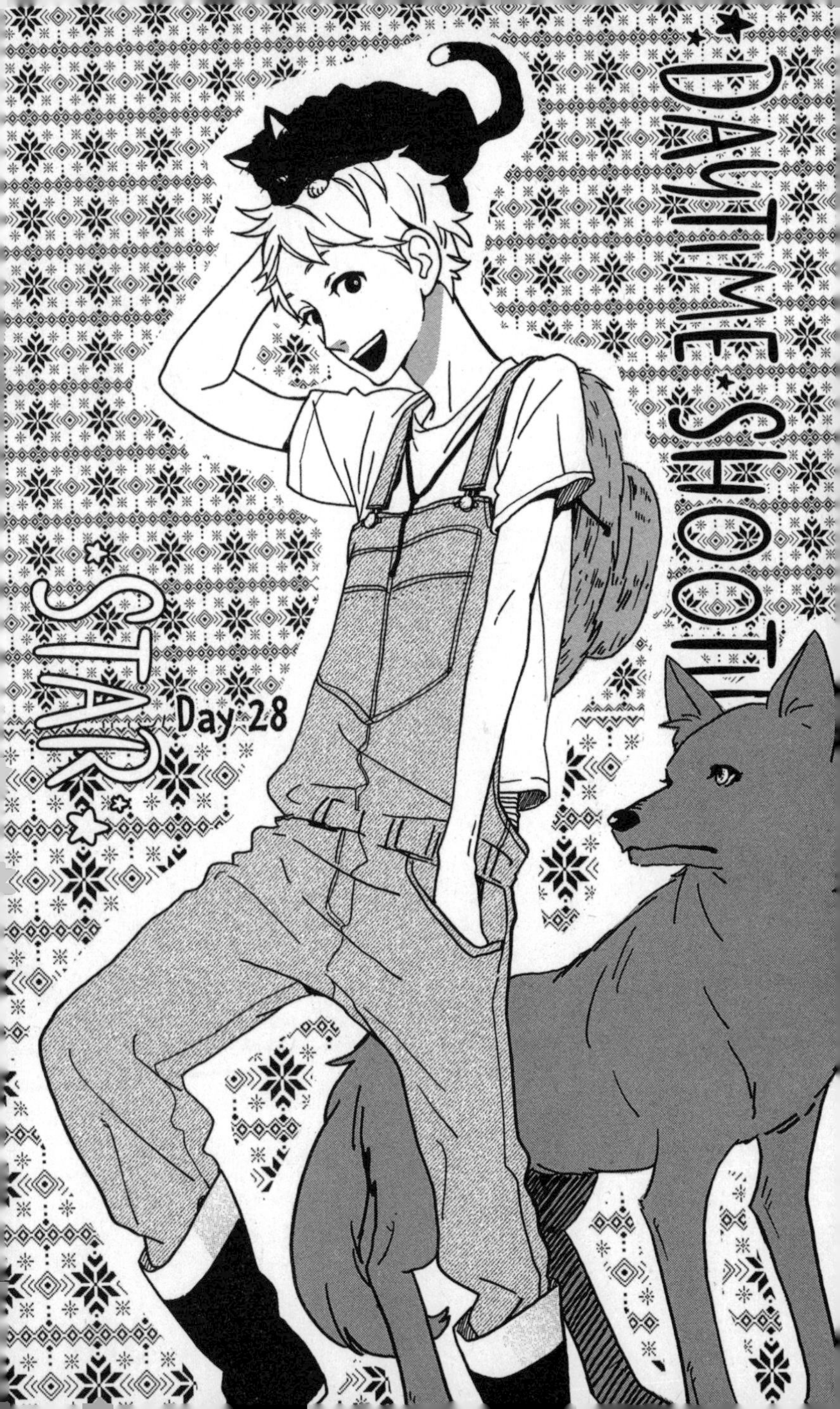

DAYTIME SHOOTING STAR
Day 28

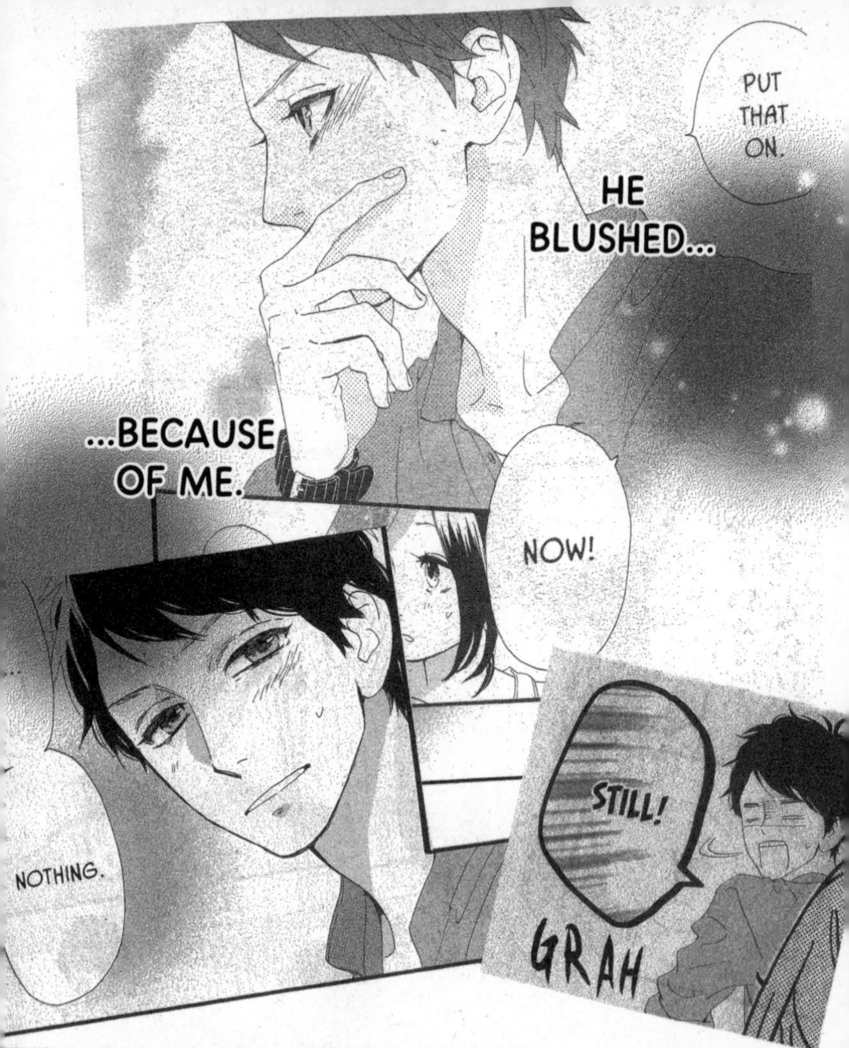
PUT THAT ON.
HE BLUSHED...
...BECAUSE OF ME.
NOW!
NOTHING.
STILL!
GRAH

Afterword How are you liking *Daytime Shooting Star*? Let's meet again in volume 5.

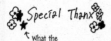

Special Thanx ★ My editor, my assistants, members of the editorial dept., designers, printer's staff, my family, my friends, my readers, and everyone else who is supporting me.

↖ What the heck is that?

Mika

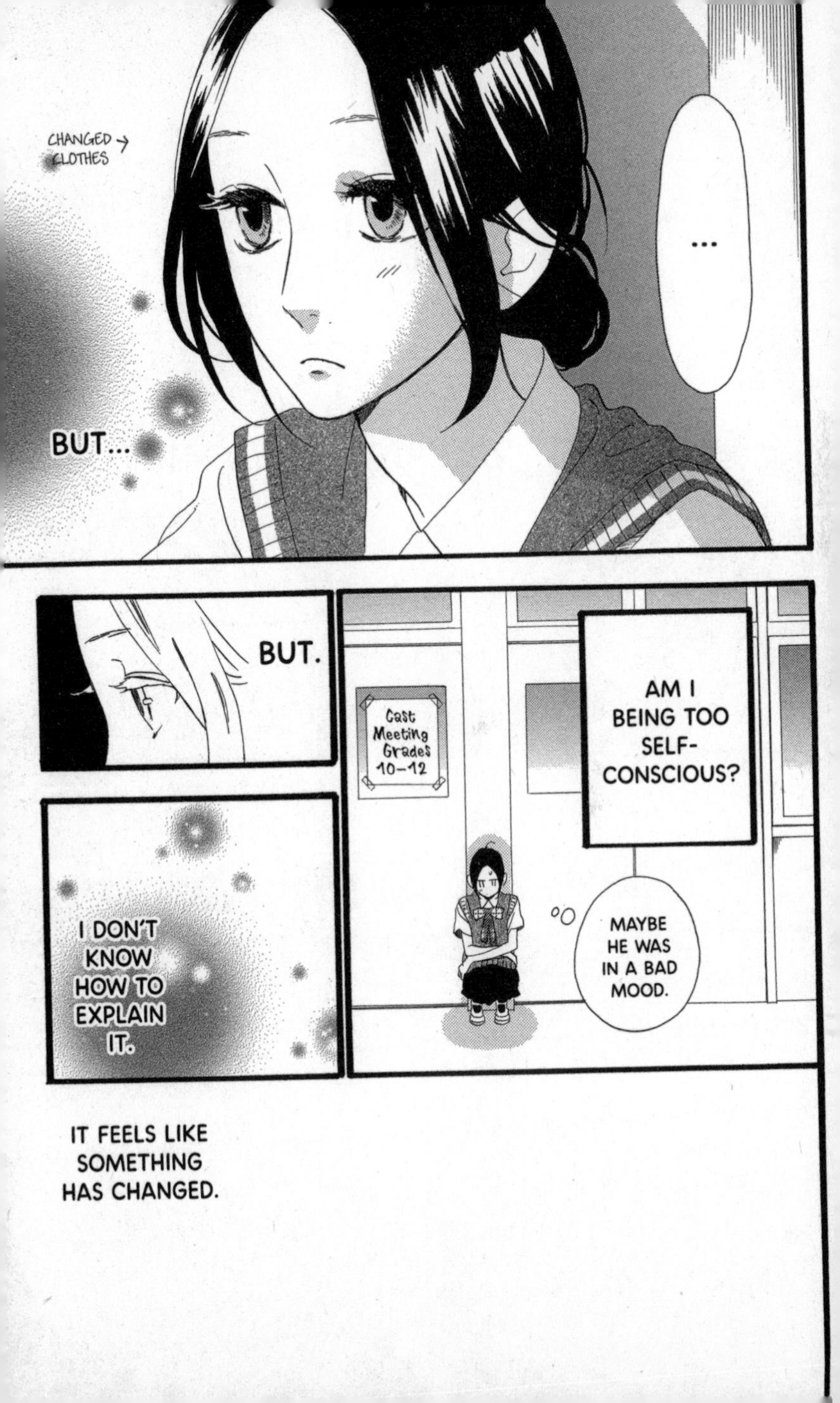
...
CHANGED → CLOTHES
BUT...
AM I BEING TOO SELF-CONSCIOUS?
Cast Meeting Grades 10–12
MAYBE HE WAS IN A BAD MOOD.
BUT.
I DON'T KNOW HOW TO EXPLAIN IT.
IT FEELS LIKE SOMETHING HAS CHANGED.

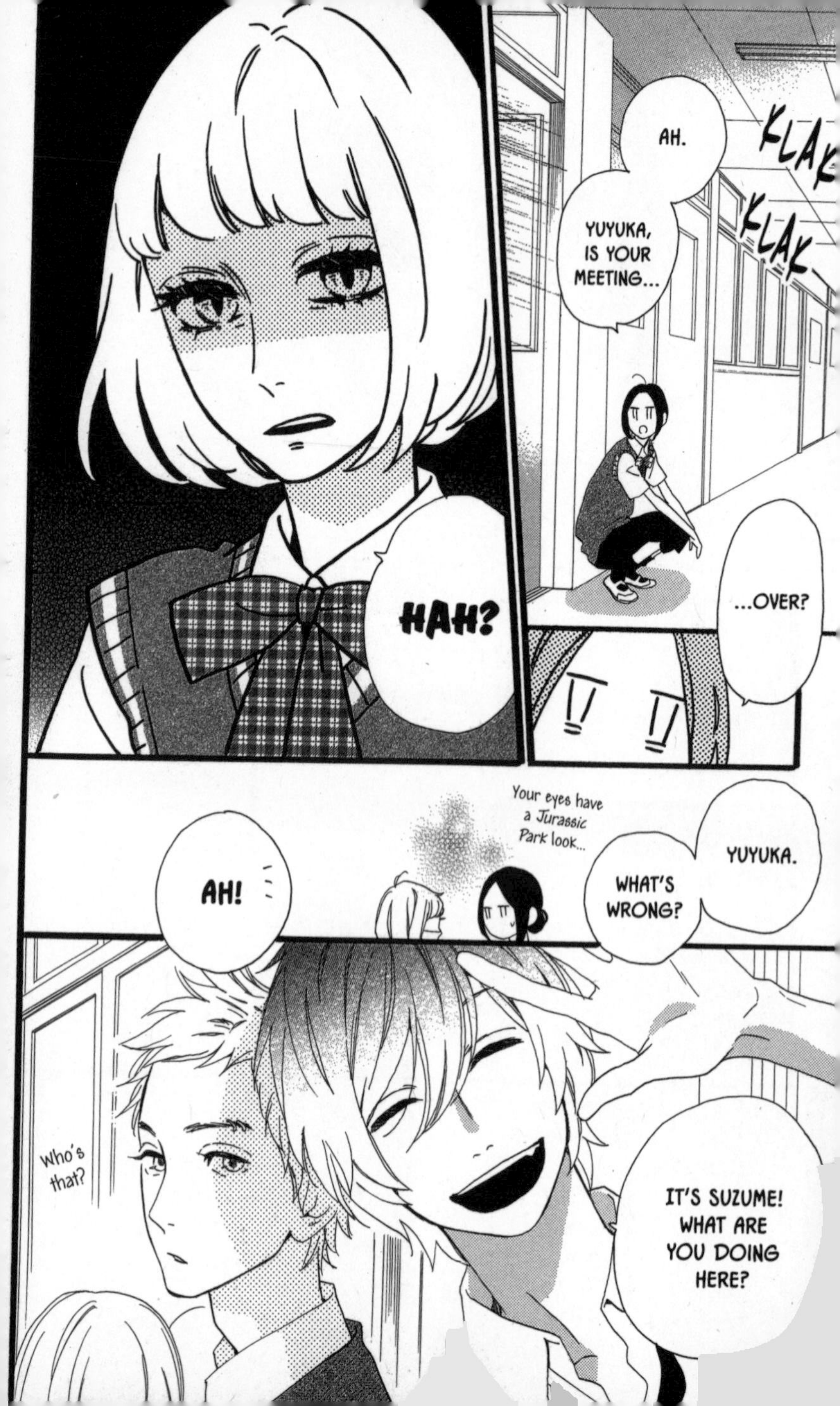
AH.
YUYUKA, IS YOUR MEETING...
KLAK
KLAK
...OVER?
HAH?
YUYUKA.
WHAT'S WRONG?
Your eyes have a Jurassic Park look...
AH!
IT'S SUZUME! WHAT ARE YOU DOING HERE?
Who's that?

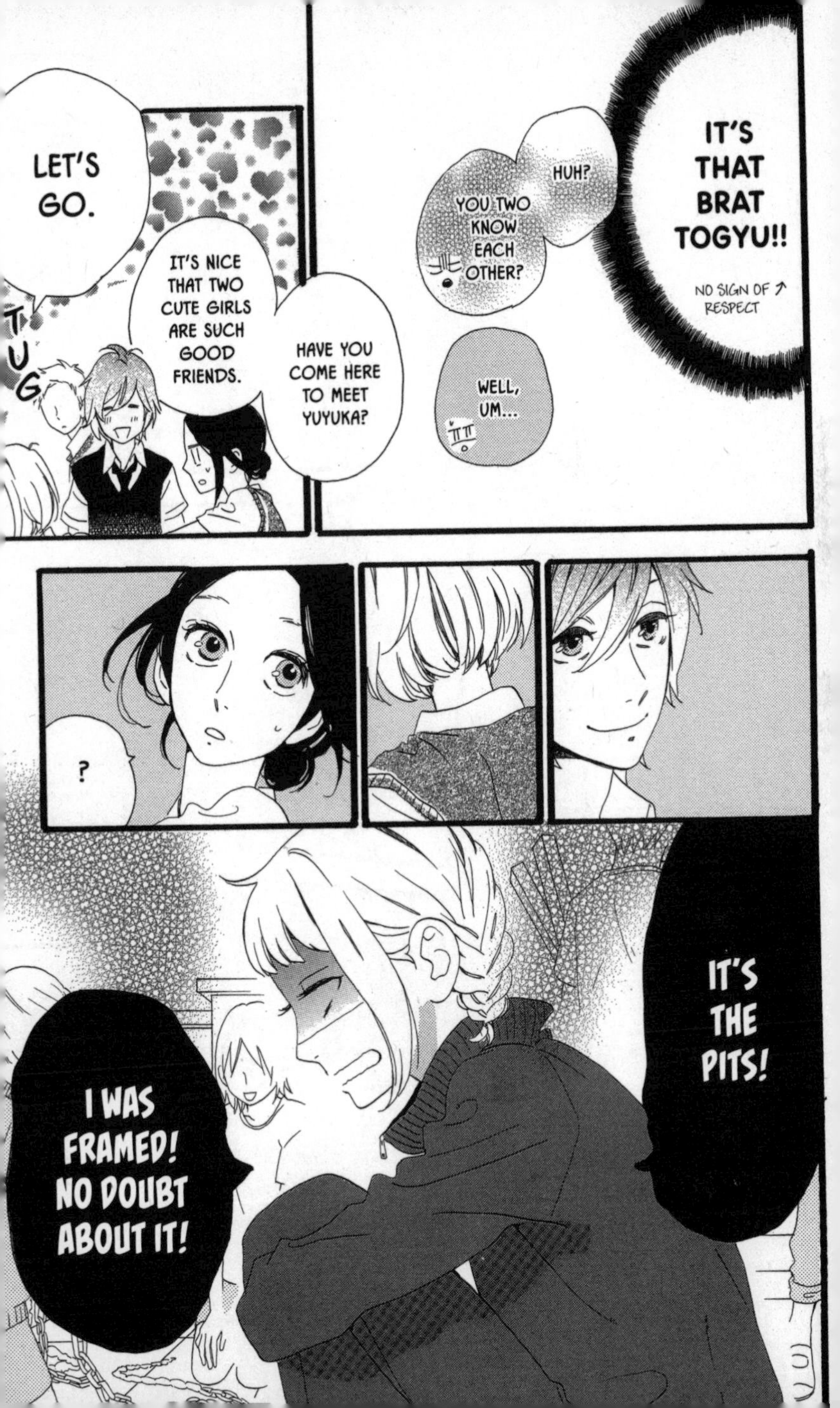
IT'S THAT BRAT TOGYU!!
NO SIGN OF RESPECT
HUH?
YOU TWO KNOW EACH OTHER?
WELL, UM...
HAVE YOU COME HERE TO MEET YUYUKA?
IT'S NICE THAT TWO CUTE GIRLS ARE SUCH GOOD FRIENDS.
LET'S GO.
TUG
?
IT'S THE PITS!
I WAS FRAMED! NO DOUBT ABOUT IT!

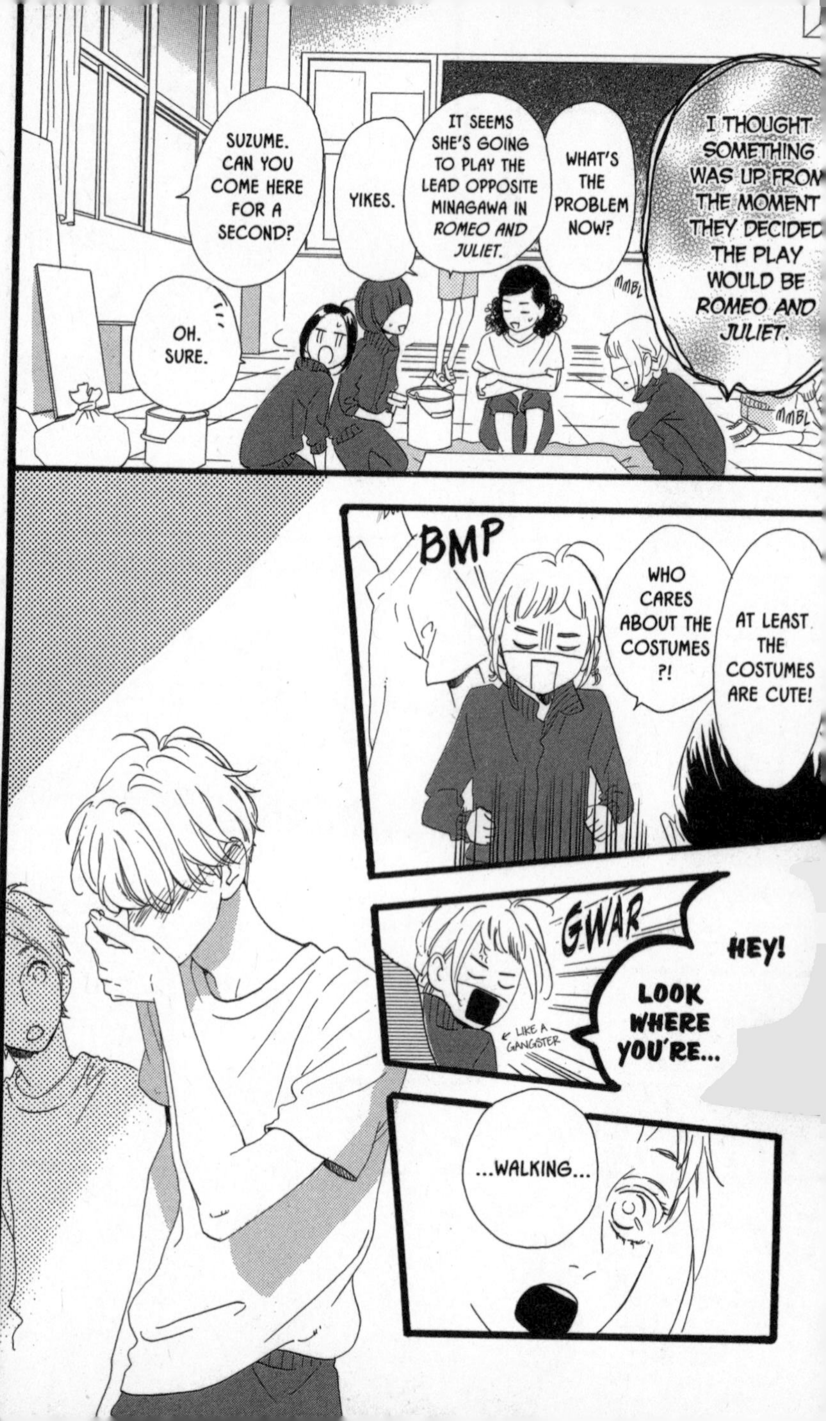
I THOUGHT SOMETHING WAS UP FROM THE MOMENT THEY DECIDED THE PLAY WOULD BE ROMEO AND JULIET.
MMBL
MMBL
WHAT'S THE PROBLEM NOW?
IT SEEMS SHE'S GOING TO PLAY THE LEAD OPPOSITE MINAGAWA IN ROMEO AND JULIET.
YIKES.
SUZUME. CAN YOU COME HERE FOR A SECOND?
OH. SURE.
AT LEAST THE COSTUMES ARE CUTE!
WHO CARES ABOUT THE COSTUMES?!
BMP
HEY!
LOOK WHERE YOU'RE...
GWAR
LIKE A GANGSTER
...WALKING...

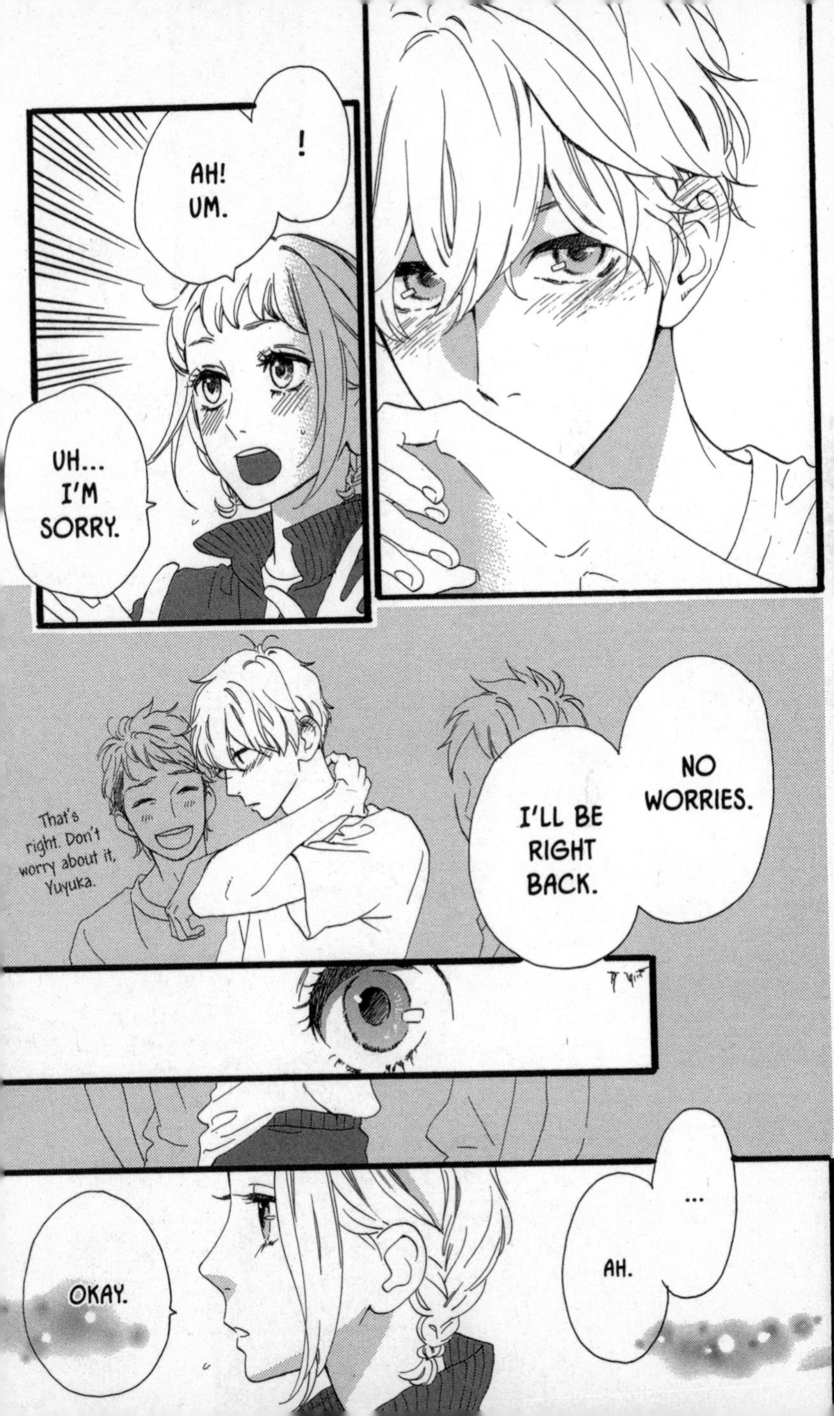
!
AH! UM.
UH... I'M SORRY.
NO WORRIES.
I'LL BE RIGHT BACK.
That's right. Don't worry about it, Yuyuka.
... AH.
OKAY.

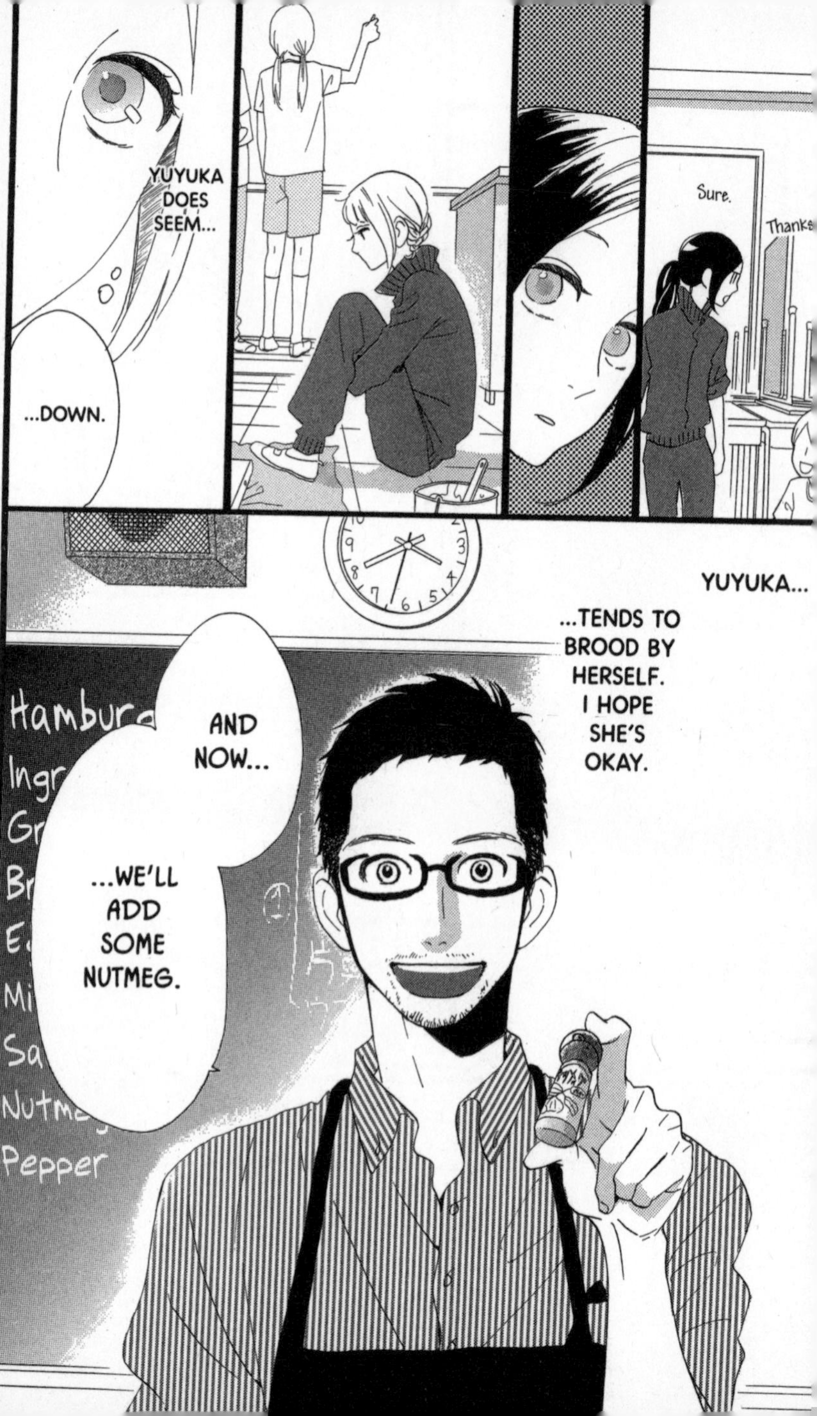

Sure.
Thanks
YUYUKA DOES SEEM...
...DOWN.
YUYUKA...
...TENDS TO BROOD BY HERSELF. I HOPE SHE'S OKAY.
AND NOW...
...WE'LL ADD SOME NUTMEG.
Pepper

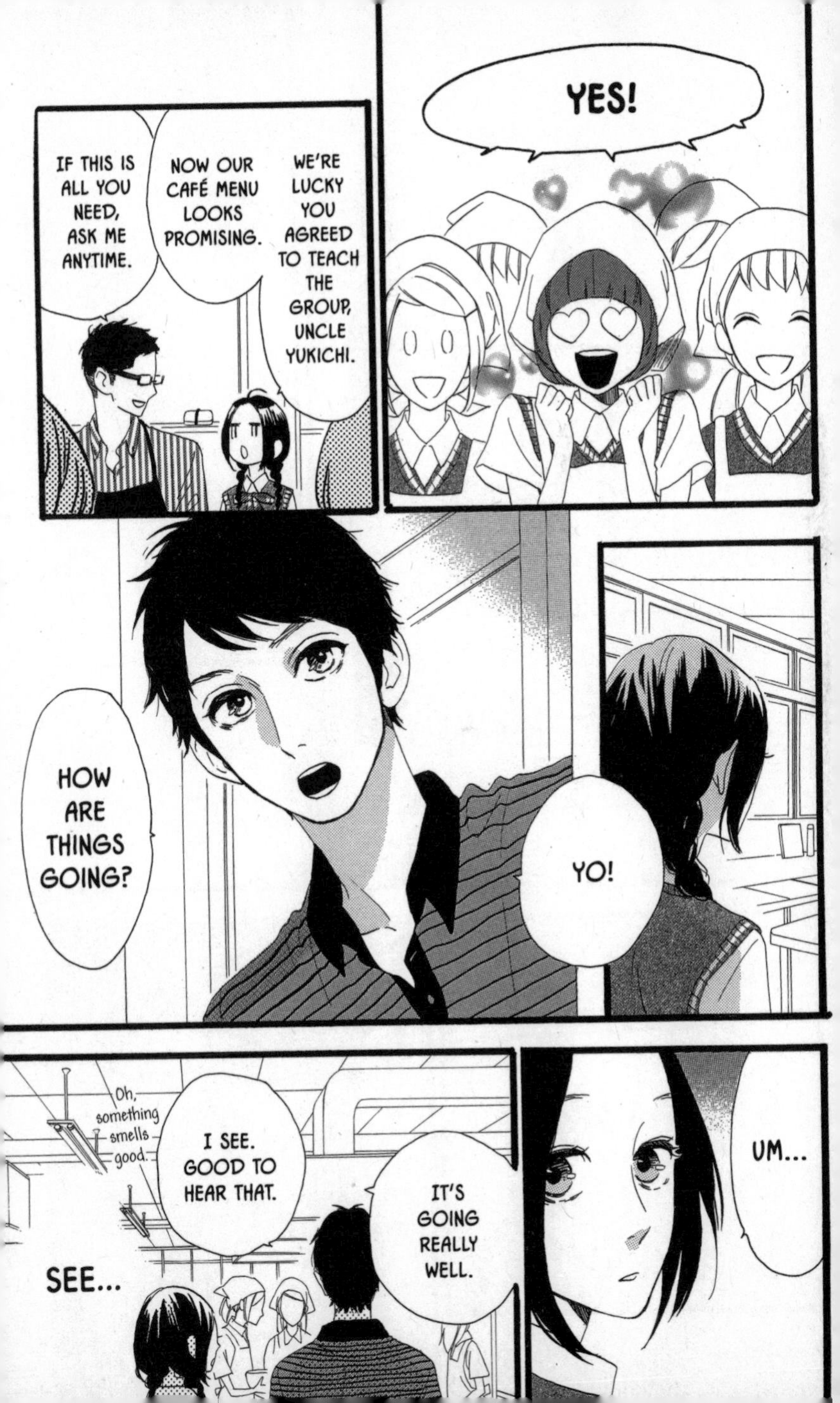
YES!
WE'RE LUCKY YOU AGREED TO TEACH THE GROUP, UNCLE YUKICHI.
NOW OUR CAFÉ MENU LOOKS PROMISING.
IF THIS IS ALL YOU NEED, ASK ME ANYTIME.
YO!
HOW ARE THINGS GOING?
UM...
IT'S GOING REALLY WELL.
I SEE. GOOD TO HEAR THAT.
Oh, something smells good.
SEE...

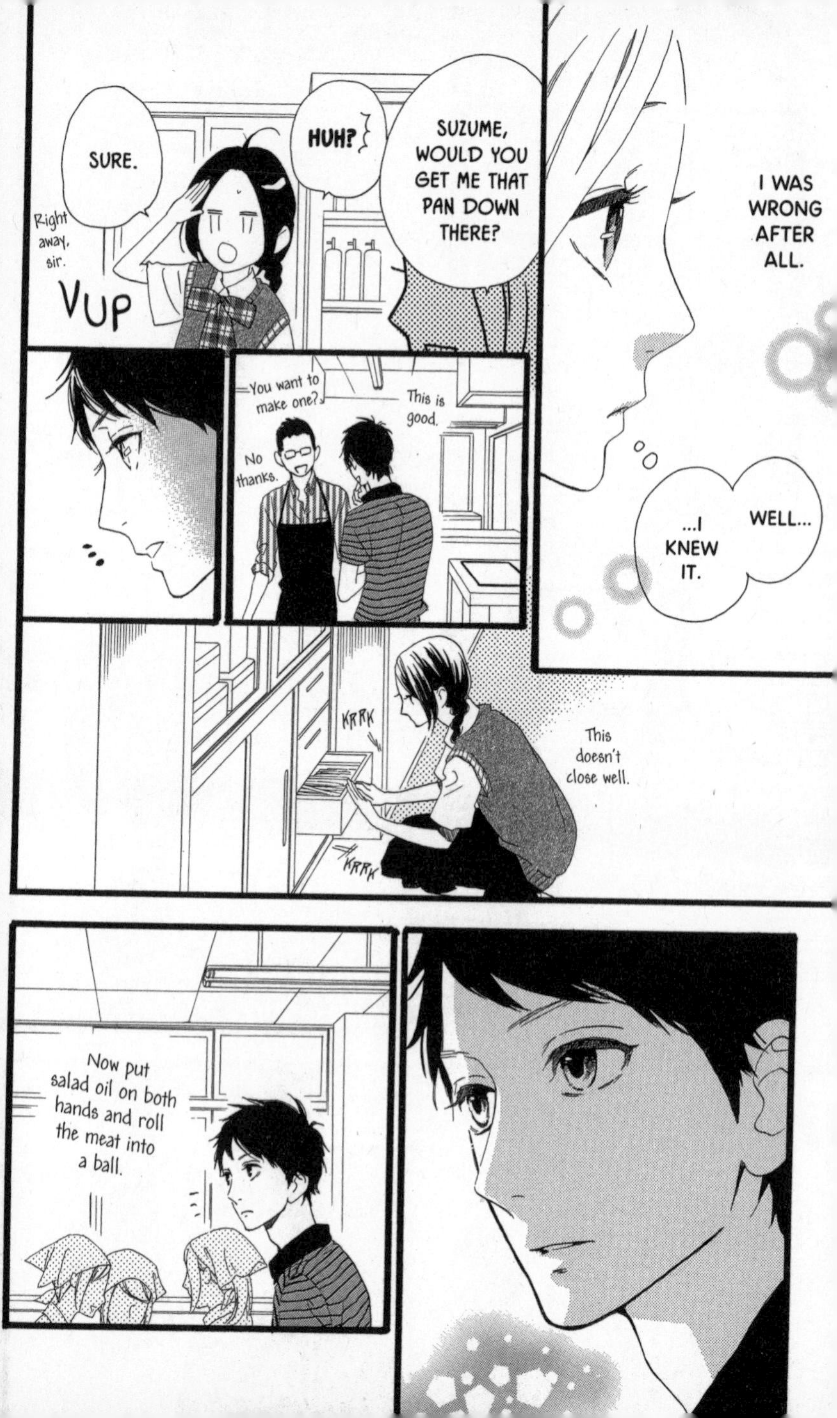
I WAS WRONG AFTER ALL.
WELL...
...I KNEW IT.
SUZUME, WOULD YOU GET ME THAT PAN DOWN THERE?
HUH?
SURE.
Right away, sir.
VUP
This is good.
You want to make one?
No thanks.
...
KRRK
This doesn't close well.
KRRK
Now put salad oil on both hands and roll the meat into a ball.

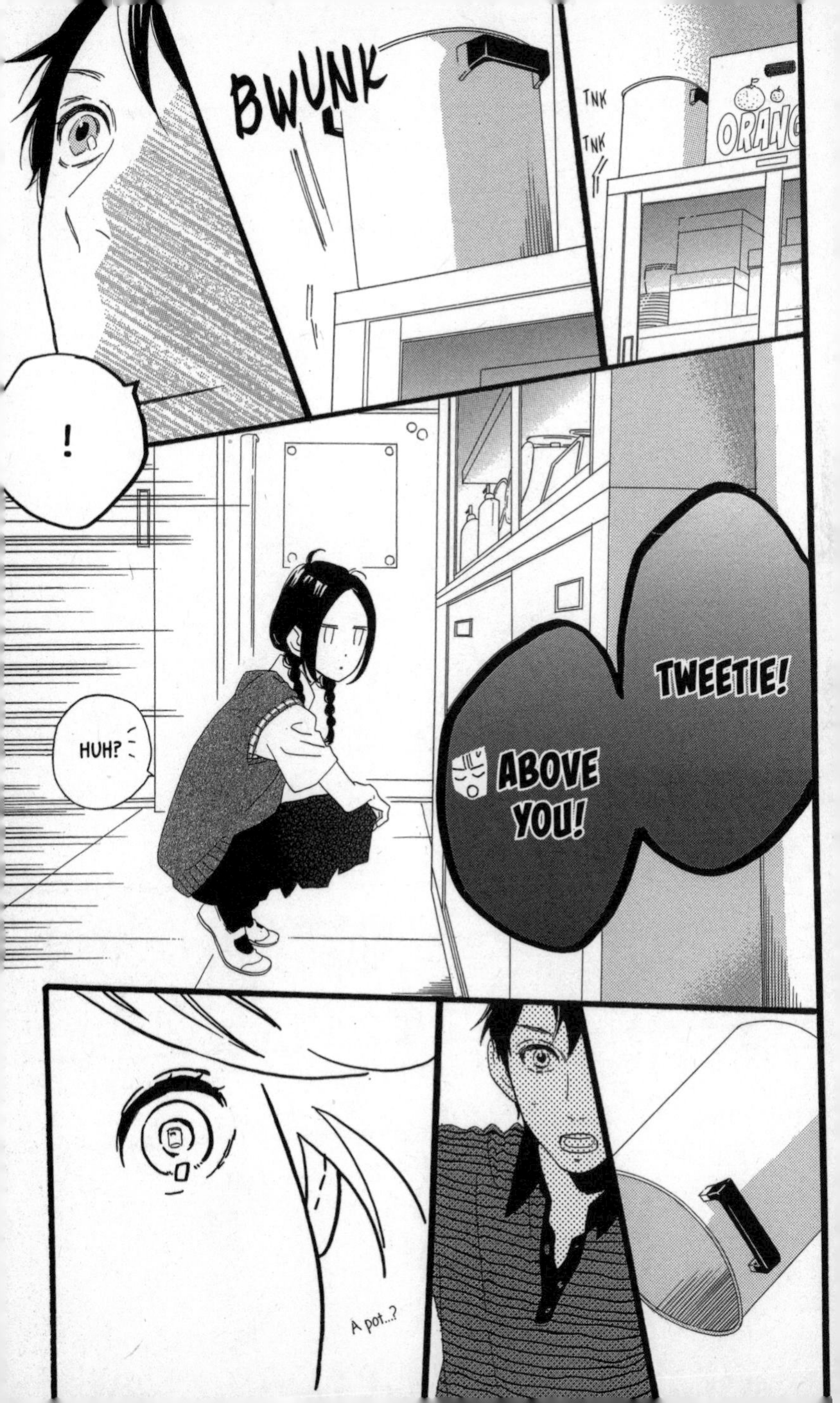
TNK
TNK
ORANG
BWUNK
!
TWEETIE!
ABOVE YOU!
HUH?
A pot...?

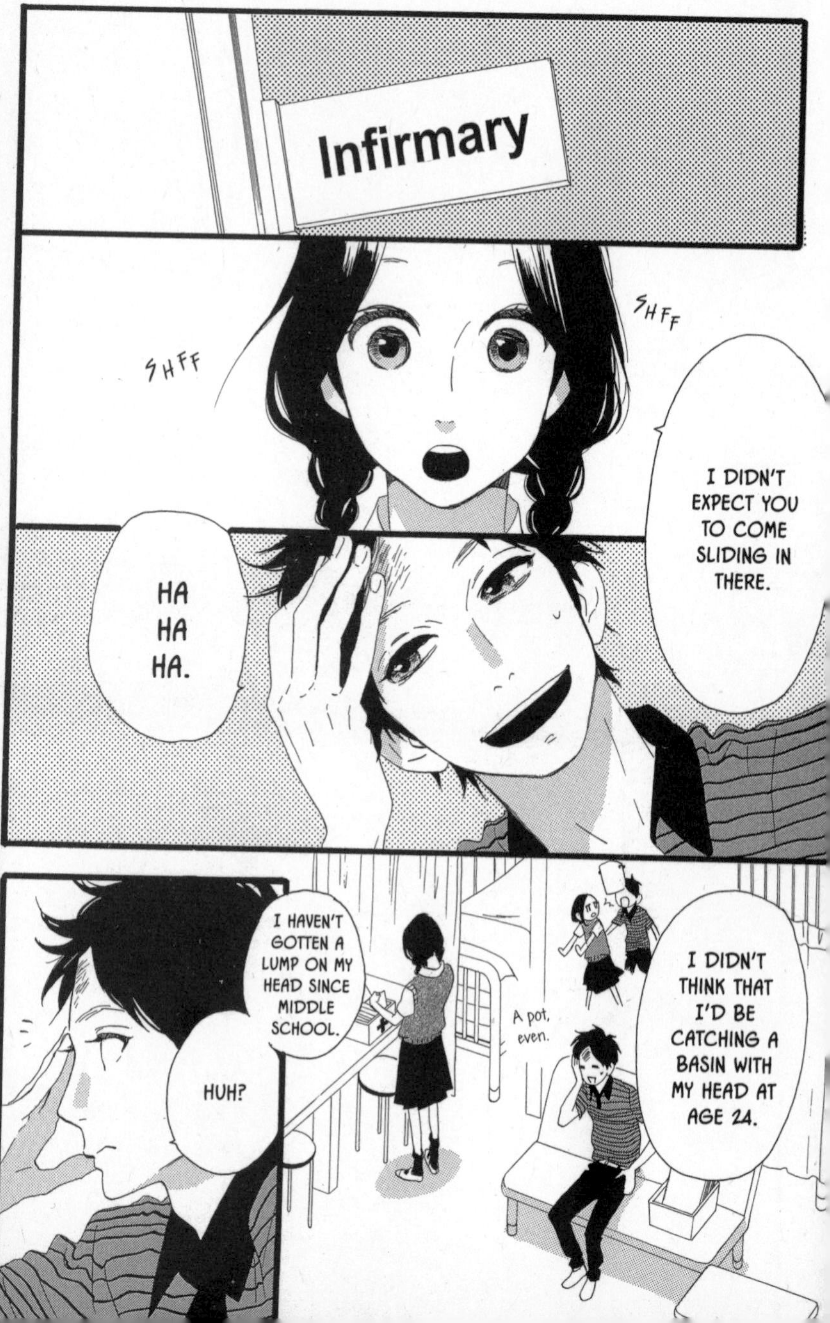
Infirmary
SHFF
SHFF
I DIDN'T EXPECT YOU TO COME SLIDING IN THERE.
HA HA HA.
I DIDN'T THINK THAT I'D BE CATCHING A BASIN WITH MY HEAD AT AGE 24.
A pot, even.
I HAVEN'T GOTTEN A LUMP ON MY HEAD SINCE MIDDLE SCHOOL.
HUH?

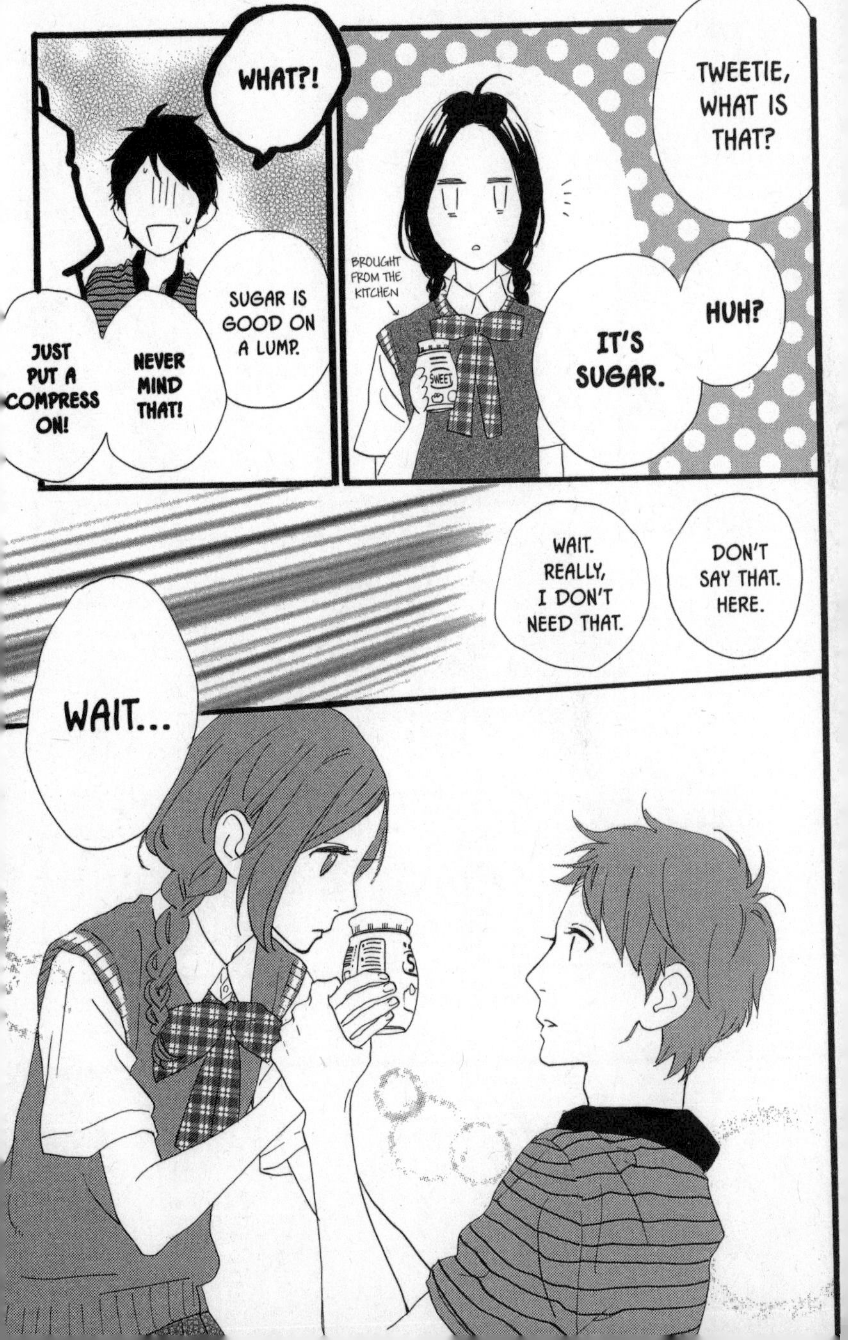
TWEETIE, WHAT IS THAT?
HUH?
IT'S SUGAR.
BROUGHT FROM THE KITCHEN
SWEET
WHAT?!
SUGAR IS GOOD ON A LUMP.
NEVER MIND THAT!
JUST PUT A COMPRESS ON!
DON'T SAY THAT. HERE.
WAIT. REALLY, I DON'T NEED THAT.
WAIT...

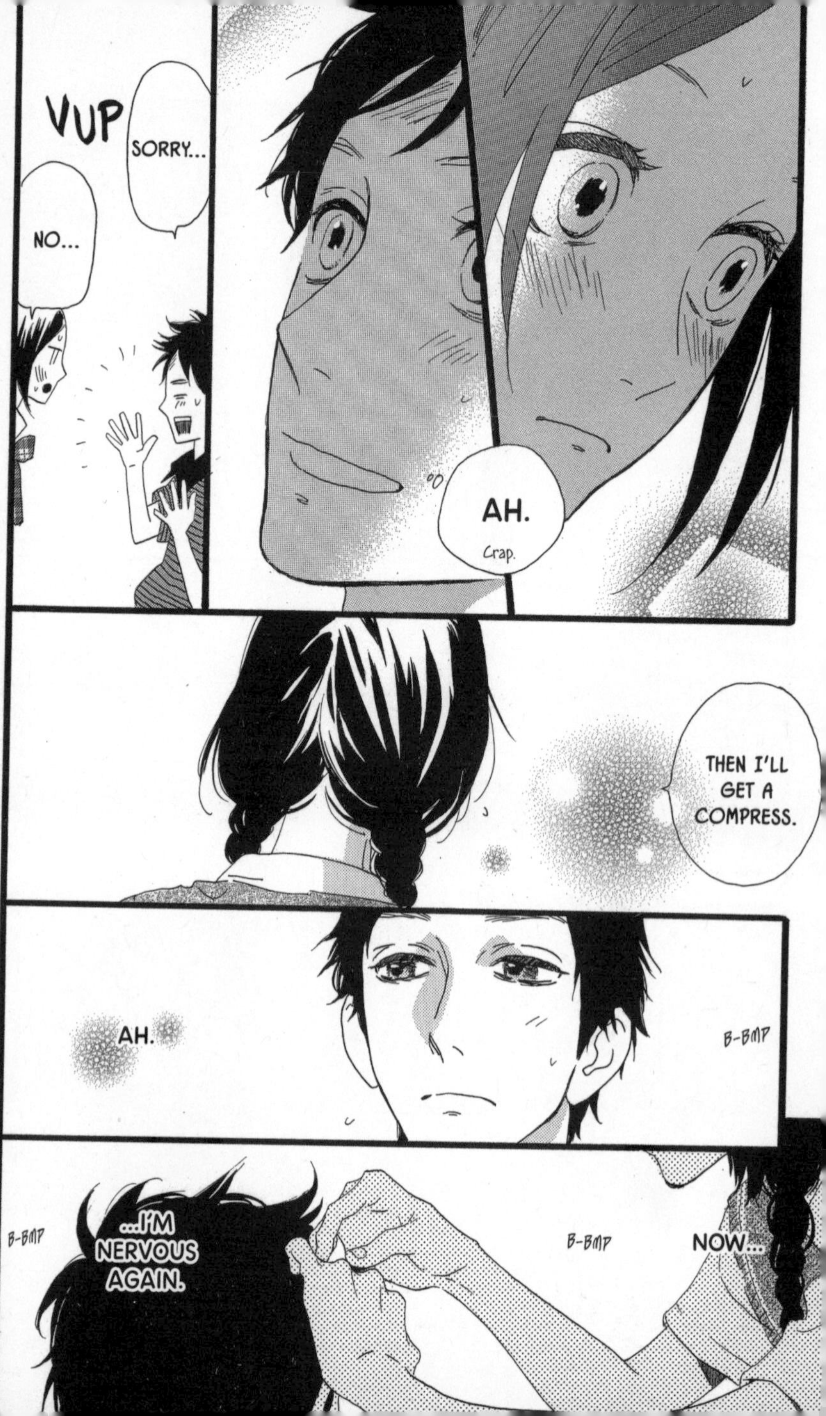

AH.
Crap.
SORRY...
VUP
NO...
THEN I'LL GET A COMPRESS.
B-BMP
AH.
NOW...
B-BMP
...I'M NERVOUS AGAIN.
B-BMP

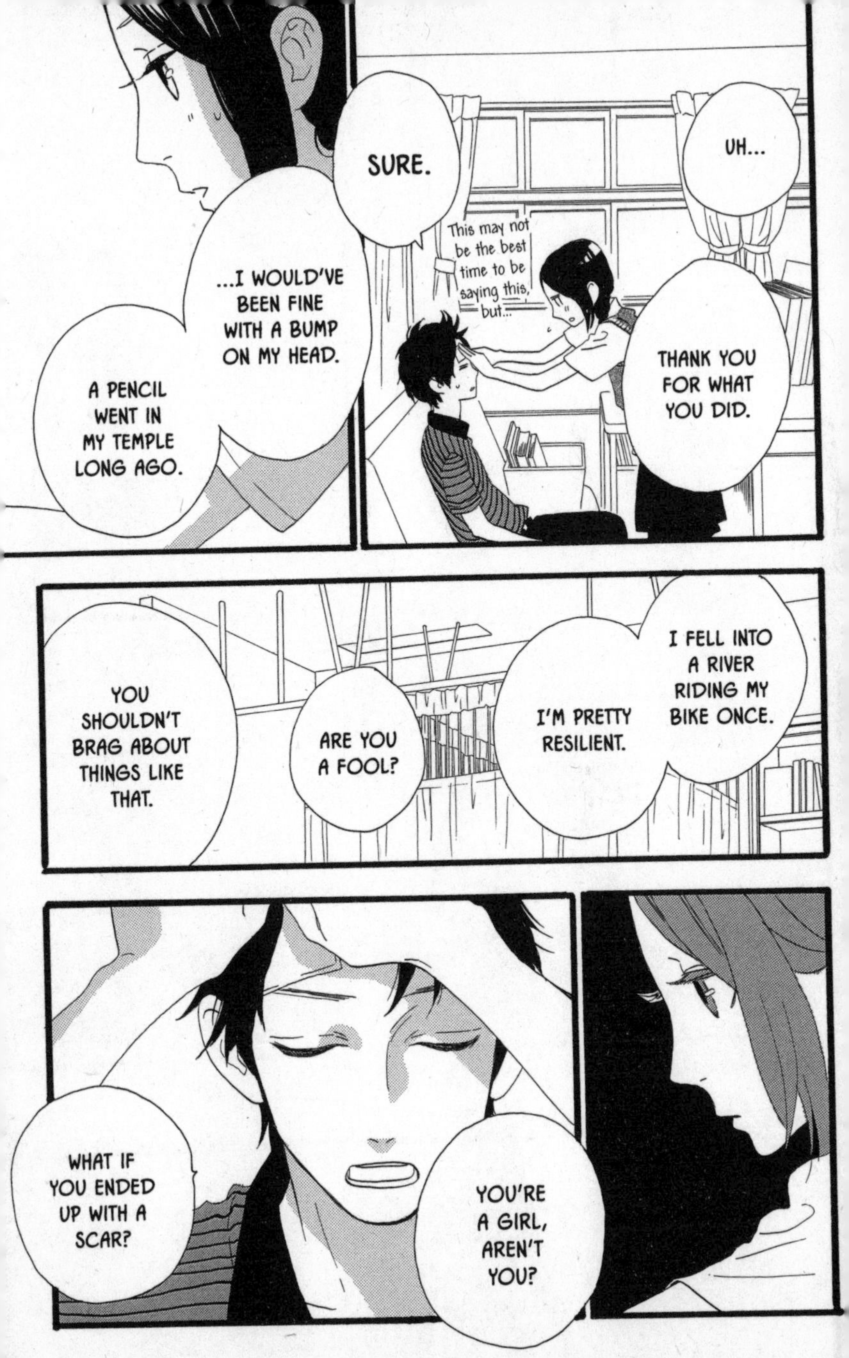
UH...
THANK YOU FOR WHAT YOU DID.
This may not be the best time to be saying this, but...
SURE.
...I WOULD'VE BEEN FINE WITH A BUMP ON MY HEAD.
A PENCIL WENT IN MY TEMPLE LONG AGO.
I FELL INTO A RIVER RIDING MY BIKE ONCE.
I'M PRETTY RESILIENT.
ARE YOU A FOOL?
YOU SHOULDN'T BRAG ABOUT THINGS LIKE THAT.
YOU'RE A GIRL, AREN'T YOU?
WHAT IF YOU ENDED UP WITH A SCAR?

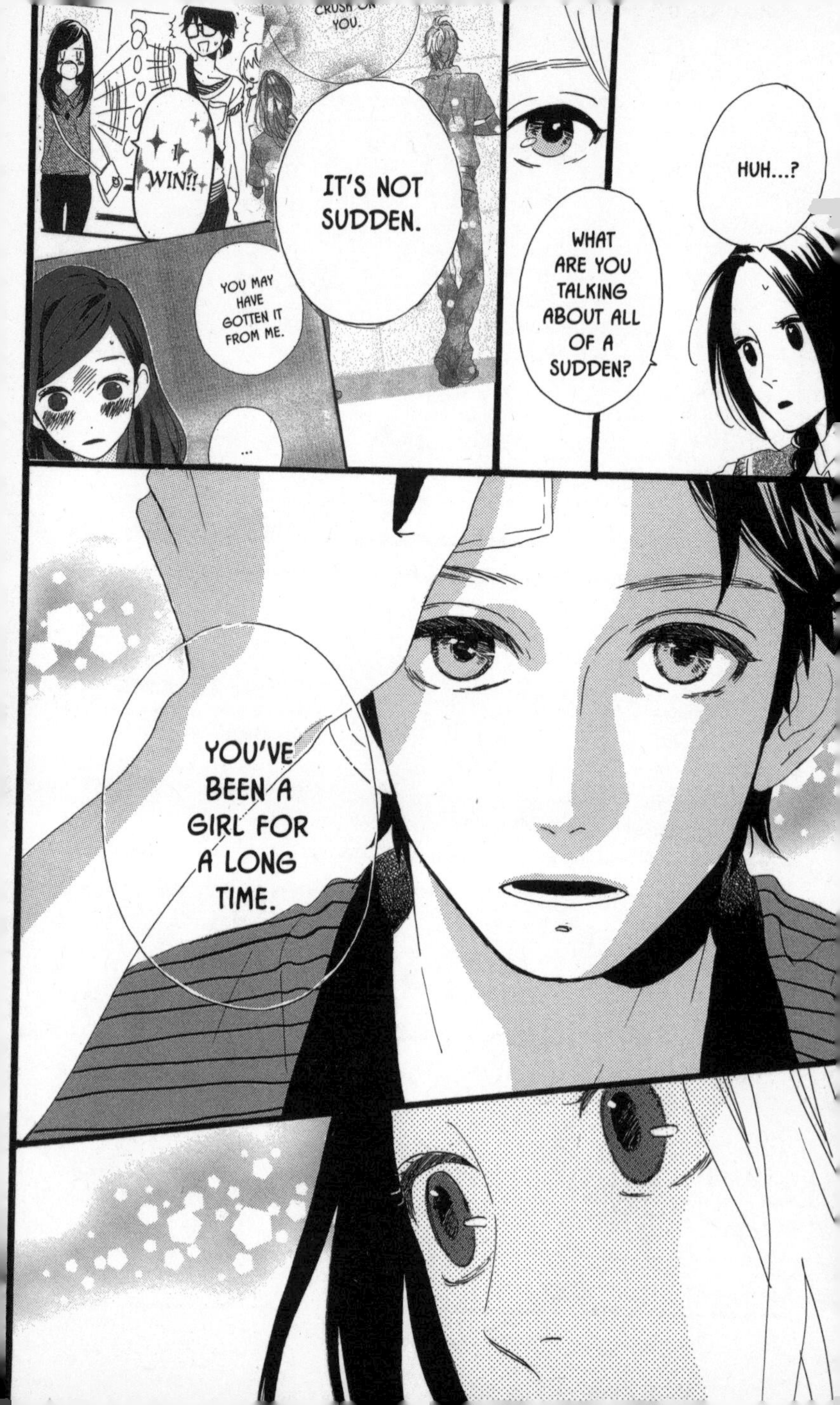
HUH...?
WHAT ARE YOU TALKING ABOUT ALL OF A SUDDEN?
CRUSH ON YOU.
IT'S NOT SUDDEN.
WIN!!
YOU MAY HAVE GOTTEN IT FROM ME.
...
YOU'VE BEEN A GIRL FOR A LONG TIME.

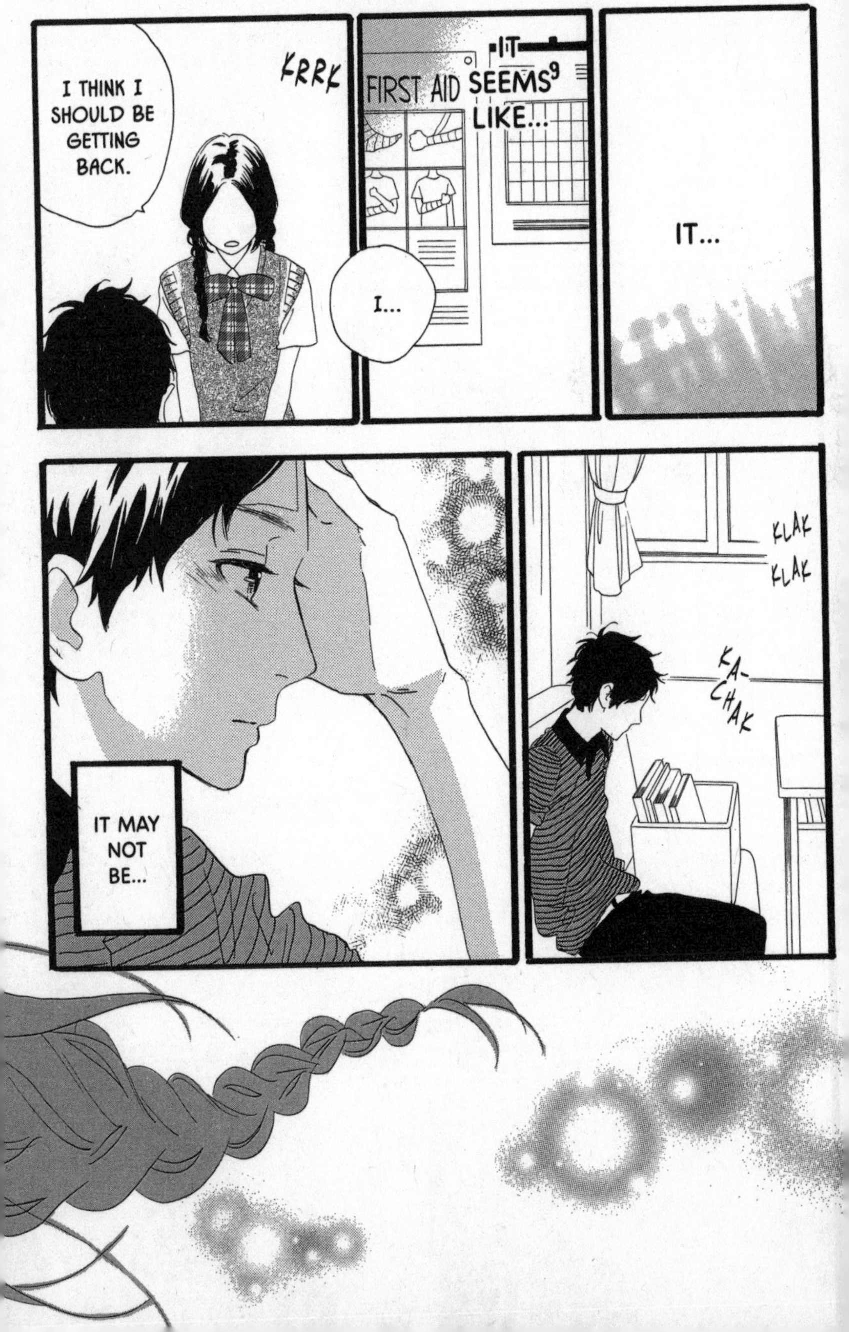
IT...
IT SEEMS LIKE...
FIRST AID
I...
KRRK
I THINK I SHOULD BE GETTING BACK.
KLAK KLAK
KA-CHAK
IT MAY NOT BE...

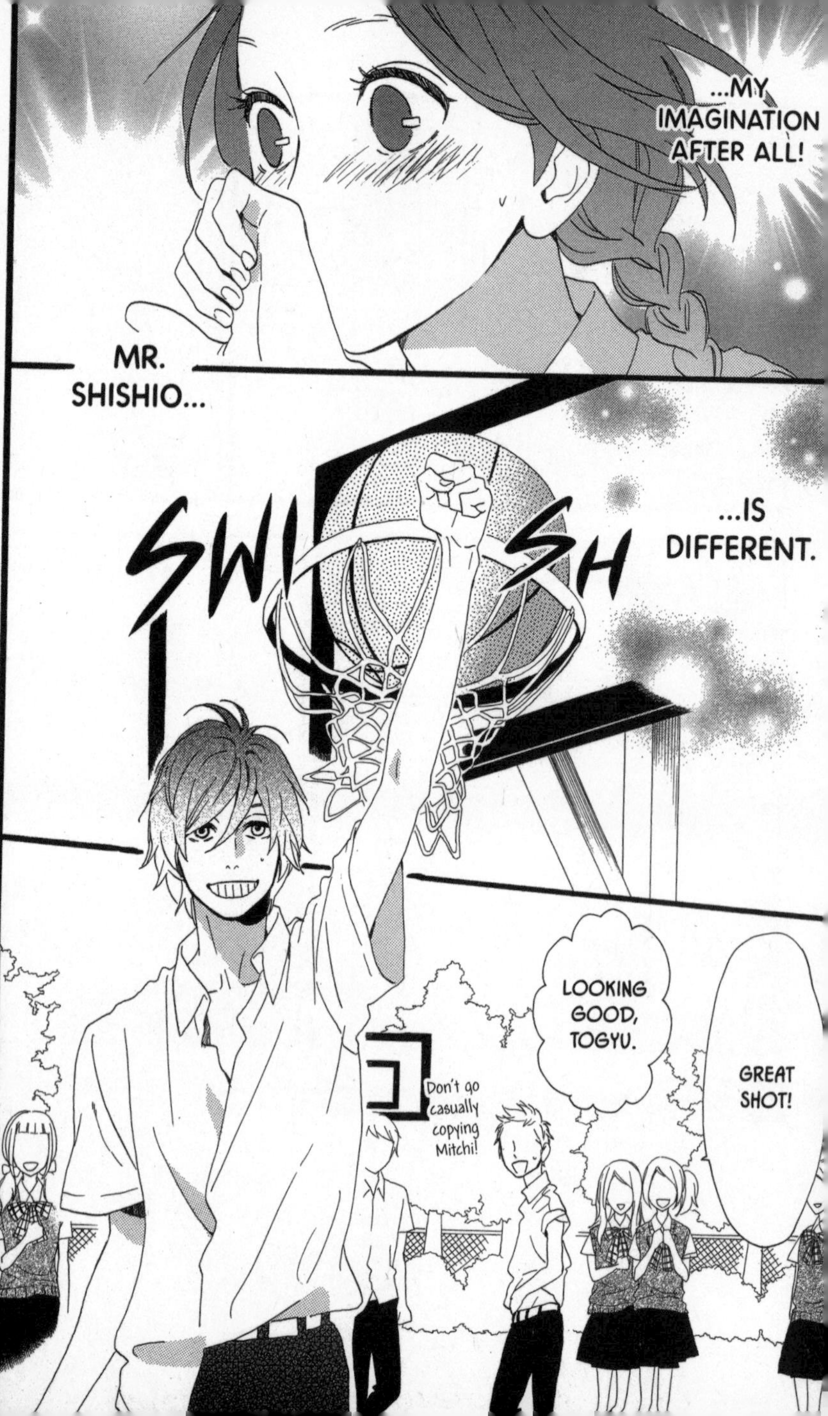
...MY IMAGINATION AFTER ALL!
MR. SHISHIO...
...IS DIFFERENT.
SWISH
GREAT SHOT!
LOOKING GOOD, TOGYU.
Don't go casually copying Mitchi!

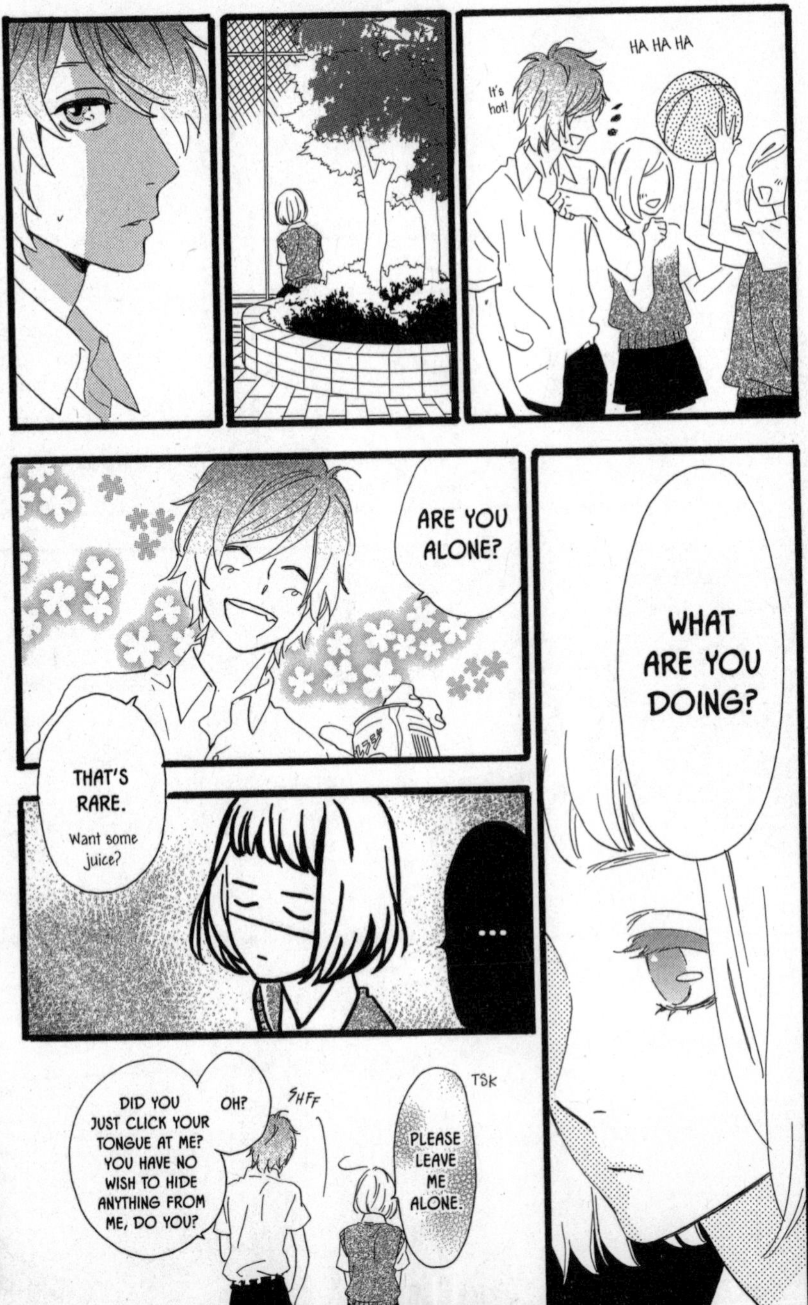

HA HA HA
It's hot!
WHAT ARE YOU DOING?
ARE YOU ALONE?
THAT'S RARE.
Want some juice?
...
TSK
PLEASE LEAVE ME ALONE.
SHFF
OH?
DID YOU JUST CLICK YOUR TONGUE AT ME? YOU HAVE NO WISH TO HIDE ANYTHING FROM ME, DO YOU?

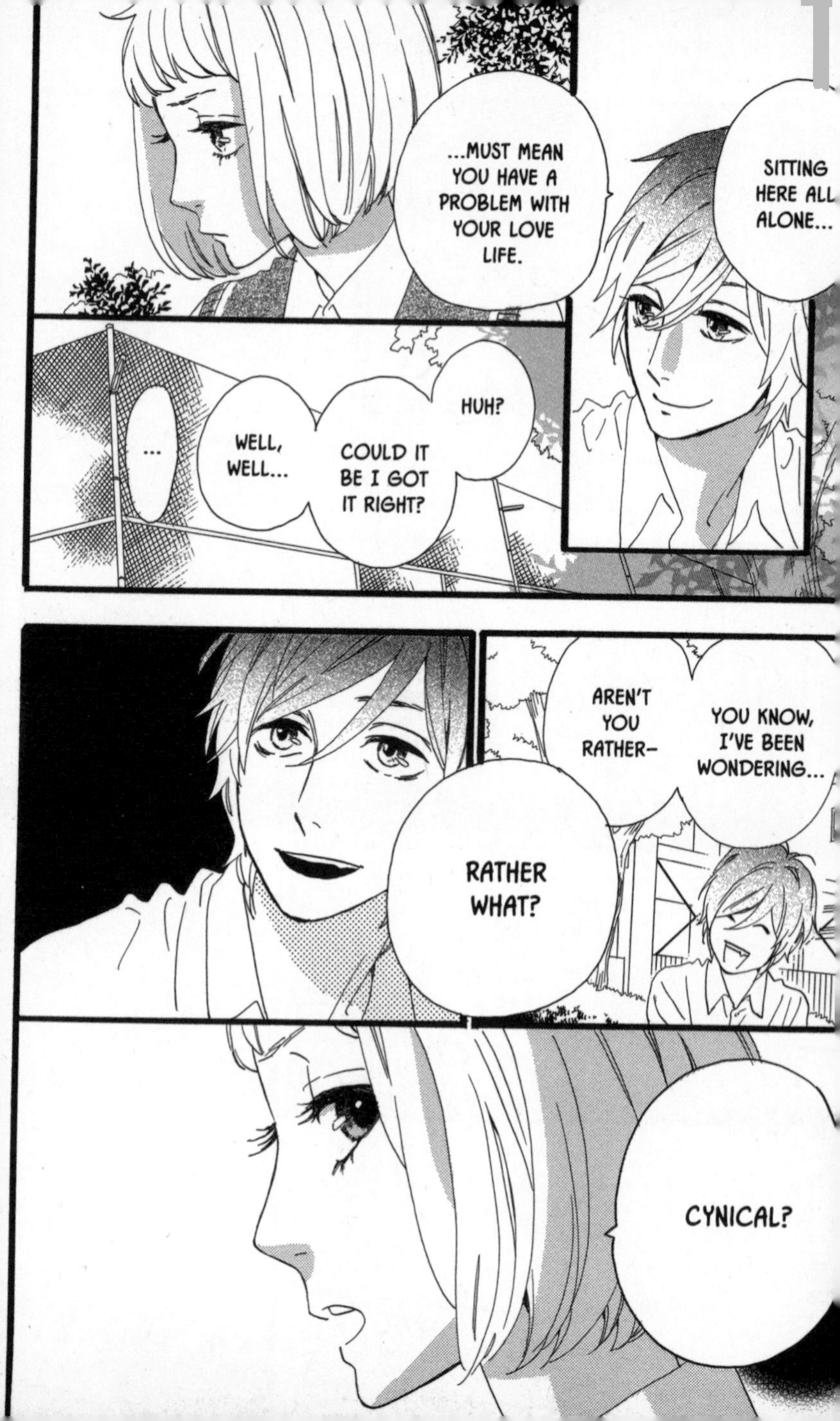
SITTING HERE ALL ALONE...
...MUST MEAN YOU HAVE A PROBLEM WITH YOUR LOVE LIFE.
HUH?
COULD IT BE I GOT IT RIGHT?
WELL, WELL...
...
YOU KNOW, I'VE BEEN WONDERING...
AREN'T YOU RATHER-
RATHER WHAT?
CYNICAL?

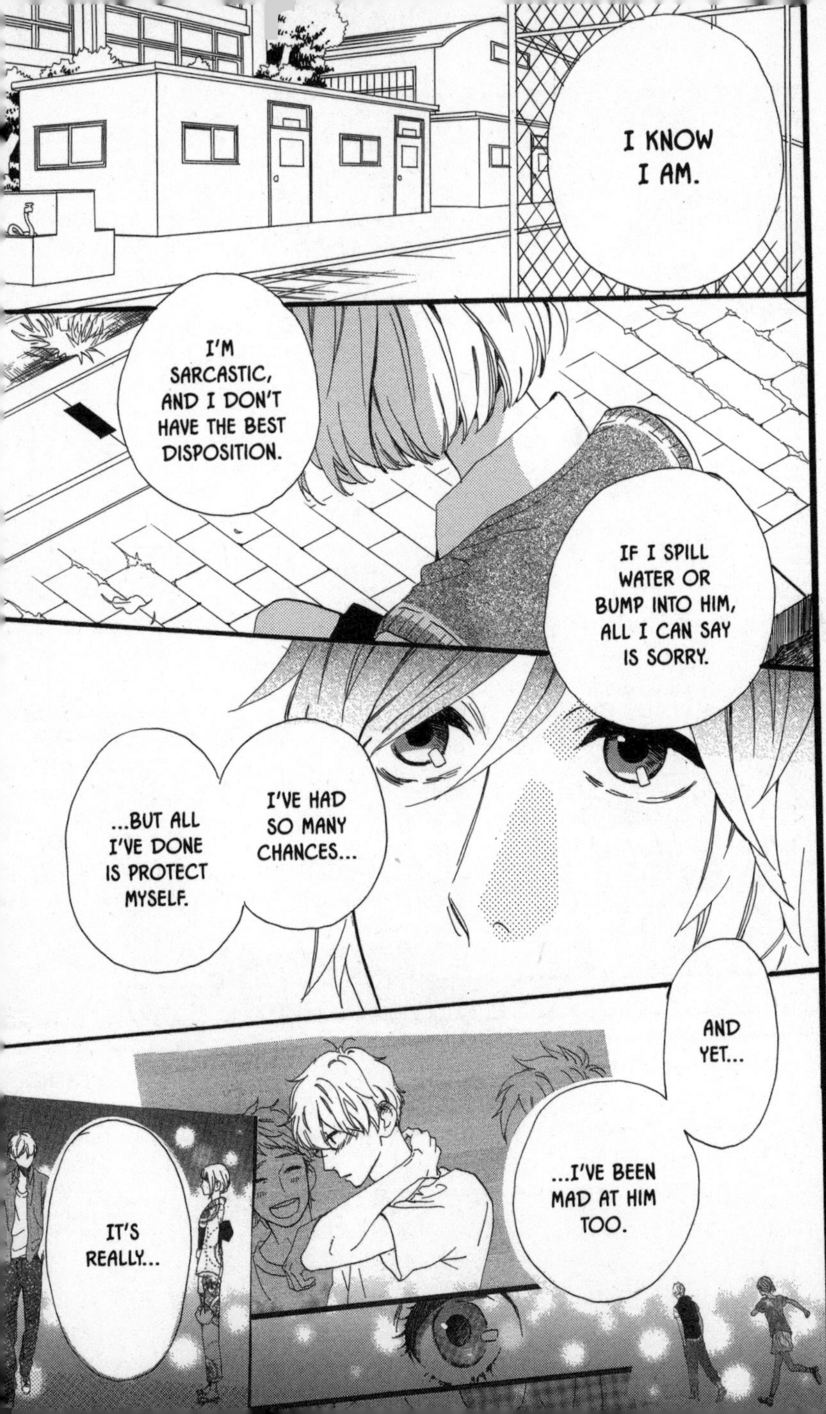
I KNOW I AM.
I'M SARCASTIC, AND I DON'T HAVE THE BEST DISPOSITION.
IF I SPILL WATER OR BUMP INTO HIM, ALL I CAN SAY IS SORRY.
I'VE HAD SO MANY CHANCES...
...BUT ALL I'VE DONE IS PROTECT MYSELF.
AND YET...
...I'VE BEEN MAD AT HIM TOO.
IT'S REALLY...

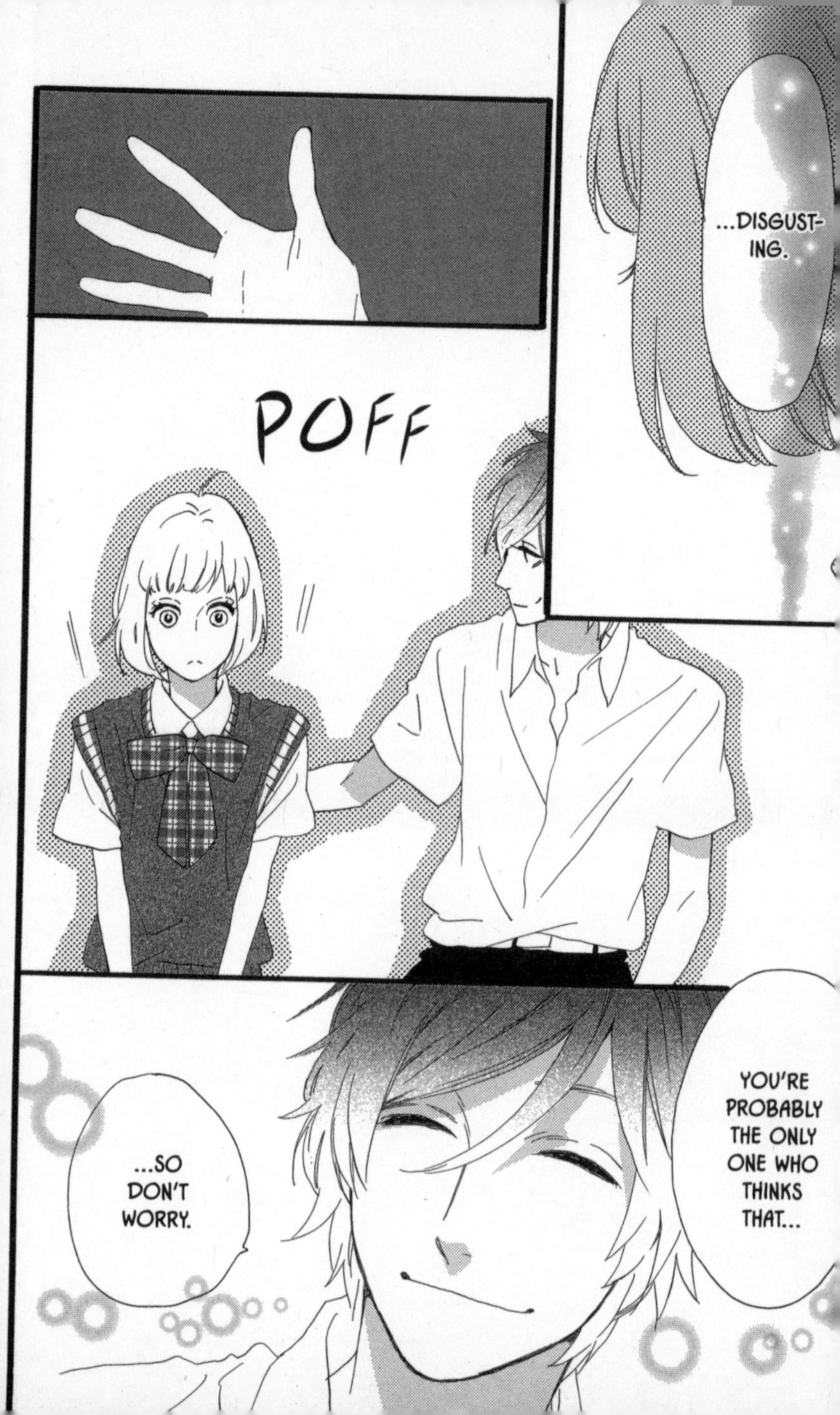
...DISGUST-ING.
POFF
YOU'RE PROBABLY THE ONLY ONE WHO THINKS THAT...
...SO DON'T WORRY.

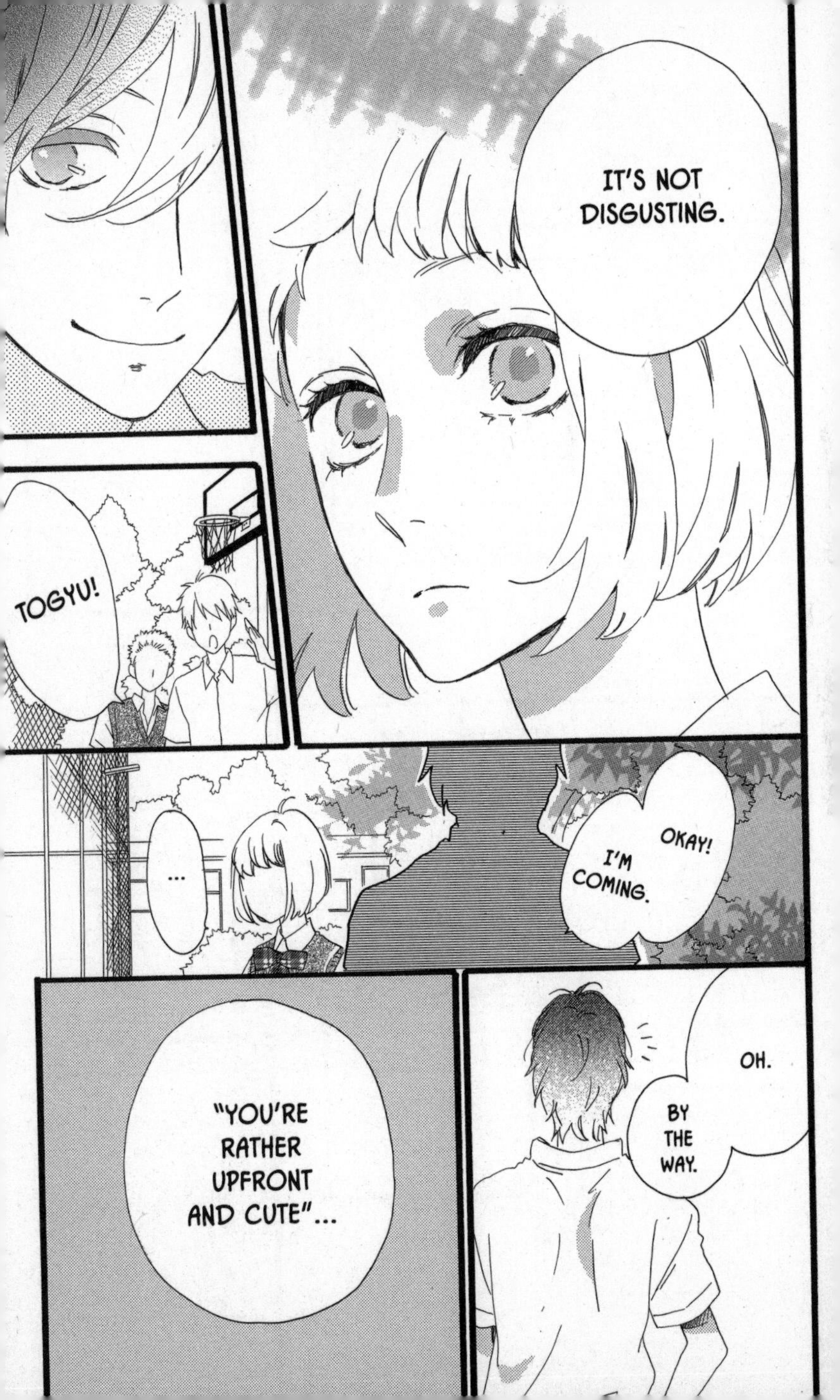
IT'S NOT DISGUSTING.
TOGYU!
OKAY! I'M COMING.
...
OH.
BY THE WAY.
"YOU'RE RATHER UPFRONT AND CUTE"...

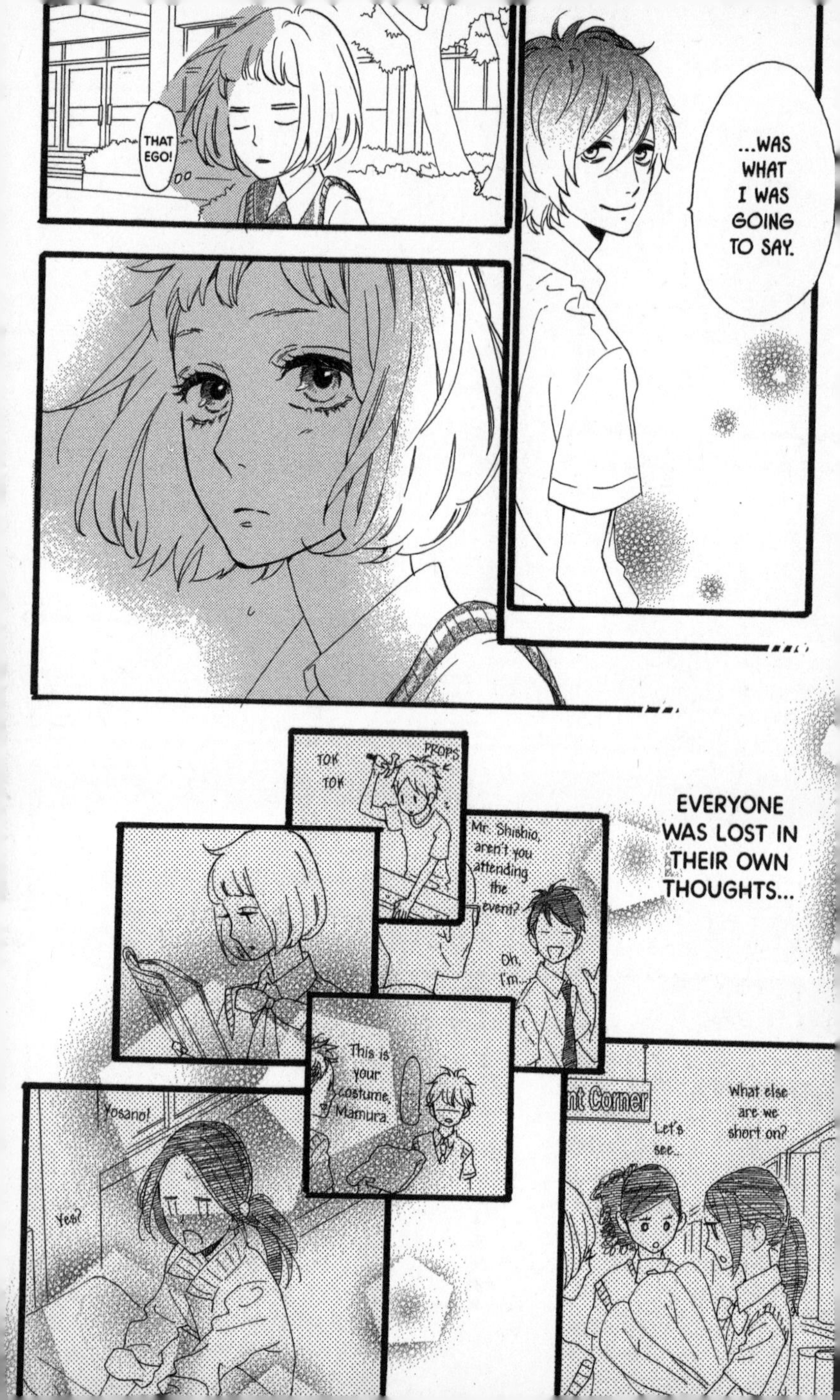
...WAS WHAT I WAS GOING TO SAY.
THAT EGO!
EVERYONE WAS LOST IN THEIR OWN THOUGHTS...
PROPS
TOK TOK
Mr. Shishio, aren't you attending the event?
Oh, I'm...
This is your costume, Mamura.
nt Corner
What else are we short on?
Let's see...
Yosano!
Yes?

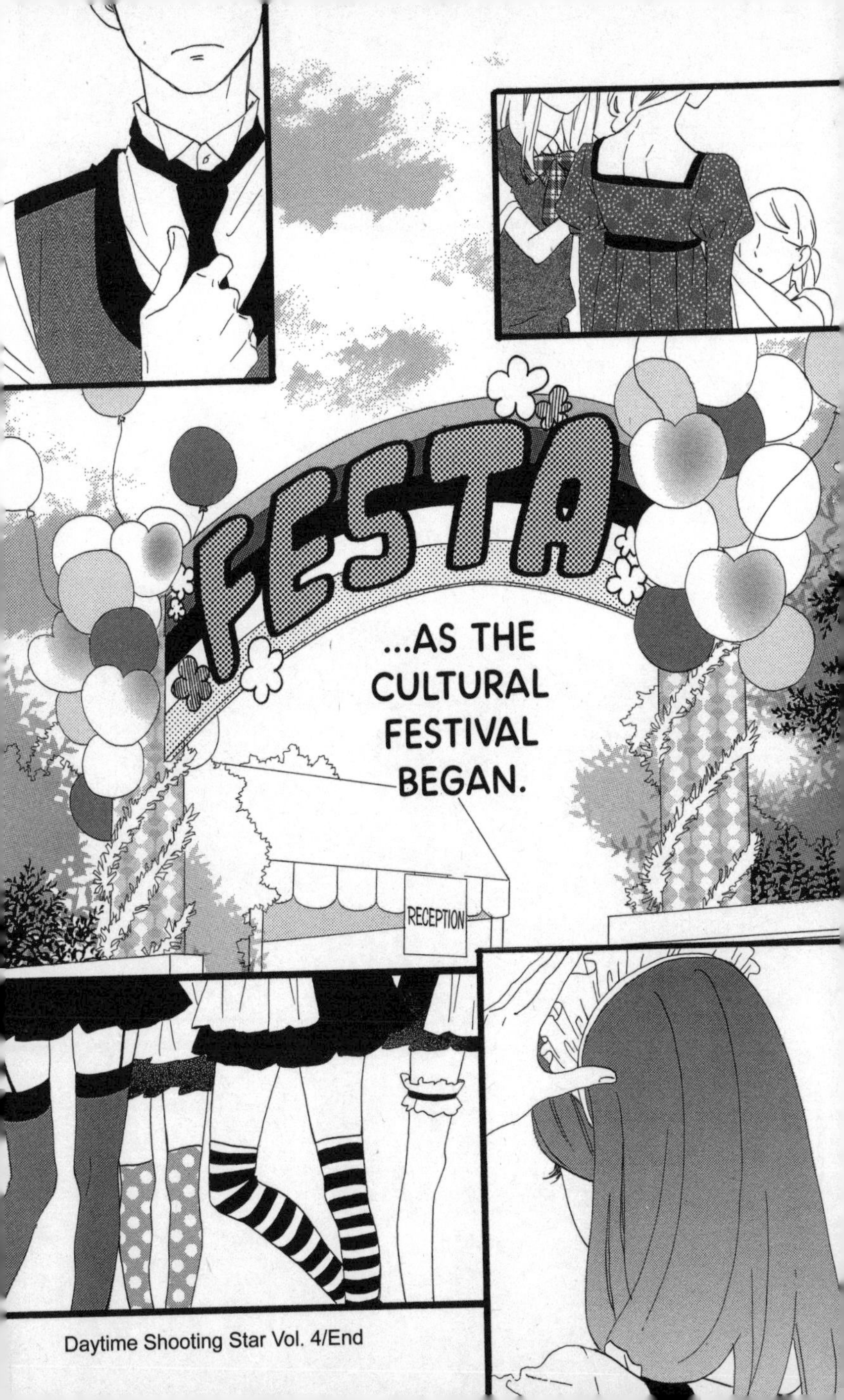
FESTA
...AS THE CULTURAL FESTIVAL BEGAN.
RECEPTION

Daytime Shooting Star Vol. 4/End

This is not the sort of story where the main character becomes cuter as we go along. She stays her same old self.

—Mika Yamamori

Mika Yamamori is from Ishikawa Prefecture in Japan. She began her professional manga career in 2006 with "Kimi no Kuchibiru kara Mahou" (The Magic from Your Lips) in *The Margaret* magazine. Her other works include *Sugars* and *Tsubaki Cho Lonely Planet*.

★DAYTIME★SHOOTING★STAR★ ★4★

SHOJO BEAT EDITION

Story & Art by
Mika Yamamori

Translation ★ **JN Productions**
Touch-Up Art & Lettering ★ **Inori Fukuda Trant**
Design ★ **Alice Lewis**
Editor ★ **Nancy Thistlethwaite**

HIRUNAKA NO RYUSEI © 2011 by Mika Yamamori
All rights reserved.
First published in Japan in 2011 by SHUEISHA Inc., Tokyo.
English translation rights arranged by SHUEISHA Inc.

Printed in the U.S.A.

Published by VIZ Media, LLC
P.O. Box 77010
San Francisco, CA 94107

10 9 8 7 6 5 4 3 2 1
First printing, January 2020

VIZ MEDIA
viz.com

Shojo Beat
shojobeat.com

STOP!

You may be reading the wrong way!

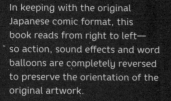

In keeping with the original Japanese comic format, this book reads from right to left—so action, sound effects and word balloons are completely reversed to preserve the orientation of the original artwork.

Check out the diagram shown here to get the hang of things, and then turn to the other side of the book to get started!

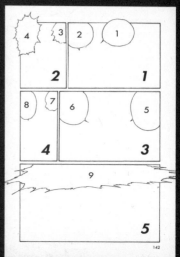